Choice People

A. E. Hotchner
CHOICE

PEOPLE

The Greats,
Near-Greats,
and Ingrates
I Have Known

WILLIAM MORROW AND COMPANY, INC.

New York   1984

Library of Congress Catalog Card Number: 83–63024

ISBN: 0–688–02215–4

Printed in the United Sates of America

First Edition

1 2 3 4 5 6 7 8 9 10

BOOK DESIGN BY ELLEN LO GIUDICE

For my son, TIMOTHY,
who is one of the truly Choice People

Contents

CONTENTS

Hurried and worried until we're buried,
and there's no curtain call,
Life's a very funny proposition, after all.

—George M. Cohan

Choice People

1

From Faulkner to Ferber
at Three Hundred Dollars a Head

In the beginning, I was a literary bounty hunter. I don't know of anyone who had ever had a job quite like that. Its creation was a tribute to the generosity and ingenuity of a friend of mine, Arthur Gordon, who had been on *Air Force* magazine with me, and postwar had assumed the editorship of *Cosmopolitan,* then a literary magazine, in the years before its sexual defoliation by Helen Gurley Brown.

My problem was that instead of returning to the United States after the war, I had elected to shed my major's leaves in Paris, and bolstered by a hefty sum of severance pay, to live in blissful cohabitation with a young soprano whom I had met toward the end of the war. During this period of ambrosia and croissants, I had received several letters from Arthur, offering me a variety of editorial positions on the *Cosmopolitan* staff, but I had scorned such mundane matters as gainful employment, preferring to dwell in romantic splendor with my *belle chanteuse* in her elegant Neuilly apartment, overlooking the chestnut trees of the Bois de Boulogne. I did not mind the hours she spent trilling at the piano with her voice coach, or having to sit through endless performances of *Thaïs, Pelléas et Mélisande,* and *Tosca* (I must have seen her fling herself off the parapet to escape the evil Baron Scarpia at least twenty times), which were the bellwethers of her repertoire. It was Paris, and I was in love— and at the same time learning from her and her coterie of sophisticated friends, about a way of life that was a far, far cry from what I had known in St. Louis, Missouri, which is where I had been raised, during the Depression.

But eventually, hard economic facts of life impinged on my Paris idyll, and realizing, one winter's day, that my bank account had dwindled precariously, I faced the grim reality that returning to the States and gainful employment had been thrust upon me. My lady love, whose name was Clarice, tempered my sorrow by revealing that she had been approached by the Metropolitan Opera and that there was a good chance that she too would be going to New York within the near future. It was agreed, over a particularly satisfying dinner of asparagus vinaigrette and poached turbot at La Méditerranée, that I would go back immediately, take up a position on the *Cosmopolitan* staff, find a pleasant apartment, and be all set for her when she came.

Although I should have been more discreet with my limited resources, I nonetheless felt so secure about my prospects that, virtually depleting my resources, I bought a first-class ticket on the *Queen Elizabeth* for my return trip to New York. It was a heady brew I had been drinking in Paris, and reality had not yet sobered me up. In fact, I became even more intoxicated when I was assigned a deck chair directly in front of a group that included Elsa Maxwell, Noel Coward, and Gertrude Lawrence. They were in their lap-robed chairs every afternoon at teatime, and so was I, ears alert, absorbing every syllable of their mesmerizing conversation. To my surprise, Elsa Maxwell—a corpulent gossip who had achieved a certain notoriety despite dumpiness of body and mind—had the most witty and entertaining voice in the conversational clatter that reached my ears, although the comment that made me laugh aloud (followed by blushing embarrassment) belonged to Noel Coward, who said to her at one point: "Elsa, you're the only person I know who runs people down without getting behind the wheel."

I went from the boat to the Hotel Shelton on Lexington Avenue, which had small rooms and rates to match (now the Halloran House), intending to stay only a few days while I got settled in at *Cosmo* and found an apartment, but, alas, it didn't work out that way. To begin with, I had a glum lunch with Arthur, who informed me that all the editorial positions on the magazine had been filled by those who had been on hand to fill them, and he warned me that the same situation prevailed at most all of the publications I would be interested in. "You are the last chap to arrive at the ball" is the vivid, disgusting way he explained it, "and all the dance cards are filled." Of course, I didn't take his word for it until after I had canvassed six or seven magazines, whose responses were firmly negative. Naturally, without employment there was no point in apartment-hunting, despite the fact that Clarice phoned from France at 4 A.M. (my time) one morning, joyously to announce that Edward Johnson, the general manager of the Metropolitan Opera, had signed her to a contract and that she would be arriving within six weeks. I felt simply dreadful, drained of energy, a listless leg-dragging weariness that I attributed to my grim predicament, but when my appetite disappeared and my urine turned as brilliantly yellow as the sun in a Van Gogh sky, I went to see the hotel doctor who had an office in the lobby. He was a natty fellow with neatly plastered white hair and a moustache to match; he wore a tattersall vest, and a red carnation in the lapel of his blue serge suit. His nurse, whose breasts bubbled above her white uniform like twin loaves of Wonder bread, looked like one of those extravagantly sexy ladies Petty was then drawing for *Esquire* magazine.

"Now, Miss Higgins," the doctor said after he took one look at me, "let's see if you can diagnose this one." He smiled unctuously at me and explained: "It's a little game we play." My stomach growled at him.

"Well," Miss Higgins said, in a voice that nicely blended Betty Boop and Minnie Mouse, "he don't look good."

"Right!" the doc enthused. "Now look at his eyes."

She came within one-sixteenth of an inch of my face and virtually touched her eyeball to mine. "It's yellow," she pronounced.

"Yes, yes! Oh, you are learning!"

"What does that mean?" I asked.

"The patient wants to know why he's yellow," the doctor said.

"Well," said Nurse Higgins, pouting up her full lips and staring at me intently, "we had one of these yellow ones in here last week."

"Exactly! And what was the diagnosis?"

"He had to eat candy."

"No, no—that's the treatment. What was wrong with him?"

"Oh, well, now what was that called? Oh, yes—John deuced."

"You hear that? Right on the nose!"

"I've got John deuced? What the hell is . . ."

"That's why you're yellow and so debilitated. Jaundice means bile is dumping into your liver and we've got to get it back into the bile duct. Now what I want you to do is go into the candy store in the lobby and buy a couple of pounds of rock candy— take it to your room, get in bed, and for one week I want you to stay in bed and eat all the candy you can."

As I went out, having placed ten of my precious dollars onto Nurse Higgins' outstretched hand, I heard the doc telling her how proud he was of her. I bought the candy, went to my room, and phoned someone I knew who said he would check the rock candy treatment with a doctor friend at Mt. Sinai. Physically I felt that some demented wrestler had been endlessly kneeing me in the groin. Mentally, I was ready for the nearest funeral home. My friend eventually called back and said that the doctor at Mt. Sinai had said that the accepted treatment for jaundice was bed rest and all the sugar I could ingest, rock candy being as good as anything.

"That's all? No medicine?"

"That's all."

What I discovered during the following six weeks that I spent in my jaundiced bed at the Shelton, in a paint-peeling room that barely accommodated a skinny bed, a dresser, and a chair, was that jaundice produces a depression so constant and deep-seated that many times I contemplated suicide if only I had had the strength to get to the window, open it, and hoist myself over the side. During this entire period, I had only two visitors: one was Ernestine Evens, a corpulent semi-toothless love of a woman who was a free-lance book reviewer for the *Herald Tribune*, and the other was Ernestine's friend, Monica Flaherty, a patrician beauty who was the daughter of the great documentary film-maker Robert Flaherty. They brought me bowls of Jell-O and homemade fudge, and Ernestine often brought books she had reviewed but didn't have to return. Ernestine was an ebullient, generous woman who, according to her, had been the first Western journalist admitted to Russia after the 1917 revolution. She was churchmouse poor, always concerned about rent and vittles, but somehow maintained a cheerful salon in her book-cluttered apartment.

Monica's swift mind and clear beauty were more restorative than her cherry Jell-O, but her effect on me was to produce a certain awed paralysis that made me appear doltish as well as jaundiced. But she seemed not to mind my doltishness as she sat on my bed and regaled me with stories about all the places she had lived as a girl while her father made such historic films as *Nanook of the North* and *Elephant Boy.* I was later to meet Robert Flaherty in their home in Vermont, a huge, tousled man of anecdotal charm and delicate fondness for the subjects and places he had photographed. But he seemed spent far beyond his years, and in fact died much too soon to the detriment of the ambitious projects he had been planning. For years Monica moved lightly in and out of my life, alighting for a dragonfly's moment, always producing in me that doltish awe, but eventually she disappeared, I know not where.

About the time my bile duct began to behave itself and a semblance of life force started to reassert itself in my veins, I received a visit from Arthur Gordon, who, obviously moved by the pitiable sight of my Jell-O– and rock-candy–wracked body, said that he had a job that I might be interested in. With a residue of $106 in the bank, and an unpaid hotel bill of $220, I was more than interested.

"There are a lot of good writers who used to write for *Cosmo,*" Arthur said, "but who have not written anything for us for a long time. I've made up a list of them, and your job would be to go see them and try to get them to write stories for us. You wouldn't get much of a salary, but I could pay you fifty dollars a week plus expenses, and give you a bonus of three hundred dollars for every writer you could bag. What do you say?"

"Could I get an advance of two hundred dollars?" I asked.

"Okay—I'll mail you the list."

"And the advance, please."

"Right."

And that's how I became a literary bounty hunter.

The list arrived the following day (and the advance), and these were the names: William Faulkner, Edna Ferber, Dorothy Parker, Somerset Maugham, John Steinbeck, Ernest Hemingway, E. M. Forster, J. P. Marquand, Evelyn Waugh, William Saroyan, Agatha Christie, and across the bottom of the page Arthur had written: "Although we have never published anything by Margaret Mitchell or Eugene O'Neill, nevertheless, contact them also."

If Arthur had asked me to climb Mount Everest I would have thought it more feasible than the prospect of locating and confronting these great literary figures of my St. Louis school days. However, what I *was* able to locate on the day I received Arthur's check was a meagerly furnished one-room apartment over a noisy garage on Seventy-second Street, at seventy-two dollars a month, utilities included. I winced at the thought of escorting Clarice and her Vuitton luggage into that room, but I had every confidence that before she arrived I would upgrade my living quarters to an acceptable level with my first three-hundred-dollar bounty.

I consulted Ernestine Evens about my author list, and she advised that I begin by going after the two ladies on the roster, Dorothy Parker and Edna Ferber, because they lived in New York City. She warned me, however, that they both had the reputation of speaking with spiked tongues, and that they did not lightly suffer strangers who came knocking on their doors with asinine requests. "I have seen Edna Ferber reduce bold men to jelly with her acerbic fire, and Dottie, of course, is notorious for her lethally witty sarcasm. Oh, you're going to have such fun with them!"

The prospect of bearding these lionesses in their dens (can one beard a lioness?) seemed like anything but fun, but incipient poverty was also not fun and in the end poverty won out. With trembling voice, I telephoned Dorothy Parker at the Hotel New Weston. To my surprise, she was quite civilized.

"Oh, yes, *Cosmopolitan,* it's been years, hasn't it? Why don't you come round for a drink around five?"

On my way to her hotel, I thought about her short story "Big

Blonde," which I had first read as an assignment in Hilda Levy's English Lit. class at Soldan High School. "Big Blonde" had a shocking, personal meaning for me: when I was twelve, and living in one room in a run-down, cheap hotel in St. Louis with my parents, the Depression having dumped us there, there was a time when I had to live alone in that dismal room, for my mother had been taken to the Fee-Fee Sanitarium, suffering from what was then called consumption, and my father was on the road, trying to sell watches. We lived in room 309, and every weekend the room across the hall, 310, was occupied by two middle-aged men, one of whom, the bellhop told me, was the most important criminal lawyer in St. Louis, and a buxom blond woman who was always laughing and singing and cracking jokes. They came on Fridays, around five o'clock, and immediately began drinking and laughing and having a three-handed good time. I knew what went on in 310 because it was terribly hot that summer, and in those days before air conditioning most of the rooms, including theirs, left their doors wide open to get ventilation. I had to pass their door to get to our room, and I always hurried for fear that they would see me, which they sometimes did; when I was spotted, I was hailed and dragged good-naturedly into their room. The big blonde wore nothing but a slip and the men were in their underwear. The big blonde always fixed a glass of ginger ale with ice for me with her nicotine-stained fingers, and they let me help myself from a pile of sandwiches which came from the corner delicatessen and which they rarely ate. Since food was terribly scarce at our table, in fact often nonexistent, the sandwiches were my reward for enduring those rather frightening visits.

Occasionally, the big blonde would sing for me if the two men were not too drunk and did not stop her. She called me "Big A, little a," and there was a gentle, lost quality about her that I liked, although she was the kind of woman I had never seen before except in the movies. Ben, the bellhop, assured me she was not the wife of either of the men, and I certainly suspected what went on in that room every weekend but I couldn't help liking her and wondering about what kind of life she led during the week.

That's when I came upon "Big Blonde" in English Lit.; it was such a shock because there she was, every detail of her life, a different woman in a different place, but after reading the story I understood the big blonde in 310. Everything I had previously read, and I read a lot, was about make-believe people; fiction was something *imagined*, unreal, far removed from life as it was lived in the St. Louis neighborhoods of my boyhood. The characters in the fictions of Jules Verne, Hawthorne, Dickens, Poe, P. G. Wodehouse, H. G. Wells, Dostoyevski, Sabatini, Robert Louis Stevenson, Melville were fictitious people who existed only between book covers. As were Hemingway's romantic heroes, Lieutenant Henry, Jake Barnes, Harry Morgan, and the characters created by Scott Fitzgerald.

None of these writers, whom I idolized, had ever written about anyone I had ever met in St. Louis, and I believed that that was the object of fiction—to create make-believe people who didn't really exist in real life. So you can see what a revelation it was when I read "Big Blonde," not only to encounter someone I knew in real life, but to have her presented in such a way that I felt I knew everything about her. It was a sad story, brutally sad, a story of wretched despair, but as much as anything I read in my early years, it caused a writer's stirring in me, this power to evoke a person's life so vividly that you know the person, and know her well, stranger though she is.

The New Weston, long demised, was one of those lived-in, frayed hotels, like the Algonquin, which had a base clientele of permanent residents, a good dining room, a well-attended oak-paneled bar, and a small, discreet lobby designed to discourage loitering. Dorothy Parker was one of the permanent cadre; she lived on the third floor in a two-room suite facing Madison Avenue. When she opened the door to my knock, I was surprised at how small she was, a petite woman in a simple black dress, flat shoes, her hair haphazardly wispy. She shook my hand firmly and smiled while her large eyes, underscored with prominent puffs, appraised me.

"Let's sit here away from the windows," she suggested. "They're unbuttoning the street." A steady tattoo of jackhammers assailed the room through the open windows.

A tall, muscularly handsome young man, around thirty, I judged, came in from the bedroom; Miss Parker introduced him as Ross Evans and suggested he make us some drinks. She asked me what I'd like, at the same time gesturing toward her bar, which contained a bottle of vermouth, a half bottle of vodka and two bottles of Scotch.

In the course of our conversation, I learned that Ross Evans had been a paratrooper, that he had writing aspirations, and that he was cohabiting with Dottie, which is what she asked me to call her but I preferred Dorothy. It was also apparent that he was trying to discourage her from drinking too much, and from talking about her husband, Alan Campbell, who was in Hollywood and whom she either was about to or had just divorced. In either event, she spoke of him glowingly and attributed her lack of writing anything for the past two years to her bust-up with Alan, with whom she had often collaborated on screenplays. It occurred to me, watching her indifference toward Evans, that perhaps she had taken him on to prove to Alan that at fifty-four she could still allure an attractive man twenty-four years younger than she. Although she looked all of her years, nevertheless she had a salient attractiveness that was rooted in a kind of smiling gentleness which, from her reputation, I had not at all expected, a quality of pathos, of vulnerability, of having been abandoned by her talent.

Evans was all in favor of turning out something for *Cosmopolitan,* several times using the pronoun "we" when speaking of the short story which he thought *they* might write, don't you think, Dottie?, maybe that idea *we* had a couple of weeks ago, yes, that might be just the thing.

Dorothy was noncommittal; she said that her writing joints might perhaps be atrophied from disuse. I was disturbed at the way things were going because I didn't know if my bounty was covered by a coauthored story. When I left, Dorothy was on her third highball, and she said she wasn't at all sure if she could get back to the typewriter.

"Don't worry about that," Evans said. "*I'll* handle the typewriter." He was standing in front of her, a paratrooper at parade rest, legs akimbo, chin forward, exuding ambition.

Arthur said he would accept a coauthored story if Dorothy Parker's name was first, but, having no confidence that any such story would ever be produced, I immediately turned my attention to Edna Ferber. My encounter with Dorothy, although perhaps not productive of a story, at least produced an acceptance of me on her part, and that made my Ferber approach a bit more confident, but when I reached her on the phone at her country home in Stepney Depot, Connecticut, I was set back by the flinty irritation in her voice, crackling at me over the wire.

"It isn't clear to me just what you want to see me about," she said.

The duress of her voice had indeed garbled my explanation of why *Cosmopolitan* had sicked me onto her. I tried for the second time to describe my mission.

"Well, I regret," she said, "that I don't have any manuscripts to peddle." Her voice was totally intimidating and I stuttered a rather profuse apology for my intrusion. I must have sounded rather pathetic because she softened somewhat and said: "Well, I suppose I can find time if you want to meet when I'm in New York next week, but there's not much point in it."

Before that meeting, I quickly read all of her books and plays, since my only previous knowledge of her work had been limited to having seen (from the remote free seats of the Muny Opera in Forest Park) a production of the musical *Show Boat,* which was based on one of her novels.

Of all her books, which included *Cimarron* and *Saratoga Trunk,* I particularly liked her novel *So Big,* a deft, autobiographical account of growing up which had won the Pulitzer Prize. She was certainly one of the most widely read and handsomely remunerated writers in the country.

I was to meet her at the Sherry Netherland Hotel, at noon, and having learned from Ernestine Evens that Ferber was fiercely punctual, I got there on the minute. I found the door of her suite slightly ajar, and when I rang, her voice told me to go in and wait in the sitting room. The entry hall and sitting room were elegantly furnished with antique Chinese furniture and artifacts, and wall hangings of spectacular beauty, but when I entered the sitting room I was stopped in my tracks by what stood in the dead center of the room: as prominent as the obelisk in the Place Vendôme, with a shaft of sunlight slanted on it from the window, there was a thin, lacquered, mother-of-pearl, high-legged table on which stood a water glass in which three toothbrushes were sunning. I was puzzling over the sunning toothbrushes when Miss Ferber entered the room, and immediately the toothbrushes became comprehensible, for the only physically attractive thing about her were her teeth. She was small and, it seemed to me, somewhat misshapen. Truncated. Her large head was slightly out of proportion with her torso, and her eyes were set too high on her face, but they were penetrating eyes, bright and evaluating. Her gray hair was carefully sculptured in curls, and she wore a simple black dress with pearls. She entered the room smiling, displaying the most perfectly configured, whitest teeth I had ever seen.

"Do you mind if we have lunch?" she asked. "I skipped breakfast and I'm famished. I've reserved at the Plaza."

This was a cordiality which, from what I knew of her reputation for brusqueness, and from how she had sounded on the phone, was totally unexpected—as was, it turned out, the nature of our conversation at lunch.

She said that she was really grateful that I had contacted her because for several years she had been living in unproductive isolation. Since the beginning of the war, she said, when she first began to read about the Nazi outrages against the Jews. She said she was the kind of Jew who hadn't set foot in a temple or synagogue for years, but who nevertheless had an aggressive pride in her Jewishness. "I have never told anyone what I'm about to tell you," she said, as best I can recall from memo notes I kept for Arthur, "but the Nazi atrocities have created a paralysis in me. I have always been a forceful, positive, productive person, but for five years now I have been hog-tied by a bleak depression. On the few occasions when I have forced myself to sit down to write, my mind has simply rebelled at writing anything. Not a word. The last time I was at the typewriter, all I produced was a bucket full of tears. For someone who was always prolific, who worked every day and who enjoyed writing, this has been the most awful time for me. I'm not by nature one of those tortured writers who chew their nails and refer to blank typewriter paper as the enemy. That is, I haven't been until now. I apologize for unburdening myself on you, but you are the first person who has shown any interest in my writing production. I have not heard from my publisher since my last book, and I don't have the kind of friends who would sympathize or even understand what I'm talking about. I suppose they are not really friends, but rather acquaintances who are only comfortable on smooth surfaces. I always thought of them as friends until I fell on these bad times. It is easier to talk to a complete stranger than to them, some of whom I've known for twenty years. Moss Hart. Kaufman. Woollcott. Frank Adams. Either you are on the top rung, wittily crowing, or they don't want to listen to you."

She had ordered enthusiastically but when the dishes came she only picked at them. I didn't eat much either, ill-at-ease as I was at being confronted with this totally unexpected confession from a winner of the Pulitzer Prize. Right on top of my experience with Dorothy Parker, it was incomprehensible to me that both of these women were so tortured about not being able to write. I had expected confident goddesses in their literate towers, passing judgment on me, likely disdainful, but instead I had encountered two insecure women for whom, inexplicably, I was a welcome listening post. I found them appealing, like childhood aunts I had not seen for years, confiding in me about family problems. I was surprised, and I suppose somewhat flattered, that they did not see me for what I was—a green kid just out of uniform and not yet into a way of life. I had practiced law for a year in St. Louis before going into the Air Force, and although I had renounced a legal career in favor of a literary life, it was a declaration based on hope rather than accomplishment.

However, even while going to law school at Washington University, I had been heavily engaged in campus writing— editor of the literary magazine, a columnist for the campus newspaper, librettist for original musicals and sundry similar endeavors. I had taken a course in playwriting from a splendid teacher, Professor William G. B. Carson, who, for our final grade, required the writing of an original one-act play. Three of these plays would be selected for production in the campus theatre before a panel of drama critics from the *St. Louis Post-Dispatch,* the Chicago *Herald-Tribune,* and the St. Louis *Globe-Democrat,* with the winning playwright awarded a plaque and fifty dollars in cash.

All during the semester, Professor Carson read our exercises, and it was my foregone conclusion that the prize would be won by a student named Thomas Lanier Williams who was an "older" man who had dropped out of school for a few years, to work. I first became acquainted with his writing through his cousin, Louis Triefenbach, who was on my staff during the year I was editor of the *Eliot,* the literary magazine. Triefenbach was a tiny, impeccable fellow who wore lavender shirts with white collars, tattersall vests. He would occasionally present me with poems written by his cousin, Tom Williams. Williams himself never came to the office, only his poems as couriered by Triefenbach.

Here, from my old *Eliots*, are a few of those poems written by Tom Williams in his college days, long before he adopted the sobriquet of Tennessee:

Recollection

It was a steep hill that you went down,
calling back to me,
saying that you would be only a little while.
I waited longer than that.
The little grasses continued to stir in the wind
and the wind grew colder.

I looked across the deep valley
and saw the afternoon sun
was yellow as lemon upon the dark pines,
and elsewhere pools of cool shadow
crept down from the hills like stains of dark water
widening slowly as the sunlight dimmed . . .

Someone called I think.
I do not remember clearly.
I only know that a long time afterwards
I rose from the grass
and walked slowly back down the path by which we had come,
the small, winding path,
and noted, here and there, your footprints,
pointing upwards, narrow and light.

CHOICE PEOPLE

Sonnet for Pygmalion

For you, Pygmalion, no silver-bought
Woman of Cyprus with kohl-darkened eyes!
For you, Pygmalion, a vision caught
In its first blinding moment of surprise
And therein crystallized: no less than this:
Perfection carved by your own hand from stone,
The lips forever lifted toward the kiss,
The breast immutable and still unknown!

And so think twice: in making her alive
You stain her with the dust of time and change,
While you should have, in taking stone to wive,
Her loveliness forever new and strange,
Her palm a chalice and her lifted face
A fire, a sacrament, an altar place!

Mummer's Rhyme

Put away the painted masque
    Of poet or of clown,
The judge's wig, the warrior's casque,
    And ring the curtains down!
Some things were said in earnest and
    Some things were said in jest:
The princess had the whitest hand,
    The harlot's heart was best!
The prophet shouted loud and long—
    Who knows what he was saying?
The blindman starved amidst a throng
    Of honest people praying. . . .
Now hang the masque upon the wall
    And ring the curtains down,
For shadows fall upon the hall
    And silence on the town!

The exercises that Williams wrote for the playwriting class were deft, touching, fragile exchanges between an eccentric St. Louis mother and her slightly crippled homebound daughter.

My exercises, and the play I eventually wrote, became a campus farce about a beleaguered student who wrote a gossip column for the newspaper. I knew in my heart that my gossip columnist didn't stand a chance up against Williams' mother and daughter.

But when time came to submit our full one-acters, the shock was that Williams totally abandoned the people he had been developing and instead submitted a play called *Me, Vashya!* which was about an egomaniac who was the munitions czar of the world. He sat in his office with a map of the world at his back, deciding where on earth to foment war to the benefit of his nearest munitions factory. It was melodramatic, bombastic, and silly, a subject Williams knew nothing about, and obviously it was not selected as one of the three plays to be produced. Williams was so outraged at this rebuff that he abandoned Washington University midterm and transferred to the University of Iowa, where the redoubtable Professor George Pierce Baker was head of the drama department.

Later, Williams repeated this bizarre behavior when he first tackled the professional stage. His play *Battle of Angels* was a melodrama that folded in Boston,* but then, righting himself, Williams wrote *The Glass Menagerie,* which finally made use of all those exercises he had been writing in Professor Carson's class.

When I reported to Arthur on my two meetings, he said that in his experience writer's block was more pernicious than anemia, and he suggested that I forget Parker and Ferber and concentrate on other writers on my list. Specifically, he wanted me to go down to Havana and try to persuade Hemingway to write an article for *Cosmopolitan* on the future of literature, which Arthur wanted to incorporate into a series he was planning on the future of everything from Henry Ford II on the future of the automobile to Picasso on art to Frank Lloyd Wright on the future of architecture. The prospect of asking the great Heming-

---

*It is not uncommon for writers to commit the youthful sin of substituting artificial melodrama for the real dramas they have lived. I was certainly one of those sinners. My first novel, *The Dangerous American,* written while I was living in Rome, dealt with a deported gangster and the underworld of Venice—subjects about which I knew absolutely nothing, and thinking back on it, I can't for the life of me figure out why I thought I could deal with such an egregious subject.

way to write anything so asinine was repugnant to me, for I shared a kind of Hemingway awe with most of my generation; we had grown up doting on his books and short stories and on the universally glamorous life which he led, as colorfully reported in the press.

I was momentarily rescued from this bleak fate by a phone call from Dorothy, who asked me to come see her. This time Ross Evans was not there. Dorothy seemed more subdued than on my previous visit; she rarely smiled and her fingers nervously picked at each other. She told me that she had started a short story called "The Game," about a couple who try to stick verbal barbs in each other while playing charades at a party, and she wanted to know if it was acceptable to *Cosmopolitan* for her to put Evans' name on it as coauthor. I said it was all right so long as her name came first. "He keeps me from drinking while I work," she explained.

She said the story would have been further along except for an interruption she hadn't counted on—the woman who was presently in her bedroom. She identified her as Mrs. Lynn Spiegel, the wife of the movie producer Sam Spiegel, who, because of the anti-Semitism engendered by the Nazis, was now calling himself S. P. Eagle. Dorothy explained that the Spiegel-Eagles had a rather tumultuous relationship which often erupted into violence, and that Lynn had shown up at Dorothy's door, battered and bruised, and had dramatically installed herself in one of the beds in the bedroom—that was four days ago and she showed no signs of stirring except to order drinks and food from room service. Of course, Dorothy was much too indulgent to suggest that she and Ross were being inconvenienced, but the fact was that Lynn Spiegel-Eagle's room service bills were a serious matter since Dorothy had no funds, nor any prospect of any, not having written anything for so long. She said she was six months in arrears with her rent and that she hadn't left the room for weeks for fear of being accosted by the manager in the lobby.

There was a little-girl-lost quality about Dorothy that I found endearing, an innocent pilloried by a manipulative world, and I felt an urge to rescue her, to try to get her a respite from being imprisoned in that room with the encamped Mrs. Eagle-Spiegel.

I invited her to lunch, assuring her that under cover of the noontime crowd in the lobby we could quietly get out the door without her being seen.

She was very nervous going down in the elevator, and even though the lobby was filled with lunchtime people, she clung tightly to my arm as we moved past the desk toward the door. We were almost there when a man at the reception desk called out: "Mrs. Parker! May I see you for a moment?"

She froze, took a deep breath, then turned to face him with the sickly look on her face of a condemned approaching the guillotine. I followed her, feeling awful that I had led her into this humiliating trap.

"We have all this mail for you, Mrs. Parker, that hasn't been picked up for weeks," the receptionist said, handing her a large sheaf of letters. She thanked him in her shy, gracious way, and casting a fleeting look of relief in my direction, she led the way toward the door.

When we were seated at the restaurant, she glanced at the envelope at the top of the bundle and was surprised to see that it was from her publisher, whom, she said, she had not heard from for several years. "He's probably offering me my unsold books at a discount." She opened the envelope and a check fell out. She picked it up as if it were ticking, and holding it gingerly at arm's length, studied its numerals.

"That can't be," she said, handing the check to me. "I didn't go to school the year they had decimals." It was a royalty check for $4,016.

"I wonder how long it was sitting in my box," she mused, without any of the emotion I would have expected from someone severely strapped for funds.

She had three drinks before ordering lunch, and she only ordered then because the captain had come to our table four times to ask if we were ready for him. She talked a great deal about Alan Campbell, who was living in Hollywood, but I still could not figure out if their divorce was final or in the works. She said that what she missed most about Alan, to whom she had been married for fourteen years, was that he was the only person in her life to whom she could truly talk.

"The people I know are only interested in a performance,

see Dottie jump through the verbal hoop, watch Dottie hit 'em in the solar plexus with a *bon mot,* good ol' Dottie, witty poems and one-line zingers, the pride of the Algonquin. The last time I tried to have a heart-to-heart with one of my so-called friends, she told another of my so-called friends: 'Dottie's not much fun these days—she's drinking too much and wallowing in her problems.' "

Listening to her, I had the eerie sensation that I could just as well be having lunch with Edna Ferber. "What about Ross?" I asked.

"Ross is a space-filler, a towel carrier. My friends think he's my gallant young stud, servicing me nightly, which, God knows, I wish he were. But bi-yearly is more like it. And then he picks the goddamnedest times! A few nights ago we were visiting friends of mine for dinner, then afterwards we sat around drinking and talking. It got to be a bit late, around two or so, and suddenly there was Ross beginning to move in on me. He hadn't molested me since last March, but there he was on the sofa, with our friends right there, starting to have a go at me. I was too startled—or perhaps I should say grateful—to protest, even though it somewhat embarrassed my hosts, who talked to each other and pretended not to notice; they are old acquaintances, indulgent, by now, of my peccadillos."

Later on, I puzzled over why Dorothy had not seemed pleased at receiving an unexpected windfall of over four thousand dollars. Perhaps an interruption in her unrelieved suffering over Alan Campbell's defection.

Two unexpected events conspired to alleviate my destitution. One was that Ferber presented me with a short story that Arthur Gordon immediately accepted for publication, thereby providing me with my first three-hundred-dollar bounty; the other event: the ceiling of my dismal one-room apartment fell down.

When I told Arthur that Ferber had completed a short story, he invited the two of us to lunch at "21". It was a pleasant lunch, Ferber witty and quite gay, frankly reveling with relief that the long arid spell in her writing career had ended. Arthur said that he hoped a flow of stories would now be forthcoming.

"I've been thinking of something longer," Ferber said, "but

I'd have to do some research on the King ranch in Texas. I know that Mr. Hearst is close to the King family, and I thought you might be able, through him, to arrange for me to stay on the ranch for a while. Anything I write, I'd give you first crack at it."

Arthur said he'd certainly do what he could. As it turned out, Bill Hearst did arrange for Ferber to be a guest on the ranch, and there came a time, several years later, when Ferber presented *Cosmo* with a huge manuscript entitled *Giant,* which, because of its length, *Cosmopolitan* wasn't able to publish. I had no association with *Cosmopolitan* by then, but I had a godfather feeling about *Giant* as a result of having helped Ferber back on her writing track. I saw Ferber quite often and we became friends. On one occasion, she even invited me to one of her legendary dinner parties at her 730 Park Avenue apartment, an evening spent in mute fascination in the company of Moss and Kitty Hart, George Kaufman, Franklin P. Adams, Cornelia Otis Skinner, and Marc Connelly.

Ferber's *Cosmopolitan* short story only produced the three-hundred-dollar bounty for me, but the collapsed ceiling was an eight-hundred-and-fifty-dollar bonanza from the Firemen's Insurance Company that allowed me to move to a decent apartment. The ceiling fell in a thunderous white cloud of powdery plaster early one evening while (thank God!) I was in a nickel poker game in the Village. I had no possessions of any value, save one—an oil painting entitled "Nude Woman Seated," which I had bought in Amsterdam at the Rijksmuseum, the great national museum of Holland. Its paintings are ordinarily not for sale, but just after the war ended, all the canvases of the old masters were removed and the museum was given over to an exhibition of works by underground Dutch, French, and Belgian artists who had painted during the war in defiance of the Nazi edict that no artist could paint who was not a member of the Kulturkammer, which had strict rules and regulations as to what could and could not be painted. The penalty for painting in defiance of this edict was death, so that every canvas on exhibit in the Rijksmuseum (almost all interiors) was a testament of bravery.

One of the most moving moments of my life occurred during that visit to the Rijksmuseum. Rembrandt's great canvas "The

Night Watch" is exhibited in a room by itself, but when I entered that room, expecting to see the Rembrandt, I found that the painting had been removed and in its huge black frame were the names of all the Dutch artists who had been put to death by the Nazis for not having joined the Kulturkammer: S. Garf, Gerrit van der Veen, Moos Cohen, Joop Narinx—hundreds of names embossed in white against the black background, the walls draped with flags and black bunting. Some of the visitors in the room were sobbing, and I was so affected by this simple tribute to these brave artists that I was determined to buy one of the hundreds of paintings that were for sale. "Nude Woman Seated," by an Underground artist named J. Franken, was one of the few canvases I could afford on my captain's pay, but it could have been a Rembrandt the way I lugged it around with me everywhere I went after that.

The reason I had gone to Amsterdam as the war was ending was to fulfill a promise I had made to a Dutch ballet dancer named Tina de Roos, whom I had been seeing while stationed in New York City on the staff of *Air Force* magazine. Her Jewish parents and other relatives had been gassed to death in Auschwitz, with the exception of her only brother, who had been married to a Catholic and had successfully hidden from the Gestapo. Tina had heard from him and knew that he was starving, as were most of the Dutch, and she had made me promise to bring him some GI food. As chief of the European bureau of *Air Force,* I was able to move about freely, so, good to my promise, I went to Air Force headquarters in Wiesbaden, where I stocked an open Jeep with mess-hall boxes of food and supplies, and took off for Amsterdam, going by way of the German cities of Koblenz, Bonn, Cologne, and Krefeld, all in ruins, the people famished, desperate, without shelter, picking through the endless mounds of rubble for whatever they could scrounge, and there was I naïvely driving through their midst in an open Jeep crammed to the gunwales with clearly marked cartons of GI food. Whenever I had to stop in traffic, or because of a partially obstructed road, I became increasingly aware of the stares people fixed on me and my cargo.

The most chilling incident of this incautious journey occurred on a desolate stretch of road outside Neuss where I had a flat tire. Dusk was approaching and there was just enough twilight to change the tire before dark. I found I had a good spare but when I opened the side panel that should have contained the tools, I discovered that it was empty. There was no habitation in sight, and although I was wearing a side arm, I knew that I would certainly not use it to protect my cargo. Dusk was fast closing down, it was bitingly cold and windy, and I felt very apprehensive about what might happen to me in the night, baited as I was. There was not much traffic on the road—horse-drawn wagons, a few bicycles, a truck running on ersatz fuel, farmers in wooden shoes pulling handcarts—but certainly enough observers to pass word along that a solitary officer with a Jeep-load of food was stranded for the night. I pulled the gimpy Jeep off the road, trying to use the trees for cover.

Night fell and I was very cold and despairing of being rescued when two strong headlights approaching me illumined the dark. I was relieved to see it was a truck with a U. S. Army insignia on its door. I stepped onto the roadway and flagged it down. There was a corporal at the wheel, another riding shotgun. The truck itself was packed with human cargo—German war prisoners, their uniforms tattered and covered with grime. The corporals had tire-changing tools in their truck but we found that the jack was much too big to fit under the Jeep.

I had just about decided to abandon my foodstuffs and go on back with them to Cologne, which was their destination, when I became aware that one of the corporals had lowered the rear gate of the truck, and that he was directing the prisoners to form a circle around the Jeep. When it was completely surrounded, he gave a command in German, and the prisoners took hold of the Jeep and lifted it a couple of feet off the ground. They held it aloft while the corporals removed the flat tire and replaced it with the spare. A few minutes later I was on my way, awestruck by GI ingenuity.

The neat, brightly painted houses of Amsterdam, untouched by bombs, came as a welcome shock after driving for days through the rubble and ruin of northern Germany. But although cosmetically Amsterdam gave the appearance of prosperity, in reality the Dutch were just as destitute as the Germans. Wooden shoes were a luxury. I saw many children wearing pieces of flat board strapped to the bottoms of their stockingless feet with string. Tulip bulbs were being eaten in place of potatoes, which were scarce and expensive. The streets of the city were ravaged of their trees, which had been used for cooking and for heat, the black circles of soil mordant reminders of where the majestic trees had once stood.

I located the house of Tina's brother on a street of small identical houses. The brother, Voon, was a short, compact man with nervous mannerisms, predominantly a giggle which preceded virtually everything he said. His wife, Rinka, was a slight woman of considerable beauty, much of it emanating from her extraordinary eyes. Their sallow-faced daughter, an only child, was painfully shy. The brother and I carried my cargo into the narrow living room, and as I opened the boxes and extricated the contents I expected a joyous reaction, but instead they were stunned speechless by the parade of these objects which had become figments of their memory, everything from mess-hall–size tins of beef stew to bars of soap. I picked up a large bar of Hershey's chocolate and proffered it to the child, who took it hesitantly after a little prodding from her mother.

"She doesn't know what it is," Rinka said.

"Tell her it's chocolate."

"Yes, I told her, but she doesn't know what chocolate is— there hasn't been any for the six years of the war, and she's only seven."

There was an exclamation of delight from Voon, who had located several rolls of toilet paper in the bottom of one of the boxes. He clutched them happily against his chest.

"There has been no paper for several years," Rinka said (she was the only one who spoke English), "and the toilet paper means more to him than all those other things." One box contained six cartons of American cigarettes, and Rinka said that they were the most valuable of all the things I had brought, for American cigarettes were a medium of exchange in Amsterdam, better than money for the purchase of such scarce and expensive items as fuel, meat, and clothes.

That night we ate dinner in the kitchen, which was the only room that had heat, and it was a feast of beef stew, succotash, bread, butter, cheese, milk, coffee, and stewed fruits, all from green GI ration tins. The child, Annika, took a probative nibble of her chocolate bar, her face responding with a big smile, then she ravenously consumed the rest of it to our amusement.

My room was on the third floor, so cold I huffed plumes of white air, but after ten minutes under the plump eiderdown coverlet, I was comfortable and slept away the rigors of my journey.

The following day, Voon and Annika went by train to visit his only surviving relatives in Rotterdam, which, unlike Amsterdam, had been ruthlessly bombed by the Germans. Voon took a portion of the things I had brought, for his Rotterdam relatives. Rinka took me on a sight-see of Amsterdam (that's when I made my purchase of "Nude Woman Seated" at the Rijksmuseum), and later I took her to dinner at the Café l'Esta, which featured a Hungarian band, songs in English, and a discreet black market menu. Rinka and I drank Bols gin and she told me about the harrowing years of Nazi rule when unexpected Gestapo sweeps were made in the neighborhood, at which times Voon had been hidden in secret attic alcoves in various houses on their block by courageous neighbors.

"All those years, we never once touched each other as man and wife. I made myself understand what being so hunted would do to his psyche. But now, the war, it is ended, the Nazis are done for a considerable time, but there is still nothing . . . nothing between us. I so try to understand, but in my heart, where my womanness is . . ."

She looked toward the violinist, who was bent furiously over his instrument, but her eyes were seeing something else.

"Have you talked to him?"

"He doesn't want to discuss . . . it makes him angry. I am so afraid the war has permanently wounded him. He has been through much hell . . . but so have I . . . but I do not wish to inflict more pain on him. . . . It is very nice of you . . . I wish to thank you for listening . . . there is no one I can talk to—not about this . . . I am no longer allowed confession because of having a Jewish husband. . . . I don't know why I tell you these things which are so intimate. You are a stranger, yet I have a familiar feeling toward you. You are a very sympathetic gentleman, is that how Americans are? It is a gift to be able to talk to you."

"I enjoy listening to you, Rinka. Perhaps that's why you feel all right talking about these things. How long have you been married to Voon?"

"We were married, Voon and I, in the spring of the year 1937. It was very difficult, the wedding, because of my father. I was nineteen, then, and my father was a very strict man who did not like me to be having dates with boys and going to parties. So I used to see Voon very slyly—is that a right word, slyly? He was ten years older than was I, and very well educated, and I was always most attracted to the brains of a man, not to his physical. Voon's family was in shipping and they had a truly beautiful house on the Prinsen Canal. Voon was a graduate in architecture from the University of Brussels. He had a wicked sense of humor and we laughed a lot and I loved him much, oh yes, very, very much. But I could not possibly allow him to call on me at my house because another thing about my father was that he was anti-Semite. He owned a big store on the Kalvertstraat, what you call a department store, but he never permitted a Jew to work for him. Jewish customers, yes, he welcomed them, but not Jewish employees. But that is not to say that with me he was not quite a good father, for he was. But he wanted to keep me a little girl, *his* little girl, what a cliché that is about fathers, perhaps a bit sexual, do you think? Coveting one's daughter?

"It was ironic, of course, that the first and only man I really got to know was a Jew. I made all kinds of subterfuges to get out of the house to see him. I was overwhelmed with him. I yearned so to be free of the strictness of my father, so when Voon asked me to marry, I don't truly know if I said yes because of loving him or because it was my way to freedom. Of course, now I had to tell my father. My mother came with me when I went to see him in his study. My mother is a very gentle woman, open of mind, easygoing, just the reverse of my father. Well, I barely had the words from my mouth when he said, very firmly, that I was to leave the house. It was treachery, he said, for me to have deceived him like this, and for a daughter of his, of good breeding, to deceive him with a Jew was totally offensive and he never wanted to lay eyes upon me again. My mother begged him to be more temperate but he left the room and . . . and . . . true to his word, I never saw him again. Not until his funeral, when I saw him in the open casket."

Her delicate features were pinched with sorrowful remembrance and I expected tears but there weren't any. "Voon and I were married in his family's house and we went to Paris on our honeymoon and stayed at the Ritz; when our daughter was born a year later, it was a joyful time. But then . . . then . . . oh, God, to have lived through that . . . the Nazis came and it was like a black storm that swept everything away . . . Voon's parents and brothers and all his relatives were overnight removed . . . disappeared . . . the house on the Prinsen confiscated, the business confiscated . . . and my father—oh, this is the most strange of all that happened . . . my father, who hated Jews, who never accepted Voon or my daughter, what he did was so . . . so . . . well, there was a Jewish lawyer, Ibik Cohen, who lived in a nearby house, and one night when the Gestapo was sweeping the neighborhood for Jews, my father took Cohen in, with his wife and his two little children, and hid them, but the Nazis raided my father's house and found them and for that my father was taken to the *Sport terrein* along with four others and put against the old wall there and shot to death. It will forever be something that will not explain itself to me. I needed him so badly and he gave his life to help strangers. Why? Is there any answer? I am twenty-seven years old now, but I know so little about life. How old are you?"

"Twenty-six."

"Ah, you see, we are the same but you have been places and experienced things, while I . . ." She shrugged.

"You are still young, Rinka—your time will come."

"You think?"

"Of course. You are intelligent and beautiful and resourceful —just give yourself time."

"And Voon?"

"Wounds heal. Some take longer than others."

At midnight, when the Café l'Esta closed, we rode in my open Jeep through the freezing, deserted streets without speaking; she had a thick wool scarf twined around her neck, and a little wool cap perched on the back of her head. She glanced at me occasionally, but I could not see her remarkable eyes in the dark.

As we crossed the canal, she said: "That's the house where I was born."

I stopped the Jeep and we looked at the house which was like all the other houses along the canal.

I parked the Jeep in front of her house, and she held my arm as we walked up the steps.

We said good night awkwardly on the first-floor landing; it seemed colder inside the house than out. She thanked me for the evening—it was the first time she had eaten in a restaurant, she said, since the Germans occupied the city. She turned toward her room, then impetuously she put her arms around me, hugged me quickly, and just as quickly disappeared into her room. I slowly mounted the steep flight to my room. The icy sheets under the eiderdown again melted pleasurably and I was just drifting asleep when her small, cold body slipped in under the coverlet. She was trembling, but not from the cold. She grasped me and buried her head against my chest and wept and wept. Her weeping was noiseless and the room was so still I fancied I could hear her tears drop. Her full breasts felt wonderfully soft and firm against me. She wept for her lost years and for a little girl who had never tasted chocolate and for her excommunication from a life she could never have.

I held her very tightly as her tears moistened my chest. It became very warm under the eiderdown. She wept for some time.

I left early the following morning, after we breakfasted on GI coffee, powdered eggs, and American bacon. As I waved farewell to her face in the Vermeer window, framed by the white sash, I had a distinct feeling that I was taking away with me much more than I had brought.

2

Clark Gable Has Blisters on His Feet

A position on the editorial staff opened up, but Arthur let me know that even though he was making me an associate editor with a regular salary, my duties as a bounty hunter would have to continue. He was pleased with the Ferber story, and with the fact that Dorothy Parker was also writing, but his dominant interest was in getting a contribution from the most alluring and allusive name on the list—Hemingway. And I was just as intent on avoiding this assignment, for I had a worshipful awe of Hemingway that bordered on the fearful—this gargantuan literary god, omnivorous, immortal, impervious to the ravages of war, pestilence, rampant bulls, and debauchery. I was not alone in this. My generation had been weaned on a mixed pablum of his writings and his tumultuous exploits, and the very thought that I would have to confront him with my *Cosmo* hustle made me weak at the knees.

After several skillfully contrived postponements, however, I finally had to go down to Cuba to try to see him, but I think that if I had not had my Clark Gable experience to embolden me, I would not have had the courage to go. Gable and Hemingway resembled one another physically and in the macho impact of their public personalities, but, in truth, there was no self-generated machismo about either one of them. Before I met him, Gable inhabited the same he-man niche as Hemingway, but he was no more real as a screen hero than were the heroes and

41

antiheroes of Hemingway's books and Hemingway himself. But getting to know Gable for the simple, straightforward guy he was did help me face up to the trauma of approaching Hemingway.

I met Gable on a bus stop bench in Miami. It was the summer of 1942, the hottest summer in the weather annals of Miami (before or since), with daily temperatures well over a hundred degrees. Miami Beach had been sequestered by the Air Force and I was there to undergo thirteen weeks of the rigors of the Officers Candidate School, thirteen weeks of the most grueling mental and physical hell imaginable, the theory being, I presume, that if a man could survive the classes, the parades, the obstacle course, the impromptu full-pack hikes, the firing ranges, calisthenics, night patrols which were crammed into those eighteen-hour days, then he could survive anything the war might throw at him. We were kept in a constant state of nervous and physical exhaustion, the purpose being to crack us if they possibly could and wash us out as potential officers.

Every day at four o'clock, the hottest part of the day, we would have to parade with rifles on a parade ground where the temperature was easily 130 degrees, often being required to stand motionless in ranks for extended periods of time. If a man fainted once, he got a demerit; twice, he was washed out. As we stood erect with our chins on our chests, the sweat pouring into our eyes, we could hear the sound of the ambulances, called meat wagons, as they skirted the rear files, picking up the cadets who had passed out. If one of our fellows fainted during the parade march, we were required to keep stride, even if it meant stepping on him, and sometimes an entire company would march over an unconscious body.

Also quartered at Miami Beach was the Air Force's Officers Training School, which was looked upon with scorn by those of us in the OCS, for these were the dentists, lawyers, Hollywood big shots, doctors, politicians, et cetera who were given direct commissions and were only in Miami long enough to get outfitted in their custom-made uniforms and given a few lectures in a country club atmosphere. The big story of that summer was that Clark Gable had been offered one of these cushy OTS commissions, but that he had turned it down in favor of enlisting as a GI private and going through the thirteen weeks of OCS like an ordinary GI. His induction had been widely publicized, and besieging mobs along the route of the train that brought him from Hollywood made him a day late arriving in Miami.

I had entered OCS a few weeks before Gable, and I had seen him from afar on the day he arrived as he strode down the street on his way to his assigned barracks (hotels that had been requisitioned), a handsome, erect figure moving purposefully as a phalanx of reporters strove to keep up with him. But I hadn't seen him again until late one afternoon, after the daily parade, when on my way back to the Plymouth Hotel (Q Company's barracks) I came upon a rumpled, sweated cadet seated on a bench in a bus stop with the shoe and stocking removed from his left foot. "You wouldn't have a pin on you, would you?" the soldier asked.

It was Gable, but I recognized the voice more than the man himself; his famous moustache was gone (OCS regulation), he had a semi-crew cut (also a regulation), his khaki shirt was soaked through, and there were blisters on his foot the size of half dollars. I was surprised to see vestiges of gray in his hair. There was an angry-looking pimple on his nose. He looked wilted and old (to my young eyes), and I recall my amazement at how much younger he had looked a couple of years before in *Gone with the Wind.* He was forty-one, almost twice my age, and it was obvious that the ordeal of trying to keep up with kids in their twenties was taking its toll on him.

I always kept a needle pinned inside my belt loop (for my own blisters), but after looking at his foot I suggested he go to the infirmary and get proper treatment.

"Well," he said, "I'd like to, but there would be such flak over my coming down with a few blisters . . ."

I understood. If you're Clark Gable you are not allowed to get blisters; the heroic seaman of *Mutiny on the Bounty* would not get blisters. I punctured the blisters with my needle and gushets of liquid ran down his foot and dripped onto the bus bench. There must have been a dozen blisters.

Afterward we went to the canteen and had a Coke (we were allowed one hour of free time each day after the parade). Looking as he did, bereft of his moustache, his crew cut giving prominence to his wide ears, his uniform sagged with perspiration, he didn't get any attention from the soldiers in the canteen. It was suffocatingly hot—in those days there was no air conditioning anywhere in Miami Beach. Gable said he was having a tough time. "I didn't realize I was such an old fart until I got here with you kids," he said. "I thought I was in pretty good shape . . ."

I assured him he'd tough it out.

"I may not. That hike today, my backpack felt like four hundred pounds. My legs were gone. They woke us up at three o'clock in the morning and gave us two minutes to fall out in the street in full uniform. I forgot my goddamn garters and got two demerits. I'll have to march an hour of penalty on Saturday. Why the shit do they make us wear garters?"

"So they can give us demerits."

"The heat's really getting to me—and I've got twelve weeks to go. I really don't know if I'll make it."

"Sure you will—you're the last person they would flunk out."

"Yeah, well, maybe they want to—just to demonstrate that OCS is so tough and impartial they can even flunk Clark Gable."

I had to admit that was a possibility.

I saw Gable once more, two weeks later, at a mustering for guard duty on the beach. A German mini-sub had landed on the beach and disgorged three potential spies who had been expeditiously captured, but now, to make the beaches more secure, we were being assigned to four-hour night patrols. Gable was in the group I was assigned to, and we wound up paired for the midnight to 4 A.M. shift on one of the beaches. The password for the night was "American Eagle." We were instructed to shoot anyone who appeared on the beach and didn't know the magic words. Our weapon was a heavy, clumsy gun that had been used in World War I. All the modern Garands were being supplied to combat forces overseas, and the antique Enfield was the best ordnance could do. (We also had to lug them around the parade grounds in that beastly heat.) It was a backbreaking four hours, patrolling the desolate beach with our heavy boots sinking into the wet sand, the Enfields weighing a ton on our shoulders, the night air equatorially hot and steamy. The moon glinted innocently over the placid water.

"You got your needle?" Gable asked.

"Always at the ready."

"My feet feel like I'm going to need it. Can you imagine having to shoot this gun and hit anything? I hope one of those OTS dentists comes along—I'd like to test it."

Each time we reached the perimeter of our area, we put down our rifles and took a short break before turning around and retracing our steps. After a couple of hours of this monotony, Gable dropped his rifle and plunked himself down on the sand.

"Pa's gotta rest his weary dogs."

I plopped down on the beach beside him.

"That's what she used to call me—Pa, and I called her Ma," he said softly. He started to smoke a cigarette, carefully cupping his hand around the glowing end. And he started to talk about his wife, Carole Lombard, a movie actress who had recently died in a plane crash while on a tour to sell war bonds. He said that for the past hour, as we silently tramped the beach, he had been reliving wonderful times with her. He told me about their first duck shoot, early in the morning, the fog too thick to see the ducks, although you could hear them. Carole asked what they could do about it—just sit here in the blind until it clears, Clark told her. She said she had just thought of something they could do while they were waiting—we made love, Clark said, which ain't easy in a duck blind.

He made a funny little sound—I thought he was chortling over the incident—but in the moonlight I could see his tears. He continued to weep as he told me about the evening that Carole, dressed in a smashing white evening gown, had jumped fully clothed into a fishpond, and he told me about the dogs they had given each other, the silly picnics Carole arranged, the Sundays alone on their ranch, their ludicrous attempt to go into the egg business, all the while making little observations about films and Hollywood life that I didn't really understand, but what I did understand was the enormous love Gable had had for this woman. In a sense, it was unreal that Clark Gable was sitting there on the wet sand weeping over the loss of his movie star wife, but the pressures of OCS had pushed him close to the edge.

"They think I don't know," he said, "but I do—what they

found of her—I know . . . decapitated, and the rest of her burned to nothing." He fished inside his shirt and brought out two chains, one that held his dog tag, the other a small locket that he opened. It contained a fragment of jeweled metal. He said that that was the only thing of hers that hadn't burned—the fragment was from a diamond-and-ruby clip he had given to her.

He put the memento away and we were just getting up to resume our patrol when a piercing shot exploded in the night, followed by shouts and a form running at pell-mell speed along the sidewalk at the crest of the beach. We learned that Gable's wish had been fulfilled—some OTS instant captain who didn't know the password had gone for a stroll and had run afoul of the sentry on the adjoining beach, who had fired at him but missed.

Gable got a good laugh out of that, and for the rest of our tour he talked about various hunting and fishing trips, but didn't mention Carole Lombard again.

That was the last time I saw him.

I have recounted these rather inconsequential incidents with Gable because in retrospect it seems to me that meeting Gable contributed importantly to my awareness that even the famous were vulnerable. Later on, when I began to write about these "name" people who were envied and seemingly impregnable to the worries and woes of ordinary man, I'm sure I was subconsciously affected by Gable, heartbroken and weeping on that beach in Miami. As a matter of fact, there was an incident in my boyhood, when I was twelve, that also must have contributed to the attitude I brought toward those I was to write about.

The incident involved Louis Armstrong, who was appearing at the time with his band on the stage of the Grand Theatre in St. Louis, one of those opulent movie palaces that flourished during the Depression. For fifty cents a person could escape the dismal world of unemployment, evicting landlords, and bare cupboards, and be momentarily distracted by the pomp and glitter of ornate, rococo theatres festooned with crystal chandeliers, marble staircases, and lush pseudo-Persian carpets. On the screen was a world of beautifully groomed people in rich surroundings, on the stage musicians in tuxedoes, a team of elegantly attired ballroom dancers, a comedian who made you laugh. I didn't have the price of admission to these theatres, but I was skilled in slipping through exit doors when a show broke, and easing past the usher who guarded the door.

That's how I got to see Louis Armstrong, whose music I knew from the radio. At the Grand I enjoyed the way he laughed and blew the piercing high notes on his trumpet and sang in that gravelly voice of his, smiling all the time; the way his head jiggled a little when he spoke as if his words were dancing; and the way he always held a crisp white handkerchief with which he mopped his brow. I just loved to sit there in the cavernous dark of the Grand and feel good because Louie seemed to be having such a good time singing and playing for us. I would bring a couple of sandwiches, usually white bread with sandwich spread on it, to sustain me while I sat through two shows. I couldn't get enough of Louie Armstrong. He was at the Grand for several weeks (the movie changed every week) and I snuck in to see him every chance I got.

One evening, after sitting through my customary two shows, I left the theatre and went to the Walgreen's on the corner for an ice cream cone. I had just sold two of my best cigar bands to Bob Tyzzer, so I had the scratch for a nickel cone. I was standing at the end of the soda fountain, waiting my turn, when in walked Louie Armstrong with two members of his band. They stood at the end of the counter where there was a TAKE-OUT ORDERS sign. The counterman, who had pimple craters on the back of his neck and wore his soda jerk hat cocked over one eye, was scooping out my tutti-frutti cone while Louie and his men waited patiently. But after he handed me my cone and took my nickel, the soda jerk paid no attention to Louie, didn't even look his way, just stood with his back against the coffee urn chewing on a toothpick. I watched all this, licking my cone.

Finally, Louie said: "Excuse me, could I please give you a take-out order."

Without looking at him, the counterman said: "We don't serve niggers."

"We don't plan to eat it here . . ."

"You heard me," the counterman said; he had red veins on his nose.

"We're appearing down the block at the Grand," Louie said.

The counterman finally looked at him. "There's a nigger restaurant down on Biddle with chitlins and all that shit."

One of Louie's bandmen said: "The other counterman filled our order yesterday."

The counterman ignored him.

The other bandman said: "Come on, Louie, Buster and me knows a place."

"I told you not to come, Boss," the man called Buster said.

"It's okay, I needed the walk," Louie said.

Louie's face did not show anger or rankle as he walked out with his two musicians. I followed them as they headed back toward the Grand. I could hear Louie saying that there wasn't enough time to go all the way to Biddle for sandwiches and that they'd just have to wait until after the last performance.

When they stopped for traffic at the corner, I found myself standing beside Louie, who looked down at me, my mouth ringed with ice cream, and he smiled. "Mr. Armstrong," I said, startling myself, "I'll get those things for you."

"Well, that's real nice of you, my man, but it might cause some trouble . . ."

"He'll have to serve me."

The two musicians agreed and Louie gave me his list and some money, and Buster said he'd wait for me while Louie and the other man went back to the theatre.

I was really frightened when I walked back into that Walgreen's, and I regretted having acted so boldly, but as luck would have it, there was a different counterman at the take-out section when I got there. Buster waited outside on the sidewalk. As he was filling my order, the other counterman spotted me and yelled out: "You getting that for those jigs?"

"No, sir!" I was an accomplished liar, as were all Depression kids.

The pimply counterman started in on me but the one who was serving me said: "Lay off him, will ya?" and that shut him up.

My order filled two brown bags, which Buster and I carried to the backstage entrance of the Grand. I followed Buster to an area under the stage where Louie and members of his band were sitting around. Louie got up delightedly when he saw us and asked me my name. "Aaron? How you spell that?"

"Big *A*, little *a*, r-o-n," I told him.

"Well, Big A," he said, "you gonna blow a solid horn some-day." I loved the silken rumble of his voice.

He introduced me to his band en masse and made me share some of his french fries. When it was time to go on for the next show, he placed me in the wings and let me watch the show from there, which was the most thrilling thing that had happened to me up to that point in my life.

On the streetcar, going back to our room at the Westgate Hotel (I snuck on streetcars the same way I snuck into theatres), I thought about what had happened at Walgreen's. Of course, having been born and raised in St. Louis, I knew that Negroes were segregated and not equals, but what I couldn't understand was how Louis Armstrong, who all those white people had paid good money to see, how he could be treated like that. I asked my father about it but he said the counterman was right—if you let down the barriers for one of them, then all the other Negroes would come flocking into Walgreen's. Besides, he added, he didn't think Louie Armstrong had much of a voice.

3

Dorothy Parker Is at the Plaza in Dire Straits

It took Dorothy Parker two months to finish "The Game," but when I went to the New Weston to get it and congratulate her, I found her in a surprisingly somber mood. With a quick little thrust of her head toward the bedroom, she immediately communicated the problem—Lynn Spiegel-Eagle was still ensconced in one of the beds. Three months! and, Dorothy confided, no sign of departure. I asked her whether she had discussed the future with Mrs. Spiegel-Eagle, but she said that Lynn was in such an abysmal state it would be cruel to do so. Dorothy thought it might be helpful, however, for her to introduce me so that I could possibly convey to Lynn, as gently as possible, that she ought to be making other bed arrangements. Ross had tried, Dorothy explained, but Lynn wouldn't speak to him. I really didn't want to go in and face this Lynn person, but I felt so sorry for Dorothy's haplessness I consented.

The sheet was pulled up over the inert form on the bed, face and all, as if it were a freshly deceased body. "Lynn, dear, I'd like you to meet my good friend A. E. Hotchner, called Hotch," Dorothy said brightly.

The sheet descended like a reluctant stage curtain, Lynn Spiegel-Eagle revealing herself in slow stages: first the jet-black hair, then large black eyes, followed by the shock of the recognizable nose and mouth. The face was thinner and the skin had lost its luminosity, but she was unmistakably Lynn Ruth Baggett of Wichita Falls, Texas, also known as Flavia. In a convoluted way, I was responsible for Lynn's being in Dorothy's bed.

Wichita Falls was the town adjacent to Sheppard Field, a huge Air Force induction center into which four thousand draftees poured daily, to be inspected, outfitted, and drilled before being assigned to various branches of the Air Force. I had made a valiant effort to avoid this miserable fate, by trying, with a pal of mine, to get into the Navy Air Force, which I had chosen as a result of having been cinematically brainwashed by the hundreds of films I had watched at neighborhood movie houses. To be honest about it, all the history books I had studied in school had made no real emotional impact on me, but Hollywood's schmaltzy versions of history, studded with such glamorous war heroes as the devil-may-care flying ace, the intrepid submarine commander, the duty officer lashing himself to the wheel—this was the real stuff of history that had charged my imagination.

So now that the time had come to embark on my own military career, I chose the one Hollywood war hero whom I had found glamorous above all—the naval combat pilot. I had been particularly influenced in this choice by a movie I had seen (several times) in which Dick Powell performed heroic aerial acts while wearing an exquisite white tunic, gold-buttoned at the throat, epauletted, festooned with gold braid; Dick Powell in rocketing descent, on the attack, looking right and left, coolly firing his machine guns, then up and away, leaving in his wake a smoking enemy plane spiraling out of control, that white-and-gold uniform as crisp and romantic on landing as it was at the start of the film. I had never set foot in an airplane but in looking through the recruiting brochure of the Naval Air Corps (I had assembled every available piece of material on all the commissions being offered by all the services) I concluded that that uniform of the Naval Air Corps was reason enough for choosing them above their competition.

I sought out my friend Myron Gollub, who was scheduled to be drafted about the same time I was, and reminded him what a favorable impression Dick Powell's uniform had made on us when we had seen the film.

"You mean you're choosing the Navy Air Corps because of the uniform?" Myron asked. Or, rather, growled. Myron was short, with the build of a middleweight wrestler (which he had been in college), and when irritated, he actually growled. We had been friends for many years.

"I know that seems superficial," I said, "but no matter what we go into it's a gamble, so we may as well wind up in a terrific uniform."

Myron did, but I didn't. The last test we were given on the physical was for depth perception. I tried every which way, before lunch and after, but I could not line up the two pegs at the end of that long table.

Undaunted, I talked another good friend, Carroll Donohue, into applying for an ensign commission in the Navy's V-12 program, but again, Donohue made it but I didn't, this time flunking because I had (imagine!) flat feet. I had played collegiate baseball and basketball but the Navy doctor said my flat feet could never take the pounding to which they'd be subjected on the metal deck of a destroyer. I also tried the less glamorous Judge Advocate branch of the service but there were too many experienced lawyers in line before me.

So I had to face the grim reality of being drafted, a fate I equated with being sent to prison. The best I could do was to wangle a couple of induction postponements thanks to my being an attorney for an indigent defendant in a criminal proceeding, but even that didn't work out for as long a time as I had hoped.

My firm did not handle criminal litigation but in this case I had been appointed by the court. To defend indigent people accused of crimes who could not afford a lawyer, judges in the criminal courts picked lawyers at random from the bottom of the rolls of the Bar Association—in other words, from among the young, inexperienced lawyers who had just passed their bars and been admitted to practice. In this manner I had been directed (court-appointed lawyers had no choice in the matter) to take on the defense of one Steve R. Cysmanski. I went to the city jail, where Mr. Cysmanski was being held without bail. The Cysmanski file and Cysmanski arrived at about the same time. I was seated in the lawyers' room, at a wooden desk behind a foot-high divider, and had just opened the file when the elevator slowly rose into view from the cellblocks below. Out stepped a guard followed by a 6-foot, 8-inch Frankenstein dressed in gray jail pants and a dirty undershirt, over the top of which cascaded a Niagara of ominous chest hair. I presumed that this huge object hulking toward me was Cysmanski and I rose to greet him as he approached, but he did not shake hands or acknowledge my presence. He sat down, leaned forward across the barrier, and said, in a guttural, heavily accented voice: "This whole thing's a crock of shit."

"Mr. Cysmanski," I said, looking at the open file, "I have not had a chance . . ."

"Little whore doin' it for two bits a throw with every little fart in the neighborhood . . ." I was reading the indictment as fast as I could. ". . . Takes after her whore mother . . . rape—ha! I don't no rape her—she just mad I don't give her money she want . . ."

As I quickly read, I could feel a distinct icy flow starting at my coccyx and moving up my spinal column toward the base of my skull. This was my first litigation, my first criminal proceeding, and what was the case? A father charged with the statutory rape of his fourteen-year-old daughter on not one but on eleven separate and documented occasions; in the State of Missouri statutory rape carried a *mandatory* death sentence. Cysmanski was a steelworker who lived in one room in a boardinghouse with his fourteen-year-old daughter and his nine-year-old son. The mother was a streetwalker who, after slim pickings on the streets of St. Louis, had left the family circle the previous year to return to her original and more lucrative beat in downtown Milwaukee. Cysmanski, the indictment charged, followed a pattern of Saturday afternoon intercourse with his daughter (referred to as Saturday "rapes" in the file); the alleged pattern was that the son was sent out of the room at one o'clock while Cysmanski got in bed with his daughter, after which Cysmanski gave the daughter fifty cents to take her brother and herself to a double feature at the neighborhood movie house. There were detailed statements in the file by the daughter, the son, the landlady, and a quartet of social workers. The daughter was currently being cared for by nuns in the House of Good Shepherds, and the son had been placed temporarily in an orphanage.

When I cited these various indictments to Cysmanski, he became enraged. He roared a couple of expletives and pounded his flat hand on the table so hard I thought the walls would come down. So did the two floor guards, who came running. "She is a tramp, I tell you! I do nothing, nothing, NOTHING! She want a raise to one dollar and that is why she call the social worker and make all this troubles. Is blackmail—is for the one dollar. Two-bit little whore think she worth one dollar!"

In response to my request for another deferment, I was summoned to appear before my draft board. Ten middle-aged men, eight with paunches, six with glasses, all wearing vests, behind a long wooden table. One folding chair facing the table for me to sit on. I described my involvement in the Cysmanski case to the board, and pointed out that although I had tried to induce Cysmanski to plead guilty and to let me plea-bargain for him with the prosecuting attorney's office (the prosecutor had indicated he might consent to five years), Cysmanski was adamant in maintaining his innocence and rejecting any kind of deal involving admitted guilt. (Actually what Cysmanski had said was "Me cop a plea? You crazy or something?! Wait I tell the jury —they see Cysmanski good honest fellow, hard of work, not guilty. Then afterwards, that little whore, that liar, that chippie from her mother, she better watch out. Oh, I get my hands on her! I break her everything!" But I didn't go into detail with the draft board.)

What I told the board was that I was in the midst of preparing for Cysmanski's trial and I asked for another six months so that my client would be properly represented. The gentlemen of the draft board were very interested in some of the details of the case and asked quite a few questions that had nothing to do with my draft status. Two days later, notification of another six-month deferment came in the mail. I wouldn't have to deal with my military fate again until February of 1942, and by then, I figured, Hitler would have conquered Russia and the war would very likely be over.

I worked hard preparing for Cysmanski's trial. My investigation disclosed that his daughter, a ripe, robust fourteen-year-old who looked five years older, was indeed the neighborhood chippie, doing it in the bushes with kids on the block for two bits a throw, but that was no legal solace for Cysmanski. I knew there would inevitably be a verdict of guilty which I would appeal, and since appeals take a year or more to be heard and decided, I felt it might be allowable grounds for a further draft postponement.

But after the jury was impaneled, the prosecuting attorney made an impassioned opening statement to the jurors, predominantly women, demanding that Cysmanski burn in the electric chair for his dastardly crime, and so well did he lard it on that Cysmanski caved in, grabbing my arm, and in a strong voice shouted: "Cop the plea! Cop the plea!"

I asked for a recess and conferred with the prosecuting attorney, but since the trial had already started, he upped the ante to ten years, which Cysmanski eagerly embraced. So Cysmanski went to state prison and I became a buck-ass GI private and went to the "prison" outside Wichita Falls. For miles in every direction, there was not a tree, shrub, sage bush, cactus, not an animate or inanimate impediment to the sand-blown wind. Whoever in Washington had boondoggled this miserable, worthless sandy expanse into the huge complex known as Sheppard Field (could Sheppard have been the boondoggler?) should have had a statue erected in his honor.

There is no more miserable fate than being drafted. Cattle on the Texas range were treated better in their herds than we were in ours. For example, no sooner had we been disgorged from the pre-World War I trains in which we had been packed, and unloaded into barracks as primitive as horse stalls, than we were herded en masse to a huge hangar where we were told to drop our newly acquired GI pants for a short-arm inspection. As I stood there at the entrance to the hangar in the Texas pre-dawn, my pants on my shoe tops, trying to protect my genitalia from the sand-stinging wind with the medical form which each of us was carrying, I recall feeling demeaned to the point of anger. Sonsabitches! Don't they realize I don't belong here? I am an educated man. A.B., Doctor of Law. I can type. I debated Cambridge University. There was an article about me as a playwright in the *St. Louis Post-Dispatch.* I'm a lawyer. I kept Cysmanski from the electric chair. God knows I did everything I could to avoid this miserable fate. Sonsabitches!

Inside the hangar, I found myself at the beginning of a long, wooden runway on which the assembly line of bare-assed GIs were being examined. What stretched before me, as far as the eye could see, under blindingly bright illumination, was a mass short-arm inspection. Standing on each side of the runway were military doctors and orderlies. The elevated ramp put the GI penis at the doctor's eye level.

The first doctor I encountered poked a hernia-seeking finger beside my testicles and told me to cough. Twice. Marked my medical form. I moved on. Doctor pushed his thumb into the liver area of my stomach. Two hard thrusts. Hurt. Marked my form. Moved to another doctor, who put his icy fingers on my penis, pulled it up, side to side, examined the tip. Penis shrank.

The doctor next to icy fingers said: "Jesus, look at this, Phil."

Phil looked, and so did I. The doctor had stripped back the foreskin on the penis of the GI next to me whom I recognized as Lamar Ottersby, one of the toughest of the hillbillies in my barracks. There was a dirty, heavy crust all around the head of the penis, which the foreskin had covered.

"Don't any of you guys ever wash?" his doctor asked. "Just take a look at his." He pointed to my penis, which shrank even more. "Now that's the way a penis should be."

Lamar looked contemptuously at my penis. I knew there would be hell to pay. I was the only circumcised penis in the barracks and there had already been a lot of derision from the Texas, Kansas, Ozarks, Oklahoma backwoods types who populated my barracks. The luck of the draw. Tens of thousands of men pouring into Sheppard Field every week from the Pacific to the Mississippi and I wound up in a barracks where I was the only circumcised city boy among a concentration of fully sheathed hillbillies.

"Move on down to Post Three," the doctor said to Lamar. "They'll strip that crust off there and disinfect you. How come you don't strip back and wash?"

"Because Ah doan play with mahself lahke some people," Lamar said, looking squarely at me.

The last section on the elevated ramp was devoted to gathering urine specimens in small glass bottles. An orderly admonished: "Don't piss it full." I was about to urinate in my bottle when a slightly familiar voice whispered in my ear: "Hotch, I'm in a jam." It was Harry Greensfelder, whom I knew from the tennis team at Washington University. Sweat was running down

Dorothy Parker Is at the Plaza in Dire Straits

Harry's face and he looked like he was in the third set of a tough match. He was clutching an empty urine bottle. He looked frightened.

"I can't piss," he whispered.

"What's wrong?"

"I've been trying like hell but I got this block I can't piss in public."

"Well, maybe they'll let you . . ."

"No, I asked but they just yelled at me. I can't even piss in urinals if someone's at the urinal next to me. I've been standing here for ten minutes with my dong in this bottle."

I could see that Harry was on the point of cracking up. I looked around at the doctors and orderlies—they were all busy and the ramp was crowded with GIs pissing into bottles. I took Harry's bottle and quickly peed in it. Then I shut off and peed the rest of what I had in mine. I gave Harry his half-filled bottle.

"Hotch, I'll never forget that you did this for me," he said, oozing gratitude.

"You've got whatever disease I've got, Harry."

"You're a helluva friend," he said.

Soon after that short-arm inspection, a directive came out that said that the commanding general of Sheppard Field had determined that it was in the best interests of the Army Air Force that personnel be circumcised. This would have to be on a voluntary basis, but as an incentive, those complying would be given a three-day pass.

"Shit, man," Lamar Ottersby said, "little snip o' skin and we got us three days to raise hell. We get paid tomorrow and we could have us a high ol' time."

Our pay was twenty-one dollars a month, which was only seventy cents a day, but it could buy a lot of hell in Wichita Falls, where a room in the hotel was two dollars a night. One after another, the hillbillies signed up. Our barracks chief, a hung-belly corporal who had been in the peacetime army for fifteen years (following his discharge from San Quentin for armed robbery), led the group to the infirmary. The corporal was an illiterate, sadistic, sour-faced man but he was disconcertingly pleasant and cheerful the morning he took the group to the infirmary. I was left all alone in the barracks and, believe me, I was glad to see all of them go. After the incident during penis inspection, I had been given the nickname of "Short-Arm"—the circumcisions of my tormentors should put an end to that.

I would have three blissful days without them. Without the blare of "You Are My Sunshine," "She'll Be Comin' 'Round the Mountain," and "Turkey in the Straw" coming from dozens of competing radios. Without farts, teeth-grindings, sour smells from food packages, belches, disgusting jokes, and latrine stenches.

The day after the group's departure, the corporal sent me to the infirmary with their medical records. The sight in the infirmary ward was one I shall never forget: row upon row of hospital beds, each with a moaning GI lying on his back, no covers, his penis heavily bandaged. Bandaged penises to infinity.

"They can't stand the slightest pressure," the ward orderly explained, "like the touch of a sheet or pajamas—drives 'em crazy. Poor bastards, thought there was nothing to it—hell, circumcising an adult is fuckin' painful."

"That was a dirty trick," I said. "The army should have warned them about that."

The corporal smiled at me, and I felt silly for having said it.

The group returned to the barracks four days after their circumcisions. They were still not very chipper and some of them complained that it hurt too much to pee.

"All right, Corporal, here we are," Lamar Ottersby said. "They really took us on this one but leastways we get our three-day passes."

"What three-day passes?"

"The ones we was promised for gettin' our dongs clipped."

"You've just *had* your three-day passes—in the hospital," the corporal snarled. "Now let's scrub up this place, it's a real shithole."

In the days that followed, a lot of incoming GIs were similarly induced into getting themselves circumcised, but none of the circumcised veterans ever spilled the beans. It remained a steadfast, silent conspiracy, and those who had so painfully lost

their foreskins and their three-day passes got a measure of re-
venge out of watching the new lambs being led to the slaughter.

You probably think that I have forgotten Lynn Baggett in this
lengthy detour, but, no, she's about to appear—I just wanted to
color in the background. That cold, sand-swept winter at Sheppard Field, I was miraculously rescued from the short arms, the
suffocating sandstorms on the punishing drill field, kitchen police, latrine duties and a paranoic barracks chief by an angel of
mercy disguised as a staff sergeant who summoned me off the
drill field and Jeeped me to Headquarters Building, where I was
ushered into the august presence of a full colonel. He was en-
grossed in my qualification card, a large yellow biographical
sheet that followed every GI throughout his military career.
"You're just the man I'm looking for," he said, to my astonishment. "I see you wrote an original campus musical when you
were in college and that's what you're going to do for us."
   President Roosevelt had decreed that an event, to be known
as "I Am An American Day," be commemorated by every state-
side military installation with an entertainment that was to be
staged in a nearby town with proceeds going to Army Emergency Relief, a fund that took care of widows and orphans of
servicemen. I was assigned to help write the Sheppard Field
offering, which was to be a musical comedy; it had to be ready
within a few weeks for presentation to the citizens of nearby
Wichita Falls.
   The colonel informed me that I was being detached from my
training group and placed in a special unit of musicians, writers,
composers, actors, directors, choreographers, set designers,
and such, which he had set up in its own barracks as a separate
entity. I wound up writing the book for the musical, as well as
lyrics for some of the music, but it never occurred to me to
perform in the show until Jack Thomas, an ingratiating fellow
who wrote the music, pointed out that we would be back on the
drill field when the show went into rehearsal unless we were
members of the cast.
   Jack's second inspiration was his insistence that we not have
a chorus line of muscled GIs with balloons in their sweaters, but
the real thing—a dozen Texas beauties. "These are serious

times," Jack told the colonel, "and we should not be in front of the public in drag." The colonel agreed, and that is how Jack and I wound up with the enviable assignment of looking for girls in Wichita Falls. Finding chorus girls with dancing experience was no problem (we placed an item in the local paper and five hundred girls and their mamas mobbed the hotel ballroom where we held the auditions) but we needed one girl for the cast who was strikingly beautiful and could act. None of the girls we auditioned was what we were looking for, but I accidentally found her in the hotel's drugstore, working behind the counter. Lynn Ruth Baggett was her name, and her father owned the drugstore. She was nineteen, and Jack and I agreed she was one of the most beautiful girls we had ever seen. She was not very good at reading her lines, but it didn't matter, not the way she looked.

The show, which was called *Three Dots with a Dash,* was only supposed to run for a couple of weekends, but the commanding general of the entire Southwest, who bore the Dickensian name of Fickle, came to one of the performances with his wife, who, as fate would have it, was an aspiring songwriter. She and the general were enthusiastic about the show, and Jack, in another burst of inspiration, said that as one composer to another he'd like to hear some of her music. Which he did, with the result that one of her songs found its way into our score, and General Fickle decreed that we should go on tour throughout the Southwest in a convoy of army trucks, taking our chorus girls and the beauteous Lynn Baggett with us.

The tour was a wonderful adventure for me, as a theatre experience (I played the comedy lead), and as a Baedeker of the towns and cities all over Texas, Kansas, and Oklahoma, where, of course, I had never been; but there were two incidents that were profound shocks. The first was my discovery that most of the actors, technicians, and musicians were homosexuals who formed liaisons with one another, leaving the chorus girls and Junior League ladies to Jack and myself and a few others. (Jack and I took two of the chorus girls, hard-bitten Texans, to one of the Junior League after-theatre parties, a very proper affair— but when my chorus girl was offered asparagus, she said in a loud, clear twang: "Asparagus? Thank you, no, it makes my piss stink.") In my St. Louis world, I was only dimly aware of gay people; back then homosexuality was a taboo that was rarely spoken about, much less observed. That I should find it in such a large group, and in the military, no less, was indeed a shocking revelation.

The other shocker occurred during our performances in Fort Worth. We had heard that our fame had spread to the West Coast and that a talent scout for Warner Brothers was coming to see a performance. The advent of the scout got much less of a reaction from Lynn than from the chorus girls, who had squealing visions of being the second coming of Betty Grable. I had gotten to know Lynn quite well. Her father had not wanted to let her tour, for obvious reasons, but I had given him my word that I would be her big brother, and he had trusted me.

We got along fine—she had a good sense of humor, an attractive, self-effacing quality, and an intelligent maturity unusual for a girl of nineteen who had never been out of Wichita Falls. So nothing about Lynn had prepared me for the shock I got on the evening we came to the theatre for our final performance in Fort Worth and found that she had checked out of her hotel and gone off to Hollywood with the talent scout, without telling a soul.

Her understudy filled in for her but I could never understand the completely masked ambition that must have motivated her to leave us in the lurch like that. I suppose she was afraid we'd try to talk her into staying, that we might phone her father. I don't know. During the war, in various Air Force movie houses, I saw her in a few films, small parts, but then she had disappeared from the screen and now here she was immovably in Dorothy Parker's bed, and here was Dorothy telling Lynn that she would like her to meet me.

Lynn raised her head from the pillow and looked at me with clouded eyes. "Well, if it isn't Jeep," she said. That was my name in the musical.

I started to reminisce about the show in an attempt to get her attention, but her head returned to the pillow and she never said another word. Talking to her was like trying to revive a corpse with mouth-to-mouth resuscitation. After a while, Dorothy mo-

tioned to me to give up and we returned to the living room to
have a drink.

The way Dorothy finally rid herself of Lynn was rather drastic
but certainly effective—she simply packed up and moved to the
Hotel Volney without telling Lynn where she was going.

Lynn's reaction was to take a taxi to the airport and return to
Hollywood. Existence in Los Angeles is impossible without a car,
so one of Lynn's friends, the actor George Tobias, lent her one of
his. The first day she had it on the road, she ran over a small child
and was jailed for vehicular homicide. Not long after that, she
committed suicide. All these years I have felt a residue of guilt at
having induced that young, pretty girl to leave the cosmetic
counter to become an actress. The stories about Sam Spiegel's
treatment of her were not pretty. How much better off she would
have been in the limited but safe confines of Wichita Falls.

Dorothy too eventually moved to the Coast with Ross Evans,
and I lost touch with her for a while, but one afternoon she
phoned me from the Plaza Hotel and asked me to come see her
as soon as possible since it was practically an emergency. "I am
in straits," she said, "maybe not yet dire but damn near to it."

She was ensconced in an enormous suite with several bedrooms and baths. She was in one of the bedrooms with the
blinds drawn, sitting up in a four-poster bed, surrounded by
pillows. On the floor beside the bed were two cheap straw bags,
and a single cotton dress was hanging in an open closet. There
was a bottle of Scotch on the bed table from which Dorothy
replenished her glass as she told me her story, an occasional tear
dripping into the whisky.

She and Ross had gone to Hollywood hopefully to get a
screenplay assignment, but none was forthcoming. They decided to go to Mexico, where they could live cheaply while
writing a play with which they hoped to make their fortune in
New York. But when they arrived at the airport, with absolutely
no forewarning, Ross had left her standing on the sidewalk as
he got into an automobile and drove off with a woman who ran
a dress shop in Acapulco. And to add insult to her injury, he took
Dorothy's two dogs with him. Dorothy said he left her at the

airport with no money, no luggage, and no good-bye. Tears coursed regularly down her cheeks as she recounted this lugubrious tale.

I asked her what had happened. Had they had a fight?

"No," she said, "I think Ross did it because I'm half-Jewish. He really hated Jews."

It was obvious that she was too distraught to think clearly. She was fifty-six now, a sensitive age to be deserted by a young lover in favor of an Acapulco shopkeeper. She said she didn't have a penny to her name and that she didn't know what to do since she could no longer write screenplays or short stories. I asked her how she planned to pay for the opulent suite she occupied, but all she said was that she hoped to "manage," her usual vagueness where money matters were concerned. I asked her how I could help, and she said by giving her my handkerchief for her runny nose. As I watched her pour more Scotch in her glass, the tears running down her face, a sentence from "Big Blonde" came to me: " 'Oh, Lord, oh, Lord,' she moaned, and tears for herself and for life striped her cheeks."

I was there only a short time when a contingent of three of her lady friends came boisterously into the bedroom, clucking condolences. Dorothy obviously had summoned everyone in her address book to commiserate with her tragedy. It was my impression that she was enjoying her misery.

Within a year Dorothy had returned to Hollywood and remarried Alan Campbell, but after her name had been dragged before the House Un-American Activities Committee, they were not employable as a writing team. For two years they drank heavily and squabbled, and finally Dorothy went back to New York by herself. I saw her often then. She was writing a play with Arnaud d'Usseau, who was a playwright whose collaborator had died, and he took Dorothy on to supplant his deceased colleague. The play was called *Ladies of the Corridor,* and the work seemed to exhilarate Dorothy. She was in excellent conversational form, and those evenings we spent in the D'Usseaus' living room, Dorothy holding forth on a variety of subjects while her toy poodle, Misty, frolicked on and over the furniture and us, were memorable. She was almost sixty but there was a glint of youth in her voice and her laughter.

But the play was a failure on Broadway, and Dorothy withdrew into a state of alcoholic indolence, pretty much the way she was when I first met her. I did not hear from her during those years, but soon after Hemingway's death, I received a call from her. We met for lunch and I was sad to see that although she was making an effort to sound like her old self, the remarkable light in her eyes had gone out and her spirit was forced. But there was a plucky quality about her, a sparrow trying to maneuver with a broken wing. Her face was puffy and her hands unsteady. She told me that Alan Campbell had died of an overdose of sleeping pills, which I hadn't known, but now I understood her absorption with the details of Hemingway's suicide. She idolized Fitzgerald and Hemingway, especially the latter, who, she had often mentioned, was precisely the writer she had always wanted to be. That such an enviable man should take his own life baffled her, in fact angered her. She went into a long diatribe about the obligation of the artist, not at all characteristic of her, a tourniquet of words to stem her bleeding emotions over Campbell's suicide.

"Well," she said, when she had finally cooled down, "I really should be immune by now—what's one more disappointment?"

I never saw her again, although she lived another six years. They were years of lonely exile from the life of celebrity wit and flop plays, love affairs and sexual debacles, Hollywood affluence and New York penury, literary accomplishment and writing paralysis. She had a warmth uniquely hers, and I always felt better after I had seen her even when things were going badly for her. She was gracious and graceful under the most hideous circumstances, and she never blamed anyone for her plight.

I just wish she had been happier. She deserved it.

4

When Hemingway Hurts
Bad Enough, He Cries

New York City is surely the busiest, most distracting city in the world, but it can also be the loneliest place in the world for an outsider. It was Christmastime but Clarice's engagement at the Met had been postponed, and as I walked along Park Avenue that Christmas Eve, the esplanade alive with lighted trees, I certainly did not feel I was a part of the city, or of the people in it.

In fact, at that time my only social life revolved around a Wednesday night poker game in Greenwich Village. The game was held at Don Congdon's apartment on Charlton Street, after which we'd adjourn to Chumley's for beer and conversation. Don was a bright, attractive young man who at that time was a fiction editor on *Collier's* magazine. I had met Don through a short story I had written, "Candle in the Poolroom Window," which I had submitted to *Collier's*. He liked the story, which I had written in Runyonesque style, but he could never quite convince the editor to take it for publication. But Don and I struck up an acquaintance over my story, and he invited me to join his weekly poker game, a modest nickel-and-dime affair. The other players were a revolving collection of out-of-work editors and unpublished writers, one of whom was a lanky, darkly handsome young man named Jerry Salinger.

It didn't bother Jerry a bit that his short stories were being rejected. He had an ego of cast iron. Many's the Wednesday we sat in a booth at Chumley's after a game, nursing the single beer we could afford when we hadn't won, which was often. We'd sit there and Jerry, who used his initials, J. D., as his by-line, would arrogantly condemn all the well-known writers from Dreiser to Hemingway. In fact he was quite convinced that no really good American writer existed after Melville—that is, until the advent of J. D. Salinger. I used to listen to his angry discourses, utterly fascinated with his opinionatedness and with the furious belief he had in his own literary destiny.

At first I thought that his anger was rooted in the impecunious have-not state common to all of us, but I found out that Jerry lived in a luxurious Park Avenue apartment with his parents, and lived well. I also found out that he had been kicked out of a succession of good Eastern schools, and that he had had a "nervous breakdown" while in service during the war. I never felt that he was a friend, he was too remote for friendship, but on a few occasions he invited me along on one of his nightclubbing sprees—he particularly liked the Blue Angel and the Ruban Bleu, two of the clubs that featured young, unproved talent. On those occasions, we stayed up late drinking beer and enjoying the endless parade of beginning performers, some of whom were destined to have successful careers. In between the acts, Jerry talked, mostly about writing and writers, but sometimes he took on institutions, like the posh schools that had dismissed him, country clubs, writing classes that duped untalented boobs into thinking that one could learn to be a writer in a classroom, and so forth.

Despite his staunch condemnations and self-acclaim, I felt that down deep Jerry was as insecure as I was and had no firmer a grasp on his destiny than I had on mine. My impression was that he was just whistling in the dark to keep his courage up. But he was an original, and I found his intellectual flailings enormously attractive, peppered as they were with sardonic wit and a myopic sense of humor. I had dinner with him a few times (when I had a little money), at his favorite restaurant—in fact, it was the only place I knew him to eat—Renato's, an old Italian restaurant with a garden that had been a speakeasy during Prohibition. It was there at Renato's, at Jerry's insistence, that I ate my first clam and my first frog's leg.

Jerry had written a short story, "Holden Caulfield on the Bus," which *The New Yorker* had rejected but he talked endlessly about how he would rework it and how eventually they would realize that it was a new kind of writing and publish it. He had read "Candle in the Poolroom Window," and another short story of mine, "An Ocean Full of Bowling Balls," both of which he found amusing, but he was nevertheless appalled that I would waste my time writing about something that was not connected with my life. "There is no hidden emotion in these stories," he said. "No fire between the words." He was right, of course. I was doing precisely what Tennessee Williams had done when he wrote his one-act play at Washington University, rejecting the writer's most precious tool, his own experience.

As a result of Jerry's expostulations on his theme that writing as an art is experience magnified, that Christmas, as I have said, feeling alienated from the yuletide world around me, I sat down at my typewriter on Christmas Day and wrote a short story, "The Christmas Canaries," which really wasn't fiction but a rather faithful account of how, when I was living in that hotel with my parents and my brother, Selwyn, with no money and dismal prospects for Christmas, I attempted to commercialize our canary, Skippy, by mating him with a female that a school friend had given to me (females don't sing and have no commercial value). The pet store was paying three dollars each for young canaries, a princely sum in those Depression days, and since there are as many as six eggs in a hatching, there would be enough for a tree, ornaments, presents for all, and, most importantly, food for a Christmas dinner. But after all the travail of mating the canaries and raising the baby birds in that small hotel room, after all the plans Selwyn and I had made for Christmas, having even picked out the presents we were going to give to our parents, we had the crushing bad luck of discovering, when we took the birds to the pet store, that all six were females—and worthless.

This time Don got an immediate acceptance from the editor-in-chief, and "The Christmas Canaries" became my first published short story, and my first object lesson in the importance of staying within the perimeter of what one has experienced for himself.

Salinger's perseverance with his own recorded experience also paid off in stories he began to sell to the *Saturday Evening Post,* and even, on resubmission after rewriting, the Holden Caulfield story for *The New Yorker.* Of course, that story was the progenitor for Jerry's classic, *The Catcher in the Rye.* But back then, when all of us were just beginning, only Salinger had complete confidence in his destiny as a writer—a writer he was and a writer he would always be, and, what's more, an *important* writer. Not so with the rest of us. Don Congdon left *Collier's* to become a literary agent (today he is one of the most successful ones in the business), and I myself quickly accepted Arthur Gordon's offer of an editorship on *Cosmopolitan.*

My first official act as an editor was to ask Jerry if he would write something for us, and he did, a fine short story called "Scratchy Needle on a Phonograph Record." With his usual arrogance, Jerry attached a note to the story that said if published not one word could be changed or deleted. I told Arthur that it was important to me that we adhere to Jerry's condition, and to that end I checked the galleys carefully, but what had escaped my attention was the title of the printed story, which I didn't see until the prepublication copy of the magazine, stamped "Not Made Ready," reached my desk and by that time no further changes could be made. I don't recall the banal title Arthur had put on the story, but it certainly was unrelated to scratchy needles on phonograph records.

Salinger was furious. Never spoke to me again.

Not long after that, Jerry left his parents' Park Avenue apartment to go live alone in a house he had found somewhere in Westchester County, and that's the last that any of the Village group saw of him. Over the years he moved farther and farther north into southern, then northern New England. He married and had a child, but spent endless time alone in a little place he had built in the woods, a good distance from the house in which his wife and child lived. *The New Yorker* published many of the stories he was planning during those Village days, my favorite being "A Perfect Day for Bananafish." Eventually, after a series of Zen stories, he became a hermit, renouncing wife and child and publication. It is rumored that he still writes every day, and accumulates what he writes, but no one has seen any of it and nothing of his has been published for fifteen years.

As I think about him, it occurs to me that Jerry's literary arrogance has now precluded him from participating in a publishing world contaminated by the books being published today. His attitude may well be that readers who read the tripe now in the bookstores are not fit to read the stories of J. D. Salinger.

I can't recall ever seeing him laugh.

When Clarice finally did arrive in New York, she did not stay with me after all. The Met, wanting her to be "visible," put her in the Park Plaza, where I stayed with her quite often, but I had to be very circumspect about my comings and goings. Clarice had expected to go into immediate rehearsal for either *Thaïs* or *La Bohème*, but days passed before Edward Johnson contacted her and then it was just a ceremonial greeting with no specifics. At the end of three weeks, her money and her patience giving out, she decided to make use of a written introduction she had been given to Spyros Skouras, who was then the head of Twentieth Century–Fox in New York. Clarice was half-Greek, and Greek friends in Paris had arranged this introduction to Skouras.

Skouras was a handsome, silver-haired, ebullient man in his late fifties, who, when very young, had come to the United States with his two brothers and found work as a busboy in a St. Louis restaurant. The boys saved their money, as only immigrants can save, and were able to buy a Nickelodeon next to the restaurant, where primitive movies were shown for the admission price of five cents. From this humble beginning, the industrious brothers compounded their Nickelodeons, eventually infiltrating Hollywood and its entrenched forces to gain control of Twentieth Century–Fox, one of Hollywood's prize oligarchies.

What was remarkable about Skouras' achievement was that he could scarcely make himself understood, so obscure was his command of English, and he could but barely read and write in English, yet he was able to evaluate screen projects and make binding judgments on what should or should not be produced. Of course, he had extremely capable producers like Darryl F. Zanuck on the lot, but the ultimate decisions were his.

He introduced Clarice to New York's Greek community, and not too long after she had asked for his assistance, the Met gave her definite dates for two performances of *Carmen.* This was baffling, for Clarice had not performed *Carmen* at the Paris Opéra or Opéra Comique, but she was grateful that she had at last been given an assignment. Risë Stevens was then the Met's great Carmen, but Clarice felt that with study and concentration she could give a good account of herself.

I decided that while she studied and prepared for her role, it was a good time to go to Cuba on my long-postponed Hemingway mission. I had Hemingway's address in the little town of San Francisco de Paula, which is about twenty minutes outside Havana, but the more I considered going out there and knocking at his door and disturbing him face to face, which is what Arthur had instructed me to do, the more my blood congealed. After two days of sitting by the Nacional pool in a semicomatose state induced by pure cowardice, I finally decided, The hell with it, there were other editorial jobs, I would not go banging on his door to ask him to write an article on the future of literature; and even had I had his unlisted telephone number, which I hadn't, I couldn't have managed to phone him.

So I took the coward's way out and wrote him a note saying that I had been sent down on this ridiculous mission but did not want to disturb him, and if he could simply send me a few words of refusal it would be enormously helpful to The Future of Hotchner.

Early the next morning the phone rang. "This Hotchner?"
"Yes."

"Dr. Hemingway here. Got your note. Can't let you abort your mission or you'll lose face with the Hearst organization, which is about like getting bounced from a leper colony. You want to have a drink around five? There's a bar called La Florida. Just tell the taxi."

Hemingway arrived a little late. He was wearing khaki pants held up by a wide old leather belt with a huge buckle inscribed GOTT MIT UNS, a white linen sport shirt that hung loose, and brown leather loafers without socks. His hair was dark with gray highlights, flecked white at the temples, and he had a heavy moustache that ran past the corners of his mouth, but no beard. He was massive. Not in height, for he was only an inch over six feet, or in weight, but in impact. Most of his two hundred pounds was concentrated above his waist: he had square heavy shoulders, long hugely muscled arms (the left one jaggedly scarred and a bit misshapen at the elbow), a deep chest, a belly-rise but no hips or thighs. Something played off him—he was intense, electrokinetic, but in control, a racehorse reined in. He stopped to talk to one of the musicians in fluent Spanish and something about him hit me—*enjoyment;* God, I thought, how he's *enjoying* himself! I had never seen anyone with such an aura of fun and well-being. He radiated it and everyone in the place responded. He had so much more in his face than I had expected to find from seeing his photographs.

As he came toward the bar, greeting the barman, I noticed that on his forehead, well above his left eye, there was a large oblong welt that looked as if a patch of flesh-colored clay had been stuck there haphazardly.

"Hotchner," he said, shaking hands, "welcome to the Cub Room." His hands were thick and square, the fingers rather short, the nails squared off. The bartender placed two frozen daiquiris in front of us; they were in conical glasses twice the size of my previous drink. "Here we have the ultimate achievement of the daiquiri-maker's art," Hemingway said. "Made a run of sixteen here one night."

"This size?"

"House record," the barman, who had been listening, said.

The daiquiris kept coming as we discussed Robert Flaherty's documentary films, which Hemingway greatly admired, Ted Williams, the Book-of-the-Month Club, Lena Horne, Proust, television, swordfish recipes, aphrodisiacs, and Indians, until eight o'clock, not threatening the Hemingway daiquiri record but setting an all-time Hotchner high. Hemingway took a drink with him for the road, sitting in the front seat of the station wagon next to his chauffeur; and I somehow managed to retain in the rum-mist of my head that he was going to pick me up the following morning to go out on his boat.

There were two Pilars in Hemingway's life: one, the lusty partisan of *For Whom the Bell Tolls;* the other, a forty-foot black-and-green cabin cruiser—both named after the Spanish shrine. The seagoing *Pilar* was docked in the Havana harbor, ready to roll when we got there. It had a flying bridge with topside controls, outsized riggers that could handle ten-pound skipping bait, and the capacity to fish four rods. Ernest introduced me to her with old affection.

The big engines turned over; Ernest climbed topside and steered her out of port, past Morro Castle, and up the coast about seven miles, toward the fishing village of Cojímar, which was destined to be the village of *The Old Man and the Sea.* Gregorio, mate on the *Pilar,* set out four lines, two with feathers, two with meat bait. I was topside with Ernest.

"Feesh! Feesh, Papa, Feesh!" Gregorio was calling from the stern. We looked quickly starboard; I saw brown flashing that turned to dark purple, pectoral fins that showed lavender, the symmetry of a submarine.

"Marlin," Ernest said, "let's go." He took hold of the topside rail and swung himself down. Gregorio handed him the rod with the meat bait. "Ever boat one of these?" Ernest asked.

"Never been deep-sea fishing."

"Then cut your teeth on this," he said, handing me the rod. I felt a touch of panic. Here was one of the world's great fishermen, a lightning-fast marlin whose size I couldn't believe, a big, complicated rod and reel—and here was I, who had never caught anything larger than a ten-pound bass out of my friend Sam Epstein's rowboat off Southold, Long Island.

But I had not reckoned with a quality of Ernest's I was to observe and enjoy many times over the ensuing years: his superb skill at instruction and his infinite patience with his pupil. In a quiet, even voice Ernest guided me every step of the way, from when to pull up to set the big hook in his mouth to when to bring him in close to be taken. A half hour later we were looking down at the beauty of that boated marlin; "We just might have a new *syndicat des pêcheurs*—Hotchner and Hemingway, Marlin Purveyors," Ernest said. I realized that he had tentatively knighted me as a potential co-adventurer; for thirteen years it was to be an invigorating, entertaining, educational, exasperating, uplifting, exhausting, surprising partnership.

Many times I have been asked why Ernest was so kind to me on that first meeting in Havana; he had a reputation for being pugnaciously inaccessible and yet he had virtually overwhelmed me with his hospitality. I think the explanation lies in the fact that I was young and struggling and vulnerable. During the thirteen years of our friendship, I saw this incredible generosity toward young people demonstrated time and again, both with money and with the commodity that Ernest regarded as infinitely more valuable than money—his time.

In retrospect, I think I arrived at a time when Ernest was lonely, when he had lost meaningful contact with his three sons, when several of his close friends, Maxwell Perkins, his editor, Scott Fitzgerald, and others, had recently died, and when his work was at a standstill; he had not written anything since *For Whom the Bell Tolls* was published in 1940, and there was no stirring in him for a new book. I shared his interest in certain sports—baseball, football, prizefighting—as well as having an athletic bent of my own; I was a risk-taker, a kid from the dead-wrong side of the tracks, an idolater of his writing, a person who exuded loyalty, which he prized. And I was someone who learned quickly, shared his love of Paris, and didn't complain or offer excuses. I state none of this as braggadocio, but as a retrospective assessment of that faraway young man, seeing him today as if he were someone else I knew intimately at the time.

Ernest never did write about the future of literature for *Cosmopolitan,* but what he eventually wrote, as a result of my visit, was a novel, *Across the River and into the Trees,* which he brought to New York on his way to Paris and Venice. I went to his suite at the Sherry Netherland to get the manuscript; he said it was a pity that he was on his way to good times in Paris while I languished behind a desk at *Cosmopolitan.*

"Well, Papa," I said, "like Jimmy Durante says: 'It's the conditions that prevail.'"

"Conditions are what you make them, boy. Now here's what we do." He picked up the manuscript of his book and removed a sheaf of pages from the end of it. "Now you take this to your editor and tell him that it's all there except for the last few chapters, which I'm taking with me because they need more polishing."

When I handed the manuscript to Herb Mayes, the editor who had supplanted Arthur, and told him that, he practically leaped out of his chair. "The last few chapters! My God, you know how unreliable he is! The way *he drinks*! There we'll be, going to press with the last installment and we won't have the ending! You'll have to go with him! Keep after him! Don't let him out of your sight! We *must* have these chapters by the first of January!"

When I went back to the Sherry Netherland later that evening, Ernest was sitting in an armchair, wearing a white tennis visor and reading a book. As I walked into the room, without looking up he said: "When are you leaving?"

I had gone to Havana anticipating that Hemingway, as widely publicized, was a hot-tempered, pugnacious soldier of fortune who roamed the world knocking over all objects, human and otherwise, that got in his way or irritated him. What I discovered was that the world's impression of him as a battering ram of a man was virtually the opposite of the truth. His short stories and his two earliest novels, *The Sun Also Rises* and *A Farewell to Arms,* had brought to American literature a new style of writing, lyrically simple, direct, very realistic, and writing the world over had been affected by it. But if Ernest had been the heavy-fisted giant of his reputation he could not have conceivably also been the sensitive artist whose work was eventually rewarded with both the Pulitzer and Nobel prizes for literature.

There were certain things in his background, though, that contributed to this distorted public image. He was a member of an ordinary middle-class family in Oak Park, Illinois, but abruptly, before his eighteenth birthday, he had quit high school and gone forth in the world to seek adventure. That quest led him into the uniform of a Red Cross ambulance driver on the Italian front in the First World War, where he was severely wounded. In the early Twenties, after a brief reportorial stint with the Toronto *Star,* he had gone to live in Paris, where he became a member of the expatriate set that later was labeled "The Lost Generation." By the time I met him, he had been married four times, had been under fire in both the Spanish Civil War (*For Whom the Bell Tolls* was based on that experience) and World War II, and had traveled far and wide, fishing for marlin and tuna, hunting big game on safari, and following the bulls in Spain.

Add to these exploits the fact that physically he had a massively indestructible quality about him, and one could understand his well-publicized reputation as a kind of garrulous bear. But as Oliver Goldsmith once observed about the great writer and scholar Samuel Johnson, who also had a reputation of being bearlike: "To be sure, he has a roughness in his manner: but no man alive has a more tender heart. He has nothing of the bear but his skin"—so one could say about Hemingway: tender heart and nothing of the bear but his skin.

There were two deep currents that ran simultaneously through Ernest's life: one was to participate fully in and experience deeply the joys and sorrows of existence; the other was to assess those experiences and emotionally react to them on the printed page. Ernest was an original man. No one else's word was good enough. He had to taste, smell, see, hear for himself.

"You need the devotion to your work that a priest of God has for his," he once told a high school student. Although that devotion was a side of Ernest that the public never saw, it was the most important aspect of his personality and character. Once asked what his life's credo was, he replied: "To write as well as I can about things that I know and feel deeply about." Of all his qualities that contributed to this credo, I think that the predominant one was courage. It was a very personal kind of courage, but coupled with Ernest's physical abilities, prowess and luck under duress, it accounted, more than anything else, for the public's mistaken image of him. The truth was that Ernest was a shy man, soft-spoken, who feared the microphone, camera, and assembled audience as one fears the rattlesnake poised to strike. His personality and his style of life were as spare and understated as his writing.

As a boy of eighteen on the Italian front, wearing a Red Cross uniform, Ernest was in a trench with three infantrymen when an Austrian *Minenwerfer* scored a direct hit on them; the three Italians had their legs blown off and Ernest's right leg was hit so severely his kneecap was down on his shin. In this condition, Ernest managed somehow to hoist the one Italian who was still alive onto his back and carry him across a no-man's-land that was being raked by machine-gun fire. The soldier was dead by the time he got him to safety, but for this exploit Ernest was awarded two of Italy's highest medals.

The surgeons later removed 227 pieces of metal from his leg.

Many of the heroes of Ernest's books and stories were born out of his adventures and from observing other men as they reacted to stressful situations. Thus, soldiers in battle, white hunters on safari, athletes "putting it on the line," men facing death, avoiding death, defying death were all closely observed, so closely that their reactions and experiences became an integral part of Hemingway himself. But no man's courage fascinated Ernest more than the matador's—the slim, unprotected young man who faced savage and unpredictable animals which could kill him at any moment in the ring. In one of his memorable short stories, "The Undefeated," Ernest depicted a matador with such depth of feeling and understanding that it is virtually impossible to believe that Ernest himself had not spent his life in the bullring.

Ernest felt that of all the great and fine matadors whom he had seen and known, his friend Antonio Ordoñez was the finest. "Antonio," Ernest said, "has all three of the basics for greatness in matadoring: courage, enormous skill, and grace in the presence of death." These were the qualities Ernest most admired in *all* men, not just matadors.

There was a different kind of courage that accounted for most of what Ernest did, believed in, and respected in others— the courage of conviction—and this was another side of Ernest that escaped the public's image of him. Writing was an arduous ordeal for him, exhilarating but demanding all of what he referred to as his "juices." When he had a book in progress, he was totally consumed by it, and at the end of each workday he would almost lovingly count the number of words he had written and enter them carefully in a log which he kept. "I like to start work early before I can be distracted by people and events," he once told me. "I rise at first light and I start by rereading and editing everything I have written to the point I left off. That way I go through a book I'm writing several hundred times. Most writers slough off the toughest but most important part of their trade—editing their stuff, honing it and honing it until it gets an edge like the bullfighter's killing sword. One time my son Patrick brought me a story and asked me to edit it for him. I went over it carefully and changed one word. 'But, Papa,' he said, 'you've only changed one word.' I said: 'If it's the right word, that's a lot.' "

During the course of that trip to Paris with the manuscript of *Across the River and into the Trees,* under the combined spell of the city's seductiveness and the quality of the life Hemingway led, I confessed to him one evening, while we were having drinks at the bar of the Closerie des Lilas, that I was seriously considering renouncing my job on *Cosmopolitan* in favor of living in Paris and trying to see if I could be a writer. I reminded him of an equation he had once mentioned: hesitation increases in relation to risk in equal proportion to age, and I asked him whether he thought I should apply it to myself.

He said it was tough advice to give since nobody knows what's inside him until he challenges himself. But if he comes up wanting, the shock can wreck a man. He said that when he first came to Paris and tried to make a go of it, he suffered a lot. He was finally devoting himself to being a writer but every day his rejected manuscripts came back to him. He said there were days when he'd read one of those cold, printed rejection slips attached to a story he loved and he would weep.

"I never think of you as crying," I said.

"I cry, boy," Ernest said. "When the hurt is bad enough, I cry." He said he really couldn't give me advice on this subject, any more than he could advise me what numbers to play on a roulette wheel, but this much he said he could assure me of: "If you are lucky enough to have lived in Paris as a young man, then wherever you go for the rest of your life it stays with you, for Paris is a moveable feast."

That night I wrote down that observation on the flyleaf of my Michelin, and years later, after Ernest's death, when his wife published his Paris memoirs and was searching for a title, I remembered that sentence in my Michelin, the final words of which I gave her for the title.

5

Marthe Richard Padlocks the Paris Prostitutes

Clarice was hoping that her performance at the Met would be the turning point in her career. Her life in Paris had been a struggle; the Paris Opéra was notorious for the parsimonious amounts it paid its performers, and her family did not have the means to help her. For several seasons during and after the war, the opera house was unheated, and just before coming onstage for her arias, Clarice would suck ice to make her mouth cold enough that breath steam wouldn't form when she sang.

When we first met, I was still in uniform and living in the Hôtel Opal, which had been requisitioned as an officers' billet. We had heat and hot water and soap, all of which were virtually nonexistent in civilian Paris, and I would smuggle Clarice up to my room, where she could luxuriate in a tub of steaming water and lather herself to her heart's content.

Success at the Met would mean emancipation from the penurious Paris Opéra, with contracts for operatic and concert performances that would at last be sufficiently remunerative. I went to her rehearsals for *Carmen* and I thought she was fine. I even took her to lunch with Irving Kolodin, who had been on *Air Force* magazine with me, and who was then music critic for the *World-Telegram,* and a very influential one at that. Everything augured well for her future. She had moved into a lovely sublet apartment on Central Park South, thanks to the generosity of Spyros Skouras.

Skouras had also been generous with me. He arranged a development contract that paid me $2,500 for an original screen story; he then arranged for me to buy a Chevrolet convertible with my $2,500 so that Clarice and I could drive out to Skouras' Mamaroneck mansion for weekend visits. The house was always filled with guests but Mrs. Skouras, a low-key, faded woman, did not seem at all perturbed by the ebb and flow of weekenders.

The night of Clarice's performance, Skouras gave a party for her. The audience response had been warm but not overwhelming, with three curtain calls and a large bouquet of red roses, but the reviews were devastating. Every reviewer had compared her to Risë Stevens and found her wanting. Even my friend Kolodin wrote that Risë Stevens was a hot-blooded cat while Clarice was a rather sexless kitten. Clarice was traumatized by the unexpected ferocity of the reviews.

But despite the negative reception, Skouras was totally supportive. He maintained that she had been victimized by being cast in *Carmen*, an unfamiliar role, and now he would see what he could do about getting her performances in the roles of her true repertoire. It might take time but she should be of good heart and certainly not be concerned with the finances involved, which he would attend to. The important thing was to make her an opera star, and not to worry, he would succeed, just as he had made scores of movie stars for his studio.

Just about the same time Clarice had her disaster, I had mine —I was fired from my job at *Cosmopolitan*. Not by Arthur, but by Herb Mayes, who had undermined Arthur with the kind of scabrous power play so dear to the hearts of Hearst men. Mayes was a vain, arrogant man who for years had been editor of *Good Housekeeping;* he had an intuitive feminine viewpoint which stood *Good Housekeeping* in good stead, and it was his conceit that he could do for *Cosmo*'s limited circulation what he had done for *Good Housekeeping* with its Seal of Approval, its testing kitchens, and its home-help departments. So he maneuvered behind Arthur's back to have him fired, and immediately had a door cut into the wall between Arthur's old office and his, basking in the glory of being the only editor of two major publications. On each corner of Mayes's desk was a symbolic lamp, a large bronze bust of Napoleon with a lampshade over his head.

Instead of building up *Cosmo*'s circulation, however, Mayes's short tenure at the helm had just the opposite effect. He assigned articles whose main purpose seemed to be to assuage his many tantrums and prejudices. One morning he summoned me to his office and told me petulantly that the night before he had ordered Haig & Haig Scotch at the Waldorf and he was sure they had served him something inferior. So! I was to get an intrepid, hard-drinking writer to do an article to be called "Make Them Show You the Bottle," based on research conducted in a variety of bars and nightclubs. I gave this lush assignment to my friend Mark Murphy (he had also been on *Air Force* magazine with me), who wrote quality profiles for *The New Yorker,* and he was drunk for two weeks gathering the salient facts.*

Along with these mindless articles, Mayes brought a Norman Rockwell perception to the look of the magazine. While Arthur had still been editor, I had given an assignment to Ludwig Bemelmans to write an essay on the glories of spring and to illustrate it with some of his drawings. Bemelmans was one of the most civilized men I have ever met. He had written several charming books with Parisian locales, but he was chiefly noted for his sketches and paintings, which graced the pages of quality magazines and hung in museums on both sides of the ocean. He was an ingratiating procrastinator, and whenever I phoned to ask him about the progress of our project (or rather the lack of it), he would pretend we had a bad connection and suggest that we'd be better off discussing it over luncheon at "21". I was invariably enthralled by his urbanity and wit.

He told me fascinating stories about former editors of *Cosmopolitan,* one of whom was a repressed homosexual who idolized his beautiful wife, until one afternoon, returning to his office earlier than expected, he came upon the managing editor in the throes of laying his beautiful wife on top of his desk. "He was never any good in his job after that," Ludwig said. "Positively destroyed. He couldn't bear going into his office after that, and he began to drink heavily and indulge his homosexuality. The

---

*Years later, Mark died tragically in a remote hospital in Africa, victim of acute hepatitis.

editor who succeeded him was a phony who wore velvet jackets to the office and overcoats with sable collars. The problem was he had a pipsqueak personality that was out of joint with his eccentric garments. He eventually shot himself at the same desk on which the former editor's wife had been buggered."

I asked Ludwig which he preferred, writing or painting. He said that he could do a drawing in two hours but that for him writing was much more difficult. "It's so hard to paint with the typewriter," he said, "because it only has one color." He said that his real ambition in life was to be a fiacre driver in Paris or Rome, because then he'd only have to care about his horse and carriage, and he loved wearing top hats. He told me stories about the shops in back of Notre Dame which were in reality whorehouses frequented by horny priests, and he told me about his recent visit to France when he had gone to see Henri Matisse along with a friend of his, a photographer named Bernstein, who was bringing Matisse some photographs he had taken on a previous visit. Matisse was delighted with the photographs, which were exhibition prints especially mounted for him. Matisse's studio was chock-full of his paintings stacked solidly along the walls, and Matisse gestured to them and asked Bernstein to pick the one he liked best.

"I was stunned by this," Bemelmans said, "because Matisse had a terrible reputation as the tightest skinflint who ever lived. While Bernstein toured the walls inspecting the paintings, his eyes aglow with anticipation, Matisse took out his leather cigar case and opened it in front of my nose, inviting me to smell its aroma. I sniffed and said it was a truly fine Havana smell. 'Yes,' Matisse said, 'they are made specially for me by Partagas.' He took one and put the case away without offering any to me.

"Bernstein finally picked up a colorful canvas that depicted a kitchen table laden with fruit, and carried it over to Matisse. 'Ah, yes,' Matisse said, 'you have a good eye—that is one of my favorites.' He took the painting from Bernstein and put it back against the wall. Sometimes I wish I were as tight as Matisse and could save my money. But I was a waiter for many, many years and I cannot get over the habit of overtipping."

Finally the day arrived (over lunch at "21" naturally) when the article and paintings were finished. The paintings were simply wonderful—fishermen on the Seine watching riverboats go by, a flower cart being painted by a plump Frenchman and his wife in front of the Café du Dôme, a windy day on Fifth Avenue, and a large, exhilarating canvas depicting the spring awakening of the animals at the Central Park Zoo, all painted, of course, in his unique, primitive style.

During the long nascence of this Bemelmans project, Mayes had assumed the editorship, so it was to him that I brought the essay and the paintings. He first read the piece and pronounced it acceptable, then instructed me to spread out the art on his carpet. He took one revolted look at the paintings and exploded (he was noted for his tantrums). "You call that art! I have a twelve-year-old daughter who paints better than that! Are you out of your mind, bringing me garbage like that! Get it out of here! Out of here!"

"What do you want me to do with it?"

"Just get it out of my office!"

"Okay." I started to gather up the paintings.

"And out of the building before it stinks up the joint!"

I put the paintings under my arm and took them down in the elevator and out of the Hearst Building and right on to my apartment; I put them on the walls, where over the years they have been a source of eternal pleasure.

Mayes was the Marquis de Sade of editors. His first act on assuming the editorship was to sack half the staff. He did it piecemeal so that no one knew whose neck would be next. Finally, he called a staff meeting and announced that there would be no more firings, this was now the staff, all jobs were secure, fear no more. A few days after that meeting, on a Friday, I was in Mayes's office when he summoned the fashion editor, Kay Wister, and told her that he wanted her to take her two-week vacation beginning on Monday. It was the dead of winter. Poor Kay looked stunned and murmured something about having planned her vacation in June with her husband. Herb clucked his tongue sympathetically and said he was sorry but we'd all have to spread out our vacations for the good of the magazine.

After Kay left his office, Mayes called in one of his two secretaries and dictated a letter addressed to Kay, telling her that in her absence it had become necessary to let her go and thanking her for her years of service to the magazine. He instructed his secretary not to mail the letter until the following week.

I myself was somehow surviving this holocaust until Mayes went on a vacation. He was sickly, and his wife called me to request that we not involve him in any office problems while he was away, since his doctor said it was necessary for him to have a complete rest. A few days after Mayes had left, a literary agent I knew came to me with a manuscript that no one else yet knew about—a novel called *The Foundling,* written by Cardinal Spellman himself. The head of Hearst Publications, Richard Berlin, was a high-ranking Catholic, a papal knight, I believe, if there is such a thing, and the literary agent said that the cardinal was giving us first look at the manuscript because of Berlin's connection with the Church—but we would have only three days to make up our minds.

After it had been read favorably by the staff, it seemed to me that the proper thing to do was to forward it directly to Berlin with our comments. He bought it immediately.

When Mayes returned and heard about the Spellman novel he was furious with me for having "usurped" his position. Who the hell did I think I was, taking it on myself to send a manuscript to Mr. Berlin himself? Was I trying to get in Berlin's good favor, thereby conniving to get Mayes's job? A senseless tirade. I gave as good as I got and in the end, his voice aflutter with rage, he ordered me to clean out my desk and be out of the building forthwith. Me and the Bemelmans paintings. I strongly recall the impact of that word "forthwith," which I always associated with those cartoons showing characters being ordered from a warm house into a blinding snowstorm.*

I was both chagrined and uplifted by my dismissal. I have always taken great pride in succeeding at what I undertake, but at the same time, ever since my Paris discussion with Hemingway, I had been intrigued with the possibility of living the life of a free-lancer. I loved the sound of the words: *free-lancer*! The freedom to be in charge of one's destiny, where one goes, whom

---

*A few years later, Mayes's tyranny overtook him. He went on a vacation and on his return, without any warning, he found that the lock on his *Good Housekeeping* door had been changed, and his name was off the masthead.

one sees, what one writes—of course, I had no illusion that my free-lancing life would be anything like Hemingway's, but I had tippled the taste of free-lance freedom and it had gone to my head.

On the very day that I packed up my office gear and left *Cosmopolitan,* I discovered that Skouras' sponsorship of Clarice was motivated by more than his interest in opera. When I confronted her, Clarice said I was being naïve, that accommodating a sponsor was a commonplace in the opera world but that it had nothing to do with her love for me and the beautiful relationship we had with each other. She was right. I was naïve not to have realized what was going on long before I did. She pleaded with me, cajoled, touched my vulnerability about her in all the right places.

Just about the time I became aware of what was going on between Clarice and Skouras, thinly veiled items began to appear in the gossip columns (what movie tycoon with what opera singer). Mrs. Skouras' response to her husband's gambol with this young beauty was to check into the hospital to have a blue network of varicose veins removed from her thighs and legs.

Skouras was true to his word and Clarice did get a chance to perform Mimi in *La Bohème,* but it did not appreciably improve her potential. The critics found her voice too small for the cavernous Met, as well as too thin in its high registers. She stayed in her Central Park South apartment for a while after that, and I saw her a few times, although I tried not to. But she had meant too much in my young life for me to leave her easily. Her relationship with Skouras had ended, and she wanted me to return to Paris with her, and perhaps I might have weakened and done so if I had had any money. But with only a few dollars to my name, and my confidence unraveled, I was not able to muster up the devil-may-care attitude needed for such a precarious adventure. Besides, my heart was still battered over Clarice's dalliance, however lofty her motive, and that too was a deterrent; and to be perfectly honest, living with an opera singer was no bed of roses. The constant obsession with throat, voice, nasal drip, and breathing apparatus gets to be pretty trying on the nerves of the singee as well as the singer. In many ways the paramour of a soprano is her caddy, his pockets full of lozenges and sprays, his pores ever alert to respond to the constant question "Hotchie, do you feel a draft?" (Yes, she called me Hotchie and that in itself might have kept me from going back to Paris.) How many times we no sooner got settled at a table in a cozy restaurant, the wine being poured, the candle flickering, than came the dire pronouncement "Hotchie, there's a *courant d'air*!" (draft). We sometimes moved two or three times until Clarice found the one table immune from that dread, mysterious current of air that was blowing on her in a restaurant that had no windows, air ducts, or open doors.

Another thing: whenever she felt a respiratory affliction coming on, invariably imagined, she rushed to eat mashed potatoes. Really. And this could happen at any time. Once at three in the morning, convinced that some viral demon was about to invade her throat, she nudged me and I awoke with her plaintive voice in my ear: "Hotchie, put on the potatoes."

But despite all, I was terribly fond of her. She was beautiful and had a sparkling sense of humor to counteract her temperamental bursts. And she was marvelously civilized. During those periods when she wasn't scheduled to sing, she cared about me and relished her role as my emancipator, freeing me gradually from the bondage of my insular Midwest upbringing. She sharpened my sensuality and my sensibilities, and by not tolerating my St. Louis prejudices, she in effect purged me of many of them.

The night before she left for Paris, we stayed together, making her departure all the more difficult for me. She wept when it was time to say good-bye at the Air France departure gate, and we vaguely promised each other that we would meet again soon.

In my heavy heart I knew we wouldn't. I was still young but with her departure I felt that I was not a youth anymore. I felt that my suffering over her had given me a maturity, a stronger self-defense against attacks where I had been vulnerable.

But I was wrong. In my loneliness after she was gone, in a state I can best describe as resigned, I impetuously got married.

Clarice too married not long after her return to Paris; he was a pharmaceutical tycoon who had homes in Paris, Geneva, and

Athens, and a yacht in Antibes. He owned an important stable of horses, and I saw pictures of Clarice in *Paris-Match* at Longchamps and Epsom Downs. She never sang again. The only time I ever saw her after she left New York was on a visit to Paris when we had a brief lunch upstairs at Lipp on the Boulevard St.-Germain, but she had only oysters and wine because she was seven months pregnant and not feeling so well.

Although I had a romantic conception of my new life role as a free-lancer, a medieval knight roaming the byways with his lance at the ready, I quickly learned that reality, alas, was not very romantic. The dictionary defines a free-lancer as "a person who acts on his own will or pleasure with little regard for the conventionalities of life," but I found it necessary to have more than a little regard for such conventionalities as eating and paying the landlord. During my short stint as an editor I had had little contact with other magazine editors; as a consequence, I didn't have an entry at any publication where in fact I could start my free-lancing.

I sent letters to the article editors of several magazines, asking for an appointment to present my article ideas, but these were simply names that I had taken off the mastheads without a personal introduction to any of them. I knew it would take a while before I heard from them, if I *ever* heard from them, and in the meantime I dredged up my Paris notebook to see if I had some material stored there that I could use for an article. I was pleased to discover notes I had made about a remarkable Frenchwoman named Marthe Richard. She was a friend of Janet Flanner's, whom I had met in the Hôtel Scribe toward the end of the war. A calm, wise woman, Janet reported on France for *The New Yorker* under the sobriquet Genêt. She had befriended me when I first came to Paris to head up the European bureau of *Air Force* magazine.

Janet was as honest and straightforward as her prose, and I learned many things from simply being around her: about Paris and the French, about the techniques of interviewing, about how to detect pickpockets and phonies at the races, and about how to survive in Paris by threading my way through the seemingly impenetrable bureaucratic maze.

Janet took me to lunch with Marthe Richard because Janet thought I might be able to write about her for *Air Force,* but Mme. Richard, fascinating though she was, wasn't a proper subject for the official magazine of the Air Force. I had conscientiously saved my notes, however, and now I disinterred them to see if an article about her might sell to an American publication.

At the time of our lunch, Marthe Richard's name had been all over the Paris newspapers. Next to Mata Hari, she had been the most celebrated spy of the First World War. She had also been one of the world's first licensed women pilots, but why she was a *cause célèbre* on the day I met her was because she was single-handedly shutting down all the houses of prostitution in Paris. What excited the French press was that this *femme fatale,* who had once wrested secrets from German generals she had bedded, was now righteously shutting down France's oldest profession.

On our way to lunch, Janet filled me in on the role Marthe Richard had played when she spied for France. Most of her espionage took place in Madrid, which was then a neutral city crawling with intelligence agents. With her stunning beauty and charm as lures, Marthe set out to captivate Baron von Krohn, who was the highest-ranking German in the city. She succeeded. The baron employed her to spy for him on the French, and her life was filled with incendiary fountain pens, invisible inks, gunrunners, false newspapers, and sleeping powder.

The baron was Marthe's most lucrative source of information. He would come to call upon her at her quarters (which he paid for, together with all her expenses), and after a few hours in bed Marthe would be able to give the Deuxième Bureau the answers to all of its questions. Her spy formula was simple: convince the subject that you are madly in love with him, give him little scraps of information which lead him to believe that you would betray your country for him, and then—let him talk.

In this way she was able to tip off Allied headquarters on the presence of German submarines; the records show that twenty-three U-boats were located and sunk as a direct result of her liaison with Von Krohn.

The baron's wife became extremely jealous of Marthe and suspected that she might be a counterspy. She invited Marthe to a dinner party where she tried desperately to trick Marthe into revealing her identity. Although Marthe spoke German very well, it had suited her purposes to pretend that she knew no German whatsoever; it was a neat device for hearing conversations which ordinarily would have been kept from her. At the dinner table, the baroness and her friends alternately spoke French and German, trying to catch Marthe off guard, but Marthe was equal to the challenge. The baron became more firmly convinced that his wife's suspicions were groundless and that the beautiful mademoiselle was simply head over heels in love with him.

When Paris was occupied during World War II, Mme. Richard knew that she was too well known to be a spy, but she became very active in the Paris Underground, hiding American airmen who had been shot down and making arrangements for them to get back to England.

In order fully to appreciate Marthe Richard's assault on the houses of prostitution, it must be understood that closing the whorehouses of Paris was not at all comparable to shutting down the red light district in, say, East St. Louis or Toledo. Prostitution in France was centuries old and sanctioned by the government. The houses and the prostitutes themselves had played a big part in French literature, and the average Frenchman had always considered the brothels of Paris an indestructible part of the Parisian scene. At the end of the Rue Chabanais, for example, where it ran into the Square Louvois, there was a four-story yellow building known as the House of All Nations, probably the most famous brothel in the world. Its rooms were known for their almost classical elegance and many were considered worthy of a museum. The Edward VII Room, for instance, had been furnished by his Royal Highness when he was Prince of Wales and a frequent visitor to the House of All Nations. Before the war there were conducted tours for American sightseers twice every day.

But when I met Mme. Richard, her campaign had forced the famous old house on Rue Chabanais to post a closing notice on its front door for the first time in its history. Closing notices were also posted on the doors of the Sphinx, the One-Two-Two, and scores of other brothels which had been Paris landmarks for as long as anyone could remember. Marthe Richard's crusade had also gathered up the thousands of Paris streetwalkers in its sweep. That it was a *woman* who had single-handedly inspired, directed, and delivered this *coup de massue* was all the more remarkable in light of the fact that the French had only recently granted woman suffrage.

"My campaign is really not concerned with closing the brothels for all time," Marthe Richard said. "I am much too much of a realist for that. You can't legislate against the natural instincts of human beings and not have the law bypassed before long. I think that was the experience of American cities with Prohibition, wasn't it? My real concern, you see, is not with the brothels themselves but with the men who make their living from these houses. Do you realize that in Paris there are 120,000 men living off the earnings of the prostitution houses? The girls themselves were getting practically nothing, with the result that the houses were badly kept, disease was rampant, and procuring prostitutes had become a vicious racket."

She told me that according to a canvass made by the Paris police, there were 30,000 illegal prostitutes in the city. (Paris had a system of licensing women who engaged in prostitution, so that an "illegal" prostitute was one who had not registered with the police and obtained a license.)

"Most of these thirty thousand women," Marthe Richard said, "were brought into the city by gangs of procurers, who usually took about seventy-five or eighty percent of their earnings. Something had to be done about it and I did it. The prostitution system had become so degenerated that I saw that the only solution was to close down all the houses."

I asked Mme. Richard, a handsome, thoughtful woman of fifty-one, what had set off her crusade against the whorehouses, and she told me of an incident that had occurred the previous year when there was an abundance of American troops in Paris. The young daughter of a friend of hers was engaged to be married to an American officer. The family was of the first rank of Paris society and the young lady had recently been graduated with special honors from the University of Paris. The officer too came from a fine family. A short while after the marriage took place, the girl came to visit Marthe Richard one afternoon. She was terribly distressed and begged Mme. Richard to help her because she could not go to her family with her troubles.

The girl explained that she had just discovered that she had contracted syphilis from her newly wed husband, who without knowing it had become infected after visiting one of the "best" brothels in Paris before their marriage.

"I was furious," Mme. Richard said. "Two beautiful young people with their lives in ruins. I started an investigation. I have good contact in the military, and I discovered that last July there were 146 American GIs hospitalized in Paris with syphilis; by August that number had jumped to 637 and the rate was climbing steadily. The same thing was happening to French civilians.

"I also found out that the Paris law that required that all prostitutes be examined by city physicians at least twice a week was being totally disregarded. The city had assigned only three doctors to this job, which meant that, with 1,700 licensed prostitutes in Paris, these three doctors would have to make 3,400 visits every week if the law were enforced. Of course, the 30,000 prostitutes operating outside the law were not even involved. And the rule for streetwalkers was just as badly enforced. They were required by law to be examined once every week, but only about ten percent of the women were going to the St. Lazare special hospital where three doctors were each supposed to handle one thousand women per day.

"Small wonder that the disease rate was getting out of hand," Mme. Richard said. "And not only that but there were so many women working the streets at night that I actually saw men have to fight their way down a boulevard to resist being dragged into a house."

Bad as the situation was, she knew she could do nothing about it on her own. But one evening, a friend who had served in the same Underground resistance group as she had during World War II telephoned her and told her that the group had decided to put up her name in the Paris municipal elections, which were scheduled to take place in a few weeks.

"But I don't know anything about politics," Marthe said.

"Never mind," her friend assured her, "we just want a woman on our slate and your name would attract attention."

Marthe accepted, but she made no campaign speeches or

public appearances. Nonetheless, she was elected to the Council of Paris by a substantial margin. At the Council's first meeting she announced what she intended to do, but in the beginning no one took her seriously. The cynical French knew that in tackling the brothels, Mme. Richard was bucking a profession which had been legitimatized and state-controlled for 150 years. A campaign to close the Paris brothels was nothing new, and since Napoleon's time reformers had been exhorting the "better" elements to erase this blotch from Paris' escutcheon.

In fact, the struggle against prostitutes dated back to 1360, when the municipal authorities of Paris passed a law prohibiting prostitutes from wearing the same clothes as "honest women." A Paris decree issued on September 18, 1367, listed the names of certain streets in the city where prostitutes were allowed to stay, and flatly prohibited them from inhabiting or plying their trade in any other parts of the city. Even back in those days the city fathers were having their headaches with the pimps, and it was a well-enforced law that any man found engaging in procuring women or operating a house of prostitution would be branded with a red-hot iron and run out of Paris.

These early laws didn't help much and in 1420 Parliament passed a series of drastic measures: prostitutes were not allowed to wear dresses or suits with high collars or long queues, and at no time could they wear furs, hats, or jewelry of any kind, under threat of long imprisonment. In 1560 all buildings formerly set aside as prostitution houses were abolished, with the result that the women dispersed throughout the city, living in bourgeois houses where the landlords accepted them because the high rents they were able to pay compensated for the possible punishment involved. If the police discovered them they were obliged to vacate the premises within twenty-four hours or else their furniture and belongings were tossed out of the windows.

In the seventeenth century, for the first time, medical assistance was given to prostitutes. They were treated in a special section of the hospital La Salpêtrière. When hospitalized, the prostitutes were compelled to perform the hardest manual labor in the hospital and they had to live on a diet of bread, soup, and water.

Toward the end of the seventeenth century, Louis XIV began

to get alarmed over the welfare of his soldiers, who displayed growing signs of venereal contamination. Louis issued a stern edict that any prostitute found in the company of one of his soldiers would have her nose and ears cut off. Although a quantity of noses and ears were amputated, Louis sadly admitted that "license and corruption of morals are making steady progress every day."

A famous police decree of November 6, 1778, prohibited prostitutes from soliciting business on the streets or in public places, or from even making overtures to the passing male population from their windows. Despite this severe restriction, which carried the penalty of a head-shaving, prostitution flourished during the Revolution, the Directoire, and Napoleon's regime. The Palais Royal became a virtual headquarters for the ladies of the street.

Mme. Richard explained that the brothels, as they existed just before her ax fell, were neatly divided into five different categories. In category one were the ultrafashionable houses such as the House of All Nations, which featured girls from all over the world; the Rue de Moulon, which catered almost exclusively to bankers; the One-Two-Two, which was a very swank establishment located at 122 Rue de Provence and which featured a mysterious system of exits and entrances that assured its clients complete secrecy.

In category two were the more popular brothels known as coffeehouses. These establishments were really nightclubs where women were available, but a customer who merely wished to have a few drinks and watch the floor show was perfectly welcome. The famous Sphinx, located in Montparnasse, was a good example of this type of house. Built expressly as a house of prostitution, the Sphinx had an elaborate dance floor surrounded by the usual small nightclub tables. There were plenty of scantily clad young ladies on the premises for those who wanted company, as there were at Les Belles Poules, which figured in many famous French novels.

Category three contained the ordinary brothels, where the charge was modest. The small houses employed about sixteen women each, and handled anywhere from 800 to 2,000 visitors per day.

In category four were the illegal brothels, which operated in apartment buildings and paid off the police. In normal times there were about seventy-five such apartments in operation, employing 230 women.

The fifth category contained the aristocrats of the profession. These women operated out of "houses of rendezvous," where men chose women from photographs and arranged for some future meeting. These women were not attached to the rendezvous house but merely paid a certain amount of money for the service performed by the house. Since this type of prostitute was under no control whatsoever, it was possible for women from all walks of life to add their names to these lists.

I myself had visited only one of the houses Mme. Richard was talking about, but because of rather unforeseen circumstances it was a very brief visit. I had been taken there by an eccentric American lieutenant I knew who because of his luxurious moustache was nicknamed, of course, Lieutenant Moustache, but the pronunciation was French. Moustache was the most dedicated chauvinist I have ever known, as witness his Hôtel Scribe technique for luring attractive girls into his bed. He was living on the third floor of the hotel, as I was, when I first met him, and his idea of a fun evening was to go out on the balcony of his room and search the passing throng below for pretty young girls. When he'd spot what he referred to as "a bird of bright plumage," he would adroitly toss a packet of cigarettes or a candy bar at her feet. Of course, at that time those were highly prized enticements which would elicit an immediate, startled response from the bird, who would peer upward to spot her benefactor. Whereupon Moustache would unfurl a nylon stocking over the balustrade and undulate it at the upturned face of the bird, who more often than not responded as metal does to magnet.

I told Moustache that I thought his degrading balcony act was reprehensible, but he couldn't understand how it could be degrading when the mademoiselle invariably departed with nylons on her legs and Hershey bars in her handbag.

Which brings me to the one whorehouse I visited. Moustache loved this house, known as 32 Rue Blondel, and he was insistent that I come with him to see it. In Mme. Richard's categorization, it was a number-two house, a coffeehouse where the drinks were certainly not coffee. There was a man on duty at the door but he was casual in his scrutiny of the clients who presented themselves, only watching for drunks and men of unclean appearance, in deference to the house's motto: "The clients must be as clean as our girls."

A massive oak bar ran along one wall of the ground floor, which resembled in every respect the crowded, smoky, swilling scene of a Toulouse-Lautrec poster. The men sat crammed around small round tables and were served by attractive waitresses who wore short pleated skirts with satin blouses. Two black musicians, piano and saxophone, played languid music that barely rose above the cacophony of voices calling for specific waitresses. The piano player was large and fat and played without looking at the keyboard. The saxophonist was a small man with a gray goatee who played with his eyes closed and a puff in his right cheek. He sat well back in his chair, on his spine, and played endlessly, not even resting during the piano riffs. He just played and played and played, at the same mellow level, a velvet flow of saxophone sound.

The waitresses wore buttons with their names on them and they would sing out their orders to the barman, who repeated the order in a heavy, singsong baritone. The waitresses wore nothing underneath their skirts, so that when they moved hurriedly they sometimes flashed a bare behind. But it was a strictly enforced rule of the house that clients were not allowed to assist the skirt in its rise, or to probe beneath it with their hands. When a client decided on a waitress, he rose, often with his drink in his hand, accompanied her to the rear of the room, where at the foot of a narrow stairs there was a cashier who took his money, issued him a clean towel from a stack beside the cash register, and gave a room key attached to a large wooden paddle to the waitress. The supply of waitresses in the room was continually replenished by girls descending from the two floors above, followed by their satisfied clients, who often reseated themselves for postcoital refreshment.

Moustache and his pal Captain Derringer, who was Moustache's accomplice in dropping girl bait from the third floor of the Scribe, led me to a table near the cashier, and Moustache laughed at the look of bewildered astonishment on my face as

I took in the wailing saxophone, the shouting men, the baritone bartender, and the girls pivoting and wriggling among the tightly packed tables, with their little round trays held high. The higher they reached, the more of their body they exposed, and as one buxom blonde squeezed past me, I was faced with a close-up of her black, damp pubic hair. Moustache and Derringer ordered beer, which they advised me to drink out of the bottle.

"Is this a sight?" Moustache exclaimed, his face beaming. "Oh, I could come here every day, I really could."

"And they're all for hire?" I asked, indicating the waitresses. "All of them?"

"Every last one."

"Well, you know, some of them are not bad—not bad at all."

"Course not. And they've all got health certificates. These men want value for their money. I've been told that Madame Nicole never takes a girl from the street—that she recruits them all from farm villages in the south and factory towns like Lyon."

At an adjoining table, a florid-faced, muscular man, with a cap on the back of his head, had placed a stack of francs on the corner edge of his table. He was bellowing loudly for a waitress named Nanette.

Nanette was a plump-breasted, long-legged brunette who slithered up to the table, hesitated a moment while she eyed the stack of coins; then with a quick swing of her leg she straddled the coins for a second, then slid away, the coins departing with her in the sack of her vagina. The men gave her a big hand. The scene was repeated in other parts of the room with other girls.

Moustache ordered another round of beers from a waitress named Zizu, who smiled at him and said: "Ready for dessert?" Moustache took some coins from his pocket and put them on the corner of our table, balancing them precariously over the edge, and underneath the exposed part of the stack, where it couldn't be seen, Moustache held the flame of his cigarette lighter up against the coins.

"Here she comes!" Derringer warned, excitedly.

It didn't dawn on me what they were about to do. Zizu put the beer on our table, and then approached the stack of coins just as Moustache extinguished the lighter and slipped it into his pocket. Of course, I did finally realize what he was up to, but I was too horrified to react. Moustache's face was rigid with malicious expectation. Zizu straddled the coins and adroitly enveloped them, but as she flounced away from the table, the heat of the coins ignited her insides and she screamed as she grabbed at herself, hopping around as she tried to extricate the hot coins.

Moustache and Derringer were convulsed with laughter, doubled over, grabbing at each other's arms in merriment. But I was appalled and, sensing trouble, quickly left the table. Several of the waitresses had rallied to Zizu's aid, and they started to lead her toward the back stairs, her cries and moans having silenced the room, but the two black musicians continued to play as if nothing had happened. They had been witness to every imaginable alarm and fright during their long musical peonage and by now nothing daunted the continual flow of their music.

A large, lumpy man who had been standing at the end of the bar with his back against the wall, a matchstick between his teeth, now slowly made his way to the table where Moustache and Derringer were enjoying themselves. I watched this unfold from where I had mingled myself with a group of men at the back of the room. The man from the bar, who was obviously the bouncer, grabbed a handful of Moustache's top hair and pulled him to his feet. Moustache tried to push him away but the bouncer hit him with his forearm, and when he released Moustache's hair he fell slowly to the floor like a scarecrow released from his stick. The bouncer then grabbed at Derringer, but he managed to escape and bolt from the room. The bouncer took hold of Moustache's collar and dragged him across the length of the room to the door, where he pitched him into the street.

That was the only one of the Paris brothels I had seen. In fact, it was the only brothel I had ever visited anywhere, although, strictly speaking, there was that whorehouse in East St. Louis where I had gone when I was twelve. It was while we were living in the Westgate Hotel during the Depression, when my father was out on the road with a line of Elgin watches that no one was buying, and my mother was in the Fee-Fee Sanitarium suffering from tuberculosis. Before she had been hospitalized, my mother had been going door to door, selling silk lingerie that she got on consignment from a firm in Chicago. On one of my weekly visits I told her that one of her orders had arrived from Chicago. Children were not allowed to enter the sanitarium, so I had to communicate with my mother by shouting from the lawn below her second-floor window. She was dismayed to hear that, because it was a large order that had to be delivered to East St. Louis. I said I would be glad to take it there for her but she was very reluctant to let me go, although she stood to make a $2.75 commission, enough for me to live on for a week.

She finally said she guessed I had to go but that I should collect the money as quickly as possible and leave. I promised that I would. I thought she was concerned because I had to take two streetcars and go over the Eads Free Bridge to get there, but as it turned out that wasn't what concerned her.

The address she gave me was on an unpaved street in a run-down neighborhood. I couldn't believe anyone who lived there could possibly afford to buy silk things, but when I rang the bell, a woman's voice on the squawk box next to the bell button asked me who I was, and when I told her she buzzed me in. At the top of the stairs was a beautiful woman in a black silk flowered kimono. She led me down a dimly lit corridor, to a room that seemed like a movie scene to my twelve-year-old eyes: fringed lamps with orange shades, silks and satins everywhere, a big bed with a silk canopy and gold angels at the corners holding the silk, and tall framed mirrors mounted on carved wooden pedestals.

The woman called in two of her friends from down the hall, also as beautiful as movie stars, and they inspected the things in the box, dividing them up, and paid me the amount on the bill. While I was there the bell sounded, and as I was leaving, a short, stout, bald man was coming up the stairs and he went into the room I had just left. That's when I understood where I was. I had read enough De Maupassant to realize that.

On the way out, I passed a waiting room where there was radio music and a bar, and a couple of men were sitting on the sofas with their arms around some other girls. There was a black barmaid serving drinks. The men were laughing and rubbing their hands over the girls. I took all this in from the doorway, which was covered with a beaded curtain so that they couldn't see me peeking in at them.

I was never interested in whores; sex for pay was always

repellent to me, but even if it had not been, the fact was that I never had any money to spend on prostitutes. In high school I didn't have a nickel to my name, and despite my scholarships, college and law school were a desperate struggle. I held down campus jobs (first with the Character Research Institute of the psychology department, then in the law school library) for which I was paid by the National Youth Administration at the rate of fifteen dollars a month. I also earned occasional amounts by impersonating Harpo Marx. I performed with two friends, Bill Davis and Al Rich, who were Groucho and Chico, and we were employed by Loew's State whenever a Marx Brothers movie was about to open. We would parade around the streets of downtown St. Louis in a horse and buggy with side panels advertising the movie, and between features we'd appear in a box at the theatre during the coming attractions.

On one such engagement, heralding the advent of *A Day at the Races,* we were cruising the busy noontime streets in our buggy, Bill Davis at the reins, when one of the wheels caught in the streetcar tracks and was wrenched from its axle, the three of us getting dumped onto the pavement. Traffic became snarled for blocks as we unhitched the horse and pushed the disabled buggy to the curb. And then came the long, ignominious trek back to the theatre on foot through the hordes of pedestrians. Bill led the horse and we followed, but without the sign announcing our purpose, we looked like three kooks escaped from the local nut house, especially me since my costume consisted of a long flannel nightgown, the Harpo top hat and curls, and a honk horn tucked in my belt. But we earned twenty dollars a day, astronomical pay for those times, so we never complained about our job's vicissitudes.

We got so good at our impersonations that in the summer we played a circuit of St. Louis beer gardens; for those engagements we added the services of a gorgeous, chesty blonde who was Bill's girl friend, but we were paid so poorly that we eventually disbanded. However, we continued to perform for various organizations who occasionally booked us to entertain at their affairs.

As for nonpaying sex, in the St. Louis of my youth this was consummated in the cheesy motels that dotted the outskirts of the city. Perhaps they are still there. No registration was required, and the door key was passed to the driver through his car window in exchange for the required fee. But even if I had known a girl willing to accompany me to one of these love nests (which I didn't), I had neither of the two additional essentials for such a sex mission—money and a car. When I was in my second year at the university, I almost had a car, a Marmon coupe with brass headlamps as big as manhole covers, and a rumble seat that automatically popped up when you pressed a button on the dashboard. My grandfather had thrust this Marmon upon me for the express purpose of selling it to "one of those rich snotty kids on your campus."

My grandfather (maternal) was a short, stocky man with a bristling moustache who had the most explosive temper I have encountered in a human being. In addition to which, he was arrogant, bigoted, opinionated, unforgiving, ignorant, and Hungarian. He devoted his life to operating a succession of Hungarian restaurants, with my poor grandmother slaving in the kitchen, each restaurant a more abysmal failure than the one before. With one of these restaurants, in order to bail himself out of his usual financial troubles, he contracted with a couple of arsonists who guaranteed results for a fee of 20 percent of the amount that would be paid by the insurance company. These arsonists attacked their job too zealously, however, causing an explosion that leveled the entire block, and causing my grandfather to flee to Oklahoma City for a couple of years until the police cooled off in their search for him.

One reason that my grandfather's restaurants failed was his habit of extending credit to customers who were shaky risks. After running up a sizable tab, these customers would disappear, or pay off my grandfather with objects other than money. That is how he came to acquire a chow dog who was so vicious that no one had the courage to feed him. And that is how he happened to come into possession of that Marmon coupe, which had two significant defects, the first being that it ravenously consumed gasoline, the second being its total lack of a foot brake. The hand brake worked, but if you have ever tried to stop by using a hand brake you know that it is an abrupt jolt that sends you catapulting forward. There was no way I could reduce the speed gradually with a hand brake. I did drive it to the campus a few times with a FOR SALE sign in the window, jolting myself silly hand-braking my way there, banging my head against the steering wheel a few times, but after a week or so even the hand brake gave out and the only way to stop the car was to ram it against the curb. But it was a beautiful automobile, and I loved stopping it (when I could) in front of coeds waiting at the bus stop in front of Brookings Hall, and popping up the rumble seat.

After a couple of weeks, my grandfather took back the Marmon and sold it for twenty-five dollars to a junkman who ate at his place. Thus I really never had the car or the money necessary to visit the Heavenly Rest or Dew Drop Inn motels. It really wasn't until the United States Air Force liberated me from St. Louis's puritanical clutches that I was free to have unrestrained relations with what we used to refer to as the opposite sex. And, of course, once I became a member of the touring company of *Three Dots and a Dash,* between our chorus line of Texas beauties and the Junior League's young ladies who were present in every city we visited, I was baptized with a vengeance.

I apologize for this long digression from Marthe Richard, but I wanted to explain why I had not seen any of the wondrous Paris brothels that Mme. Richard shut down. I asked her if the pimps and madams had tried to get in her way, and she said that indeed they had, that from the very start of her campaign the procurers tried every trick they knew to get her off their trail. She received scores of threatening letters, and anonymous telephone calls warned her to lay off. She was hauled into court on a trumped-up charge of swindling 300,000 francs from a French widow whose German lover she had allegedly promised to get released from a Paris jail. In final desperation, the proprietors of the various houses, who were banded together into a legally registered group known as "The Association of Owners of Furnished Rooms and Hotels of France and the Colonies," offered her six million francs in cash if she would go away for a six-month vacation and just forget the whole thing. When I met her, Mme. Richard had been provided with a twenty-four-hour police bodyguard.

"The dignity of the Frenchwoman is at stake," Mme. Richard said. "Three-fourths of the women working in the various Paris houses are married and have families. We've got to see to it that we restore the dignity of all Frenchwomen by helping to bring some dignity to these families. Also, if there is any monkey business in the closing of these houses, I have so many leagues, clubs, and labor unions lined up on my side that I don't think the government will be able to withstand the pressure. With all of us pulling together, I can't see how we can fail. The married prostitutes should try to settle down into regular family life—it will do their husbands good to have to provide for themselves for a change."

Although as a realist Mme. Richard expected the brothels to return in all their glory, that has not happened. There is an abundance of streetwalkers, and the doorway girls of Pigalle are as thick as ever, but thirty-seven years after her remarkable coup, brothels like the ones that flourished in her day are still absent from the Paris scene.

6

Ingrid Bergman Has Only
One Regret

I did not write the article about Marthe Richard because I received an immediate reply to one of my magazine letters. This from a man who was destined to become a great friend of mine as well as the provider of a home editorial base. His name was Brooks Roberts, and he was articles editor of *This Week* magazine, a Sunday supplement that ran in hundreds of newspapers across the country.

I walked out of Brooks's office after that initial meeting with my first assignment, my first commission as a *free-lancer;* over the next decade I was to write over a hundred articles for *This Week* on a wide spectrum of subjects: politics, theatre, crime, sports, sex, trials, pets, romance, space, revolutions, self-help, medicine, psychiatry—any- and everything from the Hungarian uprising, which I witnessed in Budapest, to the first lift-off at Canaveral. It was a splendid proving ground for me, and a pleasurable one, thanks to Brooks, a mild, sweet-tempered man, perspicacious, polite, and eminently fair-minded. There was a steady consistency in both his editorial judgment and his personal life; for example, in all the years I knew him, he never deviated an iota from his Brooks Brothers look. Lapels widened, vents deepened, pockets patched, ties flowered, lengthened, and fattened, shirt collars spread like butterfly wings, cuffs came and went, two-button jackets jumped to three and back to two again, but through it all Brooks held fast, leading his own buttoned-down existence, going in and out of style every few years but happily above the battle. When I went to live abroad, often for a couple of years at a time, it was always a joy to discover on my return that Brooks's personality, his point of view, and his values had held their own, unchanged by what was or wasn't fashionable.

Thanks to *This Week*, and then other magazines—the *Saturday Evening Post, Esquire, Redbook,* et cetera—the promised freedom of free-lancing became a reality. Article assignments took me all over the world, and I often geared those assignments to mesh with rendezvous with Hemingway in such places as Paris, Madrid, Málaga, Ketchum, Key West, Venice, and Havana. We usually met for some enjoyable pursuit—a steeplechase, bullfights, hunting, *ferias,* fishing, prizefights, the World Series. But sometimes when we met it was not for fun and games; that time, for instance, when I went to see Ernest in Venice after his plane crash.

I was in Holland, researching an article on the royal *scandale* of the day—Queen Juliana's admission that she conducted her affairs through the occult guidance of a fortune-teller who was in residence with her at the royal palace in Soestdijk. I was also in Holland to write an article about the rumored existence of the highly prized but long-elusive black tulip; an audience with the queen had been arranged for me to discuss the tulip, not the fortune-teller, but it was my hope that while at the palace under cover of the black tulip story, I could get some stuff about the fortune-teller—or, with luck, meet her.

While I was in one of the palace salons, waiting for my appointment with the queen, I had walked out on a balcony that overlooked an elaborate flower garden. An Alice-in-Wonderland apparition suddenly appeared, a Jeep bouncing wildly along the footpaths that wound all through the flowers. At the wheel of the Jeep, her blond hair flying in the wind, was a teen-aged girl. In the seat beside her, a military attaché was holding his hat with one hand and desperately clinging to the windshield with the other. The footpaths curved and circled, and occasionally the driver, as her wheels cut too sharply or not sharply enough, lopped off some of the flowers and sent them flying.

Absorbed in watching this astonishing sight, I had not been aware that the queen had joined me on the balcony. She too was watching the bouncing, careening Jeep, but with a look of pleased satisfaction on her face.

"She's doing quite well, isn't she?" the queen said pridefully. "My daughter, Beatrice—only her second lesson."

The Jeep now completed the circumference of the garden, leaving a residue of battered flowers in its wake, and pulled up before the balcony in a shower of pebbles and dust, skidding sideways in the process. Princess Beatrice hopped out and bounded up the stairs to the balcony to greet her mother. She wore jodhpurs and was on her way to the stables. She acknowledged our introduction in perfect English before dashing off.

Queen Juliana had just started our interview when Beatrice reappeared, this time astride a spirited, mottle-gray horse, which she galloped over the garden's pathways, following the tracks of the Jeep. Juliana watched her, bemused. (Beatrice, of course, is now the queen of Holland.) In the process of my interview on the rumored black tulip (not true), I did get to meet the palace soothsayer, who looked like a skinny Gertrude Stein.

While I was at the palace, the press attaché handed me a cable. It was from Ernest, asking me to phone him at the Gritti in Venice that evening, which I did. He had just arrived in Venice, as a passenger on the S.S. *Africa,* after a series of violent misadventures in the dense jungle near Murchison Falls in Uganda. There had been two crashes, the first less serious than the second, but it had been the first that had set off the universal mourning and the obituaries, which had abruptly changed to cheering and, in fact, disbelief when Ernest had suddenly emerged from the jungle at Butiaba. But a few hours later, a rescue plane that had been sent to fly the Hemingways back to their base in Kenya had crashed on takeoff and burst into flames, and this was the crash that left its marks on Ernest.

But over the scratchy long-distance phone Ernest's voice had sounded surprisingly strong. "How long you going to be lounging around that palace?" he asked.

"I think I've lounged out my welcome," I told him. "The palace guards have begun fingering their weapons when I approach. Does that strike you as unfriendly?"

"Yep. I think you should flee the royal life and come down here. You've got to see that Venice hasn't been damaged since we left her. I'm going to leave in a couple of days to meet Mary in Madrid and I thought you might like the ride. I have a beauty Lancia and a good driver who can race it or not. I prefer not, as we have plenty of time before the start of the Feria of San Isidro in Madrid. I could make the run alone but I'm pretty beat up from those kites falling all over Africa. We've kept it out of the funny papers but what I drew as cards when we burned the second kite was a ruptured kidney and the usual internal injuries, plus full upstairs concussion, double vision, and so on. Now the left eye has cut out and we had a very bad bush fire down on the coast, which I had to fight, and I burned the hell out of the left hand—the good hand—and because I was weaker than I figured, I fell over and so burned belly, some of legs, and forearm. Genitals okay. But, Hotch, times are just faintly rough now. To top it all off, with these few disabilities I hired on to write fifteen thousand words for *Look.* I don't mean to sound like a morbid, but I'd sure as hell like you to be along for this ride so I could cheer up."

When we set out in the Lancia for the voyage across the Riviera to Madrid, we first detoured to Milan to see Ernest's old friend Ingrid Bergman, who was then appearing at La Scala in the role of Joan of Arc in an opera by Arthur Honegger, directed by Ingrid's husband, Roberto Rossellini. In the automobile on our way from Venice to Milan, Ernest wondered whether the terrible ordeal Ingrid had been through had broken her spirit.

He was referring to the uproar caused by her flagrant affair with Rossellini at a time when both of them were married. It had happened at the height of her career, when she was undisputedly "Hollywood's First Lady," and when she was married to her first husband, a Swedish dentist, Peter Lindstrom, and the mother of ten-year-old Pia. Ingrid had gone to the island of Stromboli in Italy to make a film with Rossellini; the group of journalists who were on the island to cover the movie had also provided full coverage of Ingrid's romantic involvement.

At that time the world was far less permissive with its heroines than it is now, and Ingrid was roundly condemned by powerful groups, including the Vatican. And then with the even more shocking revelation that she was pregnant, the howls of condemnation intensified. No studio would touch her, the audiences that had flocked to her performances in such films as *Spellbound, Notorious, Gaslight,* and *The Bells of St. Mary's* now shunned her movies, and even many of her erstwhile friends renounced her. The only place where she could still find occasional work was on the stage.

For me and my generation of young men who went into military service, Ingrid had been a personification of radiant purity—the fresh, untouched beauty of *Intermezzo* (her first starring role, with Leslie Howard) was unique in the Hollywood of that day. But it was her portrayal of Maria in *For Whom the Bell Tolls*—the quality of the love she exuded for Robert Jordan (Gary Cooper)—together with her role in *Casablanca,* with Bogart, which had made her unique on the roster of those ladies of the screen who helped make unbearable stretches of the war somewhat bearable.

Five years had passed since the beginning of her affair with Rossellini. They were married now, with three children, but the motion picture world was still unforgiving, she was still classified as "box office poison," and it was this ordeal about which Ernest was concerned.

When we stepped off the elevator at her floor, Ingrid was waiting for us in the hallway outside her door. She was radiantly beautiful in a high-necked white silk blouse, the top six buttons of which were undone. Her short Jeanne d'Arc haircut was very becoming. She hugged Ernest and they were very happy to see one another. We went into the living room of her suite, where every possible surface was ablaze with long-stemmed red roses.

"You are riddled with roses, Daughter," Ernest said.

"They were sent by an official on the Stock Exchange. I have never met him but he was so moved by my performance he sends roses every day."

"How do things go?" Ernest asked, looking at her closely. "How do they really go?"

"Oh, when I think how it was a few years ago and how it is now! If only in a crisis one could learn to have patience, everything would be fine. Look at my children. . . ." She took a picture from her handbag. "Robertino, four; the twins are now two. Did you ever see such beautiful children? Oh, how I love little children when there are a lot of them. To have only one, like my first child, is sad by comparison."

"What about her—your first child?"

"She's . . . unforgiving," Ingrid said.

"Have you been skiing much?" Ernest asked, to change the subject. Then he said to me: "She's a beauty skiier."

"Haven't been skiing at all. I love it so, and I miss it, but I've been pregnant ever since I came to Europe. I was going to go last winter during my one nonpregnant lull, but I figured up what it would cost to outfit the children and the nurse, and it didn't seem worth it."

I asked her whether there were any movies for her to perform in. "No, none," she answered. "But I really don't care. The way things are now I could just concentrate on being a housewife and be perfectly happy because I have a husband who is in the theatre and talks movies, and artists are around all the time, and that would be enough for me. I could not be happy being a housewife married to a merchant, but to Roberto, yes."

"Listen, Daughter," Ernest said, "I have looked into Dr. Hemingstein's crystal ball, and a housewife is one thing you ain't gonna be. When they are starved enough for your talent, they will come to get you. In the meantime, anything I can do with my checkbook or my sixteen-gauge Winchester or maybe just to cream a couple of characters who need creaming, you have only to say the word. Okay?"

"Okay, Ernest."

"I am sincere, Daughter. I am not prone to making idle offers."

"I know, I know . . . and I love you for it."

Twenty-seven years after that visit in Milan, not having seen her since but having heard that she was suffering from cancer, I went to see her in London, where she was completing the last scenes of a four-hour television movie in which she portrayed the former Israeli prime minister Golda Meir. Hemingway was dead, Rossellini was dead, Ingrid's marriage to the Swedish producer Lars Schmidt had been dissolved, but in her courageous way she was carrying on against unconquerable odds, refusing to be vanquished, squeezing the last drops of achievement out of her exemplary life. I admired her enormously, and this visit would be an homage to her as an artist and as a woman.

My London cab pulled up in front of a hotel facade that said PALMER HOUSE, but which was in fact a London hotel that had been "dressed" to resemble Chicago's Palmer House. Ingrid, now sixty-six years old, virtually unrecognizable, was standing in front of the hotel, costumed as Golda. Vintage American automobiles, borrowed from a London collector, drove along the street as Ingrid walked toward the Buick that was waiting for her at the curb. She was dressed in a nondescript boxy coat, her hair pinned up in a bun behind her pillbox hat; a worn leather handbag hung from her arm, and she walked with a straight-backed, measured step.

As the camera moved in to record a line of dialogue that she spoke to her aide, the closeup revealed how adroitly makeup had given her an uncanny resemblance to the late Golda Meir. It was the last day of shooting after weeks of arduous photography in Israel, where the heat had been oppressive, and although there was some fear along the way that Ingrid would not be able to finish the film, she had not faltered despite her pain and debility.

While the crew set up for another take, I followed Ingrid into the hotel lobby, where she sat in a corner awaiting her call. I had been warned that her long bout with breast cancer had ravaged her beauty, but it was still a shock to see how little of the vibrant woman of Milan remained. But she smiled as we shook hands and the smile eased my memory. However, her voice was low-pitched and tired, and her right hand and arm were severely swollen.

I said that going from Maria of *For Whom the Bell Tolls* to Golda Meir was certainly traveling the gamut for an actress.

"Well, this kind of part," she said, "is like nothing I've ever done. In fact, when it was first offered to me I said: 'Now, really, how can a tall, thin Swedish Lutheran portray this short, plump Jewish lady?' But the more I learned about Golda Meir, the more I was attracted to her—or, I should say, to the experiences we had had in common. We were both workaholics, devoting our lives to our work rather than to our homes; we both initially married men who were at odds with our life styles and whom we eventually left; we both loved our children but were separated from them periodically because we were not willing to put them before our work—as a result, we had enormous guilt about them.

"And other things: we both gave up our native tongues and our native countries, we traveled incessantly, and we both attained a high degree of success in our fields. Yes, I finally admitted, the tall Swedish Lutheran could play the plump Jewish lady."

There was another similarity that Ingrid didn't mention—in fact, it is depicted in a scene in which a doctor informs Meir that she has cancer of the bone, a scene that required Ingrid to react and pull herself together; just as Golda Meir continued to function as prime minister while undergoing treatment, so did Ingrid continue her acting career after her first mastectomy in 1974.

The production manager informed Ingrid that they were ready for her; she took a last deep pull on her cigarette as she rose stiffly from her chair. On her way to the door, the production photographer approached and said that he'd like to have her for a photo session as soon as that take was completed.

She nodded wearily.

Late that afternoon, after the last shot in the hotel dining room was completed, Ingrid joined the cast and production crew at the corner pub for a wrap-up celebration. Having shed the thick eyebrows, gray wig, and clothes of Golda, Ingrid was enjoying this farewell champagne with the people whom she had lived with and worked with for many long weeks. At her side stood her companion-nurse, who lived with her in her London flat and who was with her all during the shooting in Israel.

I was standing at the bar with Gene Corman, who was the producer and who was the one who with quiet persistence induced Ingrid to play this role. "How I admire the courage of this lady," Corman said. "You've no idea . . . do you remember the famous picture of Golda when at the moment she was elected prime minister she covered her face with her hands and burst into tears? Well, the script called for a duplication of that scene, but Ingrid's right arm and hand were so swollen we were prepared to use a stand-in's hands in place of hers. I'm told that swelling like that often occurs after a mastectomy. But you know what Ingrid did? She was so intent on playing the scene herself that the night before she tied her arm in an up position and slept that way in order to bring the swelling down. By morning the swelling had indeed diminished and she was able to use her own hands in the scene."

The production manager rapped for attention and raised his glass in a toast to Ingrid, everyone echoing his sentiments as Ingrid beamed her lovely smile at them. But I detected a pervasive undercurrent of sadness; more than the film had ended.

As Ingrid prepared to leave, I said: "We haven't been able to talk much today. Would you mind if we meet tomorrow for a while?"

She invited me to her flat at noon, but apologized that she didn't have the energy to offer me lunch.

Ingrid lived in a modest flat in Cheyne Gardens, a quiet, residential district of London. In the small, comfortable living room, three clustered Oscars on a bookshelf signified the glory of her achievements. Outside the tiny kitchen a silver shovel, inscribed to her, commemorated the planting of a tree in her honor. But these were the only visible adornments of her past. Everything about the flat reflected Ingrid's direct and simple way of life.

"That day Ernest came to visit me in Milan," she said, "he was still concerned about my well-being, wasn't he?"

"Yes. We were driving from Venice to Madrid but Ernest detoured to Milan because he wanted to see for himself how you were bearing up under the attack, and to give you a show of support. He loved you very much."

"Did you know that Ernest came to see me in Paris when I was playing in *Tea and Sympathy*? It was the only thing that had been offered to me at that time, and he came backstage and said: 'Daughter, I know you're going back to the States to face the rotten music, and I'd like to be on that plane with you when you arrive in New York to protect you. I'll knock down the first reporter who gets out of line, that way the press will behave themselves.' It was just like Ernest to want to protect me, but I said, 'No, absolutely not, don't you see I must arrive there completely alone, no friend, no secretary, no public relations man, no one, completely alone, or else they'll accuse me of being so afraid I need protection. I *am* afraid, but if they attack, I'll handle it.' "

She looked out the window, remembering that day, her eyes a bit misty. "In my life, I have never been afraid to face things alone. It was always like that. My mother died when I was only three, and my father, who was away much of the time, died when I was thirteen, so fending for myself was nothing new."

"Ernest said you wore your courage on your sleeve. He admired you for that, very much."

"Ernest was a true and loyal friend. When the press asked him what he thought about me being pregnant outside my marriage, Ernest said: 'I hope Ingrid has twins. I will carry them into Saint Peter's and be their godfather.' But those were dark, dark times for me. I had not been prepared for the terrible consequences of falling in love. In fact, I wasn't even prepared for falling in love. I cried all the time. I had a terrible guilt about deserting my daughter, Pia, and leaving Peter like that. But I was honest with him—that is my way—to be as direct and honest as I can. I wanted Peter to know I was leaving him, that I was unfaithful, so I wrote him from Stromboli and told him the truth. I said I knew that my letter would fall like a bomb on our house, our Pia, our future, our past so filled with sacrifice and help from him. I acknowledged that now he stood alone in the ruins that I had created, but that I couldn't help him. Or myself. I said that what I was asking for was more sacrifice and more help from him."

"You married Peter when you were eighteen, didn't you?"

"Yes."

"Do you think he was a father figure for you?"

Ingrid looked at me with a puzzled expression on her face. "That's never occurred to me," she said. She thought for a while. "Well, yes, perhaps he was a continuation of my father. He was ten years older than I, which in my young mind made him quite old, and he had an established career, a car, an impressive life style, *and,* most important, he exercised a very strong control over me. Instead of teaching me to be independent, to act for myself, he so tied me down by being helpful, by doing everything for me, making all the decisions for me that I lost my self-reliance.

"Of course, onstage or before the camera I always had total control over what I did, but not otherwise, and that has been a handicap. Men make women helpless by usurping their independence. Beginning with my father, then, after he died, Uncle Otto, who was terribly strict with me, and then Peter, who took over my life even before we were engaged— But I was somewhat to blame, for in the beginning I constantly asked Peter for his advice and guidance, and completely relied on him.

"But later on, Peter's dominance began to irritate me. I'd come home after a long day at the studio and be telling him all about what had happened that day, but he'd be nagging me: 'Don't wrinkle your forehead,' 'Sit up straight,' 'Don't twist your fingers'—precisely as if I were his child, not his wife. And the way he nagged me about not gaining weight, keeping his eye on everything I ate, even forcing me to get on the scale for him!

"To be truthful, I was afraid of him—and certainly it was a craziness to be married to someone I was afraid of. I remember one time when he expressed his displeasure with something I had done, and I said: 'All right, I made a mistake, but everyone makes mistakes now and then—you make mistakes, don't you?' He became furious with me. '*I* make mistakes . . . *I*?' 'Well, don't you?' He was really steamed. 'I certainly do not! I think a thing over very carefully before acting.' That's when I knew I would have to divorce Peter—it was wrong to be married to someone I feared, and who honestly believed he never made a mistake."

"And Rossellini?"

"He was the exact opposite of Peter in that respect—and in many others."

"So it was like running away from home with a boyfriend."

"Well, yes, somewhat like that. I suppose I had been waiting for a long time for somebody who would compel me to leave Peter. Roberto did that, but I didn't think it would upset the entire world. But the fact was I didn't have the courage to leave Peter until I fell in love with Roberto. He was so different from any man I had ever known before. He made everything larger than life. He had enormous courage and his courage was contagious. I probably had it in me, but Peter throttled it, wouldn't allow me to let it out. He kept saying: 'Be careful, play it safe, take it easy.' But Roberto said just the opposite: 'Take risks, be spontaneous, let yourself be free—if we want to have that child in your belly, then we have our child and the hell with scandal and what people think and what they'll try to do to us.' At first, I was terribly frightened but he'd say: 'Frightened of what! What is there to be frightened about? We have each other, and we have talent, and who can take any of that away from us?' I couldn't have had that kind of bravery without him beside me. You have no idea how many people said to me, people I cared about: 'How can you be so foolish, why don't you have an abortion?' It never crossed my mind. This was our child, we loved each other, and this child would be a product of that love. I say that rather easily now, but it certainly wasn't easy for me back then. I cried all the time. I felt that the newspapers were right in saying that I was an awful woman, abandoning my husband and only child. I had terrible guilt about that, and it was destroying me, along with all the mail I received from people who wrote that I'd ruined the movie business, ruined myself, that my career was gone and done with. Roberto stood by me, but curiously I felt very much alone, as if I had cut myself off from all that mattered."

She stood up. "Let's have a glass of wine," she said as she headed into her kitchen. She returned with a bottle of wine, which she handed to me to open as she lit another cigarette. "The curious thing about my life with Roberto," she continued, "was that he eventually became as restrictive as Peter, but in a different way. In Roberto's case it was—how shall I say?—artistic jealousy. He would not let me make a film with anyone but him. After we married and produced our brood of three children, the world began to relent and I was offered pictures by several directors I was dying to work with, men like De Sica and Zeffirelli, but in Roberto's mind, to make a film with any other director was the same as being unfaithful to him. But the pictures I made with him during those years were all failures—insofar as film-making was concerned, we were really not at all suited to one another, so when Hollywood finally decided to take the risk of casting me in *Anastasia*, to be filmed in London, I decided the time had come to face up to Roberto. I had been in professional exile for more than seven years by then and that was long enough.

"When I told him I had accepted the *Anastasia* part we had a terrible quarrel, which wound up, as usual, with Roberto threatening to commit suicide by driving his Ferrari into a tree. That was his standard threat, but when you have three children and a husband with a volcanic temper, you do not take it lightly, for I didn't want his suicide on my conscience, but this time, suicide threat and all, I decided to defy him. We had no money, an untold amount of debts, and besides, I was dying to get back to the kind of acting I was good at. I simply could not pass up this wonderful part—for which, eventually, I won an Academy Award.

"But actually the relationship with Roberto dissolved for many reasons, not just my defiance over *Anastasia*. At the time of our divorce, he made it very difficult for me with our children, but once we had that settled we remained good friends until his death."

"Do you have regrets over those nonproductive years wasted with Rossellini?"

"Oh, they weren't wasted! No, no, I really have no regrets about Roberto."

"About anything?"

"Well . . . yes . . . about Pia. I have a lot of guilt about her. When I tried to get legal permission for her to visit me in Italy for the summer—Peter had refused to allow it—my request had to be taken before a court in the United States. The answers she gave the lawyers that day will bother me forever. When she was asked, on the witness stand, if she loved me, she said no, she didn't love me, but she liked me.

"When she was asked if she missed me, she told the court no. They asked her if she wanted to see me, but again she said no, she'd rather spend the summer with her father. And when she was asked if she felt her mother cared about her now, she said, Not too much, that I wasn't interested in her when I left our family, and only became interested in her when I had married and had kids. Needless to say, the judge denied my request. . . . It hurt—very deeply."

"Did you have a good relationship with Pia before you went off with Rossellini?"

"To be honest, I really didn't. I was too young to be a

mother, not so much young in years as immature. I was so wound up in my career, and Hollywood's star system and all that, that I didn't find time for the little girl in my house. She'd wait all day for me to come home from the studio, and then when I did arrive, often much later than expected, I was either too tired to give her much time or hurriedly dressing for some function or other. There's no doubt in my mind, I neglected her, and for that I have a lasting sense of guilt.

"Of course, now that she's an adult, I've talked about all this with her, but to this very day, though she can understand my explanations intellectually, I fear she still does not accept them with her heart."

(When I returned to New York, I told Pia Lindstrom, now a television news reporter, what her mother had said about her, and asked her how she now felt toward Ingrid.

"What happened between my mother and me," she told me, "after she left my father is something I will never get over—one doesn't erase such emotions—but I have tried to understand what occurred so that I could deal with those emotions without a residue of rancor or anger. That humans make mistakes—I concede that *intellectually,* but emotionally I was hurt and I suppose the hurt is still deep down inside me. But it is not something I dwell on or that has affected my life. I am not bitter about it. It is not a barrier to the enjoyment of my own life and my own children. Of course, I regret that my mother did not stay with my father. There was a pain in that rejection of us and a humiliation caused by all the notoriety, and when I do think back about what happened I still feel a surge of those emotions.

"When I was a child, I was, as my mother told you, neglected. She was super-devoted to her career and my father was very busy with his dentistry; he had gone back to dental school in Los Angeles, and he was doing a residency in dental surgery. So I was alone a great deal of the time, and lonely. But the fact was that as a child I knew nothing different from the life I had; that's how life was: lonely, empty. No one around the house. No one to play with. Or talk to. Or to make me laugh. Just a big, empty house and a succession of nannies none of whose faces or names I can recall. In Beverly Hills there is a built-in isolation for kids

—big houses with high walls. I didn't have any expectation of human companionship, and certainly not love. Even when my mother and father were together we never made any noise as a family. I have no vivid memory of family happiness, and my mother's leaving certainly did not rip apart a blissfully happy family life. It simply robbed me of the fantasy that someday things might be different, that someday we might become a happy family that did things together like other families.

"I was at school when, after all those years abroad, my mother came back to New York for an award. I phoned and told her how much I longed to see her after so many years apart, but she asked me not to come to New York because she'd be so busy, so many press people and photographers and all that, and she'd like to wait and have a reunion with me when she had more time. I guess, in a way, I was more hurt by that rejection than by her originally leaving me."

I asked Pia if by now she had been able to forgive her mother.

"It isn't a question of forgiving her—there's nothing to forgive. I do not blame her and yet I cannot exonerate her for the pain and isolation and rejection which are still deep inside me.")

I asked Ingrid if she had any regrets other than her regrets about Pia.

"Oh, well, I suppose that in my life I could have been more discreet," she replied, "more diplomatic—I never was. I have always been completely straightforward, as honest about myself as I could be. I simply can't hide my feelings, or pretend—I was often accused by the press of pretending to be honest, pretending to be simple, especially in Swedish publications. But I don't pretend. I am direct and simple and outspoken. It's just that people aren't used to it—they're used to sham and artifice and pretense and they think I'm putting on an act."

Ingrid had certainly been straightforward about her bout with cancer, which first struck her while she was performing in *The Constant Wife* on the London stage. It had been a protracted, debilitating struggle that resulted in a radical mastectomy; and after intervening operations on her remaining breast, a recent second mastectomy with attendant radiology, the doctors told her that the swelling in her hand and arm could either be attributed to this operation, a frequent occurrence after a mastectomy, or it could be an indication that cancer cells were still present.

Ingrid was facing this latest and most challenging threat with the same determination with which she had faced the other crises in her life. The operations had left her too weak ever to perform on the stage again, but she still hoped to be able to perform occasionally in movie roles.

"Time is shortening, but every day that I challenge this cancer and survive is a victory for me and I am thankful for it. I have accepted it and will make the most of what's left of my life while I can. Cancer victims who don't accept their fate and learn to live with it will only destroy what little time they have left.

"Six months ago I announced my retirement. I thought my acting days were over. But just look—I've now completed a strenuous four-hour film that has been an acting challenge from beginning to end. I honestly didn't think I had it in me. But it has been a wonderful experience, as an actress, and as a human being who is getting more out of life than expected.

"Last night, the producer gave a farewell dinner for the actors, the director, the cameramen, and other people involved in the Golda Meir film. We all exchanged our reminiscences about the trials and tribulations of the movie, especially the filming in Israel, and a good time was had by all. A lovely group of people. Afterwards, I came back here to this quiet, empty apartment, and I suddenly realized, This is my reality now, this is how it is—and I felt drained and very sad; the ending of the film, I thought, was like a death in the family. And standing here at this window, looking out at the streetlights, I started to weep. Isn't that strange? I couldn't stop crying. I have made so many movies, you'd think I'd be used to it by now—these abrupt endings to something that only yesterday had so much life and vitality. But there I was, weeping my heart out. People who have been so close to me who I will likely never see again.

"And maybe . . . well, who knows? . . . this may be the last time I face my dear, old friend, the camera."

Leaving Ingrid's flat that afternoon, in London's gathering twilight, I was reminded of what Hemingway had said when we left her that time in Milan. First he said: "Have you ever seen such honest beauty, grace, and intelligence in one package?" He looked out the window of the car for a while at the passing scenery, thinking about her, and I could tell from the sad look on his face that he was commiserating with her unkind fate.

Finally, he said: "I'll tell you something, Hotch—if they ever have an Olympic event for courage, Miss Ingrid is a cinch for the Gold Medal."

Ingrid died a short time after I saw her, and the world mourned her passing, as did I. In memoriam, television played many of her old movies, and again seeing her in *Intermezzo* and *Casablanca* and *Anastasia,* I was happy to realize that a vital part of her still lives.

7

The Night I Got Caught in the Hungarian Revolution

With each assignment, editors became more confident in my ability and so did I. Whereas in the beginning I was restricted to "safe" pieces such as "You Cannot Afford a Divorce" and "The Scandal of Our District Attorneys," I was now given much more freedom in my assignments. I was in Germany doing research on the "war" between our Occupation forces and the Germans in the locales where our GIs were stationed when I received a cable from Brooks Roberts informing me that the Hungarians had started an uprising against the Russians in Budapest, and asking that I cover the event.

I first went to Vienna, where I acquired a translator and accreditation documents, then proceeded to Traiskirchen, which is a small town situated on the border between Austria and Hungary. Hungarian refugees were streaming into the village unmolested by the border guards, who ordinarily allowed no access to Austria.

As these refugees crossed the border they were gathered up by volunteer workers and taken to one of several camps which had been established along the border. But instead of heated rooms, hot food, and some semblance of civilization, these crude camps inflicted more privation on the people who took shelter there. In one of the camps, Eisenstadt, where two mobile kitchens out in the freezing cold dished out what little food there was, I saw a small boy hiding the bread and cheese that were his lunch ration. As I stood watching him, a young priest who was also a refugee stopped and joined me. He mumbled something to himself in Latin and shook his head. I asked him what he had said. He repeated it slowly: *"Exoriare aliquis nostris ex ossibus ultor."* I asked him if he could translate that into English.

"Yes," he said. "It's from Virgil: some avenger will sometime arise from our bones."

My translator was an attractive young woman named Christine Bottomore, a doctor of philosophy from the University of Vienna who spoke eight languages. After the war she had been briefly married to a British airman named Bottomore, which was a name she preferred to her own hyphenated, convoluted Austrian name. She spoke fluent Hungarian and somehow arranged to get us places in a convoy of Red Cross vehicles that were leaving for Budapest.

All the villages we passed through were alive with celebrants, and in Budapest it seemed that every inhabitant was in the streets, singing, dancing, drinking wine, an orgy of happiness over the liberation from all those years of Russian oppression. The Russian military presence, especially the loathsome tanks, had rolled out of the city and headed back to Russia. In front of the parliament building I saw a huge mass of people who were chanting "Good-bye, Russians!" and while I watched, they attacked a gargantuan bronze statue of Stalin that occupied the square in front of Parliament House. They attached a rope to the statue and tried to pull it down but the rope broke and the statue didn't budge. Then some men appeared with a roll of steel cable but the mob still couldn't topple the statue. Finally, a group of welders put their torches to Stalin's feet, melting them away, and the statue crashed to the pavement. It was explained to me that pulling down the statue was symbolically important, because an ancient church that had stood on that spot had been pulled down by the Russians to make room for the statue.

The revelry continued all through the night, in and out of houses, restaurants, bars, and hotels. It had all started with student protests, and fleeting attacks by the emboldening Underground, but in their wildest fantasies the Hungarians never expected the Russians to turn tail and run. But that is exactly what had happened, and the Hungarians were overcome with a long-absent national pride over their achievement. They sang songs that had been banned and shouted obscenities toward the departed Russians as they wept and laughed and danced in one another's arms, but with the dawn of the new day they were about to realize that they had been victimized by one of the cruelest hoaxes ever perpetrated by a bully conqueror on his victims.

We were in the dining room of one of the hotels, having breakfast with some Swedish Red Cross people, when one of their group came dashing in with the sketchy news that the Russian tanks had turned around and were headed back toward Budapest. At first there was disbelief as differing rumors darted in and out of the lobby, but by midafternoon the first of the tanks began appearing in the suburbs, and the euphoria of the previous night turned to panic.

The previous day, I had met an engaging man named Sandor Noly, who was one of the leaders of the Underground, and Christine and I now went to find him. My plan was to attach myself to his group and write about their exploits as they dealt with the Russians' new assault.

We found Sandor at his house, where he and several other men were hurriedly assembling their guns and putting rounds in ammunition belts to be slung across their shoulders and chests. We could clearly hear the sound of bombardment by the cannons of the approaching tanks. I told Sandor my plan but he wouldn't allow me to do it. "No, no—you would create danger for yourself, and for us. You do not realize the seriousness of this. I beg you, quickly find some way to leave—quickly, while one end of the city, the end that faces Austria, is still open."

Christine also urged me not to stay, and I realized that they were right. Without an operational base, I knew I could not function; so we returned to the hotel. But there I discovered that the Red Cross convoy had already pulled out, and there was no other available transportation to Austria. However, I had learned a valuable trick from Janet Flanner on how to resolve such predicaments—a large bill pressed firmly onto the palm of the concierge. One phone call and we were told to wait on the sidewalk in front of the hotel.

The crowds of the previous night had completely vanished;

now the streets were filled with flight. Bicycles laden with belongings were being pedaled toward the highway that led to
Austria. It was a noiseless exodus, the only sounds coming from
the wheels of the bicycles and carts, an infrequent automobile,
and the distant thunder of the tanks. Not a word was spoken, the
people fleeing in utter silence, more ashamed than angry.

Inside of ten minutes, a small rickety truck pulled up in front
of us. It had a cargo of sacks of cement and bricks. The driver
got out and immediately informed us how much he wanted to
make the trip. It was steep but since there was no alternative I
told Christine to accept. The driver wanted full payment in
advance, and he made it clear that he was not guaranteeing we
would make it to the Austrian border; in the event we were
arrested along the way, he wanted it understood that there
would be no refund.

We both sat up front with the driver, who never said another
word to us or looked at us until he got to the border. He stopped
a short distance from the guard post, telling us that as foreigners
we'd be better off approaching on foot and showing our papers.

Several days later, while I was at the Eisenstadt camp taking
pictures and talking to some of the refugees, I saw Sandor in a
group that was just arriving. The entire left side of his face and
one of his hands had been burned. That evening, after medical
treatment, he told me what had happened to his little band of
resistance fighters in the three days since our departure. "You
are fortunate to have left when you did," he said. "The Russians
took as prisoner an American woman from the *Reader's Digest*
and locked her up in the jail where she is now."

This, then, is an account of the three-day Russian assault on
Budapest, based on what Sandor told me:

It was light enough to see by six-thirty. In the back of an alley
that had been blocked off by a heap of bomb debris, the early
dawn revealed a hideout that had been formed by the tenting of
two walls of the shattered building. It was beautifully camouflaged.

Inside the shelter, on the white-powdered, hard-rock
ground, three young men were asleep. Sandor, unshaven and
inadequately clothed against the morning cold, as were the men
asleep on the ground, sat in a corner of the shelter where a crack

in the rocks gave him a commanding view of the approach. Stacked against the back wall were scores of gasoline cans and empty glass bottles and a number of wooden crates. Two tommy guns hung by their slings on the wall, and there was a circle of rifles in the corner. But there was no food and nothing to drink. These men hadn't eaten in two days.

Outside the shelter there was a slight stirring, but Sandor, recognizing the tall man in the beret, did not move. The tall man, whose name was Janos, silently entered the hideout through its camouflaged entrance. He was carrying a small but heavy wooden keg.

"How's it, Sandor?" he asked.

"Quiet," Sandor said. "Belo and Josef got all the cans filled —they got several liters by siphon out of a couple of wrecked tanks, and the rest they got at Polgar's paint shop."

"Good," Janos said. "How's Polgar?"

"The secret police hanged him in Petoefi Street yesterday morning. His wife told Belo."

"We'll put his gasoline to good work for him," said Janos grimly. "I see you got bottles—very good."

"What's in the wooden keg?" Sandor asked.

"Liquid soap. And look at this." Janos pulled a mound of shoelaces from his leather jacket. Sandor's face broke into a smile, but suddenly, from somewhere outside the shelter, there was a low whistle followed by a high, thin young boy's voice calling out: "Panzer!"

The three sleeping men were quickly on their feet. Gasoline was poured from the cans into several of the glass bottles. Gyula took one of the tommy guns from the wall, fitted it with ammunition, checked it carefully. Josef slung a rifle over his shoulder and picked up one of the gas-filled bottles. Sandor and Belo also filled glass jars with gasoline, and Janos took the other tommy gun from its wall hook. The men all dipped into one of the wooden crates, which contained hand grenades, and hung as many from their belts as they could carry. Janos passed out shoelaces to everyone.

Now, without a word, they filed out of the shelter with Janos leading the way, five young men with makeshift equipment, taking on the biggest tanks in the Russian army. Ten days ago they had been students at the Budapest Polytechnic University, studying to be engineers, but now they were experienced antitank fighters. At first they had made costly mistakes—Janos had started with a group of twenty—but for two days now there had been no casualties.

They knew how to fight the tanks, for, ironically, the Russians had taught them. "How to Fight an Enemy Tank in a Partisan War" was a required course at the university, and they had been shown Russian-made training films that had proved very helpful. By now they had added several ingenious inventions of their own.

Janos led them cautiously through the protective cover of backyards, most of them a shambles. They climbed through the battered windows of a tailor shop, and reaching Izabella Street, they went up the fire escape of the tallest building. From the roof ledge Janos could see the approaching tank, one of the new thirty-six-ton models that mounted a big 100-millimeter gun. It was closely followed by an open-top armored car that had a machine gun on a swivel mount; there were four Russian soldiers in the car. The Russians had learned that their tanks were vulnerable from behind, where they had a blind spot, and the armored car was following for protection. Janos shielded his eyes against the sun and carefully studied all the surrounding streets. Everywhere he looked he could see tanks grinding along in a crisscross patrol pattern. "They've brought up a lot of reinforcements," he said. "We're going to have a busy day."

The big T-54 now turned into Izabella Street, its metallic roar filling the air. Its top turret was shut tight, and the two men at the panzer car's machine gun were scanning the building tops. Janos pulled back out of sight. His four men took up positions along the roof ledge. Gyula readied his tommy gun. The other three men took shoelaces from their pockets and inserted one end of the shoelace into their gasoline bottles. Janos took three grenades from his belt. They were Hungarian grenades, so tooled that they could be fitted together to form a chain. Janos screwed the three of them together, then signaled to his men to light the free end of the shoelaces.

The tank was now directly in front of them, four stories

down. "Ready," Janos said. He pulled the pin in the top grenade, held it for a two count as he took a sighting on the panzer car, then gently tossed it forward. At the same moment, the three bottles of gasoline, their shoelace wicks aflame, went flying through the air in the direction of the back of the tank, where the motor and fuel tank were located. The grenade hit the panzer car dead center with a roar. One bottle missed the tank, spilling its flaming contents all over the street; but the other two were on target, and as the glass broke, the gasoline was immediately ignited by the burning shoelace and raced its flames all over the back of the tank.

The panzer car wheeled over, a twisted wreck, its four soldiers dead. The tank now caught fire within and skidded to a stop. The turret was flung open, and the sergeant driver, choking from the smoke, was first out. Janos held up his hand, indicating no action. The four other members of the tank crew got out as fast as they could and as the last man stumbled down from the burning tank Janos and Gyula opened fire with their tommy guns and shot them all dead.

Janos quickly led his men away from the area. Their next destination was a building on Wesselenyi Street. A convoy of three tanks had been spotted headed in that direction from Dembinski Street, where they had indiscriminately leveled every building on the street, with no warning to the women and children inside them. Janos and his men stopped off at the hideout and took five cans of their precious gasoline. Now they dumped the gasoline all over the street, bathing it in gasoline from gutter to gutter. The tank rumble was very close as they ran into a building and climbed to its roof. Belo had made a torch out of a broomstick with a turban of rags; he saturated the rags with the last of the gasoline. Janos waited until all three of the tanks were in the gas-soaked stretch. Then he nodded to Belo, who threw his flaming torch to the street. As the torch left Belo's hand he was an easy target, and there was a burst of machine-gun fire from the lead tank. The bullets caught him across the chest, and he fell backward onto the roof just as the street below burst into flames. The undercarriages of the tanks caught fire, and two of the tanks rammed together as they went out of control.

This time Janos did not wait for the crews to abandon the tanks. As the turrets opened, he shot down the drivers struggling to get out, thereby blocking the passage and trapping all the other crew members inside the burning tanks.

Janos' band of freedom fighters, now down to four, got one more tank that morning, and a panzer car containing five AVO secret police. But at one o'clock in the afternoon they suffered another casualty.

This time a tank appeared unexpectedly and there was no time to prepare for it. So they tried a daring assault. Josef hid in a doorway at street level with a two-grenade stick held ready. Up on the roof, Janos fired a burst at the tank to make it turn its 100-millimeter cannon to the side, away from the protective machine gun which faced front. As the big cannon fired a blast at the roof, Josef dashed forward and jammed the hand grenade in the mouth of the gun, which was being reloaded. The grenade roared its destruction, setting off the tank's ammunition, but Josef was hit in the head by a piece of flying steel. He died in the street beside the twisted tank he had killed.

At two o'clock, Janos' teen-age sister Johanna came to the hideout with two loaves of bread and a huge cut of cheese, and the men ate for the first time in two and a half days. Johanna was afraid of the tanks and the Russian soldiers riding grimly in their iron automobiles, but like the other children in her neighborhood she was brave and helped as much as she could.

Twice more that afternoon they made forays against the ever-increasing tanks. They disabled one tank by throwing a four-grenade stick into the rubber wheel at the front of its track, but the Russians stayed inside the tank and there was no way to get at them. The other foray almost ended in disaster. Sandor had hidden in a doorway, holding the end of a rope that was attached to a gasoline can on the other side of the street. As a tank approached, Janos, also from a hidden position, set fire to the gas tank; Sandor then pulled the burning gas tank across the street so that it would come to rest underneath the passing tank and ignite it. It was a maneuver they had used successfully in the past. But this time the tank's track hit the gas can, flipping it in Sandor's direction. The flame burst up, burning Sandor severely across the face, and at the same time the tank, having spotted Sandor, opened fire with its machine gun.

Luckily, the turret of the tank was a few inches open, and Janos, taking dead aim, hit the tank driver between the eyes. The tank lurched, ruining the machine-gunner's aim, and Sandor was able to escape.

The left side of Sandor's face was in bad shape and Janos wanted him to go to the nearest aid station, which was in the basement of a drugstore, but Sandor refused.

Now the gasoline was gone, but they had not used the keg of liquid soap. They chose a small street in advance of a tank that was headed toward the Kilian Barracks, where a big battle was in progress. They broke the keg open, and the syrupy soap ran from the center rise of the street toward both gutters, leaving a slippery band across the asphalt. The three men then took up positions on a rooftop overlooking the street and waited for the tank. Janos still had ammunition for his tommy gun, and Gyula and Sandor were ready with grenades. Down below, the tank came rumbling into view. It spun and skidded to the side as its tracks found the soap. The tank driver speeded up his engine, trying to overcome the slipperiness, but the tracks only spun round in place. Cautiously, the driver opened the turret and looked over the side, but there was nothing to see. He hoisted himself out and climbed down the side.

Now was the moment to strike. The turret was open, the tank was stopped, the men were inside, sitting ducks. Gyula stepped forward and leaned over the roof gutter, holding his activated grenade out in front of him, aiming it for the turret opening. Janos too was forward, his tommy gun pointed toward the tank driver, who was slipping and sliding comically on the soapy surface.

Intent on their prey below, the men on the roof did not notice the panzer car as it swung swiftly into the street. But the panzer saw them immediately. Its machine gun exploded. Gyula, hit hard, pitched forward with his grenade still in his hand and exploded with it on the street below. Janos and Sandor threw themselves to the roof, but Janos had been hit along his side and thigh and the blood came fast. Down below, the machine-gunner of the tank joined the panzer in directing a concentrated fire on the rooftop position, and the tank, slowly spinning around into position, despite the soap, was preparing its cannon for action.

"Get going," Janos said. "I can keep them distracted with my fire and you can get out the back way."

"No," Sandor said. "I've still got grenades."

"Don't be silly. They've got the tank buttoned. What good are grenades? Go on. What's the sense their getting both of us?"

"But I can carry you."

"Where?" Janos asked.

Lying there close together on the roof, the machine-gun fire digging into the bricks and stone over their heads, Janos reached out and touched his friend on the cheek. They had been good friends.

"Leave me a grenade," Janos said. Sandor wanted to say something but he started to cry, so he turned on his belly, and using his elbows, squirmed along the roof to the back of the building. Going down he heard the quick rattle of Janos' gun, and as he reached the backyard, he heard the explosion of the last grenade.

Now the heavy roar of the tank's cannon took over, firing point-blank into the first floor, then the second, and when, with a heavy rush, the building caved down, showering everything with its white mist, the tank fired a final round for good measure.

Then it wheeled its gun back into position, turned, went on its way, leaving behind it a huge mound of white and gray rubble —a monument to a rebel's courage.

On my last day in Vienna, I had a farewell lunch with Christine Bottomore in a charming restaurant next to the Opera House. As a good-bye present, she had brought me a book which had recently been published, the memoirs of an Austrian woman named Maria von Trapp, which Christine had translated into English.

"You told me that someday you would like to write a musical," she said, "and I think this book would be wonderful for that. Maria von Trapp is a friend of mine. I talked about you and she would like for you to write it as a musical if you are interested."

I promised to read it and I carried it around in my luggage for quite some time. But I never got around to reading it. A year or so later, Richard Rodgers and Oscar Hammerstein did read it and wrote *The Sound of Music.*

8

Frank Sinatra Says He's His Own Worst Enemy

Despite my success with articles on general subjects, I was not having much luck in getting assignments to write about interesting people. There were well established writers who specialized in these so-called personality pieces, and since these profiles were usually tied in with the magazine's cover they were of prime importance. *Redbook* was one of those magazines. I had developed a good working relationship with Bob Stein, the articles editor (now editor-in-chief of *McCall's*), who finally gave me an assignment that several writers had already failed at—a piece about Frank Sinatra. "None of these experienced writers was able to get to Sinatra," Stein warned me. "He's arrogant and rude and surrounded by a bunch of tough guys who will push you around. But if you want to take a crack at it, we'll pay expenses."

I spoke to Sinatra's agent but he said that Frank was in the midst of shooting *The Man with the Golden Arm* in Hollywood, and would see no one. A Broadway publicist I knew said the same thing. "Too much fame, too much dough" was his capsulated opinion.

My first awareness of the original teen-ager Sinatra phenomenon had occurred one afternoon early in 1943 when, while on leave in New York City (I had just graduated from OCS and was on my way to Westover Field in Chicopee Falls, Massachusetts, where I was to become the adjutant of the 13th Anti-Submarine

Wing of the Air Force), I had tried to walk past the Paramount Theatre on Broadway.

It was an impossibility. What seemed like thousands of teenage girls choked the sidewalk and spilled over into the street. Special police details could not handle them. Some of them had been standing on line since the night before. They were all there answering the call of Frank Albert Sinatra. His name was engraved on their jackets and many of them wore limp bow-ties fashioned after their hero's.

It was hard for me to reconcile the bobby-soxers' Frankeeee!, "The Voice" of the Forties, with the "serious" actor who had won an Oscar for his role in *From Here to Eternity.* By the time he signed for *The Man with the Golden Arm,* his income was in the millions as a result of a string of successful films—*Suddenly, Young at Heart, Not as a Stranger, The Tender Trap*—and also, he was number one in the recording field, with two of his records, "Learnin' the Blues" and "Young at Heart," each up over a million.

But only two years before, the only thing that Sinatra was collecting was trouble. The government was after him for $110,000 in back taxes, the sales flow of his records had become a trickle, his second marriage, to Ava Gardner, had failed, and emotionally and physically he was shot; the press, never very friendly to him, was digging his grave. But Frank refused to show up for his funeral.

I checked into the Beverly Hills Hotel and put in a call to R.K.O. I had discovered that all the other writers who had tried to interview Sinatra had first contacted either his personal press agent or the R.K.O. press agent, but nobody seemed to have made an attempt to contact Sinatra directly. When the studio operator came on the line, I asked for Mr. Sinatra's trailer, and after a few rings he answered the phone. For a moment I was flustered by the success of my boldness, but after telling him why I was calling, he asked: "What kind of an article you got in mind? If it's another of those that proves that I'm wild, eccentric, swellheaded and fulla talent, I think *Time* gave me all the lumps I need for a while, don't you?"

He was referring to a recent cover article in *Time* magazine that made him out to be a wild spender (carried nothing smaller than a hundred-dollar bill) who looked, talked, and acted like a gangster in real life, dressed in gaudy imitation of George Raft, had a neurotic obsession about cleanliness, constantly surrounded himself with a gang of rough "boys," always took one of his men along on dates, mingled with notorious gangsters like Joe Fischetti and Lucky Luciano, frequently threw crying fits and temper tantrums (sometimes while sitting on the lap of his secretary), and claimed he was going to do exactly as he pleased in life. "I don't need anybody in the world," *Time* quoted him as saying. "I did it all myself."

"No, I'm not interested in that kind of article," I said. "I'm not trying to prove anything. I would just like to know how, after everyone said you were all washed up, you managed to make such a spectacular comeback. I mean, what went on inside you."

"Good enough," Sinatra said. "Come on the set tomorrow and we'll have a talk between takes."

That simple. The following day, when I presented myself at the studio gate, there was a pass waiting for me. I was immediately taken to the sound stage, where Otto Preminger was directing Sinatra in a scene in which he was explaining to the girl he loves how he got the dope habit. Preminger called for action, the camera rolled. Sinatra was sitting at a scarred kitchen table in a dingy flat, sipping a cup of coffee. "You only do it for kicks, first," he said. "You don't *need* it, you can take it or let it alone. So you keep takin' it. 'N' then there comes a time you don't find on any clock ever made. Not day, not night—just Fix Time. It rolls toward you like a wave 'n' when it hits you you're gone. You're so sick, nobody can stand bein' so sick. 'N' you know then that you're hooked. There's a forty-pound monkey on your back 'n' the only way you can get through the day under that load is by leanin' on a fix."

Sinatra had worked his way inside the character he played, and as Preminger called out: "Print it!" I felt the excitement among the grips and electricians watching the scene. "Have you ever seen such dedication to a part?" Preminger said to an assistant. "He's a great actor. I've always said it. A great actor."

Sinatra now came over and shook hands, and I got my first chance to study him up close. He stood about 5 feet 10, and couldn't have weighed more than 130 with lead sinkers in both pockets. Contrary to *Time* magazine's pronouncement, he bore no resemblance, in my eyes, to "the popular conception of a gangster, model 1929." As a matter of fact, as he chatted amiably with one of the grips about the potential of an up-and-coming prizefighter named Floyd Patterson, I was reminded of something Harold Hobson of the London *Times* had written about Sinatra on his first visit to the Palladium in 1950: "To a people whose ideal of manhood is husky, full-blooded and self-reliant, Sinatra has chosen to suggest that, under the crashing self-assertion, man is still only a child, frightened and whimpering in the dark."

Frank wore a hairpiece to cover inroads of baldness, and there were even white caps on his teeth. His makeup, however, could not completely cover several deep scars alongside and in back of his ears (the result of his head having been torn by forceps at birth—what had actually happened was that the doctor had given up on Frank as a stillborn, and it was his grandmother who saved his life by snatching him up and holding him under the cold-water tap).

Sinatra and I entered his portable dressing room, which was a few yards away from the set. There were no tough bodyguards around—in fact, no one at all. He sat on a chair with his back to his makeup table, lit a cigarette, and said, over an ingratiating smile: "Shoot."

"How about this picture?" I asked. "Isn't this a strange role for you to be playing?"

"Well, it's pretty far from *Guys and Dolls,*" he said, "but it's a part I've had my heart set on for a long time. John Garfield first wanted to do it, and after he died I tried to buy the book. It doesn't matter that I didn't get it, it only matters that after all these years of waiting, I get to play the part. It looks like we can't get a seal of approval for it, but the movie people are just being stupid. Every manner of thing's been on the screen—drunks in *Lost Weekend,* insanes in *The Snake Pit* and *The Shrike*—but about narcotics, everybody's supposed to stick their heads in the ground. Well, it's time we came out and showed people how awful this thing is. I wanna play this part so they feel what a terrible thing it is to do to a human being.

"I remember back when I was a kid in Hoboken, there were a couple of older guys on the block who acted funny and later I found out they were on the junk. Tough, poor neighborhoods like that, one peddler can ruin a lot of kids' lives. That's why this is such a good part. It says something. That's what I'm looking for. Those kinds of parts, but I'm not forgetting that song and dance and light comedy will always be my bread and butter. However, I need a lot of variety and a lot of work to keep my interest going.

"That's why I steer clear of the stage. After opening night I'd go nuts repeating the same show night after night. I can't repeat. I got to go at a thing with all I got, burn it up, and go on. That's why I've worked out this schedule I've got. Why, hell, I won't have ten minutes between movies for the next coupla years. I go into my first Western, *Johnny Concho,* the day after I'm through here, and this time I'm going to produce the picture with my own company. And after that, I gotta get from Hollywood to Madrid with only forty-eight hours between finishing the one picture and startin' the next. I'm movin'! One of the pictures I'm especially excited about is the life of the nightclub comedian Joe E. Lewis—I'll play Joe and what a part that is!" Sinatra shook his head, thinking about the part, and then his smile faded.

"To think, coupla years ago, I couldn't 've *bought* my way into a film." He thought about that. "Time takes care of many things," he said softly.

"What happened back there?" I asked him. "What put the skids on you?"

Sinatra's eyes snapped up at me. "Me," he said. "I did it. I'm my own worst enemy. My singing went downhill and I went downhill with it, or vice versa—but nobody hit me in the throat or choked me with my necktie. It happened because I paid no attention to how I was singing. Instead, I wanted to sit back and enjoy my success and sign autographs and bank the heavy cash. Well, let me tell you, nobody who's successful sits back and enjoys it. I found that out the hard way. You work at it all the time, even harder than when you were a nobody. Enjoyment is just a by-product of success—you get a kick out of it, fine, but the only real fun in being successful is working hard at the thing that brings you the success. That's what I had to learn. You hear all the time about guys who showed big promise or who even made the top and then suddenly they flub out. Everybody says they must have developed a block or lost their touch or one of the guys at the office was out to get them or whatever. Well, maybe that's just a fancy way of saying the thing I found out: the only guy can hurt you is yourself."

The phone rang. It was Marlon Brando, calling from the Paramount lot, which was nearby. "Okay for lunch," Sinatra said, "but tell the guy at the gate I'm comin'. I got on some strange clothes and he may give me a hard time."

He hung up, looked down at his beat-up clothes, and laughed. "Who says I'm a clotheshorse?" he asked. He made a date to see me later that day and went off to his lunch date.

"The only guy can hurt you is yourself," I wrote down on my note pad, and I thought about how badly Frank Sinatra had hurt Frank Sinatra back in 1951 and 1952. The head of steam that finally blew had been building up quite some time. Sinatra had made a number of fairly undistinguished but remunerative movies, among them *Higher and Higher, The Miracle of the Bells, It Happened in Brooklyn, Take Me Out to the Ball Game,* and *The Kissing Bandit,* but the gossip in Hollywood was that Frank often went off to Mexico for weekends that spilled over into the week and forced the studios to halt production.

He was seen on dates with an unending succession of beauties—Lana Turner, Judy Garland, Marilyn Maxwell, Gloria Vanderbilt, Anita Ekberg—and it was commonly accepted in Hollywood that Sinatra's marriage, which dated back to his Hoboken days and which had spawned three children, was done for.

And then along came Ava Gardner and put the finisher on it. In his own vernacular, Frank flipped for her, chased her all over two continents, finally induced his wife, Nancy, to give him a divorce despite the fact that she was a staunch Roman Catholic.

All this activity was murder on Frank and his career. One night in Reno he was rescued from an overdose of sleeping pills, and when he and Ava were married in Boston in 1951 Sinatra got into a scrape with one of the photographers that almost turned the wedding reception into a brawl. The marriage to Ava was tempestuous, to put it mildly. Loud and frequent battles alternated with loud and passionate reconciliations. MGM canceled out on Frank's movie contract. CBS followed suit on his television show. Nightclub owners heeded *Variety*'s word that "The Voice" had turned into "The Croak," and a tired croak at that. Some music stores didn't even carry Sinatra records in stock, so infrequent were the demands for them.

When he and Ava left for Europe on their honeymoon, an editorial in the Richmond *Times-Dispatch* proclaimed: "Goodbye, Frankie and Ava, and don't come back." The New York *Daily News* inquired: "Anyone know of a bigger bore just now than Frank Sinatra?" At Toots Shor's, a favorite Sinatra hangout, the word was that Frank was washed up.

This, in brief, was the sinking ship from which Frank had to rescue himself. To try to understand how he did it, what inner forces suddenly came to life in him, I searched for clues in where and how he grew up.

If ever a man reflected his environment, Sinatra is that man. He was born an only child, in a roisterous neighborhood in Hoboken, New Jersey, on December 12, 1917. His parents, Anthony and Natalie, were Italian immigrants of vastly different temperaments. Anthony was a reserved little man who fought as a bantamweight under the sobriquet "Marty O'Brien," worked in a shipyard, toiled as a boilermaker, ran a nondescript bar, and wound up, thanks to his wife's remarkable career, a captain in the Hoboken fire department.

Frank's mother, whose nickname was Dolly, was a two-fisted, astute woman who became involved in the politics of her neighborhood, which was predominantly Italian Catholic; by the time Frank was born she was already a political power. She had little time to devote to Frank, who was raised by his grandmother, at whose house he lived. But Dolly tried to make up for her lack of mother attention with a plethora of material things. By the time he was twelve, Frank owned six bicycles and fourteen sports coats, and as a teen-ager he ran through five automobiles. So there was Frank, a virtual crown prince in a neighborhood of rough and ragged kids. At Frank's school, where the wearing of socks was normally regarded as a show of ostentation, he showed up in a different suit almost every day of the week. "With a silk handkerchief flapping out of the pocket, yet," one of his schoolmates is reported to have said.

Needless to say, this frail little bundle of chic was a frequent target for the neighborhood toughs, but Frankie was an awesome scrapper, with his fists or the jagged top of a glass bottle, and those opponents he couldn't beat off he bought off. This formula was so successful that Frank became leader of the gang on his block and he kept them busy rifling dime-store counters and candy-store cash registers. His followers became so impressed with the thoroughness with which he planned his junior-sized heists that they nicknamed him Angles. Sinatra admitted that "If it hadn't been for my interest in music, I'd probably have ended in a life of crime."

But Mama Sinatra finally became aware of what young Frankie was up to, and she moved the family to a better neighborhood, where Frank's delinquencies were limited to bedeviling his high school teachers to the point where they booted him out of school.

Frank worked for a short time as a newspaper delivery boy, but when he was eighteen he found the *raison d'être* for his future existence. He took his girl, Nancy, to a Jersey City theatre where Bing Crosby was appearing in person, and he was struck with the fact that this was precisely the manner in which he wished to make his mark. "You know what he is," Frank remarked to Nancy, "he's a troubador, that's what. He sings friendly like. He tells a story in every song. He's relaxed but he makes you feel like he's singing just for you. I'm gonna sing like that. I'm gonna practice and I'm gonna sing just like that."

Frank won an amateur contest at the Academy of Music, a run-down movie house that was located on Fourteenth Street in New York, and from that triumph went on to greater heights when, as a member of the Hoboken Four, he did well enough in a competition on "Major Bowes Amateur Hour" to be sent on tour in one of the Major Bowes units. This was a third-rate troupe that played one-night stands in remote whistle-stops, and after a couple of months on the trail Frank gave up and returned to the relatively lush surroundings of Hoboken. "There was no class to that," he explained to Nancy. "All they wanted you to do was to sing loud and funny for laughs or else that Mother Machree shit. The thing I ought to do is to get on radio."

Frank broke into radio in a unique manner: he offered his voice free of charge, and before he knew it he was singing on eighteen sustaining programs per week for stations in Jersey City, Newark, and New York. The only income he received from all his labor was seventy cents a week, which one station paid him for carfare.

In 1938, Sinatra got his first paying job as a singer when he was hired as a headwaiter and singing M.C. at a roadhouse just outside Hoboken. He started at fifteen dollars a week and worked himself up to twenty-five. On this beneficence, he and Nancy got married. One evening, a trumpeter named Harry James, who was leaving Benny Goodman's band to start one of his own, heard Frank sing and signed him as vocalist at seventy-five a week. Sinatra was then hired away by Tommy Dorsey at twice the salary. While he was with Dorsey's band, Frank made the discovery that he could phrase his singing and glide his notes in pretty much the same manner the maestro handled his trombone. During this period with Dorsey, Frank learned a lot about music, although he never learned to read a note. By the beginning of 1942, Sinatra was attracting as much attention as the great Dorsey, and in the summer of that year he finally managed to get out from under his contract, but at a terrible price—43⅓ percent of his gross earnings for the next three years had to go to Dorsey and his manager.

Frank struggled valiantly under this yoke for a year but then managed to buy his way out of it. In December of 1942, Sinatra got what was supposed to be a routine booking at the Paramount Theatre on a bill headed by Benny Goodman's orchestra, but teen-agers mobbed him, and under the inspired guidance of the late George Evans, a peerless press agent, Frankeeee! became a national phenomenon, his income was well beyond a million, and over the course of the next couple of years he managed to pull many a symphony orchestra out of the red by simply appearing with them.

At the height of his popularity, Frank devoted much of his considerable energy toward promoting interracial harmony among teen-agers. He indefatigably toured high school audi-

My first $300 bounty: Edna Ferber, here performing in one of her hit plays, *The Royal Family,* with Louis Calhern

Dorothy Parker was a gentle, compassionate woman with a devastatingly witty tongue and a tilt toward melancholia.

Tom Williams, later "Tennessee," front row, left, when he was writing poetry for our literary magazine at Washington University. (I'm at the extreme right.)

Clarice introduced me to the world of opera and to the joys of living in Paris, but also to a "reality" I couldn't accept.

Clark Gable as I knew him at O.C.S., without moustache and with blisters on his feet.

We sat on the beach and Gable wept over the memory of his lost love, Carole Lombard.

Louis Armstrong shared his french fries with me and let me watch him from the wings of the Grand.

Our Air Force musical, *3 Dots with a Dash,* eschewed GIs in sweaters with balloons for a chorus line of Texas beauties.

We discovered Lynn Baggett in a Wichita Falls drugstore; here she plays a scene with me.

One year later, Lynn had become a Hollywood starlet, but when I next saw her, she was in Dorothy Parker's bed, en route to her eventual suicide.

Jerry Salinger played poker with us in the Village, equated himself with Herman Melville.

Marthe Richard, a spy who slept with German generals in World War I, single-handedly closed down the Paris whorehouses after World War II.

"Bemelmans paints like a twelve-year-old," cried the editor of *Cosmopolitan.* "Get his pictures out of here!"

Sinatra and Ava Gardner at their wedding, two people who couldn't live with or without each other

Between takes of *The Man with the Golden Arm*, Frank confessed that he was his own worst enemy.

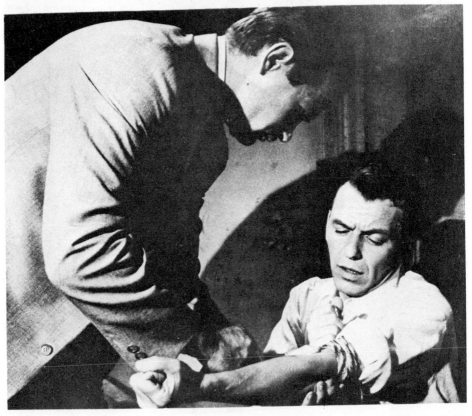

Dietrich and Hemingway spoke a language all their own.

Dietrich was incensed that
The New Yorker portrayed her as
a charwoman. Some charwoman!.

At the right, next to her father, Prince Bernhard, is Beatrice of Holland, now the queen, then a rambunctious princess who took wild Jeep rides through the palace tulips.

At the bullring in Ciudad Real, with my manager, Ernesto Hemingway, and the world's two ranking matadors, Antonio Ordoñez and Luis Miguel Dominguin

Ingrid Bergman had a special place in Hemingway's affections.

A rare photo of Ingrid Bergman with the two men who dominated her life—Peter Lindstrom and Roberto Rossellini.

Ingrid at the stake in
one of her many
portrayals of Saint
Joan

Her career and her life
ended with a memorable
portrayal of Golda Meir, the
Israeli prime minister.

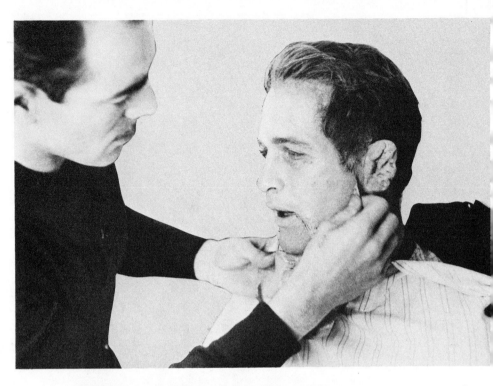

Paul Newman and I met in 1956 when he acted in *The Battler*, a *tour de force* that catapulted him to stardom.

Paul and I have had many madcap adventures, the madcappest of which was this historic moment when we mixed our first batch of salad dressing.

The cast of *Last Clear Chance*. In Paul Muni's ear is the converted hearing aid that fed him all his lines.

Gary Cooper with Hemingway and the renowned hunter Taylor Williams.

The incomparable John Barrymore would not sign for a film until my aunt Marie Hotchener consulted her astrological chart.

Richard Burton and Maximilian Schell in *The Fifth Column*. One of their scenes was held up to allow rigor mortis to set into a murdered cat.

John Frankenheimer at right, Robert Ryan on the cot, attended by Ann Todd. In a tree above Ryan were the three abused vultures, and just beyond John, the Land-Rover he attacked.

Maureen Stapleton and Nicky Persoff, foreground, with Jason Robards, Maria Schell, Eli Wallach, and Steve Hill in *For Whom the Bell Tolls.* On one fateful night it tolled for Jason, Nicky, and Maureen.

toriums, flailing away at prejudice and delinquency, and although the audiences were invariably disappointed that he did not sing for them, they listened respectfully.

But as the war ended and servicemen began to return (Frank was rejected because of a perforated eardrum), the shrill cry of the teen-age female abated, and with it abated the popularity of Frankie Sinatra. His record sales took a nose dive, but Frank had an explanation for it: "I signed on with Columbia Records, whose head guy was Mitch Miller. Well, came the age of Millerism. Mind you, I'll admit he's a great musician, but I couldn't go along with him. Instead of a real interest in the lyrics or the melody, all Miller cared about was gimmicks. One day he said to me: 'Frank, we're going to make a record with a washboard.' I looked at him and said: 'Mitch, you're kidding.' But he wasn't. I refused to do it. I guess I did a lot of refusing between 1949 and 1952. In fact, I rejected so many tunes my business managers began to hound me to accept one. Finally I said: 'Okay, the next song Mitch suggests, I do.' You know what it was? 'Mama Will Bark'—and I sang it with Dagmar. I growled and I barked on the record, and I guess it sold, but the only good it did me was with the dogs."

And that's where Frank's career was headed—to the dogs. Two nerve-wracking years with Ava culminated in a night at Palm Springs when Frank sent her packing. They never cohabited again, but they were a long time divorcing. Physically, Frank was scraping the bottom: his weight was down to under 120 pounds, his temper was an open wound, his voice was a rasp.

But then a curious thing happened—Frank read a book that was destined to change his life: *From Here to Eternity*. Frank had started to read it solely for enjoyment, but before he was half through it he was fired with a desire—to play the part of the rollicking little Italian, Maggio, when the book was made into a movie. Frank identified with many things about the character in the book, and although he had never before played a straight dramatic role, Sinatra dedicated his fierce ambition, long dormant now, toward procuring this part. He was in Africa visiting Ava, who was making *Mogambo*, when a wire came offering him a test for the part. He took the next plane home. There are stories about pressure being applied on the studio by some of

Sinatra's unsavory friends, but they are unsubstantiated and probably apocryphal. "I just woke up one morning," Sinatra told me that day we talked, "and I suddenly realized what I was doing—I saw it all. From that minute on, I began to get in shape, the way a fighter gets in shape. I worked hard on my voice, trying to improve my execution, making it more resonant. And I worked hard on the part of Maggio. I switched to Capitol Records. I left M.C.A. and put my career in the hands of the William Morris office."

Sinatra's performance in *From Here to Eternity* won him an Oscar and opened the door to a new career, but he vowed to do as little television as possible. "Let's face it—I'm just not fond of TV. It takes too much energy—too much tension, havoc, and rehearsals—for the results you get. Everything moves so fast you're not even conscious of what's going on—like the guy who gets belted out in the first round but gets up and fights the rest of the fight and then when it's all over he asks: 'What round was I knocked out?'

"That TV is a killer. Man, I've seen it kill the incentives of a lot of great people. The talents I've seen it chew up. I *know* what it does to your insides. I had a one-hour weekly show for CBS for a whole year. Only guy can survive it is someone like Ed Sullivan, the modern Rudy Vallee. Ed is pegged at a 1905 vaudeville level. Show him Fink's mules and he'd grab 'em up and put 'em out there.

"TV can't work until they fatten up the executive and creative side. How can you put your career in the hands of some idiot who in the course of a lousy hour can blow up your whole future? The way fine artists get thrown around! Take that last Judy Garland show—I adore Judy and think she's one of the greatest living performers but look what they did to her! A tasteless, hack show for an artist like that!

"It's probably not tactful for me to talk out like this, but who ever won a war with tact? I'm an outspoken guy, always have been. My blood boils when I see the mediocres who are sitting at the top of the TV networks, refugees from ad agencies who think that show business is stuck together with spit and gimmicks. And these mediocres at the top hire other mediocres to work for them so that there isn't any contrast to make them look bad. In TV Land the mediocres have already inherited the earth."

I asked Sinatra about *Time* magazine's allegation that he always took one of his buddies along on a date. The blood rushed to Frank's face. "Can you imagine anyone printing a thing like that! Me? Me? Frank Sinatra? I gotta take a guy with me? For Chrissake, I'm a simple guy, when I go out on a date I go off somewhere quietly for dinner, a movie, maybe one of the night spots. I'm single now, no ties, what the hell do I want with a male chaperon? It's a fantastic, childish thing to say. And look how they quote me as saying I got where I am by myself and I don't need anybody in the world. How could I ever say that? Why, for the last three years I've gotten so dependent on Abe Lastfogel and Burt Allenburg of the William Morris Agency that when I go into a men's shop I don't pick out a tie without calling them on the phone and checking if it's okay. And my music—this comeback I've had. Don't you think I realize how much of it I owe to the people over at Capitol and Nelson Riddle, who has handled arrangements and all that for me? I posted a ten-thousand-dollar bond with Hedda Hopper to be paid to anybody who can prove I ever said that line about doing it alone, doing it all by myself. I don't see anybody on *Time* coming around to claim any of that easy money."

I believed him when he said: "I'm the most contented I've ever been. I seem to have worked something out, something inside me. What I need is hard work, and plenty of it. Every night I come home to my apartment in Beverly Glen, pooped out from having done a good day's work, from having given something of myself. Weekends I drive to my place in Palm Springs and I sit around the pool and rest up.

"Three times a week I see my kids, and I have them with me on Sunday. Nancy is fifteen now, Frank's eleven, and Tina's seven. I have a wonderful relation with them. I had them all to dinner last night, and each one was loaded with his own problems and that's all they want to talk about. That's fine with me. They're swell kids and I get a lot out of them and try to give back."

*　　*　　*

That day on the R.K.O. lot, I had eaten lunch at the studio commissary while Sinatra was lunching with Brando; during lunch I had thought about what I would ask him in the afternoon, but when I returned to the sound stage, I found a large, unpleasant man blocking the door of Frank's trailer. I told him my name and he opened the door a little and tossed my name into the room out of the corner of his mouth. I could hear Sinatra say: "Okay." But it wasn't okay. Three or four rather sinister-looking characters were in the room and all of them looked at me suspiciously when I entered. This was obviously the entourage I had been warned about. They seemed to have a profound effect on Sinatra, who had shed his easygoing affability of the morning, and made caustic remarks that made his henchmen laugh. It was apparent that any further interviewing was pointless, and when Sinatra was summoned to the set to shoot the next scene, I left.

I felt sad that I had not been able to talk to him some more, but I liked him nonetheless for in the morning I had seen the man who lived beneath the facade. Just before my piece about him ran in the magazine, with his picture on the cover, I received a letter from the film's press agent that said: "After you left the set on the day that you saw Frank here, he told me how much he liked you and suggested he would like to do whatever he could to 'fatten up the piece' for you." Unfortunately the offer came too late, but after the article was published, I found that magazines were eager for me to write profiles for them, and I was at last able to indulge my desire to write about those people who fascinated me.

9

Marlene Dietrich Wants to Sue The New Yorker, *Yes,* The New Yorker

I first met Marlene Dietrich in Hemingway's suite at the Sherry Netherland Hotel when he came to New York with the manuscript of *Across the River and into the Trees,* which we ran in three installments in *Cosmopolitan.* Ernest's suite was well attended when I got there. In the center of the sitting room, which was furnished in lacquered Chinese, was a round table on which rested two silver ice buckets, each containing a bottle of Perrier-Jouet, a huge blue tin of Beluga caviar, a salver of toast, a bowl of finely chopped onions, a bowl of lemon slices, a salver of smoked salmon, and a thin vase containing two yellow tea roses. Around the table were Marlene Dietrich, Mary Hemingway, Jigee Viertel, Charles Scribner, senior, and George Brown. Off to one side, with a stenographer's pad in her lap, sat Lillian Ross of *The New Yorker.* Jigee Viertel, formerly Budd Schulberg's wife, at that time married to Peter Viertel, had known the Hemingways for many years and was booked to cross on the *Île de France* with them. George Brown was one of Ernest's oldest and best friends; the genesis of their friendship was George's demised Brown's Gymnasium, once the hangout of the boxing elite. Ernest always said that George knew more about prizefighting than all the managers and trainers operating in New York put together. Lillian Ross, in her corner, was taking rapid shorthand notes for a profile of Ernest she was doing for *The New Yorker*. ("It was a shorter hand than any of us knew," Ernest was to say a few months later.)

Ernest introduced me to his guests, and then to the decor. "Well, look around, Hotch," he said, "you won't often find yourself in the midst of authentic early Scarsdale Chinese."

"It's later than that, lamb," Mary said, piling high a square of toast.

"All right, then, authentic Pelham Manor Mandarin."

"That's more like it," Mary said. "I don't like it when Papa exaggerates."

"Little did you think," Ernest said to me, "when you left St. Louis as a callow and disillusioned youth, that one day you'd be eating caviar and swilling champagne surrounded by authentic Rickshaw Renaissance."

"You from St. Louis?" Dietrich asked.

"I once had a fighter from St. Louis," George Brown said. "He could hit like lightning but he always got hit first."

"George," Ernest said, "I have a piece of a new fighter, in Havana, who can hit harder than Sandy Saddler and keep hitting for three minutes. But he doesn't know anything and we have to strengthen his hands. The way he goes now he would as soon hit an elbow as your jaw. You see, Charlie, these cultural pursuits keep me happy after I quit work. I work when the spirit moves me—and it moves me every day." Everybody laughed. "I pinched that crack from Faulkner," Ernest confessed.

The floor waiter came in with two replacement Perrier-Jouets, and everyone's glass was replenished.

"Papa, I think you're making a terrible mistake not letting me list you with Dr. Richter," Marlene said, obviously returning to a conversation that had preceded my entrance. "What have you got to lose?"

"My amateur standing," Ernest said. "Once you let the professionals work you over with their crystal balls . . ."

"Now, Papa, Dr. Richter does *not* use a crystal ball. He is a very reputable astrologer and it's a very exact science. All I would do is give him your birth date and place of birth and he would keep me informed. He wouldn't have your name, just that much information, and he would get in touch with me if anything threatened you."

"The kind of things that threaten me, by the time he got in touch with you and you got in touch with me I'd be laid out in the Frank E. Campbell funeral parlor with makeup."

"Listen, Papa, the moon pulls great masses of water, so why not accept the fact that it also pulls us insignificant mortals? May I give you an example? One of the dearest friends I ever had was Grace Moore.* She felt the same way about astrology as you do, just didn't believe in it, but I kept after her and after her and finally, just to please me, she let me give her birth date to Dr. Richter. Well, one evening I was at a dinner party in New York when Dr. Richter phoned me from Hollywood, which is his home base, to say that he had just had a reading and that whoever belonged to such-and-such a birth date had to be contacted immediately. 'That woman must not put foot in an airplane for sixty days,' he said.

"Well, I didn't have my book with me so I had to leave the party and rush home to see whose birth date that was. When I found it was Grace's, I immediately put in a call to her in Paris. She was scheduled to fly to Monte Carlo for a concert but I carried on so on the phone that she promised to take the train instead. And she did. But the day after her concert she took a plane and that was the crash that killed her."

Ernest said that that was a very impressive anecdote and to extend his compliments to Professor Richter, but that he had to give astrology a pass because when he was on *Pilar* he navigated by the stars and if he started to confuse them with his life story it might cause him to wind up in some very strange ports.†

As Ernest moved among us, refilling our glasses, Marlene mentioned her new role as grandmother, how she had become

---

*An opera and film star who had scored spectacularly in the movie *One Night of Love.*
†Marlene persisted, however, and a month later, when the Hemingways and I were at the Ritz in Paris, Richter's five-page astrological assessment of Ernest arrived with a note from Marlene urging him to take it seriously. Ernest rang for the floor waiter and gave it to him to translate into French, since, Ernest said, it was his long-established practice to read his horoscopes only in French.

an occasional baby-sitter and *femme de ménage* for her daughter, Maria. She had photos of her eighteen-month-old grandson in her handbag, and she proudly showed them to Ernest and the rest of us. She talked about places in Europe where she had bumped into Ernest when she was entertaining the troops for the U.S.O. She recalled in particular a chance meeting at the Ritz bar in Paris when Ernest had shown her a poem he had recently written about Mary, a poem Marlene read aloud while the barman, Bertin, who was also listening, wept.

Ernest had told me that Dietrich was coming to the Sherry Netherland, so I was somewhat prepared for the impact of her extraordinary beauty (I had seen her once before*), but I was totally unprepared for her intelligence and her concern for others. She was a caring, involved woman, refreshingly outspoken, not actressy, caustic, well read, self-centered, quick-witted, and liberally affectionate although she treated fools and sycophants with stony rebuff. She and Ernest obviously adored one another, but I was inclined to believe Ernest when he told me they had never had an affair. "The thing about the Kraut and me," he said, "is that we have been in love since 1934, when we first met on the *Île de France,* but we've never been to bed. Amazing but true. Victims of unsynchronized passion. Those times when I was out of love, the Kraut was deep in some romantic tribulation, and on those occasions when Dietrich was on the surface and swimming about with those marvelously seeking eyes, I was submerged. There was another crossing on the *Île,* years after the first one, when something could have happened, the only time, but I had too recently been in and out of love, and the Kraut was still somewhat in love—we were like two young cavalry officers who had lost all their money gambling and were determined to go straight."

Not long after that evening at the Sherry Netherland, *The New Yorker* published an account of Ernest's visit to New York,

---

*When I came to Paris for the first time, as chief of the European bureau of *Air Force* magazine, a major I knew took me to dinner at the Méditerranée on the night I arrived. Facing the door as we entered, seated side-by-side on a banquette, were Marlene Dietrich and Jean Gabin—a sight that forever more endeared Paris to me.

written by Lillian Ross. Before I had a chance to read it, the phone rang and an infuriated Marlene Dietrich was on the other end. "Hotch, have you seen it? That piece of garbage in *The New Yorker*! Why, I had no idea that girl who was sitting there was going to write about us. Did Ernest know that? Why didn't he tell me? Why, it's so despicable! We talked about so many things, but the only thing she writes about is how I steal towels from the Plaza and . . ."

"Marlene, listen, I haven't read the article yet . . ."

"Then I'll read it to you: 'She lived at the Plaza, she told him, but spent a good deal of her time at the apartment of her daughter, who lived on Third Avenue. "Papa, you should see me when they go out," she said, and took a sip of champagne. "I'm the baby-sitter. As soon as they leave the house, I go around and look in all the corners and straighten the drawers and clean up. I can't stand a house that isn't neat and clean. I go around in all the corners with towels I bring with me from the Plaza, and I clean up the whole house. Then they come home at one or two in the morning, and I take the dirty towels and some of the baby's things that need washing, and, with my bundle over my shoulder, I go out and get a taxi, and the driver, he thinks I am this old washerwoman from Third Avenue, and he takes me in the taxi and talks to me with sympathy, so I am afraid to let him take me to the Plaza. I get out a block away from the Plaza and I walk home with my bundle and I wash the baby's things, and then I go to sleep." '

"Can you imagine writing about me like that? I am disgraced at the Plaza—they think of me now as a common towel stealer. And this Lillian person makes me out to have the mentality of a cleaning woman. Well, I am going to sue her and *The New Yorker*. I won't let her get away with that. I did not give my permission to write about me, and this is *eavesdropping*, I mean to be sneaky like this, pretending to be part of a social gathering when you are really an informer, and a distorter, as if that's all I had to talk about, scrubbing up for my daughter. Well, listen to me, Hotch, I've talked to my lawyers and I've told them I want to teach them a lesson. I don't care what it costs. I have my rights. Will you testify? Ernest told me you were once a lawyer, so a jury would certainly believe you. Can I count on you? It's an outrage! *The New Yorker,* supposed to be so reputable, why, they're worse than the worst of those gossip magazines because they have this *pose* of being literary and better than anyone else. Can I count on you?"

Before the day was out, Marlene must have called a half-dozen times. I finally succeeded in convincing her to avoid precipitous action, but it was a slow process; she spoke to me several times during the week, still seething, still talking about suing. I told Ernest how incensed Marlene was over Lillian's piece; he felt bad because he then realized that Lillian's presence was a "breach of security."

Ernest said: "Lillian didn't understand anything, did she? She's a good girl who should have been practicing the dead man's float in the shallow water and had no business on the high dive. I had just finished *Across the River and into the Trees* and New York was a release. But all she saw was the irresponsibility that comes after the terrible responsibility of writing and she cartooned me into a gin-crazed Indian."

I told him that Marlene was so furious she wanted to file suit.

"Hope you talked her out of it. But don't blame her for being furious—can you imagine that after having spent the whole evening with the Kraut and me, hearing all the things we talked about, all Lillian could write about was that the Kraut sometimes cleaned her daughter's apartment with towels from the Plaza."

A few months later, I heard from Marlene again, this time inviting me to her Park Avenue apartment "to discuss a personal matter." This personal matter turned out to be her delinquency in delivering a piece to *McCall's* magazine for which she had received, and spent, a large advance. The article, "The Danger of Being Beautiful," was intended as the first of several articles on beauty that were eventually to become the chapters of a book to be called *The Woman Within You. McCall's* was pressing her for the article, but she did not have enough money to return their advance to them; besides, she desperately needed the full payment of the $25,000 she would receive on submission of the piece. Would I please, *please* help her write these articles?

During this discussion, Marlene wandered onto other subjects. She often referred to Rilke, her favorite poet, thumbing through her well-read Rilke anthology to find certain verses to read to me. At times she would discuss film contemporaries, often caustically: "Paulette Goddard has to collect her men carefully because they must all be able to afford precisely the kind of gem she is collecting at any specific time."

During one of these gossipy digressions, I asked about John Gilbert, the matinee idol of silent films, what kind of fellow he was off-camera, why he couldn't make the transition to the talkies. I knew that Gilbert and Dietrich, both married at the time, had had a long-lasting affair, but what particularly intrigued me was an account I had heard, attributed to Dietrich's housekeeper, of the bizarre manner in which Gilbert had died. I was told that Gilbert had suffered a massive heart attack while making love to Dietrich in their secret hideaway, that Dietrich had clandestinely left the hideaway without calling anyone (in those days such a scandal would have ruined her), returned to her home, and phoned her dressmaker, from whom she ordered three black mourning dresses. But mentioning Gilbert's name elicited no response from Dietrich.

As for the articles on beauty, I said that this was a totally unfamiliar subject for me, and that I'd have to give some thought to trying to write a book on the subject.

A week later, this letter arrived:

Dearest Ed,
please help me with at least the first article, I have been spending all my time at the studio, plodding along at a rather boring task, boring, but necessary to get the Vegas loot.

Knowing that I should do better things the task has so far seemed even more uninteresting than usual. But I am bound as far as time goes by the schedule of the studio, and if I don't do it now they will be otherwise occupied and I cannot do it at a later date.

I want them to have, I mean McCall's, the first article soon because of the money I need. I am sending you some of the things I have written and notes on the subject and please tell me if I can count on you to put them together and also tell me the financial arrangements. Letters from Papa sound fine and wonderful about you—vague about the "Readings" plan. I wrote to him explaining.

> Lots of love
> gratefully yours
> Marlene

I'll be in N.Y. Tuesday and I will bring more

The allusion to "the 'Readings' plan" referred to a stage script I had prepared, composed of excerpts from Hemingway's writings, which Marlene would perform with a small cast. I went through the pages of beauty notes that Marlene had enclosed, and after meeting with her a few times, I did attempt to write something coherent and interesting but my heart wasn't in it. Try as I could, one version was flatter than the next, but eventually I went to see her with the best I could do. As I sat beside her on a sofa in her commodious living room, I could see from the look on her face that she was reading the manuscript with increasing dismay.

I took the bull by the horns. "Not very good, is it?"

She sighed. "No."

"I'm sorry. I really tried, but it's not a good subject for me."

"I can tell." She lit a cigarette and watched the smoke; the silence was uncomfortable.

"Well, I'd best be going," I said, rising. "I'm sure you'll work something out. Perhaps you should try to do it yourself."

At the door, we shook hands. Her eyes showed her disappointment in me. "You've both let me down," she said, reprovingly.

"Both?"

"First Jean Cocteau, and now you—you've both failed me."

"Jean Cocteau tried to write this article for you?"

"Yes. A couple of versions."

I left, not at all dejected but rather elated to have been placed in such exalted company.

These last years have not been kind to Marlene. She insisted on going far beyond a sensible retirement, with the inevitable result that her cabaret act became a cruel parody, a severe fall from a stage finally forcing her to quit. She lives alone in Paris now, rarely leaving her apartment, solaced by whisky and memories. I recently received an incomprehensible cable from her, alluding to one of Hemingway's actress granddaughters. But in thinking about her, I have followed Ernest's advice: "What I learned constructive about women," he once told me, "is that no matter how they get, always think of them the way they were on the best day they ever had."

10

Paul Newman Has a Cauliflower Ear

My friendship with Hemingway was beginning to produce some curious offshoots, one of the more curious being my unexpected foray into the world of ballet. Hemingway and I were sitting in the elegant living room of a charming palazzo on Venice's Grand Canal, sipping cognac that was practically senile with age and watching the boats and gondolas drift by. Our hosts were old friends of Hemingway's, high in the galaxy of Venice's diminishing aristocracy.

There was a very expansive (and expensive) feeling in the air. Lunch had been superb—pheasant and wild rice served by liveried Venetian giants in knee breeches—and now we were chatting aimlessly about the business of converting one art form into another.

It was through this brandy-misted gateway that we entered a discussion of ballet as a story form, and this led us ultimately to "The Capital of the World," one of Ernest's short stories which has as its climax a magnificently macabre scene wherein two Spanish boys play bullfight with a chair that has two carving knives secured to its legs. It was the young, lovely daughter of the house, Ann-Marie La Cloche, who drew our attention to this danceable element of the story.

We all agreed that the episode would make an exciting and effective dance, and discussions of this nature being what they are, enthusiasm mounted to the point where everyone agreed that since I was about to leave for New York, the ballet capital of the world, I was the one to do it.

"How about it, Hotch?" Hemingway asked.

"Sure," I said, with the bravura so characteristic of that particular cognac.

"See if they'll dance it at the Met," Hemingway added.

"Why not?" I said. For all I can remember I may even have added: "There's nothing to it."

The Capital of the World was ultimately danced on the stage of the Metropolitan Opera House, but during the four harrowing, impresario-infested years that intervened, I many times chewed, swallowed, and regurgitated the glib words I uttered on that Venetian afternoon.

For when I got back to New York it occurred to me that I hadn't the vaguest idea how one converts a short story into a ballet. And at the Met, yet. I was searching my address book, trying to find someone I knew who might have some contact, no matter how remote, with the ballet world, when I joyfully discovered that my friend Alfred Katz, a ubiquitous Broadway press agent, had as one of his favored clients Alicia Markova, then one of the world's leading ballerinas.

I went to Aflred's office and explained my predicament. "Easily solved," he announced, and a few seconds later he was speaking, in that mystic jargon of his, to Sergei Denham, director of the Ballet Russe de Monte Carlo. "Sergei, you are in magnificent luck! A Hemingway ballet, superb, kudos galore, my friend Hotchner right here, carried it in his pocket from Venice, we have selected you for this honor . . ." After he hung up, Alfred turned and frowned his enormous forehead at me. "If only I could cure myself of underplaying everything," he said wistfully.

Sergei Denham, in the grand tradition of Gregory Ratoff and other Hollywood impresarios, sat in a large office surrounded by samovars and mementos. "Hove you evaire wreeten a ballet?" he asked. "No? Den I geeve you dese wan adwice: in ballet we can say: 'Dis womans, she ees my modaire.' But we cannot say: 'Dis womans, she ees my cousin.' Mistaire Hotchnoor, do me dis favors—write me no cousins."

As it turned out, that was just about the only sane advice I was to hear. That summer I got around to writing a ballet adaptation of the story, and I wrote Denham no cousins. I sent my script to him, anticipating a reply of "Thees steenks" or "Thees is wunderfuls" within a few weeks, but the leaves fell, the snow came and melted, and notes to him and phone calls went unheeded. The Ballet Russe was on tour, or he was at a rehearsal or a fund-raising dinner.

But a year later, out of a clear swan lake, I received a letter from the composer George Antheil (whom I did not know), telling me that Impresario Denham had enthusiastically presented the script to him and that he, Antheil, thought it was splendid and wanted very much to compose a score for it. "However," he warned me, "Sergei, like most impresarios, is a kind of Diaghileff, who, if you remember, was an angel-devil, able to weep pitifully and enticingly one moment, and to threaten the next. It is a special temperament. I have known him for years. One thing I can say—his taste is impeccable. He is an artist. We cannot hope for more."

The shot, as Antheil called it, was right in the pocket. For the ensuing two years Denham wept, threatened, exhorted, entreated. It was an enjoyable performance to watch, but it produced no ballet, only exasperation. However, Antheil recognized in me the maverick soul of an amateur, and he attempted through constant and voluminous letters to keep me placated while he went ahead with the score.

"Let me caution you," he wrote at one point, "that things are not conducted in the ballet world as they are in the world of writing and letters. Writers think in terms of all sorts of rights, contracts, legally binding papers. To step from this world into the world of ballet, where everything is done with mirrors and where no contract I have ever signed has ever protected me an iota, is a big step."

I would have welcomed a big step in any direction, in fact even a little step. Finally, a year after Antheil had rushed into the project, he announced that he had finished the score and that he would play it for Denham when the Ballet Russe came to Hollywood on tour. This is how Antheil described the audition: "I played the ballet for Denham alone. At the end he kissed me, wept, declared it was far and beyond anything he had expected.

He declared he would open it during his next Metropolitan engagement."

But another year passed and there was no ballet, for the plain reason that new ballets cost considerable money. Why invest thousands in a risky new work when a *pas de deux* can be performed in front of an old cyclorama at no cost at all? I was rescued from this dilemma by a friend who, I discovered, was on good terms with Lucia Chase of the Ballet Theatre. I sent her the script and within the week, to my astonishment, I found myself meeting with Miss Chase and her co-director, Oliver Smith. They had contracts drawn up for Hemingway and myself, and another for Antheil, and Eugene Loring was commissioned to do the choreography.

I was delighted that at long last I had definitive word for Ernest about the ballet, but when I told him about it and put the contract before him for his signature, I got a reaction from him I had not expected.

"I do not like Antheil or his music," he said, speaking deliberately. "His name is true box office poison, not that that would matter if his music were good enough. But I don't want him in. Correct me if I am wrong."

I was floored by his strong, negative reaction. I had met with Antheil several times, and found him an enthusiastic, energetic, imaginative little man who fondly remembered his experiences with Ernest, back when they were part of the Paris group in the Twenties that frequented Sylvia Beach's bookstore. In fact, Antheil had told me that he had contributed significantly to Ernest's literary beginning. In 1924, the way Antheil told it, when "the group" was meeting regularly at Sylvia Beach's book shop, Shakespeare and Company, Antheil had become the official Paris representative for the German magazine *Der Querschnitt*, whose editor, Count von Wedderkop, was called "Mr. Awfully Nice" by the Shakespeare regulars, for those were the only two words of English that he knew. In his official capacity, Antheil said he had submitted a short story of Ernest's and four of his poems to Count von Wedderkop, and these were among the first things that Ernest had had published.

Against this backdrop of friendship was the additional consideration that Antheil had been a respected composer since he first attracted attention with his controversial *Ballet Mécanique*. I had no way of knowing, of course, what could have caused Ernest to have backed off him so far; I told Ernest that when I returned to New York I would talk to Lucia Chase and Oliver Smith about finding someone else. But I knew that to start all over with a new composer would set us back another year and very likely lose the support of the Ballet Theatre.

After returning to New York, I procrastinated about going to see the ballet's directors, although I was fully aware that with each passing day they were further into the mounting of the ballet. Finally, on the very day I had made an appointment to see them, I received a reprieve from Ernest.

He phoned early in the morning, before he turned off his phone and started to write. "Listen, about Antheil, think it's okay to go ahead since he's already in it and I don't want to louse it up. Maybe he is better now and maybe he really learned his stuff scoring Hollywood movies. That's what he's been doing all these years, you know. I am sure he was a better musician than I gave him credit for. But scoring Hollywood movies is hardly a way to learn and practice your trade. Also he was such an opportunist and a letter-down of his friends that that could have cramped my judgment on him as a musician. So I am probably unjust about him and if it is arranged that he should do it, let him go. Maybe the horse can win once. He should have always won."

The Capital of the World had its world premiere at the Metropolitan Opera House at a gala for the Milk Fund, and it received fine notices, with Antheil's score being singled out for special praise. Columbia Records made an album of it, and the ballet was performed on national television.

Ernest was genuinely pleased with Antheil's success and said he was damn glad to have been proved wrong. "It's always more fun to come back than to never have been away," he said.

To those friends of mine who asked me what made me stick with a waffling project like that for so long and against such odds, I replied: For the money. After all, Ernest and I got a royalty check for each and every performance—he got three dollars, and I got two.

*　　*　　*

My *entrechat* into the ballet world was but the first of many forays onto new and strange terrain. On one of my visits to Havana, Ernest asked me whether I'd help him out with a problem that was robbing him of precious work time. When he was in a writing period, Ernest was combative and suspicious about interruptions, with good reason. On one occasion, when we were staying at Bill Davis' palatial estate outside Málaga and Ernest was hard at work on *The Dangerous Summer,* an account of the bullfight rivalry between Luis Dominguin and Antonio Ordoñez, who were brothers-in-law, he had made it clear that there would be no guests or social life until his manuscript was finished, but his wife, Mary, returning from shopping in Málaga one afternoon, said she had run into Eric Sevareid, who said he was on a honeymoon with a new wife. He had asked to meet Ernest, so she had invited them for lunch. Ernest was dismayed by this because he said he did not want to have to talk to newspaper and television journalists because they often pinched his stuff, but Mary assured him it would be strictly social.

Sevareid's companion was charming; after lunch she entertained us with Cuban songs which Ernest enjoyed hearing, but then Sevareid began to ask him direct questions about the fights between Ordoñez and Dominguin and the enjoyment went out of him.

Ernest said: "To tell you the truth, Sevareid, I intend to write about it and I don't like to discuss anything I'm going to write about because I don't like seeing it in print under somebody else's name before I get to it."

"Oh, for goodness sakes," Sevareid insisted, "I'm the last person in the world . . . why, I know *nothing* about bullfighting —these are the first bullfights I've seen, and I just want to learn a few things . . ."

Ernest again tried to turn him off but Sevareid kept asking things and Mary said that of course Eric wouldn't write about it, so Ernest reluctantly answered some of his questions.

A few months later, a four-page article by Sevareid entitled "*Mano a Mano,* Dominguin vs. Ordoñez: What Really Happened" came out in *Esquire,* describing the lunch and setting forth in dialogue form everything Ernest had told him about

Ordoñez, Dominguin and the *mano a manos,* as witness this passage:

> "Ernest," I said, "enlighten me. Didn't Antonio do a crossover to the far horn while patting his hip?"
> "He did."
> "Isn't that horribly dangerous? . . . Didn't he do a pendulum pass, front to back, while still moving his feet?"
> "He did, my friend."

Not bad for a nonwriting neophyte seeing his first bullfight. He even mentioned me in the article, calling me "Hutch." After he read the piece, Ernest said, among other things: "I think it would be advisable for Mr. Sevareid, if he is interested in longevity, not to find himself in my vicinity for the next twenty years."

So it was understandable why Ernest was trying to defend himself against unannounced predators. "It's mostly the TV hordes invading from the north," he said, that day in Havana. "They sweep down like the Huns with their deals and residuals; I tell them not to come when they write or phone but they come anyway, and I tell them no again when they get here, but they all want their dime's worth of publicity and they wire to the gossip columns that they have me under contract. Last week I was put under siege by a wet-palmed press agent named Richard Condon,* who came out and drank gin by the yard and sweated so heavy I thought he'd pass out, all the time trying to con me into a deal he'd dreamed up. The way I am being bombarded these days with television wheeler-dealers, was thinking this morning maybe it's something you could handle. You're in New York where you can screen the dross from the brass and I'd be willing to go on your nod."†

I said I'd be glad to do what I could but that I had never written for TV, nor did I know anything about it. "That puts you

---

*Later on, Condon gave up press agenting (and gin, for all I know) to write popular novels.

†Hemingway had no agent or other representative; he did have a New York lawyer who had no expertise in publishing, television, or films but who nonetheless in his dealings with people in those fields had a chauffeur's arrogance.

a jump ahead of all those network geniuses who think they do," Ernest said.

Not long after I returned to New York, I received a call from a gentleman with a Southern accent named Fred Coe who said that Hemingway had referred him to me. Coe was the producer of a program called "Playwrights '56," and he wanted to know if there was any Hemingway story, suited to television, that was available. He knew that all the best stories, and the novels, had already been sold to Hollywood but he wondered if perhaps I knew of something feasible that had been overlooked. I said that one of my favorite stories was "The Battler" but that it was only a few pages long and limited to three men sitting around a hobo fire alongside some railroad tracks. Coe had a quiet, polite persuasiveness (also, I learned over the course of the twenty-five years I knew him, a volatile temper), and by the end of our phone talk I found myself promising to see if I could find a way to convert Ernest's brief story into a three-act, sixty-page television play. I hadn't the slightest idea how to go about it; I had never even seen a television script, and the sample scripts Coe gave me simply filled me with a kind of paralyzed awe.

But what I soon discovered was that my association with Ernest had by now given me an intuitive insight into his way of thinking, and a feel for the pulse of his beliefs; an insight into the symmetry of his imagination and into the compassionate way he dealt with cruelty, death, and hate. I found that in exploring the spare nuances of the characters in his lean short stories, I could identify things that Ernest had left unstated and events that were undepicted, forces that he had put in motion but left unconsummated—all of which were vital to a fully developed drama.

In addition, once I began to form the structure of the playscript, Ernest himself aided me immeasurably by giving me information that fleshed out central characters and events.

Overall, there was for me a unique exhilaration in developing Ernest's people beyond the confines of his short stories, in inventing dialogue that would blend with his without showing the seams, in creating dramatic scenes that would not distort the true nature of the people he had put on his pages.

I think I achieved this best in a play I wrote for a CBS

program called "The Seven Lively Arts," which was produced by John Houseman and directed by Robert Mulligan. In that instance I took seven of Ernest's Nick Adams stories and formed them into an integrated drama, *The World of Nick Adams*, which was about an adolescent boy leaving home and growing up in a way that mirrored Ernest's own early life, as do all the Nick Adams stories. It was a live performance, splendidly acted, with a fine original musical score by Aaron Copland, who directed the orchestra as it performed during the live telecast right alongside the actors in the studio.

During a visit to New York that year to see the World Series, Ernest went with me to a CBS screening room to see a kinescope of *The World of Nick Adams*. Having to sit beside Ernest during these viewings was always extremely trying for me, but he was invariably understanding about the changes necessarily incurred in transferring one creative form to another. After that screening of *The World of Nick Adams*, he turned to me and said: "Well, Hotch, you got it on the screen as good as I got it on the page." I have never been paid a finer compliment.

But getting back to my first television effort, "The Battler," I realized that I could not convert Ernest's brief story into a full-length play without taking enormous risks—which I did, using language necessary for the characters but unwelcome to the ears of network censors, using scene changes that required instant makeup and costume adjustments that the production people would find impossible to execute, and I developed the story's implied incestuous brother-sister relationship, which was high on the list of network taboos.

I showed my script to a couple of experienced television writers whom I knew, and they both said it wouldn't have a chance if I didn't make it more "acceptable." But I decided that since Ernest never pandered his stories to anyone's taste, neither would I, and I turned the script in to Fred Coe just as it was; after a fierce battle with the network censors, he put it into immediate production.*

---

*That taught me a valuable lesson about risk-taking—either you do or you don't; there is no middle ground, for you cannot compromise risk any more than you can compromise pregnancy.

Arthur Penn was signed to direct, James Dean, fresh from his triumph in *Giant,* read the script and consented to make this his first live television performance, Phyllis Kirk was cast in a major role, and as young Nick Adams, Coe cast an actor who had been one of the thugs in the Broadway play *The Desperate Hours.* His name was Paul Newman. I was flown out to Hollywood and ensconced in the Beverly Hills Hotel to await the start of rehearsals. (This was not my first trip to Hollywood; I had been there once before, when I was in uniform, but I will come to that later on.) I began to have script conferences with Arthur Penn, whom I liked very much, and I was amazed at how easy it was to mount a television play.

But that was an illusion which I suppose deludes all rookies at the beginning of their first experience with television. For no sooner had the set builders and costume designers gone to work than the tragic news reached us that Dean had been crushed to death in an accident involving his souped-up sports car. Now, with rehearsals only a few days off, we had no lead, and this was a long and difficult part, calling for an actor to portray a punch-drunk, dangerously unbalanced, suspicious ex-pug who was once welterweight champion of the world, a part that moved back in time showing the boxer at various stages of his life. After a frantic but futile search for a star to replace Dean on such short notice, Arthur suggested that we try to perform the play with Newman, whom he had worked with at the Actors Studio, in the lead. Coe agreed reluctantly, lamenting having to go with a relative unknown in the leading role.

But when they told Newman about the casting change they wanted to make, he unexpectedly had a negative reaction—he had never played a role even remotely like this and he was afraid of it. But Coe's Southern persuasiveness again prevailed, and an actor named Dewey Martin was engaged to play Paul's part. During the beginning of rehearsals Newman was totally out of sync, floundering, trying to discover something in himself while questioning if indeed it was there at all. This was the way Hemingway described the character Newman had to play: "His nose was sunken, his eyes were slits, he had queer shaped lips . . . the face was queerly formed and mutilated. It was like putty in color. . . . He had only one ear. It was thickened and tight against the side of his head. Where the other ear should have been there was a stump."

Paul went through countless disappointing rehearsals, and I felt sorry for him, because he had been talked into this part that he knew he wasn't suited for. But, then, one morning he started to rehearse a pivotal scene at the trackside campsite, and there suddenly emerged the slurred, halting speech, the stiff-legged shuffle, the jerks and twitches of a stumblebum prizefighter. This accomplishment was not an accident. Paul had started to hang out at the YMCA in downtown Los Angeles, a run-down building that was located next to the grubby gym where the local boxers worked out. Newman had found a punch-drunk old welterweight with whom he had made friends, and now he was slowly assuming the old pug's persona. It was a thrilling metamorphosis that can be likened to the way a sculptor works on a lump of clay, refining its contours, sharpening and defining its shape until it is transformed into the form he wants it to be.

During our lunch break, it was customary for Arthur, Paul, Phyllis, Dewey Martin, and myself to go to a nearby restaurant (we were rehearsing in a room at a Hollywood funeral parlor because no rehearsal rooms were available at NBC), where we sat in a booth and discussed the morning's work. On one such day Dewey swiveled his head to follow an attractive blonde who was crossing his line of vision on her way to another booth.

"My God!" he exclaimed. "Have you ever seen a prettier ass? Who *is* that?"

"Don't you know?" Phyllis asked.

"Do you? You really know who that is?"

"Yes—Peggy Lee."

"The singer? That's Peggy Lee?"

"Dewey," Newman said dryly, "you are blowing your number-one gasket."

"Listen, listen to me," Dewey said with fervor as he wiped his forehead with his napkin, "I am going to marry that woman."

We all laughed.

"I'm telling you," he repeated. "I'm going to marry her." He got up and went over to her booth and introduced himself. And, just as he had predicted, not long after that, he married her.

The morning after the telecast of *The Battler,* Paul received a call from MGM. They had been having great difficulty casting the lead role in the film they wanted to make of Rocky Graziano's autobiography, *Somebody Up There Likes Me;* having seen Newman's performance in *The Battler,* MGM was offering the part to him. The offer came at precisely the right moment in Paul's life. He was thirty-one years old but neither his stage nor film career was really going anywhere. He was separated from his wife and very much in love with a young actress named Joanne Woodward, with whom he had become involved while performing with her in *Picnic* on Broadway, but he had three children and getting a divorce was not going to be easy. Now, suddenly, he had the lead role in a picture that was going to allow him to put all of his considerable talents on display, talents that he didn't realize he had until *The Battler* forced him to extend himself.

Since we both cut our eyeteeth on that television adventure more than a quarter of a century ago, Newman and I have maintained a steady and gratifying friendship. We live near each other in Westport, Connecticut, and we share a boat, the *Caca de Toro,* on which we have gone fishing since 1962. (Actually, there have been two *Cacas,* the first one having died of natural causes in the middle of the Sound in 1971.)

We've been out in *Caca I* and *Caca II* approximately a thousand times, during which we've consumed great quantities of beer but have yet to catch a single noteworthy fish. Anglers around us have reeled in bluefish, stripers, flounder, weakfish and blacks, while we watch with virginal envy, drowning our sorrow in Budweiser.

We once went fishing on Man O' War Cay in the Bahamas, noted for its abundance of bonefish, and for the world-famous guide Captain Sam. We spent three days at it, with Captain Sam groaning and grunting at the tiller, after which Captain Sam announced his permanent retirement.

"I been fishing these here waters nigh on fifty-three years," he said, "and you two fellers are the first ones never even got a bite on your lines. Seem like the bonefish went outa their ways to avoid you."

I don't want to give you the impression, however, that all of our ventures on the briny deep are as ill fated as that one. To our utter amazement, we did manage to snare a few bonefish at Harbour Island, where we had gone to scout possible locations for a film we contemplated but never did.

But whatever skills Newman lacks as a fisherman, he more than makes up for with his skill in the kitchen. His repertoire is a bit limited but nonetheless he cooks an exquisite scrod, an exemplary hamburger, and for years his guests have applauded his salad dressing.

As long as I can remember, Newman has been rejecting so-called house dressings and concocting his own mix. How many times I have watched captains and maître d's, and often the owners themselves, go scurrying around to assemble Newman's ingredients. When we first ate at Elaine's, one of New York's "in" restaurants, where the bizarre is unnoticed, virtually all the waiters and even Elaine herself gathered round as Paul carefully blended and tasted the ingredients that had been brought to him from the kitchen.

I have watched this scene repeated in a variety of places—in a little restaurant on the remote Bahamian island of Eleuthera, in a diner near the racetrack at Watkins Glen, at a wedding party in Oyster Bay, and in various restaurants from coast to coast. Newman's dressing. When his kids went off to school, they would ask him to fill a couple of bottles of the stuff for them to take along.

All well and good until that day, a few years back, when Paul came over one afternoon to watch a football game, and said: "Listen, Hotch, I've got a neat idea for Christmas presents this year—I'm going to give all my friends bottles of my salad dressing; they're always asking me for the recipe, so I'll fill up all the empty wine bottles I've been saving and play Santa Claus. Good idea, huh?"

"Great—they'll love it," I said naïvely.

"When can we start?"

"Start what?"

"Making the dressing. I figure you and I can do it in an afternoon—how about tomorrow?" It took us eight hours of hard labor to mix it, bottle it, cork it, and wrap it. But Newman's friends were delighted and it was a ritual Paul and I followed every year after that, each year taking longer than the year before as the list of requests for "Newman's Own Salad Dressing," written on masking tape affixed to the bottles, grew longer and longer.

But last year was the straw that cracked my sagging back. In the first place, it took us three days of sweatshop labor down in Newman's cellar to turn out enough bottles to satisfy his list, now three pages long. Meals were sent down on trays, but I have no memory of eating them. Paul refused to take desperate phone calls from Hollywood producers frantically seeking his services. My editor was getting apoplectic about the galleys of my new book.

But that wasn't the worst of it. What really caused me to blow the whistle was Newman's suggestion, at the end of the third day, as he stood in the center of the cellar happily surrounded by all those filled bottles, that we should maybe do another hundred bottles and put them up for sale in local food stores. It was as if his dressing was a gospel that Paul wanted to spread among the good people of the world.

"You can't stand the thought that on Christmas Day there will be people around here eating salad without your dressing on it, that it?"

He nodded. "Poor bastards—how can we be so selfish? Spread good cheer, I say. What's a couple more days of bottling?"

There was no need to tell him that at that point I regarded another day of mixing and bottling like being sentenced to a week in the Tombs. Instead I said: "It's against the law."

"What is? There is absolutely nothing in my dressing that's illegal."

"The pure food law. You have to have certain certificates."

"Okay, let's look into it."

That was how it started, innocently enough, but over the subsequent months Newman was driven by his desire to market his dressing, as driven as Lancelot in his quest for the Holy Grail. Scarcely a day passed but what my phone rang, Paul calling from some unlikely place to discuss a newly discovered source for the perfect olive oil, the perfect red wine vinegar, the perfect mustard, et cetera, which he constantly sought. He phoned me from racetracks, in between his races, from mobile dressing rooms on location while shooting *Absence of Malice* and *The Verdict,* from airports on his way to make speeches on behalf of the nuclear freeze movement, and even, on one occasion, from where he was shooting footage for a Japanese film crew, a background of cacophonous Nipponese chatter making it difficult to hear him.

Inside of a year, we had formed a partnership and produced a product that was sold not only all over the United States, but also in Canada, Australia, England and Japan. A second product, Newman's Own Industrial Strength Venetian Spaghetti Sauce, has been just as successful, and at the end of our first year of operation, we were able to give all of our profits—over half a million dollars—to deserving charities. We are probably the only business in the world that gives away all of its earnings.

Paul seems to be enjoying his new role as much as any movie part he ever played, his underlying zeal being to bring to the marketplace natural products without chemicals, gums, sugar, and preservatives. And the naturalness that has made his salad dressing a success also accounts for his own success as an actor, for it shines through the roles he plays. In my opinion, this factor, more than anything else, accounts for his enduring popularity. In this respect he strongly resembles Gary Cooper, who was as natural and unpretentious as any man I ever met. I recall an evening when Coops and his wife, Rocky, called for me in their limousine to go to a black tie event at the Directors Guild. The sidewalk in front of the building was packed with gawkers who spilled into the street. As our car pulled up to the entrance, the fans crushed against the windows, squealing Cooper's name. Their flushed, bug-eyed faces jammed against the glass. Cooper shook his head pityingly. "Well, Hotch," he said, "now you know how it feels to be a monkey in the zoo on a Sunday afternoon."

I first met Coops in Ketchum, Idaho, when he came out from Los Angeles to go hunting with his old pal Hemingway, whom he had originally met in nearby Sun Valley in the early Thirties. They respected each other's hunting skills and knowledge of the outdoors, and they were always completely honest with one another. They shared rough jokes, swapped philandering secrets, and enjoyed their mutual disdain for the encroaching years. When Coops portrayed Robert Jordan in the hugely successful film version of *For Whom the Bell Tolls,* it further bolstered their friendship.

In the field Cooper was not quite as fast as Ernest in getting a duck in the gunsight, but he had just as pretty a move and was almost as accurate. We went out every day, regardless of weather, until a really fierce blizzard socked us in, and on that day Cooper came over in the afternoon with a whole smoked goose, Ernest brought in a half-gallon of Chablis that had been chilling in a snowbank, and we sat around the table in front of the fire all afternoon cutting off slices of the delicately smoked goose and drinking the Chablis.

"Ain't this Mormon country wonderful!" Cooper said. "They know how to live."

"I'm practically one myself," Ernest said. "Had four wives, didn't I?" He took a sip of wine. "To tell the truth, if I were reborn and I had a choice, I'd be a Mormon."

A bit self-consciously, Cooper confided to Ernest that after all these years he had finally converted to Catholicism to please his wife, Rocky, and his daughter, Maria. But he said he felt uncomfortable about it and wondered whether he had done the right thing. Ernest said that since he himself was only a miserable, failed Catholic, he couldn't give him a reading on it but he thought it would work out all right.

The talk then shifted to work projects, with Cooper wondering whether there was anything of Ernest's that might be good for him. "When you get my age," he said, "you get scratching pretty hard for lead parts."

Ernest asked me what I thought might suit Cooper and I suggested *Across the River and into the Trees.* "Good idea," Ernest said to Cooper. "You'd just be playing Robert Jordan ten years older." Cooper hadn't read the book but said he'd get a copy as soon as he got back to Hollywood the following day.

Soliciting Coops to do *Across the River* was certainly uncharacteristic of Ernest, and I suspect that it bothered him that *Across the River* was the only one of his novels (*The Torrents of Spring* doesn't count) that was not made into a film.

Cooper reacted favorably but not enthusiastically to playing the doomed army colonel in *Across the River.* Picking up on

Cooper's lack of fervor, Ernest had an alternate suggestion which he first tried out on me. He came to my cabin in Ketchum one night with a husky book under his arm. "Every boy needs a hero," Ernest confided, "and here is mine, the man I have tried to pattern myself after."

The book he handed me was entitled *Scouting on Two Continents,* an autobiography by Major Frederick Burnham, Ernest's hero; his exploits as a scout and adventurer in the American West and in Africa were certainly dramatic and exciting. Coops was much more taken with the Burnham book as a possible television series than he was with *Across the River.* We tracked down Major Burnham's son, who lived in Idyllwild, California, and took an option on the book for one year. The program was to be billed "Gary Cooper Presents the Ernest Hemingway Theatre of Adventure."

I met with Coops quite often, both in Hollywood and New York, ostensibly to discuss the particulars of the new program, but when we got together we somehow never got around to talking shop. Coops liked to reminisce, but rarely about his film-making, and he was a surprisingly good raconteur for a man known for his laconic "yups." He had loved only two women in his life, and he liked to talk about that, and about hunting, which was also a passion, and he often discussed Ernest, whom he admired to the point of exaltation. "Ernie has done the things I keep promising myself when I finish the next picture. All my life, it's what I'm going to do when such-and-such film is in the can. But then there's another film waiting and the promise to myself ain't worth a good goddamn."

I was often in Hollywood during the period I was writing dramas for "Playhouse 90," and Coops and I would meet for a drink at the end of a day at the bar of the Luau, which used to be on Rodeo Drive. Coops liked it there because the bar was very dimly lit and he was not readily recognized.

"Whenever I see Papa," he once said (it always sounded strange to me to hear big Coops, who was a few years older than Ernest, calling him Papa), "it sets off a feeling of friendship in me that I don't have with anyone else. Like he's an unblooded brother, you know what I mean? I'm not someone who collects friends—I keep purty much to myself because I don't like film

talk and out here that's the only language anybody talks—
filmese. But acting in films is the only thing I know, that's all I've
done my whole life, and I like the acting part of it, but I sure as
hell don't like all the shit that goes with it. That's why I'd like
to do this series with you and Ernie—we could mebbe have some
fun and you guys don't talk filmese."

Unfortunately, that plan proved to be as ephemeral as all the
other escapes Cooper had promised himself. He phoned me in
New York on the day he was supposed to arrive for a conference
with CBS executives about the television series. The phone call
came from Boston, where Coops had gone for prostate tests at
the Massachusetts General Hospital. The following day, he was
operated on. I telephoned the hospital a day or so later and his
voice was strong and animated. The operation turned out okay,
he said, no malignancy, he'd be out in a few days, but he'd have
to return to his home in Beverly Hills to recuperate.

I myself had to go to Los Angeles a few weeks later to start
rehearsals for a "Playhouse 90" I had written, *Last Clear Chance*,
starring the renowned actor Paul Muni, and during that time I
saw Coops a few times. One of those times was a black tie dinner
at his house to celebrate his birthday. Almost all the guests were
actors and directors with whom Coops had worked, and I recall
how dazzled I was by the enduring beauty of Merle Oberon.

But I did not have much time to spend with Coops sitting on
the barstools of the Luau; the "Playhouse 90" rehearsal had
turned into a nightmare because poor Muni could not memorize
his lines. He had gone from New York, where he lived, to Los
Angeles by train, and had spent the entire four or five days in
his compartment studying a tape he had made of the entire
script, but his ability to remember those lines was unpredictably
erratic. This was to be a live telecast, as immediate as a Broadway play: the red light of the camera was the equivalent of the
curtain rising on a Broadway house, but the difference was that
on television it was not possible to have a prompter in the wings.
Most of Muni's scenes involved a trial, and in the give-and-take
of courtroom dialogue, improvisation was virtually impossible.
The director was George Roy Hill, as intelligent and gifted a
man as one could ask for, but he began to despair when Muni
performed a scene letter-perfect one day, only to forget most of

the lines the next. And Muni's fellow players—Luther Adler, Lee Remick, Dick York—also began to despair because it was impossible to rehearse properly when Muni was mumbling and fumbling his lines.

I liked Muni very much. He was one of the screen heroes of my boyhood, always portraying the downtrodden—on a chain gang, a beleaguered gangster, the persecuted Dreyfus—and as I had been a Depression downtrodden myself, he was a kinsman. Now meeting him in the twilight of his career and his life, I was moved by the courageous battle he was waging against his faulty memory. Each morning he began rehearsals with desperate resolve that the words would come to him, and they often did, for a delusory scene or two, but then the mind that had served him so well on the stage in such towering dramas as *Key Largo* and *Inherit the Wind* would falter, and I could see Muni stiffen and apply the whip as he tried to rescue his pride from this humiliating experience. His devoted wife, Rose, who accompanied him to all the rehearsals, tried to comfort him during our frequent breaks—quiet conferences in a corner of the rehearsal room—but there was really nothing she could to.

But not once did Muni waver from his fierce resolve to perform his role, not once did he express any feeling of defeat; he was a fighter repeatedly knocked down, always getting back on his feet and putting up his dukes. In a long and distinguished career that included an Academy Award, Muni had never taken the count and he was battling to preserve what he stood for in his profession.

However, a couple of days before our air date, Martin Manulis, who was the producer, came on the set and discussed with George Roy Hill and me his misgivings about going on air when Muni did not know his lines. Marty said he felt he had to play it safe by arranging for a standby movie to be shown in the event Muni's memorization had not improved by the day of the show. If that happened, it would be the first time in the history of "Playhouse 90," then at the height of its popularity, that it had failed to go on the air. I knew in my heart that the situation was hopeless, because Muni was not going to achieve in two days what had failed him for four weeks.

I often had lunch at the Farmer's Market, which was adjacent to the CBS building, and on the day of that depressing conference with Manulis, I was there having lunch by myself, wallowing in my misery, when Arthur Penn sat down beside me, looking as depressed as I did. He was rehearsing the "Playhouse 90" which was scheduled for the week after mine and his problem was that an actor named Tab Hunter, who was supposed to play a psychopathic killer, was coming across as soft and effeminate rather than the mad-dog assassin he was supposed to be. I swapped my Muni misery for his Hunter misery and for a while we both sat silently, not touching our tacos and beans.

Finally, Arthur roused himself to say that he recalled being in a dilemma like mine. It had happened during the beginning of his career, when he was working for a television program called "Studio One" that put on live, hour-long telecasts. Arthur was floor manager, which meant that, equipped with headphones and a receiving device attached to his waist, he communicated with the director, who operated from a glassed-in booth at one end of the studio.

It was "Studio One" 's practice to have a dress rehearsal on the afternoon of the evening's performance, and the play that Arthur was recalling was one that starred James Barton, who had made a name for himself in Erskine Caldwell's *Tobacco Road.* During the dress rehearsal, Barton, who had had a history of mental unstability, suddenly dropped to the floor of the studio and began hugging himself and weeping uncontrollably. Every attempt was made to get him back on his feet, but all failed and he was carried off. "Studio One" did not have understudies and the telecast was but a few hours away. Also, in those days, no standby film was available.

The situation was rescued, however, by Dan Petrie, who was the director. He went through a quick rehearsal, using Arthur's headset as a means of having Barton's lines read to him from the control booth. At the start of the telecast, the audience was told that James Barton had become indisposed and that the director would be standing in for him. "Now, then," Arthur said, "television is much more sophisticated today and I'm sure the CBS engineers could devise a hearing device much less noticeable than my old-fashioned headset."

"You mean that someone would read Muni's lines to him just before he had to say them?"

"That's it. Why not?"

CHOICE PEOPLE

I hurried back to the set to tell George, who immediately sent for the chief CBS engineer. That very afternoon, engineering arrived with an ordinary hearing aid which they had converted into a tiny receiving station. "Muni," George said, "you're going to play this part hard of hearing."

At the first rehearsal, Muni did just that, and brilliantly. When he wanted his lines repeated, he'd cup his hand around his hearing aid and command a witness to "Speak up!" whereupon George, who fed him every line from a script in the control booth, would repeat the line he had just given him. The transmitter for the device was in a leather pouch that was affixed to Muni's lower back, where it was hidden by his suit jacket.

After dress rehearsal, Luther Adler came over to me and said: "Hotch, mark my words: all of us dying with sympathy for Muni, all this time, not able to rehearse properly, everybody running around trying to help poor old Muni, well, tomorrow the newspapers will all have big headlines—Muni sensational! Muni gives performance rarely seen on TV! Muni this and Muni that, and all the rest of us, all of us sympathetic shmucks, if we find our names buried somewhere toward the end of the reviews we can consider ourselves lucky. Listen, it's nothing new for me. Muni and I started in the Yiddish theatre at the same time and we've been fighting each other ever since and the son of a bitch outfoxes me every time. Poor old Muni, my *tuchas*! Poor old Adler, that's who should get the sympathy!"

Of course, Luther's clairvoyance was 100 percent on the nose. Muni was brilliant, making full dramatic use of his deafness, not faltering once, playing his part to the hilt—that of an old lawyer defending his lawyer son against charges which could get him disbarred—as poor George Roy Hill sweated bullets feeding the dialogue to Muni from the control booth, not able to pay any attention to camera coverage, sound, or anything else.

And the accolades of the critics were as Luther had predicted, although Luther did get more mention than he had feared. As it turned out, *Last Clear Chance* was Muni's farewell, the final performance he gave before his death; as I thought about him on the day of his obituary, it occurred to me how aptly named my play had been.

11

Gary Cooper Wins the Race to the Barn

When Gary Cooper came to New York in 1961 to tape a television show about the American cowboy, he called me in advance of his coming to arrange to have lunch. That's when he told me that he would have to withdraw from the plans he had made with Ernest and me. "The medics have told me the truth about that operation I had," he said. "It was cancer. They say I'm not gonna hang around too long. I hope to Christ they're right."

They had told him just after Christmas, when he had started to experience severe pain, and he had asked them point-blank. Now the pain was so bad, he said, that despite all the things he took for it he could work in front of the cameras only an hour at a time.

He asked me about Ernest, who had been admitted for the first time to the psychiatric section of the Mayo Clinic. "You better tell him about me," Coops said. "We always have leveled with each other, absolutely, about everythin', and I wouldn't like him to find out from someone else or in the papers. I tried to call him but they wouldn't put me through, and I don't like to write about somethin' like that." Coops looked as good as he ever looked, and it seemed impossible to me that his days were numbered.

"Y' know," he was saying, "I never worried much about my health or how I looked—oh, maybe a coupla face tucks and a dye job to cover the gray—but I was never one to go to a doctor much or have a lot of tests—all that medico shit. I figgered on bein' around as long as I liked. I never really had anythin' go haywire with my plumbing or anythin' like that, so I didn't figure that the first time I went off the track they'd tip me the black spot." He said it matter-of-factly, no self-pity in his voice. Two matronly ladies came up to the table to get autographs on their menus and Coops obliged politely. As I watched him scrawling his name, it occurred to me that the painful price you pay for having friends who are older than you are is that you have to watch death taking them away from you, one after another.

I had first gone to Hollywood long before *The Battler* and my other television experiences, under rather peculiar circumstances. At the time I had just become a second lieutenant, newly graduated from OCS, and my first assignment as an officer was as adjutant of a squadron of the 13th Wing of the Army Air Force's Anti-Submarine Command at Westover Field, Massachusetts. These squadrons flew B-25s around the clock,* surveying the offshore waters for signs of U-boats. I was glad that finally I was away from show business and on a military assignment. A few days after I joined my anti-submarine squadron, we were put on alert for immediate overseas duty in North Africa. But on the day of our scheduled departure, the commanding colonel of the wing sent for me; when I entered his office I found him studying my classification card, that very efficient document which contained all the salient facts of one's life.

"I see here, Lieutenant," the colonel said, ignoring my salute, "that you wrote and performed in an Air Force musical when you were at Sheppard Field."

"Oh, sir, that was just . . ."

"And that you went on tour."

"Well, yes, to raise money for emergency relief, but it was just a silly thing . . ."

"I'm glad I located you before your squadron took off," the colonel said, flipping my card into his out basket, "because I am

---

*Medium-range bombers that were much too fast for the slow reconnaisance work they were being used for.

going to detach you from squadron duty on special assignment to me."

"You are?"

"I have a directive from General Larson to take immediate steps to get some recognition for our organization. No one knows what we do, they don't even know we exist. We sound like we're Navy. Now what General Larson wants is a film that shows our men in training and in combat—something that can be shown in all post theatres—of course a film that puts us in a very good light."

"Excuse me, sir, but if you're asking me to do this, I think you have the wrong man. I don't know a thing about film-making— in fact, I don't even know how to operate a camera."

The colonel's face grew dark. "Lieutenant, what did they teach you at OCS? To be resilient?"

"Yes, sir."

"Confident?"

"Yes, sir."

"Accept direct orders without assessing their consequences or dangers?"

"But, sir, that's just it—there is no more danger in making a movie than there was in touring with that musical."

"Lieutenant, this film you're going to make will have to contain footage of actual combat with U-boats—so you needn't worry about danger." He stood up and put out his hand. "Good luck, Hotchner," he said, shaking my hand. "The general expects this film to make us look very good—in fact, make us look like we're the best doggone outfit in the Air Force—get me? General Larson has been a brigadier for a long time and he wants another star—get me?"

My total staff consisted of two enlisted men, Private Walker and Corporal Brown, both of whom had been small-town photographers in civilian life. I went through the supply catalog and requisitioned five hundred thousand dollars' worth of motion picture equipment from the Air Force Supply Depot in Dayton, Ohio. I didn't know what to order, so to be on the safe side I ordered everything. We stockpiled more film in our special refrigerators than was used to shoot *Gone with the Wind*, and Walker and Brown began to use it up in our special Bell & Howell cameras like there was no tomorrow. I wrote a scenario and commentary for the film, and the Navy dispatched a submarine, *The Tuna,* to maneuver for us as Walker, prone in the cramped Plexiglas nose of a B-25, photographed simulated attack runs on the submarine. Later, we flew to North Africa, and as luck would have it, on the second day after our arrival, with Corporal Brown in one of the B-25s, a U-boat was spotted and a chain of depth charges was dropped on it as it submerged. Corporal Brown kept his camera on the entire operation, and the unsteadiness of hand, caused by either aircraft vibration or nervousness, gave the footage combat realism.

When we returned from North Africa, I packed up all the miles of footage we had shot and trundled my load out to Culver City, California, where, on the grounds of the old Hal Roach Studios, the First Motion Picture Unit had set up its film-making operations for the Air Force. I took a rather shabby room at the St. Moritz Hotel in Hollywood for three dollars a night (my per diem was seven dollars a day). The First Motion Picture Unit was run by former studio executives who had been drafted, and the lot was a stay-at-home haven for movie stars, directors, stunt men, character actors, screenwriters, and technicians who turned out a wide variety of training films and other Air Force movies.

I was assigned a cutter who would edit my footage and splice it together, a commentator to do the voice over, and a musician who would arrange the music for the titles and for scenes that needed it. The cutter's name was Jason Bernie, son of Ben Bernie the old maestro, yowsuh, yowsuh, yowsuh, who used to broadcast his band music from the College Inn in Chicago; the commentator was Private First Class Alan Ladd, and the musician was Sergeant David Rose, who, I believe, was married to Judy Garland at the time.

When Alan Ladd walked into the little office I had been assigned, I couldn't believe my eyes. I had just seen him in *This Gun for Hire* and I had expected a hefty tough guy, but in the flesh he was minuscule, certainly not more than 5 foot 2, with orange hair and a rather dainty mien. But worst of all, when he started to read the commentary, I was shocked to hear that he had a slight speech defect, not quite a lisp, rather like his tongue catching on his teeth. I listened to a playback of his voice and it sounded more like a stickup than the official voice of the Air Force. I agonized over what to do, for although I had the specter of General Larson to contend with, I also realized that despite my lieutenant's bars, I was in reality a green kid from St. Louis, and who in hell was I to fire superstar Alan Ladd.

I mentioned my dilemma to Jason Bernie, who though only a corporal had the balls of a three-star general. "Lieutenant," he said, "Ladd no more wants to stand around here and record this shit than you want him to do it. Tell him—you'll be doing him a favor."

I did, rather haltingly, and Ladd's reaction was a wordless shrug and a quick departure. His replacement was Private John Beale, who sounded precisely right. And David Rose recorded the entire score, full of soaring violins and triumphant brass, with his Santa Ana band, which had been hailed as one of the best bands of its kind ever assembled.

Jason edited the film expertly,* and we became good friends. He had an urbanity, a civilized craftiness that fascinated me. He was a handsome young man who relished his constant escapades with a slew of attractive women. One day he asked for permission to leave the cutting room early in order to meet a train that was bringing his girl friend to Los Angeles. He had often mentioned her, and had awaited her advent with great anticipation, even booking a special room at the Ambassador for the occasion.

When he arrived at work the following morning, Jason was in a foul mood, tossing filmstrips around, growling at the GI who was helping him. I asked him what was wrong. "That lousy bitch," he said, "she was a virgin! Can you imagine that? A goddamn virgin! I put her on the first train out of here this morning."

Converting raw film footage into a finished picture, which I had titled *Atlantic Mission*, with integrated sound and titles took much longer than I had anticipated, so I had a lot of time on my hands.

---

*He had been a film editor at Columbia Pictures.

I knew no one in Hollywood but there was one man I was anxious to meet, my uncle Henry Hotchener, who had not dropped the middle *e* from his name as my father had. My father had often told me about the famous coastal Hotcheners, Maurice in New York and Henry in Los Angeles; Maurice had been the attorney for Jimmy Walker, the flamboyant New York mayor of the Twenties (Maurice's official title was "Special Corporation Counsel of the City of New York"), and Henry was the business manager and confidant of the incomparable John Barrymore.

When I had been in New York on my way to Westover Field, I had gone to see Maurice Hotchener, who was then in private practice. He was a diminutive, natty gentleman, bow tie and vest, who was having his shoes shined by an itinerant bootblack when I was ushered into his office. He offered me a shine, and while our shoes were being glossed he gave me a capsule summary of the family history of the Hotcheners and the Hotchners, calling one the E clan and the other the Pretenders. I found him witty and amusing, especially when he spoke about the Jimmy Walker days. He opened a drawer and showed me one of his Jimmy Walker mementos—a peculiarly shaped piece of iron with an electrical cord on it which Walker had invented so that his valet could iron the shoulders and back of Walker's suit jackets after he had put them on, thereby molding them to his body. "Nattiest dresser I ever met," my uncle Maurice said, with admiration. "As soon as I can afford a valet, I'll start using the iron."

I asked him about his brother Henry, and he told me that when Barrymore was alive, Henry often asked him to do legal work for Barrymore. Maurice said that Henry and his wife, Marie, had been close associates of John Barrymore for seventeen years, right up to his death, which had occurred only a few months ago. Both Henry and Marie were deeply involved in the occult and in after-death phenomena, and actually had met while on psychic journeys to India. My aunt Marie was, according to Maurice, an authority on theosophy and abnormal psychic phenomena as well as being an extraordinary astrologer. Henry and Marie had both been to India many times, taking Barrymore with them on one occasion, and Marie had participated in psychotherapeutic experiments conducted by the leading occult scientists of the day in clinics in Nancy and the Salpêtrière in Paris.

Both Henry and Marie had been educated in American schools. Henry had studied law at Georgetown University and the University of Southern California, and Marie, after her graduation from Mills College in Oakland, had shown great promise as a soprano, performing operatic roles in Italy, France, and Germany, often with the composer Puccini himself conducting the orchestra. But her interest in theosophy and spiritual phenomena eventually obsessed her and she turned down all operatic engagements, including an invitation from Frau Cosima Wagner to sing at the Bayreuth Festival.

"They had enormous influence on Jack Barrymore," Maurice said. "He was dependent on Henry for business affairs, and he wouldn't make a move until Marie checked it out on her astrological calendar. You must go see them. They live in an area north of Franklin Avenue that they are developing as a real estate venture."

There was no telephone listed for Henry Hotchener at the address Maurice had given me; the two letters I had written to him had gone unanswered, so one afternoon, having nothing better to do, I decided to go and knock on my uncle's door.

The area in which he lived was north of Hollywood Boulevard, a section where there had not been much development. I had difficulty finding the house, which, as it turned out, stood far back from a massive, rusted iron gate. There was a bell on the gate but it was rusted beyond usefulness. The gate was slightly ajar, however, and it opened with a painful squeal. I self-consciously walked up the winding drive to the house, which was as unkempt as the weed-covered lawns and the decrepit driveway. All the blinds on the house were shut. I seriously doubted that my uncle and aunt, or anyone else, lived there.

I rang the bell and heard it sound shrilly in the interior. No answer. I rang again, and again, and was preparing to leave when I heard a slight rustle from within, followed by a clank of the door's protective metal. I was confronted with a man, or, to be more precise, an apparition, for this individual was dressed like a genie, a green genie, silk tunic and silk blousy pants tapering into Arabian pointed, jeweled slippers, a wide beaded and bejeweled belt around his waist, a huge gold scarab on a chain at his neck and, incongruously, a tennis visor on his forehead. He looked at me, saying nothing.

"I'm . . . ah . . . Lieutenant Hotchner, I came to see my uncle Henry if he's here . . ."

The man put a finger to his lips, even though I had spoken in a low voice, and he gestured for me to follow him. The house was dimly lit and smelled of incense and musk. I followed him across a foyer and then through what I supposed was the dining room, but in the center of the room, in place of a dining table, there was an Indian funeral bier with a stout woman, shrouded in a flowing white gown, stretched out on it. Her hair and her complexion were as white as her gown. Her eyes were closed and her arms were crossed over her ample chest. A band of jewels encircled her forehead, and a scarab, identical to the one worn by the man, hung from a gold chain around her neck.

The man stopped at the bier and said: "Dear, this is Sam Hotchner's boy, now a lieutenant in the Air Force. This is my wife, Marie," he said, quite formally.

I managed to extract a "How do you do?" out of my constricted throat, but Aunt Marie did not move or reply. She wasn't dead, however, for I distinctly saw the rise and fall of her copious bosom. I guessed her to be at least twenty years older than my uncle.

He now led me past the dining room and into a butler's pantry, where he motioned for us to sit on two high stools that he placed close to each other. He spoke to me in a very low voice, so as not to disturb his wife, I presumed. He asked about my father, whom he had not seen in twenty years, and then he asked me what I was doing in Hollywood. He knew about the First Motion Picture Unit, because, he said, in his long association with Barrymore he had become familiar with all the Hollywood studios.

I told him that I thought that John Barrymore was the greatest actor I had ever seen. My uncle said that it was difficult for him to talk about Jack because he had just died the previous May, and it was painful to mention his name, so much did my uncle love him. My uncle said that his wife had been so affected by Barrymore's death that she had been in a spiritual trance ever since. She was one of the world's greatest astrologers, he said, and Barrymore would always consult her before going on a trip or making a movie or getting involved with a woman. She once warned him on his astrological chart not to drive his automobile on a particular day, but he forgot and his car went off the road and turned over and he suffered a concussion and a fractured hip. He got so dependent on Marie's astrological readings that he would not shoot a scene in a picture without first checking the astrological signs with her.

My uncle said they had taken Barrymore on a trip to India at a time when his health was beginning to fail and alcoholism was getting the better of him. At first the Ayurvedic cure, which was given by a Dr. Murti and involved herbs and essences from the Himalayas, seemed to work, but after a couple of weeks Barrymore suddenly disappeared on one of his binges. They later discovered he had bought out an Indian brothel stocked with Eurasian girls, spent a week there, and between the bar and the obliging girls Barrymore undid all the good the cure had done him.

I sat there all afternoon on that stool in the butler's pantry, listening to my uncle's Barrymore stories, oblivious of time, feeling sad and empty when he got to the end of Barrymore's life, describing the painful and miserable way he had died, his mind and body in ruins from years of abuse.

I wanted to ask Uncle Henry so many things but we were both suddenly startled by a shrill sound that came from the dining room. My uncle immediately got off his stool and said I would have to be leaving. As we passed Aunt Marie I heard her droning a litany of strange sounds, perhaps a Hindu prayer from the way it sounded.

At the door, my uncle gave me a card on which his name and address were printed. "Tell your father," he said, "that we are developing this entire area. There's not much here now but after the war people will start to build here and he can make his fortune. I've heard how bad things were for him and your family during the Depression but this is his chance to recoup. We have building lots here for as little as a hundred dollars. Tell him. I'd like to see you again, perhaps entertain you, but you see how things are . . ."

He quickly closed the door.

I wrote to my father about Henry's offer and enclosed his card, but my father's response was that he didn't put money in get-rich-quick schemes. Of course, my father had no money, and even if he had he would have invested it in something that was a sure loser. My father was a well-meaning man, with limited dreams and a capacity for failure.

On a warm spring day in Beverly Hills, I went to see Cooper for the last time. During February and March, on his good days, he continued to try to live his life the way he always had. One afternoon he invited me to his striking house on Baroda Drive to witness in the garden a spectacular demonstration by five karate experts. And there were occasional dinner parties at his house when old-time friends would carry on as if Cooper were perfectly all right.

But by April the pain and ravages of the cancer had finally knocked him down for keeps, and when I went to see him that afternoon in May he was a wasted figure, lying immobile in his darkened room. His hair was gray-streaked where the dye had left it. His wife took me into his room, then left us alone.

"Papa phoned a couple of weeks ago," he said. He paused between words, because it was very painful for him to speak. "Told me he was sick too. I bet him that I'll beat him out to the barn." He smiled and closed his eyes and seemed to doze off. "Heard on the radio he was back at Mayo's." The eyes flickered open. "That right?"

"Yes."

"Poor Papa." His eyes shut again but he seemed to be listening as I told him how the hunting had been the previous season in Ketchum and related little gossips about people he knew there.

He was hit by a big pain and his face contorted as he fought it off; sweat instantly covered his face. When the pain had passed, Cooper reached his hand over to the bed table and picked up a crucifix, which he put on the pillow beside his head.

"Please give Papa a message. It's important and you mustn't forget because I'll not be talking to him again. Tell him . . . that time I wondered if I made the right decision"—he moved the crucifix a little closer so that it touched his cheek—"tell him it was the best thing I ever did."

"I'll tell him."

"Don't forget."

"Don't worry, Coops, I'll tell him."

I sat there for some time while he slept, my mind clouded with grief, rooted to my chair, wanting to say something meaningful, to pray, to deodorize the smell of death, to weep, anything, but I just sat there, feeling my heart thumping heavily in my chest. How strange, I thought, that these two men, Cooper and Hemingway, good friends, longtime friends, are approaching the end of their lives at the very same time but so differently: Coops wanting to live but with no hope of life; Hemingway with life as an alternative, but wanting to die. If only Coops could exchange his cancer for the years of living that remained in Ernest but which he was hell-bent on rejecting by suicide. Now that would be a formidable challenge for the transplant doctors, wouldn't it? An implant for living.

I finally stirred myself and started out of the room, but I had gone only a few steps when Coops called out my name. He had raised himself up on one elbow, the effort causing his arm to tremble.

"Hotch, listen," he said in a barely audible voice, "I'd like you to have somethin' of mine."

"I'd like that, Coops."

He looked around the room, cluttered with medical apparatus. His eyes searched the pictures on the walls, the few books on his night table, some framed photos on top of his dresser, then he spied something appropriate.

"That little TV of mine—over there."

I didn't see anything that resembled a television set, but I crossed the room to where Cooper was looking. On the floor was a leather-covered box.

"That's it," he said.

I had never seen anything like it. On close inspection, I found that there was a crease in the leather which opened at one end into a hood that revealed a recessed six-inch screen that could only be viewed by one person.

"Fellow from Philco gave it to me," Coops said.

"Thanks very much, I'm really glad to have it."

"You kin watch my old movies on it," he said, lowering his head to the pillow, a slight smile on his face. "My old movies," he repeated.

12

John Frankenheimer Cues the Goddamn Vultures

One winter I produced and dramatized a series of Hemingway-inspired television shows, several of them directed by John Frankenheimer, who had the best natural feel for the power and limitations of television of anyone I ever encountered in that medium; but along with his quite extraordinary flights of inspiration, he also was subject to seizures of madness which invariably occurred at the most inopportune times.

Johnny was tall, a bit stoop-shouldered, and very, very intense. When he fixed his eyes on an erring actor, usually placing his face as close to his victim's as possible, there was no conceivable way for the actor to look anywhere but into the dead center of John's piercing pupils. When John exploded with laughter, microphone booms tumbled. When he gave an order, brave men on the set trembled. When he wanted snow, he wanted to outdo the Antarctic, and when he wanted rain, he wanted Noah's deluge. There was no middle ground with John. Energy, ENERGY was the key, and his shows pulsed with it, throbbed with vitality, jumped across the living room to the easy chair and bear-hugged the viewer.

But, as I say, there were these madnesses to contend with. We were on a sound stage that had been converted into a stretch of African plain for *The Snows of Kilimanjaro*. Robert Ryan was lying on a cot in the shade of a mimosa tree, his gangrenous right leg swathed in bandages. Off to one side was the Land-

Rover that had broken down and put him in this predicament. In the top of the tree were three big vultures, waiting to pick Ryan's bones as soon as the gangrene did him in. Out of range stood the owner of the vultures, poised with the ends of three thin black wires in his hand, the other ends attached to the vultures. The opening shot called for the camera to pan slowly from the man on the cot up the tree to the three vultures, who, as they came into the shot, would emit bloodthirsty screeches.

In the control booth Johnny started the cameras, and when the pan shot got to the vultures, he barked: "Cue the vultures!" The vulture man gave a little tug on his wires but nothing happened. John was furious. "Cut!" he bellowed. "Why in hell didn't you cue the goddamn vultures?"

The voice of the stage manager came into the booth. "We did, John, we cued 'em."

"Well, don't tickle 'em, *cue* 'em! Now let's get set to roll 'em again."

Same shot, then: "Cue the vultures!" One vulture shuffled a little bit but the other two sat like lumps. "Cut! Goddamn it, cut!" John exploded. "Are you telling me you actually cued those fucking vultures?"

"We gave 'em a good tug, John."

"Where've you got those wires attached?"

"To their legs."

"All right, get up there in the tree and wire their tails."

There was a lengthy delay while the vulture man climbed up in the tree and rewired his birds.

Again John rolled the camera and again he cued the vultures and again nothing happened. That's when the madness overcame Frankenheimer. He turned the controls over to the assistant director and went storming out of the control booth, spewing invectives all over the set. He grabbed the floor manager's mike and snatched the three wires from the vulture man's hand as he yelled up to the control booth: "Roll 'em!"

When the vultures came into the panning frame, the assistant director said: "Cue the vultures" and John gave the wires such a mighty yank that he jerked out all their tail feathers, which went flying all over the mimosa tree, a blizzard of vulture feathers, and the birds, which were tethered to the bough, set up the kind of shrieks not heard since the time of the Borgias.

The vulture man ran up a ladder to administer to his stricken birds but they broke loose from their tethers and attacked him with such vehemence that he fell back off the ladder, narrowly missing Robert Ryan as he landed on the floor. John was now back in the booth, and calmly surveyed the pandemonium he had set loose on the set. "Hotch," he said to me, "I don't think we need that opening shot with the vultures."

I had thought that denuding the vultures would have exorcised Johnny's furies for the rest of the production, but there was still the Land-Rover madness to come. On the third day of taping, just before the lunch break, John summoned the stage manager and told him that a scene in front of the Land-Rover was going to be shot that afternoon and that the car certainly did not look as if it had been baking in the sun on an African plain for a couple of weeks. "Dirty it up, make it look broken down," Johnny said.

"Okay," the stage manager said, "but we've got to be careful because the car's on loan from a dealer and Land-Rovers cost a bundle."

"Well, fake it, for Chrissakes, you can fake it, can't you? Fake it and clean it up afterwards."

After lunch John set the scene to be shot and the cameras began to roll but when the Land-Rover came on the monitor, Johnny ordered everything to a halt. He glowered at the Land-Rover on his monitor and then, in an ominously controlled voice, he spoke into his mike and his words rolled onto the set like Moses speaking to the blasphemous Israelites.

"That Land-Rover has not been baking in the African sun for two weeks. It looks like it could win the next race at Le Mans. IT IS SUPPOSED TO BE BROKEN DOWN!" His voice suddenly dropped to a whisper. "Now, I am going to be patient— I will switch to the party scene and I will put this Land-Rover scene over until tomorrow but when I come on the set in the morning, I want to see a BROKEN-DOWN FUCKING LAND-ROVER!!"

I arrived on the set early the next morning and immediately went to inspect the offending Land-Rover. It had been sprayed with a film of dust and its wheels muddied over. The stage manager, who looked as if he had spent the night in the car, asked me if I thought it looked broken down enough and I said it looked broken down enough for me but there was no telling about John.

When Frankenheimer arrived, the first thing he did was to have a camera focused on the Land-Rover. Everyone on the set waited with suspended breath.

"Is that it?" he asked over the intercom in a very calm voice. "I gave you eighteen hours to make this Land-Rover look like it was broken down and this is your idea of broken down, is it? Well, gentlemen, I think you need a little lesson in what a truly broken-down Land-Rover looks like so that the next time you have a scene that calls for a broken-down Land-Rover, the director, who may not be as patient as I am, will not have to deal with idiots and imbeciles who do not have the foggiest notion of what it means to be *broken down.*"

All this in a steely, even voice, no more animated than a railroad conductor announcing the stations, but I knew full well that madness was in the ascendency and I followed John as he launched himself down the stairs that led to the set. By now the entire cast and crew had assembled to watch Frankenheimer deal with the Land-Rover; if there was one thing John relished above all else, it was an audience. He strode purposefully onto the set and went directly to the safari tent, which had a variety of tools scattered around it. John rummaged through these and emerged with a pickax. Brandishing it high over his head, he advanced on the Land-Rover as one would stalk a dangerous beast hidden in high grass. With a mighty heave he smashed the pickax into the radiator hood of the Land-Rover. His audience gasped and laughed nervously at his outrageous audacity, which, of course, incited John to repeat his pickax assault on the defenseless Land-Rover, scrunching a couple of fenders, the door on the driver's side, and flattening one of the tires. By now his audience was egging him on, cheering each swing of the ax, reveling in the massacre of the Land-Rover as revolutionary mobs must have enjoyed the guillotining in the Place de la Concorde.

Finally satisfied that the Land-Rover was sufficiently broken down, John tossed aside the pickax with the *savoir faire* of Ted

Williams after belting a game-winning home run, and sauntered back to the control booth to a noisy ovation from the spectators.

At the end of that day's shooting, however, the edge was taken off John's glory with the arrival of two executives from the CBS accounting division, who came into the control booth and presented John with a bill for the purchase cost of the Land-Rover, which, they said, was now his damaged property, and that they would deduct its cost from his director's fee. In rebuttal, John informed them that what he did was for the good of the production and if this bill was not immediately withdrawn he would not shoot the final two scenes of the show.

The following day, the standoff shut down the production. The Land-Rover, scrubbed and patched up, was pushed into the corridor outside our sound stage, and various CBS functionaries came to inspect it during the day. In fact, it became a celebrated curiosity, and it seemed *all* of CBS came to look at it. With his lawyer on one side of him and his agent on the other, John garrisoned himself in the control booth, where he ate pastrami sandwiches brought from a nearby delicatessen and refused all attempts at compromise. No, he would not pay one cent toward the purchase of the Land-Rover, nor would he complete the show unless he was immediately paid his entire director's fee.

CBS on its part threatened to sue John not only for the cost of the Land-Rover but for the substantial cost overages incurred by the shutdown. During the course of the day, both sides hardened their positions, and if they had had troops at their disposal they would doubtless have sent them into action. But at five o'clock in the afternoon, Fate, in the person of a black comedian named Rochester, arranged a solution.

Jack Benny was taping a show in the studio which adjoined ours, and Rochester, who was a regular on the show, emerged from that studio at the end of the day's shooting; as he walked along the corridor, he came face to face with the Land-Rover and it was love at first sight. Rochester had just purchased a ranch in the Valley and he wanted a vehicle appropriate to a ranch owner who has to oversee his spread; when he found out he could purchase this beautiful vehicle, which had immediately captured his heart, at a bargain price because it was slightly damaged, he jumped behind the wheel and drove it right out of there, thus solving the Great Land-Rover Impasse.

When John and I did *The Fifth Column* I thought that the august nature of the cast would temper Johnny's madness, but I should have known that madness is madness. *The Fifth Column*, Hemingway's only play, set in Madrid during the Spanish Civil War, had been originally produced on Broadway by The Theatre Guild with Lee J. Cobb and Franchot Tone as its stars, but the playscript had been extensively changed by a Hollywood scriptwriter named Bernard Glaser, and Ernest had been offended by the production. To write my television dramatization, I had gone back to Hemingway's original script, and although I had to make changes, adding scenes and dialogue, I made every effort to stay true to the characters and events created by Hemingway. The two leads were played by Richard Burton and Maximilian Schell, with Sally Ann Howes, George Rose, and Sydney Pollack* in supporting roles.

Sydney, who is a kind, soft-spoken man, was cast in the part of a sadistic Nazi colonel and John decided that it would help his character if he were bald. Sydney was appalled. He had just been married and, possessed of a bushy head of hair, he was fearful of going home to his new wife in a bald condition. But John was adamant, uninterested in such trivia as busting up a new marriage, and while tears rolled down his cheeks, Sydney was shorn as bald as the proverbial billiard ball.

The baldness made him more convincing as a sadistic Nazi, but when he went home to his new little wife that night, she slammed the door in his face and told him not to return until he had hair.

At the cast party, which was held after the final day of shooting, Burton was seated at a table with Sydney and his new little wife. Burton kept looking at one, then the other, the pretty girl and hairless Sydney. Finally, Burton said to Mrs. Pollack: "Tell

---

*Sydney became a director later on—*They Shoot Horses, Don't They?*, *Absence of Malice*, and *Tootsie* were among his films.

the truth, m' dear, you married him out of pity, didn't you?"

The entire production was shot in a studio on the West Side of New York that had once been a neighborhood movie house. Everything was going smoothly until we got to the third day of taping. John had been on good behavior for too long. John started the day's shooting in the mock-up corridor of a hotel but as the camera dollied down the corridor, John suddenly stopped everything because he didn't like the looks of the doorknobs, which, he said, ruined the atmosphere he wanted to create. He instructed the stage manager to rush over to Third Avenue and buy some old brass knobs in an antique store that John knew about. In the meantime, all the technicians, actors, and camera crews were biding their time while the budget clock ticked away.

When the replacement knobs were all on the doors, John cranked up the production again until we reached a critical street scene where a pitched battle was going to be fought. Barbed wire had been strung across the street and John had planned a camera angle that photographed the combatants through the strands of barbed wire, on which a cat had been impaled. John was enamored of tricky, dramatic shots like that but he was not at all enamored with the condition of the cat's carcass as he saw it on his monitor. "Cut! What in Christ's name is that supposed to be on the barbed wire?"

"That's the dead cat you wanted, John," said a voice from the floor.

"It looks like a mangled boot. You got another cat?"

"No, John, this is the only one property had."

"I want that fucking cat to look like a CAT! A real goddamn mouse-eating CAT! Got it?"

"It's hard to find stuffed cats, John. Really hard."

"Then get the real thing."

No answer.

"You hear me?"

"John . . . are you talking about a real, live cat?"

"Call the ASPCA—see if they've got a surplus cat."

While a mob of actors costumed as Fascist and Partisan soldiers stood around waiting, the stage manager put in a call to the ASPCA.

"John, I got 'em on the phone—they say they don't give out cats to be stuck on barbed wire."

"Then you're gonna have to go out and get one."

"What, John?"

"Go out in the alley and get me a goddamn cat!"

A short time later, when Richard Burton arrived to start taping his scheduled scenes, he asked me why everybody was standing around and I explained about the cat. At the conclusion of work every day, Burton and I had made a practice of going around the corner from the studio to a tavern on Ninth Avenue to have a few drinks. We sometimes had more than a few and there were evenings when Richard enchanted the winos at the bar with his Welsh songs and stories. The winos had never heard songs in Welsh before and Richard was a big hit with them. Burton and I had many pleasurable evenings in that Ninth Avenue gin mill, occasionally joined by Max Schell and on one occasion by Sally Ann Howes, but for some reason that I can't now recall, Sally wound up in tears that time and bolted off into the night. I doubt that Richard had anything to do with it, because when imbibing he was one of the most pleasurable companions imaginable. Poetry, song, reminiscence, vituperation, mimicry, fantasy, wisdom, ribald humor sprang from him in an unquenchable fount, and I would always leave him with a feeling that I had just spent a jolly evening at King Arthur's court.

Be that as it may, Burton did not believe my account about the cat. "Hotchner, you've had a few breakfast nips at our bar."

"No, Richard, so help me we are awaiting a cat for impaling."

Just at that moment, in corroboration, the stage manager appeared, disheveled and rather breathless, carrying a scrawny, yowling alley cat by the scruff of its neck. I do not know who did it or how it was done but the yowling stopped suddenly and the carcass of the now-deceased cat was affixed to the barbed wire. Frankenheimer lavished praise on the head of the cat captor and alerted everyone for action. Guns blazed away, bodies fell, grenades exploded, motorcycles zoomed, cars sped by as John photographed all this with the cat on the barbed wire in the foreground.

At the conclusion of the shot, John was ecstatic but his cameraman was not. "John," he said, "the cat was moving."

"It what?"

"Look, it's moving now."

Sure enough, the legs of the cat were moving. "John," I said firmly, "we can't use that shot—people will be throwing up all over America."

"It's the contractions that occur as rigor mortis sets in," someone said who seemed to know about such things.

"Why don't we jettison the cat the way we jettisoned the vultures," I suggested.

"No," John said determinedly. "I'm going to shoot that scene through the barbed wire. We'll just have to wait for rigor mortis to set in."

Which is what we did.

Little did I know that all these madnesses were but preambles to the *grande folie* which occurred during the filming of *For Whom the Bell Tolls*, a madness in itself. Until I wrote the script for *For Whom the Bell Tolls*, my problem had been to enlarge Hemingway short stories into full-length scripts; now my problem was to contract Ernest's massive novel about the Spanish Civil War into a three-hour teleplay. As a condition precedent to his signing on as director, Frankenheimer was assured that he could cast Jason Robards, Maria Schell, Eli Wallach, Maureen Stapleton, and Nehemiah Persoff in the key roles. The catch in this was that Jason, Eli, and Maureen were all appearing in Broadway plays, so that the show had to be performed in New York City in two studios located on opposite sides of Manhattan. There would be no exterior filming and yet this was a sprawling story that took place in the Escorial, in caves, under bridges, in horse corrals, on hilltops, and in valleys, all of which had to be simulated in cramped television studios.

As if that weren't enough, Paramount owned the basic film rights and would not permit CBS to do the show unless one pivotal scene was performed live. This meant that right in the middle of the telecast there had to be a switch from the film to a studio where Jason and Maria would give a live performance of the celebrated sleeping bag scene; at the end of that scene, there then would be a switch back to the film.* I'm not aware that any other program in the history of television has been put on the air in this manner.

But that wasn't the worst of it—both Jason and Maureen were in their heavy-drinking periods.† On Wednesday and Saturday, when they had matinees, it was necessary to film after their evening performances, but that's when they liked to open their bottles, and our problem was how to keep them away from the sauce and sober during the period of filming between 11 P.M. and 3 A.M. To achieve this, John hired bodyguards whose job it was to stay with Jason and Maureen from the moment they came off the Broadway stage and accompany them to the television studio to insure that they didn't sneak a few drinks on the way. Easier planned than done, however, because Jason and Maureen were very crafty drinkers who could conjure up booze out of thin air.

To be presented over two nights, *For Whom the Bell Tolls* was the costliest and longest special up to that time, and Hubbell Robinson, then programming chief of CBS, was counting on it to boost CBS in the ratings, but with John Frankenheimer at the helm it almost sank the entire network, and it turned out to be the beginning of the end for poor Hubbell, a man whom I greatly admired.

The first fiasco involved John's barber. Every show that Frankenheimer directed, he made his barber, who lived in Hollywood, a paid member of the cast, with travel and living expenses. John had a fetish about his hair, which he kept precisely so over his ears, and he required that it be trimmed every morning—but no one but his personal barber was allowed to perform this ritual. In order to justify the barber's cast status, John always found some menial turn that he could perform in front of the camera.

So that's how it happened that John's barber was on the Madrid set that fateful morning. An elaborately detailed section of Madrid had been built at great expense, and the action called

---

*This would ensure that no one would have a complete tape of the show.
†They are both teetotalers now, and much happier for it.

for a messenger to career up to the door of the embassy in a motorcycle with a sidecar, dash up to the door, and deliver an important document.

Looking for a way to get his barber before the camera, John said to him: "Irving, can you drive a motorcycle?"

"Yes, of course, Mr. Frankenheimer."

"You sure?"

"Yes, boss."

John had the rotund Irving fitted into a uniform, the motorcycle was placed in position, and crowds of extras were put in circulation on the street. Irving got on the motorcycle, kicked it into action, and revved up its motor. Frankenheimer activated the cameras, established the scene, and then gave the fateful command "Cue Irving!"

The stage manager signaled to Irving, who gunned the motorcycle forward, expertly maneuvered it along the busy street right up to the front of the embassy, and then shot up the sidewalk and through the facade of the buildings, tearing down the entire set, which collapsed in a shower of canvas and splintered wood on top of the motorcycle, which had overturned with its wheels spinning in the air after having pitched Irving on top of a peddler's fruit cart.

John confronted Irving, who was struggling to extricate himself from a pile of squashed oranges.

"Irving, you son of a bitch, you told me you knew how to drive a motorcycle."

"Yes, boss, I know how to drive it, but I don't know how to stop it."

This fiasco, plus others, caused delays and replacements that ran up the cost of the show astronomically, and the CBS brass became alarmed at what certainly looked like a production out of control. Hubbell Robinson was hauled on the carpet and it was decided that a delegation of executives would pay a surprise visit to the set to see for themselves what was going on. It was a Wednesday, which meant midnight shooting because of the matinees.

On that particular night, one of the most important scenes in the production was scheduled, the confrontation in the Partisans' cave between Robert Jordan and Pablo, the Partisan chief, but the filming did not start on time because Jason had adroitly slipped his keeper and an intensive search of the neighborhood bars had not yet located him. To make matters worse, while everyone was distracted by the search for Jason, Maureen had unearthed a bottle from one of her hiding places. By the time Jason was discovered drinking warm ale at Mcsorley's saloon, both he and Maureen were in a state of thick-tongued wobbliness.

Seething, Frankenheimer had as much black coffee poured down them as they could hold, and set up the scene in the cave. The action called for Nicky Persoff, as a drunken Pablo, to reject all of Robert Jordan's (Robards) attempts to provoke him. Frankenheimer ran one take after another, imploring Jason not to slur his words, imploring Maureen not to list to one side, imploring Persoff to exhibit more drunkenness, each take adding to John's exasperation until he exploded: "I got two drunks who should be sober and one guy sober who should be drunk!" Smoke was coming out of John's nostrils, a sure sign that madness was in the ascendency.

"Nicky," he said in a deadly tone, "you are going to play this scene DRUNK! And if you can't *act* drunk, which it seems you can't, then I will make you drunk!"

John produced a bottle of Scotch and filled a glass with it. Nick downed it, and in no time at all it got to him. John again put the scene in motion, and it was at this point that the delegation of CBS executives, led by Hubbell Robinson, entered the set to watch the filming. What they saw were three drunken actors staggering around a cave that reeked of booze, garbling their lines, missing their cues, getting in one another's way, but enjoying themselves as only drunks can.

The show was a success both critically and in its ratings, but after that night of the three drunks Hubbell did not have to ask for whom the bell tolled—it tolled for him.

Frankenheimer eventually left television to make feature films, but in my opinion his pictures have not been as effective as were his television shows because making a feature film is a slow, deliberate process that has no call for madness. It has no immediacy, but John thrived on that pressure, on doing the impossible in a very short time, on igniting a moment of brilliance in an actor with ordinary talent. In all the movies he has made, I warrant to say that John has never once wielded a pickax, nor have I seen a shot of his barber in any of them.

13

Barbara Hutton Will Always
Be a Princess

Mobility is one of the basic rewards for the insecurity of free-lancing. Wherever you put your typewriter is home, and new surroundings can sometimes regenerate the mysterious machinery of self-motivation which a free-lancer needs to face the daily torment of blank typewriter paper. In 1956, I discovered that Rome was an excellent rejuvenator.

Apartments were lavish, abundant, and inexpensive, good help was plentiful, and the economy genuflected before the dollar. I put my children in the American School, and quickly discovered that the languid life of Rome was a writer's paradise.

The first apartment I rented had been newly built on the roof of a building on the Via Ludovisi, just off the Via Veneto. It had an expansive terrace with a commanding view, tiled floors, a triangular living room with an elevated fireplace, and, *rara avis,* a modern kitchen. But it also had one serious drawback—congenital water failure. Engineers from the hydraulic company virtually lived on the premises, and there were daily head-scratching seminars devoted to analyzing the problem, but none of these consultations—or the addition, subtraction, or relocation of pipes—succeeded in producing a regular flow of water from the taps.

We survived there for several months, however, thanks to the diligence of the *portiere,* a genial behemoth who thrice daily carted up buckets of water in the service elevator and filled a water storage tank that perched above the apartment. The ancient Romans had been geniuses in designing aqueducts to bring in water from remote sources, but modern Romans had apparently lost the knack and couldn't even figure out how to get the *acqua* from the street to the roof.

It was a fine place to entertain, however, and I often invited members of the American and English contingents for the evening, warning them, however, to restrain their use of the bathroom facilities. There was the novelist Tom Sterling and his journalist wife, Clare; Beverly Pepper, the artist, married to Bill Pepper, then a *Newsweek* correspondent; the sculptor Robert Cook and his wife, Joanne, a playwright; and the novelist John Cheever and his wife, whose visit was particularly memorable.

We were sitting in the living room with the Cheevers, having after-dinner espresso, when there emerged from the fireplace what at first glance appeared to be a black cat. But as the cat descended the steps from the fireplace and approached us, Mrs. Cheever was the first to recognize that the cat was not a cat but a monstrous Roman rat. Her immediate response demonstrated remarkable agility, as she sprung from a seated position to a perch on top of the coffee table, a leap that was accompanied by a series of shrill screams that startled the rat and sent it scampering toward the rear of the apartment and into the bedroom where my two daughters, ages four and six, were sleeping.

Her screams also awakened Pango, my Bedlington terrier, who had been snoozing, and he opened his eyes just as the rat went scooting by him. Pango took off in hot pursuit, for Bedlingtons had been bred by Welsh coal miners to go down in the mines before the morning descent to get rid of the rats. Pango certainly appeared determined to rid the world of this one.

I too went in pursuit of the rat, grabbing a kitchen broom on the way, alarmed that the rat had entered my daughters' room. I flicked on the lights, and both Pango and I spotted the rat in a corner under one of the beds. Pango charged it head on but it scampered under him and headed toward me with Pango right on his tail. But Pango was having trouble getting traction on the slick tile floor. As the rat ran past me I belted it with the broom, slowing it for an instant, but it immediately recovered and resumed its circuit of the room before Pango could nab him.

The girls had awakened and were enjoying this funny game that Pango and their father were playing with a frisky rat. Each time I whacked the rat as it ran by, Pango almost caught up with it, but not quite; after several rat circuits, however, I changed my broom tactic and smacked the rat with the *edge* rather than the *flat* of the broom and that stunned it just long enough for Pango to grab it, give it a vicious shaking, and then toss it up in the air, breaking its neck.

I pushed the rat's carcass onto the broom with my shoe and started to carry it out when I noticed, for the first time, that Cheever had been observing all this from the doorway.

With Cheever following me, I carried the rat onto the terrace, wondering what I should do with it. It weighed a ton on the end of the broom. With a sly smile on his face Cheever said, "Render unto Caesar," gesturing toward the starry night. It was a brilliant suggestion. I reared back and with a mighty heave catapulted the rat into the night. It flew through the air in a soaring arc that carried it toward the lights of the Via Veneto. As we watched it slowly disappear, Cheever and I exchanged the conspiratorial smiles of two mischievous schoolboys.

"It should be an Olympic event," John said: "the rat toss."

We went back to the living room to check on his wife. A snifter of Strega had restored her color.

Some years later I ran into Cheever in New York and we had a drink. "That night of the rat," he said, "was the highlight of our stay in Rome. I often wondered where it landed."

We then spent an amusing half hour imagining the most preposterous situations into which our rat could have descended. I laugh even now at John's description of how the Pope was in the midst of a ceremony in St. Peter's Square when the rat suddenly descended from the heavens and landed with a thud on the altar, the event henceforth celebrated as the Miracle of the Rat.

I moved from the Ludovisi waterless apartment to an elegant penthouse on the Viale di Via Massimo, which I rented from an impecunious principessa. It was replete with fountains, and terraces with orange trees, and life in Roma was splendid indeed except for the fact that Roma is a far, far way from those publishing sources that nurture and sustain the free-lancer; in fact, the ocean seemed to stretch a few miles every day. After exhausting the supply of such native subjects as the latest Etruscan discoveries, the Calabrian Mafia, film-making at Cinecittà, the rise of the Vespa, and so forth, I found I was having to scratch to find assignments. A professional free-lancer never writes on speculation; he proposes article ideas, and on approval he proceeds on the basis of a contract that defines the length, content, and fee to be paid for his work. Occasionally a magazine or a publisher or a network suggests a subject to the writer, as CBS once asked me to do a "Playhouse 90" on the last days of Mussolini, but this is infrequent. The free-lancer who waits for assignments or inspiration to come to him is doomed.

That winter in Rome, when my letters to the States proposing article ideas were finding fewer and fewer takers, I read in the Rome *Daily American* that Barbara Hutton, the original and congenital poor little rich girl, had gone into seclusion in her palace in Tangier to recover from the trauma of the breakup of her fifth marrige. For quite some time I had been intrigued with Babs Hutton as the subject for a biographical article. What intrigued me about her was the fact that for three decades, ever since the day she received twenty-five million dollars from her Grandpa Woolworth's estate, Babs had managed to make her existence increasingly miserable.

When I was a boy in St. Louis, our family plagued by the Depression, there were two women whose moneyed exploits made life seem less dreary—Barbara Hutton and Gloria Vanderbilt. They were constantly in the newspapers, but even though our family lived in that one drab hotel room and I often went without dinner, I did not resent these super-rich young women and their profligate escapades—in fact, I equated them with film stars. There was solace in the fact that such living was still possible even though it was a never-never life for me except in fantasy, but as a deprived boy I fantasized a lot.

There was a big Woolworth's on the corner of Kingshighway and Delmar that I passed every day on my way to and from school, and the sidewalk was often filled with Woolworth sales-

CHOICE PEOPLE

girls carrying picket signs that read: MILLIONS FOR BABS, No NICKELS FOR US. Sign-carrying was endemic to the Depression; the unemployed didn't have any money for newspaper ads, there was no unemployment insurance or welfare, so they paraded the streets with signs, such as MECHANICAL ENGINEER, FATHER OF 4, WILL DIG DITCHES, ANYTHING; WE ARE STARVING, I NEED WORK; JESUS FINDS JOBS. I liked walking the streets to look at the signs (at the same time looking in the gutters for cigar bands for my collection), but I especially liked the signs carried by the Woolworth salesgirls, who sometimes sang songs while they picketed. One that I remember was sung to the tune of "Mademoiselle from Armentières":

> Barbara Hutton's got the dough, parlez-vous,
> We know where she got it too, parlez-vous.
> We slave at Woolworth five and dime,
> The pay we get is sure a crime,
> Hinky dinky parlez-vous.

All through those Depression years, the courtroom trials, marriages, divorces, and social high jinks of Babs and Gloria were steady grist for the tabloid mills, and grist too for my constant fascination with these poor little millionairesses. You never knew what outrageous or unexpected thing they would do next. Lavish parties, impetuous love affairs, court squabbles with relatives—the real-life counterpart of the movies. I recall how impressed I was with a poem that Barbara wrote when she was fifteen, which was printed in the St. Louis *Globe-Democrat:*

> Then when my soul you have garnered
> This harvest of ecstasy,
> Go gathering dreams that are tarnished,
> To fashion a crown for me.

I had proposed Barbara Hutton for a personality piece to a magazine that was all for it, but the Woolworth heiress was not. I have before me a slightly yellowed, handwritten letter dated August 30, 1952, mailed from the Royal Hawaiian, on the Beach at Waikiki, Honolulu, Hawaii: "Dear sir: The Princess Troubet-

218

skoy has received your letter, for which she thanks you. The Princess prefers you not to write any article about her. Thanking you for the Princess, Faithfully yours, M. Latinis."

Prince Troubetskoy was Barbara's second prince and her fourth husband, whom she had divorced the year before I received that letter (she had married Porfirio Rubirosa in the meantime), but symptomatic of her marital neuroses, she was still pathetically referring to herself as Princess. But receiving that letter did not dampen my interest in someday writing about Barbara, and eventually my perseverance paid off when I used the same method that had worked with Frank Sinatra—direct contact. I decided that I should go to Tangier, which is not all that far from Rome, and try to see her there.

This was my first trip to Tangier, an ancient city on the tip of North Africa, directly across the Strait of Gibraltar from Spain; I was delighted to find that the main part of the city was under French domination, so that hotels, restaurants, cafés, shops were a fine Arab-French blend. The Hutton Palace, however, was in the Kasbah, an old Arab section of the city. I didn't have the telephone number nor could the concierge of my hotel get it for me, so I wrote a note and went to the Kasbah to deliver it. Barbara had just gone through a painful dissolution of her fifth marriage, to the Dominican playboy Porfirio Rubirosa, and I thought the timing propitious for her to indulge in a little soul-searching.

The palace was of exquisite Moorish architecture with an inviting courtyard, but when I approached the entrance I was immediately stopped by a burly man, bearded and fezzed, who wordlessly moved in front of me, blocking my way. I handed him my letter; he looked at it, nodded, but kept his position. I had no alternative but to back off and depart; leaving a letter with my name, my hotel, and the purpose of my visit had worked with Hemingway, as I now hoped it would work with her.

But it didn't. I heard not a word from her although I did once fleetingly see her on the main boulevard riding with her chauffeur in a white Rolls-Royce cabriolet. My concierge said he couldn't help me because the princess rarely came to her palace and no one knew anything about her movements around the city or who her friends were, if any. I was fascinated with native life in the Kasbah, and I prowled the souks in endless absorption, but I never saw a glimmer of her.

On the evening of the third day, I conceded defeat and booked a return flight for the following morning. I was sitting at the bar of the hotel, sampling a new drink recommended by the barman, when a page came up and handed me a note; it read: "Sir, at the rear of the room, the woman in a white dress sitting alone is the woman you inquired about. The Concierge."

I paid my bar bill and walked toward her table, but the same bearded Goliath who had stopped me at her palace now materialized in front of her table.

"Your Highness," I said, trying to speak around the bulk of the bodyguard, "I'm the one who wrote you about an interview. I've come all the way from Rome to see you and it would be very kind of you to talk to me for a few minutes . . ."

The bearded hulk began to move forward, forcing me backward, but Barbara said: "It's all right." The bodyguard sullenly let me pass. As I approached the table, I got my first good look at her and I was stunned to see how dry and emaciated and fragile she looked, her narrow face suffused in a tragic mask, her body as thin as melba toast, prominent collarbones protruding starkly from the low neckline of her white silk dress; her dark eyes, arched by thick eyebrows, magnified by the sunken hollows above her pasty cheeks; her thin lips enlarged with bright lipstick.

"Thank you," I said.

She gestured toward the chair beside her, her hand as thin as a sparrow's foot. She couldn't have weighed more than ninety pounds. Only her jewelry looked healthy—twin emerald rings loose on her fingers, a matching emerald bracelet, pearl earrings, and on her breast a diamond clip in the shape of a four-leaf clover. She was only forty-four years old, but she looked ten years beyond that.

Considering her resistance to my many advances, I expected Barbara to be curt and uncommunicative, but to my surprise she seemed to welcome this opportunity to talk. She was drinking Cinzano with soda, rolling the glass between her palms as she spoke. She talked to me for almost two hours, and she came the following afternoon and spent another two hours, but she never invited me to the palace, nor did I see her anywhere but in the bar of the hotel.

When she came to our second meeting, she handed me a piece of paper on which there was a quotation by the Indian poet Rabindranath Tagore: "That which ends in exhaustion is death, but the perfect ending is endless."

"I am not exhausted," Barbara said.

I asked her if she had resented being called "the poor little rich girl" all of her life. "I hate to be called that, I hate it," she said. "In what way am I poor? I have always been extremely rich. Poor in morale? Unhappy? Well, of course I go through my unhappy times like everyone else. Maybe even more than others because God showered me with money and beauty and if He had made it easy for me on top of that, why, I would have turned into a monster. No, of course, I'm sometimes unhappy and I don't pretend to be happy when I'm not. I'm not happy now, but it isn't because I'm rich. How silly to say money brings unhappiness. Naturally being handed twenty-five million dollars when you're young puts a burden on you but most people scoff when you tell them that.

"But all this money has nothing to do with me. My grandpa made it and now it will pass along to my son, Lance. I don't have anything. What do any of us really own? The Indians know the truth; that we are nothing. Imagine pitying me as a poor little rich girl. That's ludicrous. What is it that I want from life? Just to be able to live for a moment, breathe for a moment, be happy for a moment. Is that such a crime?"

HOTCHNER: But you haven't been able to achieve that happiness, have you?

BARBARA: No, no, I haven't. Last night I went to bed early, and I lay there thinking about certain moments in my life. Our talk yesterday set me to thinking about the things that really hurt me. When I was twenty, I was really in love. He was my age, a Yale honor student, from a good family but not much money. I loved him so, and we were talking about marrying, but one night—and that's the moment I was thinking about—he told me that since I was going to inherit fifty million on my twenty-first birthday, it just wouldn't work out. I'd have all that money and he'd have nothing and it scared him to be in a relationship like that. So he dropped me.

HOTCHNER: Did you try to convince him otherwise?

BARBARA: Oh, yes, I certainly did, but his mind was made up. My money was a curse and I knew it—some men afraid to marry me because of it, others after me to get their hand on it.

HOTCHNER: Prince Mdivani was one of the latter, wasn't he?

BARBARA: Of course I knew Alexis was interested in my millions but I thought that he also liked me for myself. How wrong I was! On our honeymoon, our wedding night, he came to our stateroom—I had booked the entire deck of an ocean liner—I was already in bed in a new seductive nightgown Schiaparelli had made for me—and he sat down at the foot of the bed and looked at me in a cold, almost hostile way. He was smoking a cigarette and he just sat there looking at me. Finally he said: "You are too fat."

A truly terrible shock. We had made love many times before we got married, and he had always told me how much he loved my body, how sexy I was, all that, and then to hear him say that on our wedding night. "You are now the Princess Mdivani," he said, "and you must look like a princess. There is nothing more ludicrous than a fat princess." I pulled the covers up around me. Alexis said I would begin the following morning on a diet of black coffee and that I would get nothing else to eat. Any other diet, he said, would take too long. He watched me like a hawk. I had nothing but black coffee for two months and I lost forty pounds. I did look better slimmed down like that but later on, when I had serious medical problems, my doctors said it all began with Alexis getting on me like that with his diet.

HOTCHNER: Do you have any fond memories of your time with Mdivani?

BARBARA: Well, he made me a princess, and I liked that. I don't know why, but ever since I was a little girl I wanted to be a princess. He was sophisticated and worldly, Alexis, and some of that rubbed off. But the only real moment, besides our wedding night, that sticks in my memory was the cable I received the evening I married Count Haugwitz-Reventlow. We were at a big dinner, our wedding party, when the cable came: PRINCE ALEXIS MDIVANI KILLED IN AUTO ACCIDENT. I was too upset to stay at the table. He was such a negative influence on my life, he even managed to ruin my new marriage.

HOTCHNER: And Reventlow?

BARBARA: He gave me the most joy and the most pain; the joy was the birth of my son, Lance, after I had been warned by my doctors that I had a condition that made it dangerous for me to have a child. But then I did something foolish. I let Reventlow talk me into renouncing my American citizenship to become a Dane because the inheritance tax in Denmark would be in Lance's favor when I died if I were a Danish citizen. But when we divorced, I was a Danish wife in a Danish court, where the laws are loaded in favor of the husband, and Count Reventlow was awarded two million dollars of my money and custody of my child. That afternoon in that court was just about the worst. . . .

From then on, I only got to see him two months in the summer. When I was married to Cary Grant, we tried to keep him in Beverly Hills beyond the two months, but Reventlow kidnapped him and took him back to Denmark.

HOTCHNER: Tell me about your marriage to Cary Grant.

BARBARA: We hated each other's friends. One Christmas I gave a dinner for my closest friends and he deliberately humiliated me. We were opposites. He wanted to stay home all the time, and he refused to dress for dinner. But in the beginning we had our share of laughs and he taught me to play tennis.

HOTCHNER: He was the only commoner, wasn't he? Two princes and one count.

BARBARA: Yes, but titles really didn't mean all that much to me. I would have married Prince Troubetskoy even if he hadn't been a prince, but two weeks after we were married he told me that he had only married me for my money. He treated me like a cash register. As for sex, he never laid a hand on me.

HOTCHNER: How much did you give him?

BARBARA: To divorce? One million, five hundred. But that's when I became so seriously ill. That long time in Switzerland when the doctors told me I was at the end. I underwent four major operations, and only weighed ninety pounds when I got back to America. I spent another two years in an American hospital.

I asked Barbara why, after such abysmal failures, she continued to rush into marriages. "For one reason—loneliness. But I am not complaining. I have had happiness, and I may have it again. I think it is far more moral and decent to divorce a man, if your lives together become a torment, than to stay married and have lovers by the score, even children by a man other than your husband. I see this constantly in European society, and I must say I prefer our American way. I think it is more honest. But as for true romantic love—it has vanished from the face of the earth."

I asked her what she was looking for in a man. "Just two things," she said. "He should be a gentleman and he should be tender." And what qualities do you most admire in a woman? I asked. "Well," Babs answered, "I'd say most of all she should be compassionate, then she should have *finesse, délicatesse*—excuse the French, I find it hard to translate."

HOTCHNER: Your next husband was the Dominican playboy Porfirio Rubirosa . . .

BARBARA: Rubi had great charm, and he couldn't help it, I suppose, that every woman wanted to bed him.

HOTCHNER: Is it true that you gave Rubirosa a divorce settlement of two million for his ten weeks of marriage?

BARBARA: I wish it weren't, but, yes, it's true.

Barbara had come to Tangier to try to recover from this demeaning divorce from Rubirosa. She was lonely and miserable, and talking aloud to me probably had some therapeutic value for her. As for my reaction to having met her after such a long pursuit, I found myself surprisingly and disturbingly disoriented. I had just spent two hours with the richest woman in the world, but not as Hotchner, the grown-up, but as Big *A* little *a* r-o-n, the twelve-year-old kid who lives inside him. The kid who refused to leave that St. Louis hotel room for fear of being locked out for nonpayment of rent. The kid who would always feel the terror of those days and nights in that parched prison, the water and electricity cut off, the sadistic bellhop Ben prowling the corridor, taunting me through the transom. The kid who found an old copy of the *Woman's Home Companion* in the back of the closet, with pictures of young Barbara Hutton in a formal white satin gown, a coronet of diamonds in her hair, being presented to Queen Mary at the Court of St. James's. The kid who in that same issue cut out a luscious roast beef and ate it, and then, for dessert, ate another cutout, a picture of a Betty Crocker chocolate cake, in a vain attempt to assuage his hunger pains.

And now in Tangier, the kid had sat with this glamorous millionairess of the *Woman's Home Companion* and, fantasy dissipated, he had found her to be a sad, pitiable woman who despite her exterior emeralds was actually more poverty-stricken than the kid had ever been. Though our lives were worlds apart, we had shared a fake fantasy, and it was with that baffling realization that I had gone to meet her in the bar for our second encounter. She had changed her jewels, but the pathos was immutable.

She drank Cinzano and soda, as she had the day before, and she told me she felt a little better for having talked to me. "It was a little like talking to a psychiatrist," she said; it was the first time I had seen her smile.

"Have you been analyzed?"

"No, but I know what it's like."

I told her that in the process of talking to people about her, I had had a discussion with a friend of mine, Dr. Edmund Bergler, who was a New York psychiatrist. "Would you like to hear what he said about you?"

"Will I be upset? I am already upset enough. I looked in the mirror this morning and saw how ugly I've become. There are times I really *look* at myself."

I told her that she'd find Dr. Bergler's observations about her interesting, and I read his remarks from a notebook I took from my pocket:

"A very rich girl has three possibilities:
She can marry a normal man who loves her for herself, she can marry someone so rich he doesn't care about her money, or she can marry a playboy who has been attracted by her money. Let's consider these three possibilities:

First, that she can marry a normal man exists only in theory, for such a man knows that he cannot live a normal life when he is married to so much money. It would be impossible for him to carry on his own business or profession, for earning money would be meaningless. And a man who must carry on a regular career can't be partying all the time and traveling constantly to fancy resorts all over the world.

"Second, the very rich man who loves her would be her only real chance of happiness, but he is hard to come by. Barbara Hutton found him in Cary Grant, and she admits that that marriage came closest to making her happy.

"Third, the playboy and fortune hunter is about all that is left to her. So she enters marriage with him, hoping that despite her money he will learn to love her for herself. It is usually a hope against hope.

"Now bear in mind that a rich girl is as likely to be neurotic as a poor girl, and Barbara Hutton would appear to have her share of neuroses. She apparently has a subconscious need, common to her type, to be kicked around; perhaps it stems from a guilt feeling over having so much money while others have so little. But remember this—-money does not create a neurosis, it only aggravates it. In other words, a lot of women of ordinary means might behave like Barbara if only they had her money to express themselves."

She sat for a while, looking down at her drink. Finally, she looked up and asked whether she could have a copy of what I had just read to her.

I asked her if she thought she would marry again.

"I now say no, I've said it before, five times, five mistakes, five terrible disappointments, but then the loneliness or whatever it is sets in and it's a compulsion, like a drug addiction, a compulsion to do it to myself again. They are after my money, I know it, Dr. Bergler is right, but I hate the money, I *hate* it—it was put on me like a curse. I don't have to worry do they love me for myself or my money—it's for my money. Nobody ever loved me for myself. Even Cary liked the whole idea of being married to the richest woman in the world. If I had not had Grandpa's millions, do you think Cary Grant would have given me a second look? Or Alexis or Curt or any of the others? They were fortune hunters and I was a title hunter, so we were all hunters—it's a standoff."

"Why does a title mean so much to you?"

"They bow, they curtsey, they kiss my hand. They don't do that if you're nothing but super-rich, only if you are a princess or a countess, a somebody. Look at me now—I have my millions, but what good does it do me? What am I? I recently discovered what Barbara means. It's of Greek origin and it means a stranger, a wanderer, a seeker. So true too. And a little sad. But I am glad that I discovered it. You know what I would like to have been if I hadn't had all this money given to me? A dancer. I would have *loved* being a dancer. That's why I like bullfighting. I like it because it is a beautiful dance with death in color."

She paused and looked down at her thin, fragile hands. "I am a dreamer and a poet," she said in a soft voice. "That is my tragedy."

A few years after I saw her, Barbara became a baroness again by virtue of her marriage to the redoubtable tennis-playing aristocrat Baron Gottfried von Cramm, upon whom she settled three million dollars when they divorced.

Her seventh marriage was to an itinerant artist she met in the Tangier Kasbah, whom she had invested with the title of Prince Doan Vinh Na Champassak, thereby making herself a princess for the third time. His divorce dowry was four million.

That was the final marriage, and the final divorce. She lived the last years of her life in virtual seclusion in the Beverly Wilshire Hotel, her health in decline, and tragedies assailing her. The only people she saw were members of the Woolworth family, but she was buffeted by a succession of their deaths. And then there was the tragedy of Porfirio Rubirosa, who was killed in an automobile accident, as had been Alexis Mdivani before him.

But the worst blow by far was the death of her son, Lance, in an airplane crash, the shock leaving Barbara with paranoidal delusions—that she was being held in the Beverly Wilshire by her enemies as a prisoner, enemies who bugged her phones and read her letters and stole her money.* She constantly wore as much of her jewelry as she could so "they" couldn't get their hands on that too.

Barbara suffered a heart attack in that Beverly Hills hotel room and died at age sixty-six, deserted and alone, just as she had always feared.

---

*The same persecution furies that assailed Hemingway and drove him to suicide.

14

Van Cliburn's Finger and Bette Davis' Jaw Have One Thing in Common

There is no life lonelier than free-lancing. Sheepherders have their sheep, monks have their fellow monks, lighthouse keepers have their wireless, but the free-lancer has no connection with any person, organization, or thing, animate or inanimate, of the outside world. I knew a free-lancer who had written for magazines and television for twenty years, but when the poor fellow died in his apartment last December, he wasn't discovered until March, when his neighbors began complaining about the odor.

The only respite from this lonely, pitiable existence is the writer's agent, but not *any* agent, only one who truly cares about the free-lancer he represents. Such an agent, of which there are shockingly few, is the free-lancer's bridge to the outside world, his confidant, salesman, banker, advisor, protector, chastiser, encourager, discourager, pacifier, inciter, and, in a quasi-religious sense, his conscience. Too often, unhappily, the free-lancer's agent is not so caring, and in fact only becomes interested in his client when he has produced something that will generate a large income on which the agent can levy his 10 percent. His greed is boundless and he lusts after "package" commissions, which he gets when he represents all the parties involved in a particular undertaking. This is called multiple representation and the writer is invariably low man on that totem pole, as I can attest, for at this very moment I have discovered that I have been represented duplicitously by a William Morris television hustler who supposedly represented me in the sale of a book of mine for television but whose sense of morality would bring a blush to the countenance of a veteran White House spokesman.

But the caring, honest, sensitive agent does exist and I had the good fortune of having been represented by one of the most noble of this breed, a lady named Audrey Wood. Her specialty was the theatre, and although none of my theatrical ventures ever made much money for her, she was undaunted in her resolve on my behalf. She was a petite, courtly, Southern-bred woman whose acumen had discovered and nurtured the playwriting souls of Tennessee Williams,* William Inge, Robert Anderson, and innumerable other talented playwrights. She cared about your psyche, your marriage, your bank account, your health, your very being, and if you were wronged by one of the Broadway titans, she tore into him like a tigress defending her young. No matter that she was offending a theatrical power with whom she would have to deal in the future, with Audrey her client's welfare was always uppermost of hers.

Whenever I saw her, which was not often enough, she gentled my frustrations, my piques, my discouragements, and invariably lifted my spirits. In a profession noted for disasters, she was the town crier of optimistic tidings. She cared equally about young playwrights trying to get a leg up, and old playwrights trying to rekindle their spirits. She was the Sarah Bernhardt of agents.

My first play, with Audrey Wood as my agent, was called *The Short Happy Life,* and it was loosely based on several characters in Hemingway's short stories and novels. The setting was the African plain as described in *The Snows of Kilimanjaro,* and the

---

*It broke her heart when, toward the end of his career, Tennessee abruptly took on a new agent and terminated his relationship with Audrey, a relationship that encompassed *The Glass Menagerie, A Streetcar Named Desire,* and the rest of his memorable plays. What makes it truly sad was that Audrey was probably the most meaningful woman in Tennessee's adult life, the only woman he embraced.

leading character was an amalgam of several Hemingway heroes. In the last year of his life, 1961, it became obsessively important to Ernest that this play be produced, as well as a motion picture based on my Nick Adams television play, which Twentieth Century–Fox wanted to make. With Audrey's help I found a director for the play, Frank Corsaro, an actor for the lead, Rod Steiger, a designer for the intricate set, Jo Mielziner, a composer for the music, Bernardo Segall, and all the other people necessary for a production, including Columbia Artists, which booked a tour for us that began in Spokane, then moved to Seattle, San Francisco, Los Angeles, and which was destined to play guaranteed dates touring across the country, ultimately opening on Broadway at the Ambassador Theatre.

By the time we got to San Francisco the play was doing fine, but Steiger wasn't. We never knew from one night to the next what Rod's interpretation of his role would be. One night he'd play the part like Marty, the character from the Bronx he portrayed on "Playhouse 90"; another night he'd be Laurence Olivier or John Wayne or Alfred Lunt or Ernest Hemingway himself. Frank Corsaro, an even-tempered, patient man, tried to deal with Steiger in a rational, controlled manner but Steiger was disdainful and abusive, and Corsaro's best efforts to try to get him to settle into a defined performance only exacerbated Steiger's abusiveness as he railed at Corsaro in front of the rest of the cast, using what he probably regarded as "star" language.

Rod also acted in a surly and superior manner toward the two actresses with whom he played his important scenes—Nan Martin and Salome Jens. His behavior was undoubtedly provoked by the fact that their performances were receiving better notices from the critics than his; in fact, Nan, who was brilliant in her role as his wife, on more than one occasion was snarled at by Steiger *during* a scene; he would spit criticism at her, *sotto voce,* in a transparent attempt to disrupt her performance.

When we reached the Huntington Hartford Theatre in Los Angeles for our final two-week engagement prior to our national tour, Corsaro, on the brink of a nervous collapse, was counting his days until he left the production to go to Chicago, where he was slated to begin rehearsals for Tennessee Williams' *Night of the*

Iguana. * We had taken off a week in San Francisco to rehearse new scenes I had written, but cajoling Steiger through these rewrites had taken its toll on Frank. Steiger bucked and bleated at the new material, and along with Frank I spent endless stultifying hours with him, listening to his bombastic invectives while coddling his temper and inducing him to rehearse new scenes.

"The whole thing about Steiger is nerves," Frank concluded charitably. "He's insecure about the part, and all this abuse can be attributed to self-doubt. You see, Steiger does okay when he can hide behind a disguise—the fedora and cigar of a gangster, the dresses of a transvestite, the madness of Rasputin, whatever, but in this part there is no disguise, and Rod cannot handle it." I felt that was only part of his problem; in his successful movie roles, such as Marlon Brando's brother in *On the Waterfront*, Steiger had performed with effective restraint, but the stage seemed to provoke a melodramatic, bigger-than-life response from him, as if the artificiality of bombast gave size to his performance. If Corsaro had been a stronger, tougher director, he might have been able to counteract Steiger's bullying pretension, but as it turned out it wouldn't have been worth the effort, because in addition to the Steiger menace, we had an economic problem: Jo Mielziner was Broadway's leading set designer, and the set he had designed and built for the show was stunning but highly impractical for a traveling company. If we had been scheduled for the traditional couple of tryout weeks in Boston, followed by a Broadway opening, the set would have been accommodated by our budget, but moving it across the country for a series of play dates which paid fixed amounts made it too costly for us.

On our opening night in Los Angeles, the new material worked very well and gave the play the style and cohesiveness we had been striving for. Also, Steiger gave precisely the kind of performance that Corsaro and I had been urging upon him,† with the result that we received excellent reviews, and two weeks of full houses.

---

*Not knowing he was going from the Steiger frying pan into the Bette Davis fire.
†But his performances during the run were as vacillatory as they had been previously.

But the success in Los Angeles did not alleviate the economic problem we faced in trying to tour a show whose income would exceed its expenses. It was at this point that Audrey Wood, having kept abreast of all these developments, announced that she was flying out to the Coast. When I picked her up at the airport and saw her small, calm form emerging in the arrival area, an archangel dispatched from above, I felt confident that with her by my side we would find a solution, both to Steiger's obstreperousness and our economic dilemma.

Audrey studied our budget and concluded that since our income was fixed at an amount that was in excess of our expenses, we could survive only by reducing the expenses. Thus, all royalties and salaries would have to be reduced if the show were to survive. Corsaro and I waived all our royalties, and the actors held a meeting, as required by Equity, to vote on our proposition that they take a 20 percent reduction in pay. Harvey Lembeck was the Equity deputy for the company, and he reported that the cast had voted unanimously in favor of the pay reduction but that Steiger had not attended the meeting.

I went to see him in his dressing room prior to that evening's performance, which concluded our Los Angeles engagement. I explained that Corsaro and I were giving up our royalties for the tour's duration and that the cast had consented to a 20 percent pay reduction until we opened in New York. I asked him to take a similar reduction; his salary was by far the largest on the payroll and his 20 percent would allow us to balance our budget.

"I should say not" was his response. "I am a star and I must be paid as a star."

I turned on my heels and left abruptly to repress an overwhelming urge to bust him in the mouth.

During that evening's performance, I discussed the situation with Audrey. To cancel the tour at that late date would entail penalty payments to the theatres involved, but that loss would not be as great as going ahead with the tour.

"In my heart, Audrey," I confided, "I don't want to have anything further to do with Steiger. He has made a nightmare out of what should have been a pleasurable creative experience, and neither I nor the rest of the cast have any respect for him as an actor or as a man. What I'd truly like to do is close down the show and take the consequences."

"Then that is what you must do, Hotch," Audrey said. "The pity is that it's a good play now and just might make it on Broadway, but let's not go against the grain of integrity for the sake of Mr. Almighty Buck."

So, at the conclusion of that evening's performance, I called the cast together and told them that without Steiger's participation the show could not go on. Then I went to Steiger's dressing room. His wife of the moment, Claire Bloom, was with him. "I've just told the cast that the show is finished, Rod," I told him. "Fifteen actors and actresses are now out of work because you have to be paid as a star. If we had paid you what you were really worth, you'd owe *us* money."

As I departed, Steiger slammed his dressing room door behind me, rattling the wall, his ranting voice pursuing me as I walked down the corridor. It took me six months and a lot of sweat to pay off the bills I had incurred by that cancellation, but I was grateful to Audrey for giving me the courage to do what I had done. Integrity is never cheap.

Altogether, that was a terrible month for me, the blackest of my life: my father and Hemingway had died within a few weeks of each other, and then *A Short Happy Life,* as a requiem, shortly afterward.

Not long after the Steiger debacle I received a call from Audrey, who was known for her compassion for her playwrights in the aftermath of precipitous closings.

"This is afield from the theatre," she said, "but I have just been visited by a young man, sent by a doctor friend of mine, who has a very compelling story that I'd like you to hear. I think it's something you may want to write about."

"What's it about?"

"Have you been reading in *The New York Times* about Dr. Max Jacobson?"

She was referring to a series of exposés about an East Side practitioner who shot up the rich and famous with speed laced with a variety of other ingredients. She asked if the subject interested me. Of course, I told her. It was fascinating.

"Well," Audrey continued, "this fellow who came to see me, Harvey Mann by name, was a patient of Dr. Jacobson's, beginning at age fourteen, got hooked, eventually went to work for him when he was twenty. Mann is ready to tell everything: his own story, which, believe me, is frightening and terrible, as well as what he knows about all the people whom Jacobson treated while Mann worked for him—from President Kennedy to Truman Capote."

I said I'd certainly like to meet him, for my writing interest in speed went back to 1955, when I wrote the first major magazine article about the new "epidemic" drug, amphetamines, which at that time were referred to as "thrill pills" and were being popped by teen-agers all across the country. In connection with that article I had interviewed Harry J. Anslinger, then commissioner of the Federal Narcotics Bureau, along with other experts, all of whom had agreed that speed was a terrible menace but not in the category with heroin, hash, and the like because, as Anslinger stated, "amphetamines are nonaddictive and do not inflict withdrawal problems on their users." Of course, in the intervening years it had been discovered that of all drugs used, speed was probably the most perniciously addictive and its withdrawal pains and convulsions even worse than those inflicted by heroin.

I was further interested in the subject because over the past few years I had sorrowfully watched the steady amphetamine disintegration of a dear friend of mine, Charley Lederer, a well-known playwright and screenwriter who lived in Beverly Hills. He was a stylish man of wit and charm and considerable talent, who started using amphetamines on an occasional basis to get him "up" for writing, slowly became addicted to the extent that eventually he was no longer able to function at all, and finally had to be attended by a nurse who injected him at regular intervals.

Charley was married to the actress Anne Shirley, and the living room of their attractive home was always filled with movie colony cronies and New York refugees who played bridge and pinochle and chess and exchanged repartee with Charley. In league with the writers Ben Hecht and Charles Brackett, Lederer staged elaborate practical jokes* and gambled on outrageous athletic events. One of Charley's more spectacular bets involved tennis. There was an agent in Hollywood named Jack Cushingham who had once toured the pro circuit with Pancho Gonzales as his doubles partner. Jack and Charley had made many tennis bets—obstacles placed on Jack's side of the court, Charley to begin each game at 40–love, Jack restricted to Charley's singles court while Charley could hit anywhere on Jack's side of the net. Charley had lost all of them.

But Charley was determined to devise a tennis match at which he could best Jack, and his devious mind eventually produced his master gamble, the great elephant match which has become a Beverly Hiils legend. The ground rules were simple enough: they would play each other's singles courts, Jack's handicap being that he would be attached with an eight-foot chain to the leg of an elephant. The match was limited to one set, and it was to take place at the Beverly Hills Country Club, with five hundred dollars and an appropriate trophy as the wager.

By the day of the match, interest in the event had become so widespread that tickets were sold for charity, and Jack Benny had been named the umpire, with other Hollywood stars as linespeople. Five hundred spectators packed the grandstand. A section of the fence had to be removed to admit the elephant, which was of medium size and wore a tennis visor.

Jack felt confident that he could win his serve with aces, but he had trouble at first with the elephant, which swung his trunk and trumpeted ominously every time Jack raised his racket to serve, causing him to fault. But Jack and the elephant eventually worked out a *modus vivendi* and the match tensely followed serve, Charley's game plan being to keep the ball beyond an eight-foot radius of the elephant.

At 5–all, with a five-point tie breaker in effect and the score

---

*Many of their practical jokes were directed at their agent, Irving "Swifty" Lazar, who was noted for his clothes fetish. An entire wall of his bedroom was occupied by an elaborate walk-in closet, which contained a hundred suits in shades of blue and shoes to match. While Swifty was away in New York on business, Lederer and his co-conspirators gained access to his apartment and had the closet wall plastered over and wallpapered, thus entombing Lazar's entire wardrobe.

at 2–2, a cataclysmic and totally unanticipated event occurred: the elephant, either out of nervousness or spite, relieved himself, and when an elephant relieves himself on a tennis court, he covers a large area of the playing surface. Jack Benny took one horrified look at the yellow stream cascading across the court* and the endlessly mounting citadel of dung, and announced that the match was terminated and called a draw because of circumstances beyond his control. And then, not able to resist so obvious an opening for a comedian, he added: "I think we all agree that this has been a pretty shitty tennis match."

Although the bet was a standoff, the trophy—three feet high with an elephant on its summit, rampant trunk holding a tennis racket aloft—wound up in a place of honor on Charley's fireplace mantel.

It broke my heart to watch amphetamine addiction eat away the fiber of this vibrant man. On one occasion, the phone rang in my New York apartment at an ungodly hour, awakening me. It was Charley. He was in New York on his way to Philadelphia to do some doctoring on *Man of La Mancha,* which was breaking in there,† and he was desperate because he had run out of amphetamine spansules and could not face his chore without them. He asked me for the name of a doctor who would give him a prescription. I tried not to, not to contribute to this awful addiction that was slowly destroying him, but his anguish, his supplication was too terrifying for me to deny him.

In his final days, Charley would sit in a warm bath all day long, not able to eat or sleep or speak coherently, his body a skeleton draped with loose flesh, the surface of his skin too painful to touch anywhere, constantly searching for any place on his body where it was still possible to insert an amphetamine-bearing needle.

So, yes, I said to Audrey, I would certainly like to meet this Harvey Mann, to see if perhaps this would be a dramatic and

---

*One linesman was trapped in a corner and had to be ferried across like a flood victim.

†The show was in trouble but Charley saved it by suggesting, among other things, that they eliminate the intermission.

effective way to expose speed and the Mephistophelian speed doctors, who quietly and legally speed up the lives of their patients, faster and faster until many of them spin out of control. Speed kills, all right, totally and partially, and affects more people—from dieters to mainliners—than all other hard drugs combined. Harvey Mann might be a way to tell the story as it should be told—from the inside out.

Harvey Mann, late thirties, tinted glasses, theatrically dressed, black cigarette in holder, effeminate in manner, very bright, sharp recall, not organized but stream of details. Involvement with Dr. Jacobson began, he told me, when he was fourteen years old. Harvey acted regularly on television. This particular occasion he was in the cast of a live "Studio One" television drama being directed by Yul Brynner. Harvey contracted a bad cold. Air time was just two days away. "Listen, kid," Yul Brynner said, "go see my doctor, Max Jacobson. Tell him I said he has to get rid of that cold." Yul had first met Jacobson when they were both acrobats in a European circus.

Harvey went to Dr. Jacobson's office that afternoon. The waiting room was crammed with people, some of whom had been there for hours. They all knew one another. It was like a club. Over the years, stagestruck Harvey was to spend interminable hours in this waiting room, with the likes of Marlene Dietrich, Van Cliburn, Alan Jay Lerner, and Bette Davis.

Finally, Harvey was summoned into Dr. Jacobson's office. He was immediately struck by Jacobson's physical presence—powerful man, enormous trunk, huge steely arms, but paunchy, white shirt covered with blood blotches, where veins had spurted on being injected. Dirty fingernails. Dirty white shirt, sleeves rolled up. Heavy German accent, hard to understand, spoke five or six languages. Looked piercingly at Harvey, commanded him to sit down. "The way he looked at me, his voice, the whole thing, I just felt," Harvey said, "I was in the presence of God." Jacobson didn't examine him. (In all the ensuing years, Harvey never saw Jacobson examine any patient, new or old.) But he told Harvey he was much too fat, which he was, informed Harvey he was going to make him "look like an actor," and immediately injected him. Jacobson filled the hypodermics from a variety of colored glass jars that ranged around the shelves, one needle for each buttock, and the third shot directly into a vein in his arm. No Band-Aids on the puncture marks. Just a command to return the following week.

Harvey returned. And returned. And returned. With ever-increasing frequency. At this time he naïvely thought that he was being injected with vitamins, and that's what made him feel so energized, and why he lost weight so fast. But as time went by he began doing poorly at school, and he wasn't getting as many parts in television.

"How do you know about his practice?" I asked.

"Two ways: first, I spent the better part of my days hanging around Max's office. Secondly, when I was twenty I went to work for Max part-time, then when I was twenty-two he offered me a full-time paying job. He had me injecting patients—me, with absolutely no training of any kind. I prepared the mixes for the injections, and often injected patients myself. At first I gave both intravenous and intramuscular injections, but there was one occasion when I was giving an intravenous injection incorrectly, and luckily the nurse happened to see it and stopped me before I had injected air into the vein. After that I only gave intramuscular shots.

"I worked seven days a week, got an injection every day that kept my weight down so I certainly looked much more attractive, but what it did to me as an actor was that it gave me three times more energy than I needed so I always came on too strong at auditions, pushed too hard, and my throat was forever dry. I looked great but I wasn't getting any work as an actor. Max said that was because I wore glasses. He hated glasses, *hated* them. He yelled at me that I didn't need them, that he could cure my eyesight with shots. Max thought he could cure anything with shots. Once, after giving me shots, he tore off my glasses and broke them, telling me that I could see now, that my eyesight was cured. Of course that was ridiculous—without glasses I was Helen Keller.

"Sometimes he sent me to work in a laboratory he maintains in Brooklyn. I helped prepare some of his new, experimental stuff, like an extract from the glands of an electric eel, and an extract made from the bone marrow of beef. He tried them both on me—the marrow shot caused me to break out in sores like cigarette burns all over my body; the eel injection hurt painfully for more than a year, caused me to run a high temperature, and left me feeling numb in my hip.

"I also made up batches of the cream Max used to sell. It was composed of Nivea cream, vitamins, and all the leftovers of whatever was injected into patients that day, including hormones and what not. I mixed it all up in a Waring Blendor and sold an enormous number of those jars at forty dollars a throw. Max prescribed it for all kinds of skin conditions, from acne to cancer. We used to call it Max's chicken fat."

I asked if he had proof of his employment. He showed us carbons of income tax wage forms that had been sent in by Dr. Jacobson. No doubt he worked there. Our meeting lasted two hours. The more details we sought about Dr. Jacobson and his famous patients, the more Harvey impressed us with his knowledge of those details. Van Cliburn, for example: "When Van first came to Jacobson, he was playing piano at Asti's in the Village, the restaurant where the waiters sing arias. Van was suffering badly from colitis. Max in that godlike way of his took him over. No matter what a patient had when he came to Max, hangnails to cancer, Max was confident he could cure it. And his cure for all of them was injections that had speed in the mix. So he shot up Van and started him coming on a regular basis. He charged him little or nothing during those years when Van was a student at Juilliard. Max had a lot of creative people whom he'd carry during lean times. Max really didn't care all that much about money. What really mattered to Max were all these people being totally dependent upon him. In his office Max was king, physically dirty but dynamic; what comes to mind is Yul Brynner's portrayal of the king—for all I know, Brynner may have patterned it after Max.

"Anyway, his office was his stage, and with that needle in his hand he was emperor. Out of his office and off that stage, Max was zero, really nothing, which is probably why Max literally worked twenty hours a day. Almost any hour of the day or night, if you wanted a shot Max was there to give it to you. I sometimes came to Max's waiting room at two, three in the morning, and there'd be twenty people sitting around, waiting their turn. You see, speed people can't sleep. They're high all the time, really zipped with energy, and the big thing was not to taper off from that, because Max's injections set you up twice as high as anyone else's, but if you dropped off of that, it meant your lows would be doubly low. You can't imagine the blackness dropping down from a high like that. You'd go for two, three days, then Max would give you a strong downer that would really knock you out so you'd sleep for a day solid. But some people, like Marlene Dietrich, just maintained a level and the hell with sleep. You can't imagine the energy it gives you. You've got to keep doing things, scrubbing floors, anything.

"The injection itself gives you a hot initial flash; the needle actually feels red-hot going in and you get a reaction in your testicles just like an orgasm, your testicles feel hot as hell, your feet rise off the ground, you feel like you're in heat, like you could have multiple orgasms. It's the calcium-niacin combination gives you that and it's no wonder those injections hooked all of us.

"Well, to get back to Van, by the time he made it big with his Russian performance, Max really had him hooked on injections. In fact, when Van went to Russia for his second concert, he took Jacobson with him. It was very funny what everyone went through trying to get a visa and ticket for Max, all those people working on it, and then Dietrich came in one night and made one phone call and the visa arrived the next day.

"After the Russian concert, Van returned to New York for his Carnegie Hall recital. The day of the concert, he developed some kind of infection in the cuticle on one of his fingers, and he went to Max to have it treated. I was working there then. Max put a needle into the infection and injected it, then coated the finger with collodion, which is a substance like airplane glue. Van got through the concert all right, but by the time he got to his dressing room that finger, which had been puffy to begin with, was now the size of his wrist. It was a frightening sight, this sausagelike finger on the hand of this great young pianist. Van's manager rushed him to the Hospital for Joint Diseases, where an emergency team of surgeons went to work on his finger. Later on, Van told me that the head surgeon had said that another hour or so they might have been forced to amputate the finger.

"But you know something? A week later Van was back in Max's office getting his regular shots."

At the conclusion of our meeting, I made arrangements with Harvey for another meeting, just the two of us, to which he would bring notes, documents, whatever, and a list of all those well-known people who had been injected by Jacobson during the years Harvey was in the office.

Harvey came to that subsequent meeting with three shopping bags full of material, plus an index card box that went *A* to *Z* through Max's celebrated patients. I thumbed through the cards, pulling names at random: Cecil B. de Mille, President John Kennedy, Tennessee Williams, Otto Preminger, Lee Radziwill, Andy Williams, Eartha Kitt, Hermione Gingold, Senator Claude Pepper, Ludwig Bemelmans, Jackie Kennedy, Pablo Casals, Gertrude Lawrence, Sheilah Graham, Margaret Leighton, Katherine Dunham, Burt Bacharach, Montgomery Clift, Hedy Lamarr, Maurice Chevalier, Eddie Fisher, Elizabeth Taylor, Truman Capote, Alan Jay Lerner, Prince Radziwill, Mike Nichols, Johnny Mathis, Zero Mostel, and on and on. As we went over each of these names, Harvey would tell me which ones had turned against Jacobson and denounced him, and which ones were still his loyal defenders. I pressed him for details about these people, and his recall of incidents, names, places, actions, and reactions was excellent.

HOTCHNER: Were you working for Dr. Jacobson when he was injecting President Kennedy?

MANN: Yes. Several times I carried his black bag when he went to the Carlyle Hotel. In the bag that I carried were various bottles and disposable syringes that I put there at Jacobson's direction. Of course, I knew what was in them and afterwards I could tell, by looking at the bottles, just what Max had injected into the President of the United States. I was in Max's office on several occasions when he was talking on the phone with Kennedy. It excited Max that he had such an "in," such power with the President. There was this one occasion when Kennedy came to New York to address the United Nations and he had laryngitis. He sent for Max, who put a needle right into his throat and injected into the President's voice box. It improved his voice and Kennedy gave the speech all right. Later, Max told me with great satisfaction: "I've never given an injection like that before." He really thought he could cure anything with his magic needle.

HOTCHNER: Is it true that when President Kennedy went to Vienna for the summit conference, he took Dr. Jacobson along?

MANN: Yes, absolutely true. Max flew in the presidential plane. I can give you all the details on that.

HOTCHNER: And to your knowledge Jacobson gave Kennedy injections in Vienna, during the conference.

MANN: I can prove it.

HOTCHNER: This card you have here on Bette Davis, it indicates that Jacobson wasn't very successful with her.

MANN: Well, I've told you how Max felt he could cure anything with his God-given needle. When Bette Davis first came to him she had an inflamed jaw that Jacobson assured her he could treat with injections. She came for almost a year, but her jaw didn't get any better. In fact, eventually it got worse and she finally went to see another doctor. That year with Max had delayed proper treatment to the point where an operation had to be performed, quite a serious one, that necessitated removal of part of her jaw.

HOTCHNER: You've told me about the ravages of speed addiction. Did any of these patients die as a result of amphetamine poisoning?

MANN: Yes, some died, and some, like myself, almost died. Mark Shaw, the photographer, for instance. It was he who brought Jacobson together with Kennedy—Shaw was a Kennedy intimate who took a lot of pictures of the Kennedy family. I can document what happened to Mark. I knew him well. I was working there during his visits. I know how many vials of amphetamines and disposal hypodermics Jacobson gave him so that Shaw could inject himself when he was traveling. I have copies of the first medical reports that list his death as due to heart trouble, then the autopsy reports that proved that what he really died of was the wholesale presence in his body of amphetamine.

HOTCHNER: What about Jacobson's own family? Did he inject them?

MANN: Of course. You must understand that everyone in Max's world was on speed. The real story of Max and his family was his relation with his second wife, Nina, and their daughter, Jill. I spent a lot of time in Max's apartment. I was virtually one of the family. I got to know Nina very well. Nina was Jacobson's second wife, whom he met when she came to him as a patient when he was practicing in Europe. A woman of Garboesque beauty. When she came to Max she had some kind of paralysis in her legs. Max injected her and dominated her, in that way of his, and eventually she regained use of her legs. But she also in the process became addicted to the amphetamine mix Max was feeding her. When their daughter, Jill, was born, after they came to the United States, she had inherited this disposition toward amphetamines from her mother, and Max began giving her injections virtually from birth on. But let me concentrate on Nina. She was an artist, a truly lovely woman, well bred, intelligent, and the tragic, slow death which I observed her suffer had a profound effect on me. At the time she died she was as thin as my finger, wasted away, a terrible tragedy.

HOTCHNER: What about Dr. Jacobson himself?

MANN: If you mean does he inject himself, it's been going on for so many years Max is hard pressed to find a vein in his body that he can get a needle into. They're all collapsed. Shot out. I've seen him give himself injections on the backs of his hands, on his feet, and I can tell you those are really painful places. Max injected me on my hands several times and I screamed with the pain of it. Max literally injects himself every couple of hours, all kinds of things. I guess it's been going on for thirty years. He never sleeps. I mean properly, in a bed. Just little nods, dozes. There was the time he was giving me an injection and fell asleep with the needle in my arm, for God's sake! Another time, I came in the kitchen and there he was with the refrigerator door open, leaning against it, sleeping.

HOTCHNER: Tell me about your own experience with speed. What happened to you physically from the time you started with Dr. Jacobson?

MANN: Well, what happened to me eventually, after all those years of accelerated injections, was that one day I really began to come apart. I couldn't stop crying. I couldn't sleep, I hadn't slept for God knows how long, and I just kept crying morning, noon, and night. My mouth was desert dry, my breath stank like a fetid trench, I was taking dramamine and Tigan to fight the nausea. In desperation, I went to see Dr. Edmund Ziman, who was Zero Mostel's analyst. I told him I wanted to kill myself, sitting on his damn couch crying, I told him I didn't want to live. He said he knew of no one with less to live for—you know, trying that reverse psychology on me, giving me permission to kill myself, but that kind of game doesn't work with me.

I went home and called my parents and sister and told them I was going to the Hamptons to visit friends. I changed all the locks on the door, took a bottle of ice-cold vodka from the refrigerator, and emptied a bottle with two hundred sleeping pills into a Steuben crystal peanut bowl. I got in my big brass bed and began swigging the vodka and popping pills. Three days later, my worried sister drove in from the country and got the police to knock down my door. She hadn't believed my story about going to the Hamptons. They found me in bed unconscious, covered with my own vomit, and my body a mass of huge open sores like someone had tattooed me with lighted cigars. I was in a deep amphetamine coma and when they got me to the Lenox Hill Hospital I was declared dead on arrival.

But they kept working on me in intensive care and for forty-eight hours I was in a deep coma, barely this side of death. They kept me in intensive care for seven weeks, then three months with nurses around the clock, followed by almost five months in the hospital plus four months in therapy. I had no feeling in my legs, my body sores took forever to heal, and my face was completely paralyzed on one side—the doctors thought I had Bell's palsy until they realized that all my troubles came from amphetamine poisoning.

It took me over a year to get my legs back to normal, but the first thing I did on getting out of the hospital was to go to Max for a shot to help me get over the terror of dying. I called Phoenix House for help but they said to call back later on in the week because they were in the middle of a riot. I went back to see Dr. Ziman, just to tell him that I had more to live for than he did. I wanted to quit, to get clean, I really did, but one year later I was more hooked than ever.

One evening I went out with a friend of mine and two pretty girls who were models. We had a nice dinner at "21", then on to the Rainbow Grill, where I drank a lot of champagne. Max had given me a shot that afternoon and I had some Lotus pills with me that I mixed with the champagne and that really drunked me. I have no memory of leaving the Rainbow Grill. I woke up in a cell in the Tombs surrounded by a bunch of Bowery drunks. I found out later that my friend and the two girls had become disgusted with my drunkenness and had gone off and left me. I must have staggered out and somehow managed to get down the street to the Ziegfeld Theatre, where I pulled the fire alarm.

During the night in the Tombs I had screaming withdrawal pains, sweats, and uncontrollable twitching. I wound up in the hospital again, and Max came to visit me several times and gave me injections.

HOTCHNER: Did the hospital know what he was doing?

MANN: Of course not. They were treating me for amphetamine poisoning and he was shooting it back into me. When I was discharged, I got some vials of amphetamines from Max and some disposable syringes and I went to Nassau. I don't know why I chose Nassau—I can't rationally account for much of what I was doing then. I bought a couple of bottles of rum and checked into a seedy hotel, where I injected myself with speed and drank rum; I took sleeping pills at night but they didn't have any effect. I finally left my room, really zonked, and I fell down the stairs of the hotel and broke my collarbone and three of my ribs. I was able to get on a BOAC flight back to New York and went straight to the Lenox Hill Hospital. I phoned my parents and told them I had been mugged. I was ravaged, as far down as you could go, down below the human level.

In another couple of months, I'm sure I would have been as dead as Mark Shaw and Nina and some of the others I haven't told you about, if it hadn't been for a freaky streak of luck. I had met a girl at a party. A terrific girl, but she had a problem as big as mine—she was an alcoholic. I guess it was the old kindred souls thing, but I really cared about her, got involved, first person I had related to in years. I wanted to try to help her cut down on her drinking. Me, a speed freak, trying to help an alcoholic. Well, one day I got out of the subway to go to a party on East Sixty-second Street, and I passed a church where there was a sign that Alcoholics Anonymous was meeting there. I went in, thinking I'd get some literature for Pamela, try to get her there. There were a lot of people in the church, not Bowery bums, but chic, East Side people, a few of whom I knew from Jacobson's waiting room. There was a young man speaking to the group. He was telling them about his speed addiction, and as I listened, it could have been me up there. Well, I stayed right on, and from that day to this I've not popped a pill or had an injection. AA has been a miracle for me. At first, they had people staying with me twenty-four hours around the clock, you know, the classic AA treatment. But for speed addiction! There are quite a few of us in our group. I found I could substitute our AA group for Max's waiting room. For the first time in years my head is clear, I know who I am. But I have a lot of mending to do. I'm still unused to a life without the crutch of Max's injections. After all, that's all the life I had for more than twenty years.

HOTCHNER: What are your feelings toward Dr. Jacobson now?

MANN: Well, I'm the one who tipped off *The New York Times* and started them on their exposé, but I have no animosity toward Max Jacobson. I really haven't. I honestly believe he thinks he's doing good, that he's helping people, and he still has a lot of patients who swear by him. He's not in it for the money, he really doesn't earn all that much, and he works eighteen-hour days. No, I think it's an obsession with Max, to improve people's lives with injections. He believes he can cure anyone with his magic potions shot into their veins—cripples, cancer victims, multiple sclerosis sufferers—anyone. I'm not out to even a score with Max. I just wish I had never laid eyes on him.

I never wrote about Dr. Max Jacobson or Harvey Mann, nor anything more about the amphetamine menace, because I found out that charges against Jacobson were pending before the Board of Censors of the New York County Medical Society. I spoke to the doctor in charge of the investigation and he asked me to forbear writing about Jacobson until their hearing was completed. Which I did, but it proved to be a long, interminable wait, fourteen months of *in camera* hearings before a five-doctor panel, involving eleven counts of professional misconduct and fraud. I inquired why the hearings were taking so long (Jacobson continued practicing medicine all that time) and I was told that the inordinate length was directly attributable to the fact that Jacobson's lawyer, Simon Rose of the Louis Nizer firm, had prepared one of the best defenses the Board had ever encountered. There were four thousand pages of testimony and exhibits, and over ninety witnesses were heard, most of them former or current patients of Jacobson.

In the meantime, Jacobson continued his Mephistophelian ways. One of his prominent victims was Tennessee Williams, who shortly before his death frankly described his experience with Jacobson:

> Someone I loved very dearly and who really created a life for me had died. I plunged into a profound depression. It went on for several years. I only went out after dark, and then just to the deli to get a box of spaghetti, which I boiled. I wouldn't even have sauce on it. I don't know why I bothered.
>
> Then one of my publishers said something had to be done. He took me to Dr. Max Jacobson. His intention was very benign. I don't think he knew that Dr. Max was going to give me so much speed, enormous amounts of speed. I would get into a taxi to go home, and I would feel as if my heart was going to stop before I reached home. I would plunge right to the typewriter, and I would lose myself. The shots so accelerated my writing, I would get to the point of a sentence and then stop and leave the character in midair. That's the way people talk anyway.
>
> Gradually the mind began to become disoriented and wounded to a degree. Not permanently, I trust. I was committed to a snake pit. It really was a snake pit. My brother's excuse was that it was the only mental hospital close to where he lived. It was rough coming out of it.
>
> To come down from speed, I had to take powerful medication. It induced the most marvelous hypnosis. I would see Our Lady next to my bed. She would occupy a rocker next to my bed. I would drift off to sleep with her rocking. I was never sure I was going to wake up the next morning. Now I don't worry about that much.

Finally, two and a half years after the hearings had started, the decision was announced on the front page of *The New York*

Times under the headline JACOBSON LOSES LICENSE. "The New York State Board of Regents revoked today the medical license of Dr. Max Jacobson. The New York City physician for years used powerful amphetamine stimulants to lift the moods of patients, many of them well known in politics, the theatre and the literary world, in his East Side practice.

"The unanimous action of the Board, culminating nearly 2½ years of investigation, found the 75-year-old physician guilty of 48 counts of unprofessional conduct in eleven specifications and one count of fraud; that he endangered his patients' health with his amphetamine injections, that he misrepresented his activities to drug suppliers, and that he manufactured 'adulterated drugs consisting in whole or in part of filthy, putrid, and/or decomposed substances.'

"According to the evidence one of his patients, Mark Shaw, a photographer, died from amphetamine poisoning and a number of other patients became psychopathologically dependent on the drug."

Harvey Mann had suffered heinously from his psychopathological dependence but he had the ultimate satisfaction of knowing that by triggering this investigation he had deterred others from being victimized as he had been.

15

Jimmy Durante Don't Want No More Rawreggs

When asked what he thought was the most important prerequisite for becoming a writer, Hemingway used to respond: "An unhappy childhood." I agree, and the next most important thing, in my opinion, is total recall. An unhappy childhood and total recall are an unbeatable combination.

Of course, the talent that shapes and colors the lump of memory is something else again, but rhythms of speech, how things and people looked, the emotional sting of events, the slashes of cruelty, the awkwardness of failed love, the little deaths of disappointments—all those fragments that have caught on the spikes of memory are a good writer's stock-in-trade. Without strong recall, a writer is only a journalist, recording the day's events.

My strongest recall is for speech. In my mind's ear I can hear the precise words of people I knew, their inflections, their special vocabulary. I can sit and listen to my friend Hemingway anytime I want to, hear him tell his favorite stories, relisten to angry outbursts, moments of wisdom, words of keen advice. People who do not have a conversation trap in their memory do not understand those who do; remembered speech is so much better than taped speech because memory filters out the inconsequential and leaves only nuggets on the panning screen.

But other facets of my memory prism are not as polished as the one for speech, and I sometimes suffer lapses that annoy me.

For days now, I have been trying to recall how and when that dear man Jimmy Durante came into my life. Not because of a writing assignment, I'm sure. Well, however he and I met, it was a felicitous moment for me, for it brought one of the most natural and enchanting men I have ever known into my existence. He'd phone me whenever he came to New York and I'd phone him whenever I arrived on the Coast. When Jimmy asked how you were, he really and truly wanted to know. He radiated love, and everywhere he went people wanted to hug him—in fact *did* hug him. People from every walk of life. Cabdrivers would leap from their taxis, matrons from their limousines, elevator girls would stop between floors, construction workers hop down from scaffolds.

After spending some time with Jimmy, I'd go away with a glow of well-being, charged by his enjoyment of life, his mala-propped *esprit,* his unabashed affection for everyone he met. No resentments, no anger, no jaded rebuffs, no celebrity preening or pouting, just a little man with a big nose handing out samples of his heart.

Jimmy was important to me, for he was around during a time when I felt creased and furrowed by a dissolving family life, when I was one of the sheep who had momentarily lost their way, and I was feeling like that when Jimmy called me one morning on one of his frequent visits to New York.

"Hotchner, you are warned, Durante is in town and he will brook no delay in your gettin' your freckled ass over here."

"Jimmy! Goddamn, Jimmy! You at the Astor?"

"In the bridal suite—but wudja believe, wit'out a bride!"

"Why you here?"

"I gotta do a TV special on NBC. Whyn'cha hang around—it's gonna be fulla livelihood."

It was noon when I knocked on door 476 of the Astor Hotel. A few seconds later, Jimmy appeared. He looked worried.

"Hello, Hotch, how d' ya feel?" he asked in his sandpaper voice. "Come on in. We're huntin' the glasses."

In the living room of the suite, a man was turning over the sofa cushions and feeling along the creases at the sides. Jimmy went over to the piano and began to shuffle through the stacks of music disarrayed on top of it.

"How d' ya like that!" Jimmy said. "Had 'em on m' nose just a minute ago. I'm blind wit'out 'em."

"I got a friend has a seeing eye dog," the man searching the sofa said. "I'll ask him to lend it to you."

"There y' have it!" Jimmy said, slapping his right thigh with the palm of his right hand, "give a piana playuh dialogue and it kin only lead t' insubordination." The sofa searcher went into the bedroom and Jimmy stood in the center of the living room, reflecting, his nose pointed at the ceiling. "I had 'em on when I answered the phone," he mused, and then he closed his eyes and concentrated.

The search for the glasses must have interrupted Jimmy in the midst of dressing for he was wearing a brown sleeveless sports shirt with the word "Jimmy" sewn in white thread across the pocket, a green felt hat, white underwear shorts, brown socks, and tan shoes. He was chewing a cigar. "Jules! They're under the covers!" he said suddenly, and strode into the bedroom.

Jules came in and put two bottles of yogurt and Jimmy's glasses on the coffee table. "Where was they? Where'd y' find 'em?" Jimmy asked delightedly, putting them on his nose the better to see the yogurt.

"They were in the icebox," Jules said, "next to the yogurt."

Jimmy nodded, as if this made good sense to him, and began to eat the yogurt. "Wouldja believe it, Hotch," he exclaimed, "f' thoity-two years I always ate two rawreggs for breakfast, never missed oncet, ev'ry morning the rawreggs. Then one mornin' I stops. Just like that, I stops. I'm hungry but Durante don't want no more rawreggs. So my housekeeper out in Hollywood says, try yogurt. T' please her, I samples a mout'ful and spits it in the sink. But finely it gets me. Now yogurt's as incontestable as the rawreggs."

"Tastes like wallpaper," Jules remarked.

"This guy," Jimmy said, pointing with his yogurt spoon, "if sumpin' ain't got spaghetti sauce on it, he don't like it."

The door opened and Jimmy's manager, Lou Cohen, a one-armed man with a kind, sad face, came in, followed by a waiter pushing a room-service cart.

"Julie's knockin' the yogurt again," Jimmy complained to

Lou, and in the same breath he said to the waiter: "How's the missus, Tony?" The look on Jimmy's face showed that he really cared.

"We won't know until later on today," Tony said sadly.

"I'm gonna say a prayer right after breakfast," Jimmy said, and Tony thanked him and left. Before Jimmy could explain the nature of Tony's wife's ailment, the door swung open and Eddie Jackson, Jimmy's inseparable pal and member of the immortal team of Clayton, Jackson & Durante, rushed into the room.

"Don't touch that breakfast till I sample everything," he announced in a voice trained to carry to the back of the balcony. "CBS is so jealous they'd do anything, anything!"

Jimmy laughed as only he can laugh, his mouth, eyes, forehead, feet, and hands joining in the laughter. "That Eddie," he said lovingly, "whata sense of humor!"

"This television special's got me so upset," Eddie Jackson said to no one in particular, "I put on two neckties this morning."

At the phone Lou said: "There's a Mr. Wechsman downstairs. Wants to see you."

"Wechsman? Do I know a Wechsman?" Jimmy asked, and drawing a blank, he said: "Ask where he's from."

An NBC publicity man and two photographers came in, and Jimmy said: "How's it right here against the door, Phil?" Phil said that looked okay and the photographers started to get their cameras ready.

"He's from Passaic," Lou said.

"Who?" Jimmy asked, as he struck a characteristic pose for the cameramen.

"Wechsman," Lou said.

"I don't know no Wechsman from Passaic," Jimmy said. "Tell him to come up."

The photographers took their shots and Lou announced that Jimmy's car was waiting downstairs. A barber and a manicurist came in and began to arrange themselves around a chair in the living room. Two men from the William Morris Agency rushed in with contracts which they said had to be signed by four o'-clock. "I don't sign nothin' I don't read," Jimmy said, "and I can't read 'em now, I'm late f' Brooklyn." Lou handed Jimmy his hat and the whole room began to move toward the door.

A little man holding his hat in both hands stood in the doorway. Jimmy came face to face with him. "I'm Mr. Wechsman," the little man said.

"Who?" Jimmy asked, taking off his glasses.

"Wechsman," the man repeated slowly.

"Where y' from?" Jimmy wanted to know.

"Passaic," Mr. Wechsman said.

"Glad to know anybody from Passaic," Jimmy said, and started forward.

"The American Cancer Society sent me," Wechsman said, unhappily. "I took all those pictures yesterday afternoon."

"Oh, sure!" Jimmy said. "I shoulda reconized ya. It's just I got a problem wit' faces."

"The American Cancer Society wants to thank you for all you've done, Mr. Durante," Mr. Wechsman said, feeling a little better.

"That's fine, pardner, that's fine," Jimmy said. "Want to come t' Brooklyn?"

As Jimmy entered the elevator, he noticed that the elevator girl was crying. "Honey! Honey!" he exclaimed. "Dis will nevah do!" He took out his handkerchief. "Blow!" he commanded. She told him that she had just been fired, whereupon Jimmy stormed out of the elevator, sought out the hotel manager, chatted with him amiably for a few minutes, returned to the elevator, and rang the bell. "It's okay," he told the girl, pinching her cheek. "An' I gotcha a two-dollah raise."

The trip to Brooklyn was being undertaken on behalf of an old friend who was opening a neighborhood television store. As Jimmy's car turned into DeKalb Avenue, we were suddenly faced with a huge crowd of people being restrained from flowing into the street by thirty mounted and dismounted policemen.

In front of the Regency Television store there were cries of "There he is!" and the crowd surged toward Jimmy like a large conclave of affectionate cousins, everyone seemingly intent on squeezing Jimmy's hand, arm, shoulder, or midsection, the police trying to form a shield for him.

"Lou got angry 'cause I go t' Brooklyn on a busy day like

this," Jimmy said, "but m' friend needs me an' you know the sayin'—'A friend in need is a friend in need.'"

At the entrance to the store, while photographers clicked away, Jimmy was given a scissors with which he cut a piece of white ribbon that had been strung across the doorway. The store was packed with people who were as intent on squeezing Jimmy's anatomy as the people on the outside. Many old friends, some of whom Jimmy had not seen for as long as twenty and thirty years, came up to greet him and he was flabbergasted at seeing them. "Barney!" he shouted. "Barney! Why, he usedta run the store next to ma pop's barbershop! . . . If it ain't Coney Island Phil! Why, I ain't seen ya in twenny-five years. How th' hell are ya?"

Coming back from Brooklyn, Jimmy said: "The little bizness is the collarbone of America. Only guy who kin open a big bizness t'day is some guy who embezzled some money or up-sconded wit' it."

Jimmy rushed into the International Theatre for his television rehearsal, greeted the cast loudly, walked up to the orchestra leader, and proclaimed: "Just my luck t' get an or*ches*tra leader wit' hair!" He slapped his thigh. "All the vi'lins, go home!" he commanded.

"Gentlemen," the orchestra leader said, "there are three rhythms for this song—a fast rhythm, a slow rhythm, and a Durante rhythm, so please, *please* watch me."

"Ya better mark it Andante Durante," Jimmy said with mock seriousness. Then he said with real seriousness: "Look, Lou, all I ask, don't hit me wit' a foreign thing in the ear. Make the music blend."

Jimmy worked hard at the rehearsal. "Nobody realizes," Jimmy said, "that I woik eighteen hours a day fer a solit mont' t' make that TV hour look like it's never been rehoised."

The following day, Jimmy had a lunch date with Eddie Cantor, and he barged into Lindy's, the Broadway restaurant, with the air of a man who has exactly thirty seconds to spot his train and catch it. Jimmy ordered apple pie and milk, and Eddie had sour cream and radishes. They talked about the good old times on radio and the perilous times on television.

"This television swallahs ya up," Jimmy said, mournfully.

"Whaddya mean?" Eddie exclaimed. "Why, you got all those wonderful songs. You can go on forever. Every once in a while you add a new song. It's like a big rice pudding, so you drop in a raisin now and then. Old people like the old songs to remember and the youngsters like to discover them. The hell with Lindy's and the Brown Derby—it's the living room that counts."

" 'At's right, Eddie, I remember when Clayton, Jackson and Durante first went on the road. We was knockin' 'em dead in the Noo York nighteries so we go into Minneanapolis knowin' we'd be stupendjous. What happens? We have rigid mortis. Dat's how dead we are. What does Minneanapolis care if Broadway can't do wit'out me?"

"Minneapolis is more sophisticated today," Cantor said.

"Sure, sure, but one thing the comic's got to know. He can't be bitter. Not ever. Not about the critics, not about the audience don't laugh at a joke, not about no noosepaper big-jig. If the audience don't laugh atchur joke, it ain't their fault, it's yours. They wanna laugh. They come t' laugh. So give 'em anudder joke, an' if dat don't get 'em, give 'em anudder. Be cheerful— 'at's what counts."

"Lemme tell you, Jimmy," Eddie said. "Ida and I were watching your last show, sitting in our living room. All through it, Ida'd say: 'Oh, I could hug him!' They'd come in close on you. 'Isn't he darling,' Ida'd say. The program's over. The phone rings. It's one of my daughters. 'Couldn't you just squeeze him?' she says. See what I mean, Jimmy. *You* don't have to have the greatest gags ever written. And you know why? Because television, more than anything I've ever been connected with, demands heart. You know it in a minute on that TV screen if a guy's got it. And Jimmy, you're the luckiest guy ever walked because your heart is on your face."

They walked out with their arms linked while a waiter looked down at the table in amazement. James Durante remains the only man in Lindy's memory who eats the crust and leaves all the apples.

The dress rehearsal began at two o'clock and everything went wrong. Jimmy forgot his lines. The orchestra played too slowly. The scenery didn't move fast enough. Filled with misgivings, Jimmy called a meeting on the stage "to thrush things out."

"I don't think we hit 'em right in the op'ning," he said. "Whadabout he just comes in straight wit' his indemnification mark?" Jimmy always refers to himself in the third person when discussing his performance. Everyone assured him the opening was fine. "Okay, but I needa joke in the barbershop scene. Whadabout I say I juss took a horseback ride. The instructor says: 'Listen, Jimmy, all you gotta remember is when the horse goes up you go down. When the horse goes down you go up.' So I tries it. I gets on the horse. When the horse goes down, I go up. But when I came down—the horse was gone!"

Jimmy slapped his thigh and everyone laughed. "Lou Holtz gimme that joke twenny years ago," he said. "One more thing —in that part where I tear the shirt off'n the guy's back—it's a good joke but it ain't f' me. I don't like them kinda jokes. If he does it t' me it's okay. But don't make me no aggressor. Nevah!"

The cast was dismissed for an hour and Jimmy came down into the unlighted theatre and lowered himself wearily into a seat next to me.

"I been rehoisin' for a solit mont'," he said, "an' now, at the last minute, I gotta put m'self ina hands of strangers. S'funny business, this. Th' guys what woik the cameras show up when ev'rything's set an' tell ya it can't be done. Aw, this televising'll swallah ya. I usedter go one whole year ina sketch and I'd complain if they made us change it on the third go-round. What I got? Eight, ten routines? I dunno. I can't jus' sing a song or tella joke. It's the bizness 'at counts, th' bizness. An' I ain't gonna pad out wit' no acrobrats or jugglers. I'm gonna give 'em Durante. Dat's muh contract wit' da people."

Although Jimmy wasn't aware of it, Emerson once said: "The perception of the comic is a tie of sympathy with other men." Durante's tie was secured with a double knot. He really cared about every human being he bumped into during the course of each rowdy day. He was delighted when one of his friends turned up with a problem; whatever that problem was, Durante suffered through it as if it were his own.

On one occasion, when he was in Las Vegas, a pal phoned at 3 A.M. and said he had lost all his money shooting dice and was about to pawn his most prized possession, a ring his mother had given him.

"Don't! Don't!" Jimmy shouted, and three minutes later he appeared at the swank gambling casino in his robe and slippers. "Here's four thousand dollars I happened t' have in m' pocket," Jimmy said. "Gamble that but gimme the ring fer safekeepin'."

At four minutes after eight, James Durante settled his hat on his head, plunked a cigar in his mouth, and strode mightily onto the stage to the strains of "Start Off Each Day Wit' a Song." Durante never walked; he stormed forward. As he put himself in motion, his shoulders and arms pitched forward, his head formed an advance unit with the nose well in the lead, his mouth pursed determinedly, his feet thrust themselves at right angles, and as he got up steam, his arms swung stiffly in vigorous approval of the giant strides he managed to take. Actually, Durante's walk was a protest against motion.

Now he was center stage, weaving his rowdy magic, dispensing the boisterous warmth for which he was universally loved. He sang and strutted and mugged, infecting the theatre audience with his hilarity.

The climax of the program was a sketch with Helen Traubel, the Metropolitan Opera's great Wagnerian diva, who was a foot higher and a foot wider than Durante. Mme. Traubel and Jimmy sang a song called "The Song's Gotta Come from the Heart." Mme. Traubel began in a stiff and heavy manner, self-conscious in front of the battery of TV cameras. But Jimmy went to work on her. He pounded his fist in his palm, he exhorted, he shouted with her, he clapped his hands and stomped his foot. Here was the greatest rhythm clown in the world, giving a transfusion of his art.

Mme. Traubel began to respond to his exhortations. So did the orchestra. The number, as they say in show business, caught fire. There they stood on the bare stage, the Met's great diva and the nightclub's irrepressible roughhouse, both caught up in the gaiety of the moment they were creating, their voices fighting the horns, their feet beating in unison, their arms full out at their sides.

And then the climax, with both of them hitting their topmost notes, their faces flushed and happy, Jimmy with his hat held high in the air. And finally the shuffle offstage in a typical Durante windup with the audience going wild and the musicians rising from their chairs and applauding and whistling for they knew they had witnessed a rare moment in the theatre.*

In the wings Mme. Traubel went up to Jimmy, and bending down, she took his face in her hands and spoke directly into it. "I told my husband at dinner last night," she said, "that I get the same sort of supreme challenge from you that I get from Toscanini. You are the Toscanini of the comedians."

The Toscanini of the comedians was scheduled to leave on a midnight train for Cleveland, where he was to perform the following night, but before going Jimmy remembered that he had promised to make an appearance at a dinner party which the New York Guild of Newspaper Women was giving at the Starlight Roof of the Waldorf-Astoria. As he stepped into the crowded elevator at the Waldorf, a man turned to Jimmy and said: "Mr. Durante, I saw you on television and I just want to shake your hand." A lady in the elevator said: "Mr. Durante, I have never laughed so hard in all my life." By now everybody in the elevator was complimenting him and patting him on the back.

Jimmy was startled by this spontaneous outburst and he blushed noticeably. Finally, holding up his hands, he said: "Folks, folks—save them ajecktives—we got thoity floors to go!"

He was in motion the moment the elevator doors opened, and he continued, without breaking stride, right out onto the center of the floor, with Eddie Jackson on his heels. The formal-attired audience burst into applause. He sat down at the piano that was rolled onto the floor for him, and for fifteen minutes Durante and Jackson exploded in a dervish of songs. In a characteristic hoopla ending, Jimmy threw sheet music at the orchestra, and tore the piano to pieces, leaving it in a shambled pile as he and Jackson did a cakewalk exit.

---

*When they recorded the song for an RCA Victor Red Seal record, Mme. Traubel said: "It's a pleasure to record with a great *artiste* whose voice sounds the same with bad needles."

*   *   *

He made the train with three minutes to spare. I urged him to go inside lest he catch cold, but he said: "Aw, them micrabs can't do nuttin' t' me—I'll moider 'em!" He laughed, with his mouth wide open, his eyes enjoying it. Then he grabbed me in a bear hug and kissed my cheeks. "Thanks for everythin'," he said, "I appreciate it."

The train started to move and the people on the platform, waving to departing friends, suddenly brightened when they saw the little man with his familiar, laughing face, moving along in front of them.

The redcaps laughed too and they called out: "Good-bye, Jimmy, good-bye!" One redcap said something to his friend and in so saying wrote Jimmy Durante's epitaph. "There goes a hobo with the heart of a king," he said, and smiling, shaking his head from side to side, he pushed his cart along the platform.

16

Otto Preminger Sits
on a Python

One thing a free-lance writer can count on is the domino effect of accomplishment. One writing assignment leads to another just as surely as the domino of a best seller knocks down a movie sale or a mini series. In fact, the ultimate domino effect is a magazine piece that becomes a book that becomes a play that becomes a movie that then is turned into a stage musical that finally winds up on Home Box Office.

My earliest domino encounter occurred in 1958, the morning after the telecast of *Last Clear Chance,* the "Playhouse 90" with Paul Muni. I received a phone call from Otto Preminger, whom I had met briefly when I had interviewed Sinatra on the set of *Man with the Golden Arm.* Preminger said he had admired *Last Clear Chance* and would like to talk to me about doing a screenplay for him, if I were interested.

I went to see him in his dramatic black-and-white office on Fifth Avenue, the walls covered with Braques and Picassos. Otto had a reputation for being garrulous and abusive but I found him disarmingly Viennese. He explained that he had recently returned from Paris, where he had had the great good fortune of snaring film rights to a new novel by Pierre Boulle. Boulle was the author of a previous novel, *Bridge over the River Kwai;* he had written the screenplay for the film version* that had just won an

_____

*The film version was called *Bridge on the River Kwai.*

Academy Award for Sam Spiegel (at war's end, Sam had re-nounced Eagle for Spiegel). Spiegel and Preminger were old adversaries, dating back to their Vienna days. Friendly adversar-ies. When I got to know him better, Preminger told me about the time, after the First World War, that he and Spiegel decided to leave the privations of postwar Austria for greener pastures elsewhere. They packed their belongings in Otto's automobile and headed for the border, their destination Paris. There were severe restrictions on taking currency out of Austria, with stiff prison terms for those caught at it, so Otto had little more with him than his personal belongings.

But as they approached the heavily guarded border, Spiegel reached in his pocket and took out a huge wad of bills, which he handed to Preminger. "Otto, you were the director of the Vienna State Theatre, an important man, they would never question you, so would you please put these in your pocket because I am not a known person and they are bound to look me over."

"Sam," Otto said, passing back the hot wad as he pulled up at the border gates, "this is your problem, not mine."

Sam just did manage to whip the money out of sight as a customs guard opened the door, took their passports, and told Preminger to follow him to an inspection room. In the inspec-tion room Otto was told to strip, and his clothes were searched for contraband money. "I looked through the slats of the Vene-tian blinds," Otto said, "and I could see Sam in the auto, squirming in his seat, sweating, and I felt a certain satisfaction in anticipating all the trouble he was about to bring down on himself."

The guard accompanied Preminger back to his car, handed him the passports, and motioned him forward. "But . . . but aren't you going to examine him?" Otto asked, incredulously.

"No, if an important man like you doesn't have anything, he wouldn't either."

So in their postwar duel Spiegel started with the advantage of having operating funds, and all through their careers Sam was always one jump ahead of Otto.

They had both done very well with their films, but it rankled Preminger that although he had produced and directed such memorable movies as *Laura, Anatomy of a Murder,* and *Exodus,* he nonetheless had fallen short of Spiegel's two great films, *Bridge on the River Kwai* and *Lawrence of Arabia,* which had also won an Academy Award.

By means of elaborate espionage, Preminger had found out that Spiegel had an option on Pierre Boulle's new novel, but Otto's spies had informed him that with the option deadline approaching, Spiegel had shown no sign of exercising that option. Concluding that Spiegel must have forgotten that the option was falling due, Preminger had flown to Paris, courted Boulle in three-star restaurants, and at the stroke of midnight on the fateful day he had popped a bottle of Dom Pérignon and grabbed the screen rights to Boulle's novel for $300,000, right from under Spiegel's nose. Boulle was delighted with the sale, Otto said, but did not want to write the screenplay for this book as he had for *Bridge on the River Kwai.*

I asked Preminger what the book was about, but he couldn't tell me much since it had not yet been translated and he couldn't read French. He knew it took place on and around a rubber plantation in Malaya but that's about all. He would have the translation in a few days, he said, but since I could read French he suggested that I take a copy and read it over the weekend, by which time he would have read the translation.

It was an exciting prospect for me—my first screenplay, with a director of Preminger's standing, to be based on a book by a writer who had just won the Academy Award. But the prospect dimmed considerably when I got home and started to translate the French. First of all, the title translated as *Ways of Salvation,* and secondly, the text was stiff and disjointed, with one-dimensional cardboard characters and a plot about as exciting and entertaining as an obituary column. It seemed incomprehensible to me that the man who had written the deftly plotted *Bridge on the River Kwai,* with its skillfully depicted characters, could have written anything as banal and insipid as *Ways of Salvation.* I rang up a friend of mine who was steeped in movie lore, and sure enough, he knew all about the making of *Kwai.*

"Spiegel has done it to Preminger again," he said. "The screenplay for *Kwai* was written by a gifted screenwriter named Nunnally Johnson, but since Johnson was on the blacklist, one of the unemployable Hollywood Ten, Spiegel had to cover him over with Pierre Boulle's name. You should get a copy of Boulle's book and you'll see that Johnson didn't have much more to work with than you've got in *Ways of Salvation*—is he kidding with that title?"

When I went in to see Preminger on the Monday following our meeting, he was sitting at his marble desk with his head in his hands. "You have read the book?" he asked mournfully, without looking up.

"Yes. Does Spiegel read French?"

"I guess he does, the son of a bitch."

"Well, I'm sorry, Mr. Preminger—I was looking forward to working with you on this."

Otto sprang to life. An accomplished actor who had performed in many films and plays, primarily playing the part of a villainous German officer, he was demonstrative with his feelings and opinions. "You don't think I am giving up! Can you imagine what a laugh Spiegel would have? And what about all this money I have given to Boulle . . . have you thought of some way we could get a screenplay out of this . . . this . . ."

"Well," I said, aware of what Nunnally Johnson had done, "I can only suggest that you keep the locale and a few of the characters and invent a new story with real, believable people."

"Fine! Exactly! What ideas do you have?"

"I haven't given it a thought, and to tell you the truth, Mr. Preminger, I've never been to that part of the world and I don't think I have the background to invent a story that takes place in the jungles and rubber plantations of Malaya."

"So! I haven't been there either," Preminger said. "Why don't we go together to have a look? You can soak up background and I can look for locations. What do you say? The sooner we leave the better."

He phoned me the following day to report that he had just looked at a map and discovered that Malaya was on the opposite side of the globe. He suggested that we use this opportunity to go around the world. Before we departed, I worked out an outline for the film that involved a spectacular burning of a plantation mansion as its climax. Otto seemed pleased with it.

In London we were joined by a production manager named

Martin Schute. We stayed in London for a few days, then proceeded to Rome, Cairo, New Delhi, Calcutta, Bangkok, Singapore, Kuala Lumpur, Hong Kong, Tokyo, Manila, Honolulu, Los Angeles, thence back to New York. At each stop along the route, the local Columbia Pictures man would await us as we got off the plane, with a sack of local currency for each of us, a chauffeured limousine, and an itinerary for our stay that included all the best sights, restaurants, and meetings with local dignitaries. Otto would accept his sack of currency and go along with the dining arrangements, but he firmly rejected any activity that smacked of sightseeing. He much preferred to spend his time in his hotel suite with a couple of the local beauties (Otto was not married then, although I doubt whether that would have been a deterrent), leaving all the elaborately planned sightseeing trips to me. My only distractions from this exotica were occasional press conferences and Otto's nagging insistence that I come up with a title to supplant *Ways of Salvation* in time for the book's imminent publication in the United States.*

Singapore was still under British domination, a beautiful, tranquil colony. We stayed at the legendary Raffles Hotel, attended the races at the Singapore Turf Club (where one afternoon, thanks to the expertise of Mr. George Song, the manager of the Columbia Pictures office, I picked six winners out of eight races), became temporary members of the Singapore Swim Club, the Royal Cricket Society, the American Club, and just about every other social organization in Singapore. It was the last days of colonial glory, a way of life that exuded Kipling, gentlemen's leather bars, cricket on the esplanade, Somerset Maugham on the veranda, tea in the Raffles garden, polo ponies on the run, four golf courses, a yachting club, with Chinese and Hindu temples festooning the landscape.

In Hong Kong, Otto interviewed a continual stream of Chinese actresses, looking for the lead in our film. I was so enchanted with the city and with the Chinese quarter of Kowloon, with the Peninsula Hotel, where we stayed, with the junks in the

---

*During our flight from Hong Kong to Tokyo, while rearranging my currency, I thought of a title that pleased Otto: *The Other Side of the Coin.*

harbor, the shops and restaurants, and with my guide, Miss Mimi K. L. Sau of the *Chi Yin Daily News,* that I almost jumped ship.

When we arrived in Tokyo, where we had luxurious suites at the Imperial Hotel, we found that the city was in the grips of a *Bonjour Tristesse* look-alike contest.* I accompanied Otto to the cavernous Cala-Za movie house, where, onstage, he presented prizes to the girls adjudged closest in resemblance to Jean Seberg, the star of the film. That was our only chore, leaving plenty of time for other distractions: a geisha party at Ryukotei; falconer- and cormorant-cooked meals; the Sante Baths of the Club Elysee for steams and massages by young beauties with diplomas in the art of Japanese massage; and dinners at the homes of influential Japanese—all of which Otto lustily enjoyed.

As a traveling companion, Otto was affable and worldly, although irascible with those who tried his patience, which was in short supply. He demanded in others his own high efficiency (he boasted that he never ran a day over his shooting schedule), and when inefficient, the transgressor was subjected to Otto's withering temper.

I'll give you an example: not long after our trip, Otto got married and purchased a brownstone that he gutted and remodeled, but the contractor was dilatory and incompetent and Otto burned with impatience as he awaited occupancy while living in a hotel. A few months after he did finally gain possession of his house, I was at a dinner there when the phone rang and the maid informed Otto that the contractor wanted to speak to him.

A saturnine look stole over Otto's countenance as he took the phone. "Yes, yes, this is Otto Preminger . . . yes, Mr. Wilson . . . you want what? . . . Payment on your bill? Well, I'm going to tell you something, Mr. Wilson, I am going to pay you in the same way you did the work here—sl-o-o-wly!"

The focal point of our trip, of course, was Kuala Lumpur, which would be our headquarters while making the film. We had meetings with the deputy prime minister, Dato Abdul Razak, and with various government officials who would be useful when

---

*Preminger's latest film, which had not fared too well in the States but was an enormous hit in Japan.

production would begin. But our most important meeting was with the manager of the Dunlop plantation, where, according to arrangements Otto had made with the head office in Singapore, most of our film would be shot.

The manager of the plantation was a lean, red-bearded Englishman named Hathway, who lived with his wife and child in an exquisite Victorian plantation house, surrounded by formal flower gardens. Just beyond the house, groves of symmetrically lined rubber trees stretched on all sides right up to the edge of the dense jungle. In fact, all the rubber plantations of Malaya were planted in jungle areas that had been painstakingly cleared. Hathway took us on a tour of the plantation, showing us how the natives collected and processed the gummy white sap that dripped from the trees, and giving us a good look at the edges of the jungle where much of the film would have to be shot. The equatorial heat and humidity were stifling.

Afterward, we returned to the welcome shade and ceiling fans of Hathway's living room, where we were served cold drinks for our parched insides.

"My head office has informed me," Hathway said, "that they have made a deal with you whereby you are going to burn down my plantation house as part of your film."

"Yes, that's right," Otto said. "We will build a new one in its place. I suppose the plumbing is bad and all that."

Hathway, who was obviously fond of this graceful mansion with its enveloping verandas and Victorian peaked roofs, said: "No, the plumbing is quite adequate."

"Well, we've agreed on a price," Otto said.

"This house is over a hundred years old, Mr. Preminger, and considered one of the finest examples of plantation architecture."

"That's what makes burning it so spectacular," Otto said. "We will shoot the fire with four cameras. It's the climax of the film."

"I see," Hathway said, while he stirred the ice in his drink. After a slight pause, he said: "You know, Mr. Preminger, you may have some problems with the jungle—making it secure for filming."

CHOICE PEOPLE

"What do you mean, 'secure'?"

"Well, these Malayan jungles are probably the most dangerous in the world."

"You mean wild animals?" Otto asked, nervously straightening up in his chair. It occurred to me then that Otto, the essence of Viennese urbanity, had never before been involved with an outdoor film of this nature. Nor was he the type who had ever borne a knapsack or squatted before a campfire or faced a pair of gleaming eyes in the dark.

"Yes, quite an assortment of wild animals," Hathway was saying, "and snakes."

Otto noticeably blanched. "Snakes?"

"More varieties of poisonous snakes and pythons than any other place in the world," Hathway said. "More iced tea?"

"I have a particular . . . ah . . . concern about snakes," Otto said, weakly. "I mean, it happens to be that snakes . . ." The hand that held his iced tea began to tremble, rattling the ice.

"Well, then, speaking of snakes, you might be interested in what happened here just last year. I had an assistant named Wellfleet, very decent chap who had quite a zoological background and was forever bringing wild things into the compound and caging them up. And snakes. Knew how to handle 'em. Gaboon vipers, king cobras, boa constrictors, and what not. Well, one night, Wellfleet was coming back from a night of catting around in Kuala Lumpur—have you been to the Southern Dance Hall, Mr. Preminger? Quite a place, worth your time—anyway, there's Wellfleet driving back from a bit of debauchery in Kuala when his headlights pick up a big log dead across the center of the highway—or at least what he *thinks* is a log, but when he gets out of the car to move it he discovers it's a python, biggest damn python ever laid eyes on, stretched clear across the road like a giant tree trunk. Python starts to move off but Wellfleet wants to show it off, so he grabs it and swings it into a circle—he knew every snake trick in the book, he did—and got it rolled up neat as a garden hose. Then he took off his belt and secured it with that, rolled it over to the pickup truck he was driving—had a devil of a time lifting it—and drove it back here.

"Well, it was very late when Wellfleet got back here and he

268

was damn tired from his carousing and his exertions with the python, so he simply wheeled it into his cottage and into his bathroom for safekeeping until he could arrange a cage for it the following day. But he overslept and one of the servants came in to clean up and howled like forty banshees when he went into the bathroom, because what had happened was that the python had burst Wellfleet's belt and had gone into the toilet bowl for a drink, slithered down the pipe until it got completely wedged in, and there it was with its great tail thrashing about in the bathroom.

"We tried to pull the python out of the toilet—we must have had four men tugging on its tail—but he was too far down the plumbing. There was nothing to do but have the sewer pipes dug up because by now the python was clogging up the whole system."

"Did you get it out in one piece?" I asked.

"Oh, yes, had to crack open the sewer pipes but that didn't matter. We measured it and found out it was the largest python ever captured. In fact, Mr. Preminger, you're sitting on it."

Otto's face turned ashen as he slowly looked down at the large armchair in which he was sitting. It was indeed covered with snakeskin as was the ottoman on which Otto's polished shoes were resting.

"There was even enough of its skin to make those drapes in the window," Hathway said cheerily.

Otto rose slowly from his chair, being careful to let a sleeping snake lie, and he walked a bit unsteadily toward the door. "We'd better be on our way," he said. "Thank you for your hospitality."

"It was a pleasure," Hathway said. "Do let us know when you're coming with the cameras and all that. Quite the most exciting thing to happen here in fifty years. Life tends to be rather on the tepid side."

I took a last look at the impressive expanse of the armchair, ottoman, and drapes. "Is Wellfleet still here?" I asked.

"No, poor chap," Hathway said. "He was doing some work at the far end of the plantation when a saw-scaled viper slipped into his boot and we just couldn't get to him in time."

"You mean he's dead?"

"Yep, the vipers and kraits are deadly little fellows," Hathway said airily. "We lose a lot of natives to the snakes but Wellfleet was the first one of ours got done in. Pity. Damn good man."

I wrote a pretty good screenplay, but needless to say, Otto never made the movie.

A screenplay of mine that did get made into a film was *Adventures of a Young Man*, which dominoed from my television play *The World of Nick Adams*. As I previously said, the making of this film had become an obsession with Hemingway during the last, chaotic months of his life; he died while we were in the process of making it, and I wish for the sake of his memory it had been better but it was produced by Jerry Wald, a Twentieth Century–Fox hustler whose benchmark was expediency. The film revolved around the youth Nick Adams, who was the protagonist of many of Ernest's short stories, and who was, in fact, a reincarnation of Ernest's own young years. There was an actor named Robert Redford, relatively unknown, who was dying to do the part, and I strenuously urged Jerry to test him, but instead he cast Richard Beymer, the willowy kid from *West Side Story* who was tied to a cheap Twentieth contract, and who was as wrong for the part as wrong could be. Also, my friend George Roy Hill, who had directed *Last Clear Chance*, liked my script and wanted to do it, but again, Wald had a cut-rate commitment from Marty Ritt, left over from some aborted project, and Marty it was; Marty is a friend of mine, a very gifted director, but this was simply not his kind of film, especially the large segment of it that had to be shot in Verona, Italy. Marty's life is centered around attending the Santa Anita racetrack, and he likes to eat dinner at six-thirty, neither of which he could do in Verona. He also had no patience for auditioning Italian actresses for a pivotal role, and instead accommodatingly cast Susan Strasberg in the part, whose contrived Italian accent fell somewhere between Sophia Loren and Goldie Hawn.

The Verona scenes required large groups of extras, many of whom were Americans who came from an American Air Force base that was located just outside Verona. They were members of the families of military personnel who lived on the base, and one of the extras whom we chose was as beautiful as any woman I had ever seen. She was in her late teens, the daughter of an Air Force colonel, and her name was Sharon Tate. Her life had been confined to the military posts where her father was stationed, and she was as fresh and unworldly as Lynn Baggett had been when we first came upon her in her father's drugstore. Sharon was smitten by the glamour of our movie operation, and we were smitten by her innocent beauty, especially Richard Beymer, who enticed her into his trailer to look at stills and never let her go. If only poor Richard could have invested his part with a tenth of the passion he had for Sharon.

Winter fog rolling in from the mountains to the north made photography impossible and stranded us in Verona for weeks on end, during which time Sharon was part of our group which included, in addition to Susan Strasberg and Marty Ritt, Eli Wallach and Ricardo Montalban. Sharon was by then making plans to go to Hollywood with Beymer, to try to make her way as an actress. I asked Marty one evening, while we were dining at the Ristorante dei Dodici Apostoli, if he thought Sharon could succeed in Hollywood, and Marty, noted for his cryptic appraisals, replied: "She could, but she won't."

Of course, she didn't, but years later, reading about the manner in which the Manson crazies slaughtered her, I had an eerie remembrance of Marty's words that day in Verona. Sharon had started to get parts in films and was making a name for herself at the time she married the Polish director Roman Polanski. She was eight months pregnant at the time of her murder. The police had found her body in front of a couch in the living room, on which an American flag had been draped, bathed in the blood from her stab wounds; she had been stabbed sixteen times in her chest and back; and there was a white nylon rope looped twice around her neck, one end of the rope going up to a ceiling beam, the other end trailing across the floor to the body of a man who was lying in a pool of blood. This end of the rope was also looped twice around his neck. This man was Jay Sebring, a prominent Hollywood hairdresser; he had been stabbed repeatedly and shot at close range.

When I was writing the Doris Day book, I came upon a bizarre twist to this macabre massacre: Doris and her son, Terry Melcher, revealed that there was a good possibility that when Manson's crazed followers attacked the Polanski home on Cielo Drive, they had actually come to murder Terry, who had been the previous occupant of the house. He had lived there with Candy Bergen, and had only recently sublet the house to Polanski. Terry was a music producer for whom Manson, who was a self-avowed composer and leader of a singing group, had auditioned. Terry considered the music and the singing "below-average nothing," and consequently did not encourage Manson or see him again, although Manson tried to get Terry to hear some of his new songs.

A short time after the Manson murders, a couple of detectives came to see Melcher, and told him: "We've got a girl in custody who's spilling to us. She was with the group that lived with Manson at the Spahn ranch and she told us that the night they killed all those people—they came there looking for you. This girl says Manson was mad at you because you wouldn't record him. We've picked up some of Manson's people, but there's still a lot of them running around loose. So we've come here to warn you that you'd better get yourself some bodyguards with guns—and for your mother. You're dealing with some genuine crazies here and there's no telling what they might do."

Terry did hire bodyguards, and during that tense period he became increasingly haunted with a guilt feeling that he was responsible for the death of Sharon Tate and all the others because the Manson murderers had really come looking for him. And that meant they would have killed Candy Bergen too. Susan Atkins, one of the murderers, had told her attorney on tape: "The reason Charlie picked that house was to instill fear into Terry Melcher because Terry had given us his word on a few things and never came through with them."

A prosecutor in the District Attorney's office who had interviewed most of the members of Manson's family told Terry: "There was a kid from Texas living at the ranch at the same time, and one day Manson said to him: 'That Melcher, he thinks he's pretty hot shit, but he isn't worth a damn. I can kill him just like that. In fact, it would be better if you did it. I'll give you five thousand dollars and a three-wheel motorcycle—will you do it?' In a panic, the kid wired his mother for money and got the hell away from there."

It is possible that if Polanski had not had the bad luck of renting Terry's house, Sharon Tate would have one day realized her dream of becoming a movie star.*

As time passed, Terry brooded constantly about the possibility that the Manson crazies had slaughtered Sharon Tate in their anger at not finding him in the house on Cielo Drive, and he brooded too over a series of shocking revelations about his stepfather, Marty Melcher, who had just died. The result of all this emotional turbulence was that Terry fell into a deep depression that he tried to counteract with alcohol and drugs. He had an overpowering need to be alone with his guilt. "I broke up with Candy," he told me, "simply because I was determined to be miserable and lonely. I just didn't want anybody around trying to cheer me up. I had gone with Candy since I was nineteen, and the years with her had been very good. I have nothing but glowing things to say about her. Giving her up like that, when I still loved her, was more depressing than anything else. But Candy was someone to look after, to care for, and I was no longer able to do that."

I wondered what effect all this had had on Candy Bergen, whom I admired for the variety of her talent—as an actress, and as a good photographer and writer. An opportunity arose to meet her in 1977, when I was living in Paris, writing a novel, *The Man Who Lived at the Ritz.* A magazine asked me to go to Rome, where Candy was making a film with the Italian director

---

*Although Sharon Tate and Lynn Baggett, both of whom I had helped midwife into show business, had suffered grim deaths, I don't want to give the impression that my interest in a performer was invariably the kiss of death. In casting *A Short Happy Life,* I gave a young actor named Keir Dullea his first stage role; for another play of mine, *The White House,* which ran on Broadway with Helen Hayes, I cast a beginner, Gene Wilder; and for *The Hemingway Hero,* I saw a neophyte actor performing in a Greenwich Village basement theatre and immediately offered him a part—the play he was in was called *Eh?,* and the neophyte was Dustin Hoffman. However, before we opened, Dustin was offered a part in a movie and I released him from the play.

Lina Wertmüller; I put aside the *Ritz* and went, primarily to help finance the writing of my novel. I didn't know much about Candy except that she was the only child of the ventriloquist Edgar Bergen, and that she was, in a sense, another victim of the Manson killers.

17

Candy Bergen on One Knee, Charlie McCarthy on the Other

When the elevator doors opened, Candy Bergen was standing in the doorway of her penthouse suite. She was wearing a pale, soft-flowered kimono, her hair was pulled back severely, she wore no makeup, and she was barefoot. She looked tired, her pale robe blending with her pale complexion.

From the windows of the suite, which was perched on the roof of the Hotel de la Ville, there was a panoramic view of all Rome. The huge terrace, profuse with plants, was bathed in warm sun but Candy preferred to sit on a couch in the living room, her long, bare legs tucked beneath her. It was four in the afternoon but she was just finishing a breakfast of grapefruit juice, dry toast, and tea. Despite her obvious fatigue, she talked animatedly, but not naturally, forcing the animation, trying to appear up when she wasn't. I knew that after a while her forced chatter would skim off her nervousness and that then we would be able to talk for real.

"I was in the rain all night, until four this morning," she said, "not real rain but rain machines. I didn't get to sleep until six, hardest thing I ever did, and she just sprang it on me. When I showed up last night, thinking we were going to do another scene, she came to my trailer and told me we were going to do the big scene in the rain. You know what this movie's about? An American woman married to an Italian journalist, he's a Communist, and after ten years this is the crisis of their relationship

—the marriage is coming apart, the woman is coming apart, and in this scene, this scene in the driving rain, on the steps leading up to the tomb—I think it's Caesar's tomb—I really unravel, a kind of insanity, a madness. I didn't know if I could do it. I'd been worrying about the scene since the shooting began three months ago. I'd never done anything like it, going out of control like that. That's not me. I'm in control. I hold onto myself. But not since last fall. And that's maybe why I did this movie. My life, my real life, and the life of this woman in the script—well, we had a lot in common."

She tapped a cigarette out of a pack and lit it. The movie she was talking about was *In a Night Full of Rain,* written and directed by Lina Wertmüller, who had done *Swept Away* and *Seven Beauties.*

"I'm smoking again. I hadn't smoked in years, but I smoked in a few scenes and then all this tension . . ." The phone rang. New York. Someone named Gil. Only three days to go, Candy tells him, and then three days in San Francisco, and then it will be all over. "Gil, listen, I'm afraid of what will happen to me when it ends. Yes, would you? Oh, yes, come to San Francisco! I'm so tired now, we were shooting in the rain all night. But the way it was before . . . I've got to avoid all that, but I have nothing to do except go back to New York."

She hung up and put out her cigarette. Her voice was quiet now. Her eyes, which had been busy, now looked at me steadily. "I've been working every day for three months, not one day off. A mounting experience of slowly going crazy. Lina has forced me to go where I've never been before. I have thrown away all my defenses. Now I feel a panic over what will happen to me on Saturday when the movie ends and Lina packs it in and I must go off on my own again."

"I'm afraid I don't understand your fear," I said. "You are beautiful, intelligent, personable, a very successful actress, a published writer and photographer. What in the world are you afraid of?"

"Turning thirty. It has really done me in. I just . . . don't know how to handle it."

"When was your birthday?"

"May of last year. At first I was all right. I made jokes about it. I said in a magazine that now that I was thirty I was just hitting my stride, coming into my own. I put down people who let age affect them. After all, thirty is just a number, I said, so is forty, it has nothing to do with one's actual well-being. All last summer I was fine. Then in October, it hit me. I had sold my house in Beverly Hills and moved to New York. Hollywood was too close to the sun. New York had vitality. Enjoying my life, I thought. And then it struck me. A delayed bomb. *You are thirty.* You are alone. You have no man in your life. No children. Your twenties have been spent and what have you got to show for it? A lot of rotten movies that I did because they were being shot in interesting places where I wanted to go. The dialogue was sickening and the people were sickening but I kidded myself that the experience was broadening.

"The more I thought of myself at thirty, the more scared and depressed I became. I kept asking myself: Who am I? Where am I going? I locked the door of my new apartment and stayed there for weeks on end. Sat alone in that locked apartment, seeing no one, not going out on the street, wallowing in my depression. Not kidding myself anymore. I had led a life of no real commitment—not to acting, which for me was something to do until I established myself as a writer; not as a writer, which I had taken stabs at but never seriously, always telling myself that when this or that happened I would be ready; not to the women's lib movement, to which I only gave lip service; not to a man, not to a cause, not even to friends. Even during that brief period when I got involved with drugs it was only a *little bit* involved, not enough for it to have any effect on me.

"So I sat there in my apartment, coming apart, not telling my friends, not discussing my breakdown with anyone, watching junk television, coming to grips. I have always traded on my beauty. To interviewers I have always said: 'Oh, my beauty is something I don't know about, it doesn't concern me, I don't know what beauty is,' but the fact is I have always relied on it to pave the way for me. It brings me the flowers that fill this room—every bouquet here arrived with a hopeful note from an admirer. I am a totally insecure person and my beauty was my one security. It opened doors. It turned people on without my having to do a thing but show my face.

"But now that's going—don't you see? Look, under my eyes, around the mouth, it's beginning to crumble."

I looked at her closely. "I don't see the crumbles," I said. "Your beauty looks pretty intact to me."

"No, no, every morning in the mirror there are new, ominous signs. I used to make fun of women who suffered from mirror consultations. Now I'm one of them."

There was a knock at the door. A deliveryman stood there with a small package. In perfectly accented Italian, Candy told him to leave it at the door. "I think, signorina," he said, "I should deliver this package to your hand."

Candy tore open the wrapping paper and discovered a box from Bulgari, one of Rome's most distinguished jewelers. She was delighted and mystified. Inside was a velvet ring box that contained a ring of heavy gold, set with a large center emerald flanked by two diamonds. Uttering cries of delight, Candy slipped the ring on her finger, admired it, then read the enclosed card. "Oh, my goodness, he wanted to marry me but on Monday I told him I couldn't and now he sends me this anyway." She thrust her arm upward, catching window sunlight on the ring. "I don't wear important jewelry, but I've never had anything from Bulgari . . . it's my birthstone. You see what my beauty gets me? And in a few years when it's gone and the flowers don't arrive anymore or rings from Bulgari . . . What startles and depresses me is that I *care*. Why do I care? *Why?*"

We sat silently, the question hanging there between us. As I studied her, what came across to me was her vulnerability. Her insecurity, frustrations, and battles with her loneliness had robbed her of any defense against the assault of her own doubts. Thus, at thirty she was totally vulnerable.

"I've run all my life," she said, looking out the window. "Every time I get depressed I run to a new place, hoping to distract myself from myself. No more. I'm through running. I won't go anywhere or do anything unless I have a good reason. That's why I took on this movie. The part scared me. Working with Lina, from what I'd heard about her, that scared me too. But I knew this was something I *had* to do. To get myself out of that room. To get on the road to forty. And I'm glad I did. Last night, that scene in the rain, I was good, I was really *very*,

very good. I was so elated it took me two hours to get to sleep. I love to write but acting is the real center of my being."

"How long have you been on your own?"

"I left home at seventeen and I've never taken a penny, from that day to this—but then, my father never offered me anything. My friends used to say:

'Wait till you're twenty-one and you come into your inheritance'—my father is quite wealthy and I did expect a windfall, but twenty-one came and went and I never saw a penny."

"You said in an interview last summer that you preferred to take care of yourself and that you were past the point of wanting a husband and children. You said: 'What I value most are my options and my mobility. With a husband and children I would lose that and I'm afraid I might resent it. If I were a mom, I wouldn't want to be the kind who checked in every few days, shouting over my shoulder: "Hi, fellas, how are you doing? I'm off to Hong Kong now. See you!" as I slammed out the front door.'"

"That's bullshit—that's extreme bullshit! That's how I was talking before my breakdown, kidding myself, but then when the truth hit me I said to myself: Why am I buying a one-bedroom apartment in New York when what I want is a man who will sweep me up in his arms and carry me away? I *do* want a man, and a child, but I don't want a child without having a husband around. I'm not one of those women like Catherine Deneuve or Liv Ullmann. I'm too insecure. I must have a father for my child, a husband. But considering my life up to now, I must ask myself if I'm *able* to have a husband. I have to face some tough questions: Why have I no one in my life now? Why have I never been married? I have had only two men in my life—Terry Melcher, Doris Day's son, whom I lived with for a couple of years; and Bert Schneider, the producer, who's been in and out of my life; and that's it. Yes, I do want a husband, someone to provide for me and care for me. That bullshit I was spouting about my mobility and all that—just an alibi for being alone. I'm tired of providing for myself, of riding the bucking bronco of my loneliness, of trying to rope the fear of my insecurity. But the men I get involved with always have something built into them that is guaranteed to destroy our relationship. I set it up that way, I guess. If they don't have fatal defects, if they are possibles, men I *could* marry, I don't seem to develop any real interest in them."

"But now that you're thirty, and you've taken such good stock of yourself, maybe you'll change. Maybe you'll want things for yourself that you never wanted before."

"Maybe, but then I must not go on trying to go in every direction. I've got to know who I am. I must decide . . . look, I'm getting older now and each day I die a little, but then each day maybe I'm coming closer to knowing who I am. If I can reach that—if I can only *solve* that . . . But I mustn't sit alone and cry because I'm thirty. It has had a terrible effect on me—it *has*! I've spent my twenties and I have nothing to show for it. Oh, yes, I've done a lot of things and been a lot of places, and some of the things I've written I'm proud of—like the piece I did for *Esquire* on Bernie Cornfeld—but despite all that, I'm a lost soul. More lost than I've ever been. Sometimes my depressions are . . . well . . . more than I can handle." She had tears in her eyes now and she was very close to letting herself go.

There was a knock on the door. *"Avanti!"* Candy called out, and in came a tall man, neatly tailored in a pin-striped suit, trim black moustache, Roman-skinned, a broad smile on his face. "Oh, Pietro!" Candy exclaimed, and she got up from the couch and ran to him and embraced him warmly. Pietro giggled at her enthusiasm. She turned from him for a moment, still holding him, and introduced him to me. Then she nuzzled her nose into his neck. He looked at me and shrugged and giggled and said: "How do you do?" with an Italian accent.

We are in Candy's trailer on a piazza in front of Augustus' tomb (Candy had the wrong emperor). Candy is dressed in a revealing black silk nightgown and she is swallowing tablets of vitamin C. She is very nervous. Outside, the rumble of the huge rain machines can be heard as they are tested. It is 9 P.M. Candy is pacing the narrow aisle of the trailer and smoking a cigarette with a Bette Davis intensity. She wears no makeup. She had tried makeup the night before but the rain had run the mascara all over her face.

"Last night Lina sprang this scene on me as a surprise and I did it impulsively," Candy says, "but now we're going to do the close-ups and I've had all day to think about them and I'm scared to death."

Giancarlo Giannini, her co-star, comes into the trailer, full beard, horn-rimmed glasses, long hair falling forward across his face.

"Scared of what?" he asks in Italian.

"The bloody close-ups," Candy says. "I don't know if I can do tonight what I did last night. I don't feel it. I'm too scared."

Giancarlo puts his arms around her and she leans her forehead against his beard. "That Lina scares me pissless," Candy says.

Giancarlo pats her back and nods his head.

"I'm going to fall flat on my face," Candy says.

Giancarlo pats her sympathetically. He takes two tablets from the vitamin C bottle and leaves.

We are inside the building that houses Augustus' tomb. Lina Wertmüller, a short, solid woman, small dark glasses with white rims, dark-red hair probably dyed, plaid slacks, seared face, olive-drab raincoat over a fur coat, sits in a director's chair surrounded by her four women assistants. She is absolutely forbidding. She is waiting for the camera setup. A young woman comes over and starts to massage Lina's neck.

Candy stands just inside the glass doors, talking in whispers to Giancarlo. She is wearing a white terrycloth robe, and when Lina goes over and stands between the two of them to give them instructions for the scene, I have the illusion I am watching two prizefighters in mid-ring before the start of a main event.

It is a nippy 43 degrees; most of the crew wear sweaters and sheepskin coats but Candy is now outside in the driving rain of the machines, playing her mad scene, garbed only in a black nightgown and a wool shawl.

As the rain machines cut off, she is hustled into the building and toweled off, but again and again Lina reshoots the scene, each time Candy recoiling when the shocking cold of the rain machines hits her. Five or six times, each time more dehumanized as she is rushed back to Augustus' tomb, wiped by wet towels that can no longer dry her, trying to listen to Lina as Lina instructs her on the quality of madness she wants from her as she hurls herself on the wet pavement, down on all fours, Gian-carlo trying to restrain her. Candy's eyes are glassy. Whatever dignity she had is gone. The wardrobe people try to massage some warmth into her arms and back. But the rain machines start up again and Lina again beckons to her from under the plastic roof of the camera.

Before I met Candy for lunch the following day, I speculated over why a talented beauty with her personality and success would be so insecure and depressed over being unmarried at thirty. In fact, I wondered why she was still unmarried. She was obviously in demand as a bride—as witness the Bulgari offering of the day before—so *choosing* to be single and *suffering* because of it posed an interesting conflict that I would have to explore. But how? Certainly not head-on because at best that would simply lead us into pseudo-psychiatric jargon that would be meaningless.

In my opinion, an experienced writer is a more astute observer of the human condition than an experienced psychiatrist because his observations are based on deep explorations of the psyche of people who do not know they are being observed. Having had the good fortune of associating with a number of these writers, I was exposed to much of their wisdom about the frailties of the people whom they wrote about. I learned the most, by far, from Hemingway, who had developed an inner radar (he called it his shit detector) that could instantly identify phonies, hypocrites, and spongers, but the one who was the wisest about women, surprisingly, was Edna Ferber. Surprisingly, because she had never been married, never had a family of her own, but the women she wrote about in her fiction were truly depicted. I once told her how much I admired the way she wrote about women in her books, and she said: "I'll tell you the secret, Hotchner—if you are writing about women, especially those with strong mothers, pay particular attention to the fathers."

A few years back, I was lecturing at a summer writers' program at Indiana University, trying to get the students in my group, predominantly women, to write something that had some emotion—but the exercises they turned in were not connected to any of their nerve ends. Remembering Ferber's advice, I told them on a Friday to write about their fathers over the weekend. On Monday, I received some of the most moving, hostile, tragic essays I had ever read.

And so it was with many of the people I wrote about. Even Hemingway—controlled as he was in his appraisal of friends, rascals, and enemies, when he spoke of his father, turbulent emotions boiled up. "I often think about my father," he once told me, "even now, how sometimes he would take me with him up the lake when he made a call on a sick Indian. Just the two of us. By boat. Those were the best times. Without my mother around to poke at him, goad him toward the ambition he didn't have . . . to make something of himself. When he had already made something beautiful of himself, a simple man who had compassion for his patients, especially the ones who couldn't pay—'You'll never amount to anything . . . practicing free medicine! Nobody ever gives *us* anything for nothing!' He didn't commit suicide. He was murdered. By her. His finger was on the trigger of that old pistol, but she pulled it . . . yes . . . and I hated her.

"I had written him a letter that was on his desk the day he shot himself and I think if he had opened that letter and read it he wouldn't have pulled the trigger. When I asked my mother for my inheritance, she said she had already spent it on me. I asked her how. She said on my travel and education. What education? I asked her. Oak Park High School? My only travel, I pointed out, had been taken care of by the Italian army. This time when I left Oak Park, it was for keeps. Several years later, at Christmastime, I received a package from my mother. It contained the revolver with which my father had killed himself. There was a card that said she thought I'd like to have it; I didn't know whether it was an omen or a prophecy.

"What you should know is what my mother said that time I went back for my inheritance. 'Don't disobey me,' she said, 'or you'll regret it all your life as your father did.' "

So when I had lunch with Candy Bergen that day in Rome, I thought I might find enlightenment about her unmarried state, and her unfounded fears of getting old and losing her looks, by talking about her father. We were sitting in the salon of her suite, drinking wine. Her arms and legs were covered with black, ugly bruises incurred during the rain shots, which had lasted until two in the morning.

"I am frightened of him," Candy said.

"Now, or when you were a little girl?"

"Now."

Edgar Bergen, at that time seventy-four years old, was a star performer during the heyday of radio. The Charlie McCarthy show with Edgar Bergen. Charlie was a dummy and Edgar was a superb ventriloquist. "We loved each other, my father, my mother, and I, but we never showed it. No one in our house ever said: 'I love you.' How many times, when my mother came in to tuck me in and say good night, I promised myself I would tell her I loved her. I had it planned that I'd count to ten and then tell her, but I'd count and count, all the way to thirty, and I just couldn't say the words.

"My father took me places and sent me to good schools but there was always the *presence* of Charlie McCarthy. He had his own room and my father called him my brother and always referred to him by name and attitude as if he were a real person. Sometimes the three of us would have breakfast together. Dad would put Charlie on one of his knees and me on the other. Then he'd hold me by the neck, the way he would Charlie, and he'd make us talk back and forth, but I would just open and shut my mouth the way Charlie did and let Dad supply the dialogue for both of us.

"Dad was a very amusing man and we had good times, but he was remote, always remote. The Swedish Lutheran ethic, I guess. I enjoy my family, I love going home to visit, and often before I go I tell myself that I'm going to try to get closer to Dad, but the formal way he hugs me always puts me in my place and I never seem to get up enough courage to press him. How I wish I could! Oh, how I wish we were suddenly closer and I could say 'I love you, Dad.' "

"Do you confide in him?"

"No, just the opposite. Like when I was living with Terry Melcher—let's see, I was twenty-four, I guess—my parents thought I was living in New York but actually Terry and I were in a house in Beverly Hills just a few blocks from where my parents lived. You'd think I would have told them where I was but no, I was too frightened of my father. You know what I did? I used to get static on the radio and then phone home and pretend I was in New York, hoping the static would make the call sound like long distance. Finally, I became too frightened that my dad might see me somewhere in Beverly Hills, so I arranged with a girl friend to lend me her apartment for a night. I pretended to have just arrived in L. A. and invited my parents over for dinner. I even hung my clothes in the closet for realism. After that, I was able to drive down our road without hiding behind the wheel.

"Terry and I had a great time those two years we lived together in that house. We kept monkeys and a St. Bernard and a honey bear and we were two kids playing house. But then Terry went to pieces after Marty Melcher died. He began to get on things and drink a lot and he got so bad he'd pass out in the middle of a sentence. One time he phased out at dinner with his head bent forward over his plate. It was awful.

"Finally we moved to Doris' beach house and rented our house to Roman Polanski and Sharon Tate. Not long afterwards, the Manson people came to the house and murdered everyone. They strung up those bloody ropes on the very rafters I had decorated with Christmas ornaments. Some people think Manson may have been looking for Terry that night—I don't know. All I know is that what had been a lovely relation turned grim and we had to part."

A waiter came in and placed a bottle of Soave and a bowl of mozzarella and tomatoes between us. "Do you still think about Charlie McCarthy?" I asked.

"Oh, yes. Of course. Charlie still exists, you know. Dad performs with him all the time. I saw them on the Merv Griffin show just a few months ago. You see, Charlie was all the things my father wanted to be—witty, sassy, debonair. I really think my father cared more about Charlie than anyone else in his life. Charlie's room was bigger than mine, and Dad even gave Charlie top billing on his radio show—it was the Charlie McCarthy show *with* Edgar Bergen. Sunday evening was always a terrible time for me. At dusk, even now, I feel a sort of panic and I run around the house turning on all the lights. If I'm a guest somewhere, and it's Sunday and it starts to get dark, I just can't help myself. I try not to panic but I do; I've *got* to have all the lights on."

"That's when the Charlie McCarthy show was on the air, wasn't it? Sunday evenings?"

"Yes."

"But why would that put you in a panic? Most girls would love to hear their father perform."

"Of course. It's not rational. I'll tell you something else—I have this fantasy that someday I will have a handsome, man-size dummy whom I can sit on my knee. I will put my hand in his back and manipulate him and he will be everything I want him to be, everything I'm looking for in a man. Just like Charlie is for Dad, my dummy man would be for me."

Edgar Bergen died not long afterward, and it wasn't long after that that Candy finally fulfilled her desire to get married, but it was not to a Charlie McCarthy-like dummy, but to the dynamic French film director Louis Malle, who was quite a bit older than Candy. It occurred to me, of course, that her father's death had released her to marry his replacement. But I hear that the marriage was short-lived and that they have separated and that Candy is again living alone as she approaches forty.

18

Doris Day Is a Fatherless Child, and So Is Sophia

One of the basic commandments that a free-lancer must obey is, Thou Shalt Remain Solvent. This commandment does not preclude getting into debt but it does preclude a state of insolvency that destroys the free-lancer's ability to function. A writer is no better on a given day than his state of mind permits him to be, and if he allows himself to reach a financial point where, like an athlete in a slump who isn't producing, he starts to press and even question his ability, then he falls victim to his insolvency. And the awful consequence of this insolvency is that he must get a paying job, God forbid, and turn in his free-lance medallion.

There is an alternative that is less painful, but one that is difficult to arrange at the precise time you need it, and that is to take on a writing assignment not particularly to his liking, but one that will provide solvency and enable the writer to go back and complete the project he was working on when his bank account caved in.

Twice I have run up on the shoals of insolvency, the rocky shards lacerating my bottom, and each time I have squirmed back into the waters of solvency by taking a deep breath and signing on to write a book expressly for the purpose of bailing me out. It first happened to me when I was writing *Looking for Miracles,* an account of a summer in my life when, desperate to make enough money to go to college, I had lied about my qualifications and inveigled a job as head counselor at a boy's camp, a position for which I was grossly underqualified.*

Immediately preceding *Looking for Miracles*, I had taken two years to write *King of the Hill*, which dealt with that summer during the Depression when my family and I lived in that one miserable hotel room.

Time, which is the free-lancer's capital, had to be heavily invested in those two books, and one morning, overwhelmed by the mound of bills next to my typewriter, I forced myself to face the cruel reality that the financial larder had gone bare. I had a new wife and a new baby and an old Connecticut house whose maw opened voraciously on the first of every month. So in 1974 I laid aside *Looking for Miracles* and entreated my literary agent, Phyllis Jackson (a caring agent if ever there was one), to find me a to-make-ends-meet project. She already had one: just that morning she had been asked by the William Morrow publishing company if I was available to write a biography of Doris Day. Doris Day? Miss Happy-Go-Lucky, the Girl Next Door, Apple Pie and Bright White Teeth? How could there be a book in her?

The publisher asked me to go out to Beverly Hills and meet Doris before making up my mind; a second look at my bank statement induced me to go. I found Doris more attractive and younger-looking than she appeared on the screen, certainly sexier, and as straightforward, outspoken and sunnily good-natured as one could ask.

"I came out here to have lunch with you to convince myself that there wasn't a book in you," I told her.

"Because you think it will be all sweetness and light, that it?"

"Precisely."

"You know what my mother said when she heard I might do this book? 'Doris,' she said, 'your life just hasn't been that happy that you can do a book. You know the image people have of you, but the truth is—all the terrible things that have happened to you, and all the times you've suffered, well, my goodness, when you think of all the unhappiness you've had—what's there to write about?'"

------

*I had never been off the streets of St. Louis, couldn't swim, had never been in a camp, and made myself two years older than I was.

"Why do you want the book?"

"Because I'm tired of being thought of as Miss Goody Two-Shoes, that's why—Miss Happy-Go-Lucky. You doubtless know the remark dear Oscar Levant once made about me: 'I knew her before she was a virgin.' Well, I'm not the All-American Virgin Queen—I've had three marriages, and each was a bitter disappointment in different ways. When I was thirteen, on my way to becoming a professional dancer, I had my left leg destroyed in an accident and I was told I might never walk properly again. Before that, I had had to endure the bad marriage of my parents and their divorce and the bizarre behavior of my father. At sixteen I was earning a living on the road singing with bands, one-night stands, living on a bus. Married when I was seventeen and immediately pregnant, with a husband who beat me and threatened to kill me . . . so many things I've never told anyone, things my mother, my son don't . . . after my third husband's death, to discover that not only had he wiped out the millions I had earned but that he had left me heavily in debt . . . my life, my real true life."

I was intrigued by her duality—the face that she showed the world, and the totally different face that she saw in her mirror. So I signed a contract that restored my solvency, and I moved my brood out to Beverly Hills; I was writing the book to preserve my free-lancer status, but it's possible that I might have written the book even if dat ol' debil necessity hadn't been breathing on me.

Doris and I met every day at the same time in a small cheerful room in her house on North Crescent Drive, the tape machine going. I enjoyed our time together, and often, for a break, we mounted our bicycles and zipped off to Nate 'n' Al's Delicatessen, where we ate heartily while Doris received visits from fellow diners in our booth, old pals like Milton Berle, Les Brown, Billy de Wolfe, Kaye Ballard, and Paul Lynde. Doris was devoid of artifice, a remarkable trait for an actress, devoid of connivance, of jealousy, of suspicion; her emotions were as honest as the freckles on her face, and she loved her friends with unrestrained openness.

But for all that, our daily sessions were not leading us into the subterranean tunnels that had to be dug into memory by a probing biographer. In other words, Doris was not going deep down inside herself, she was just scratching the surface and handing me the residue of that. But after four weeks of these interviews, I knew I had to do something that would bring me closer to the secret place in her memory where she kept those things too painful or humiliating to reveal. It was at this point I again embraced Edna Ferber's sage advice about concentrating on the fathers of women with strong mothers. Doris and I had already discussed her father, and she had passed over him rather lightly, a footnote to her existence. He had deserted her family when she was eleven, she said, and never cared anything about her from then on.

But now I decided to go back and press her for details about those early times in her girlhood when her father was still in the house.

HOTCHNER: Tell me how you felt after your father moved out of your home.

DORIS: How I felt? Well, it became a scandal that made life very difficult for me. Our family had always enjoyed a certain standing in the community because of my father's position at the church, but when he divorced he had to resign his post. That changed the way people thought of us. Especially when it was revealed that my father had been running around with my mother's best friend. You can imagine how the tongues wagged —this respected "professor" of the church having an affair with a married woman who was his wife's closest friend.

HOTCHNER: Tell me about this woman.

DORIS: She was tall and slender, a truly lovely woman who lived in a beautiful apartment building right across the street from St. Mark's. She had two daughters, one of whom was in my class, the other in the class behind me. The daughters used to be at our house all the time. My mother would look after all of us. How often she told me to be sure to bring Jane and Virginia home with me because their mother had to go to the doctor, or whatever. What we didn't know was that it was my father she was seeing, not the doctor. The terrible part of it is that I knew about the affair before my mother did.

HOTCHNER: Did you tell your mother about it?

DORIS: No, I have never told anyone, not even my mother,

because the way I found out about my father was so awful that I could never bring myself to mention it. It happened at a party. My parents rarely entertained but this was a big party to which they had invited most of their friends and relatives. It was a rare occasion for me, and exciting, so I was up much later than usual, spying from upstairs on what the grown-ups were doing. Finally, though, I began to get sleepy and I went to my room, which was toward the back of the house. I was in bed, not yet asleep, when I heard whispered voices outside my room, and then the door opened just a crack and I could see my father peeking in. I pretended to be asleep.

Just beyond my room was a little spare bedroom that could be entered only by going through my room. My father was apparently satisfied that I was asleep, and through slitted eyes I could see the door swing open—with the light in back of them I could easily distinguish my father and the woman I have mentioned. My father motioned for her to follow him. They came into my room, closed the door, tiptoed past me and into the bedroom beyond. There I was, with the head of my bed against the wall of that room, and I heard everything, God help me, everything. I pulled the pillow over my head and burrowed my crying face into the sheet, but there was no way to shut out the awful things I was hearing.

When it was over, I again pretended to sleep as they came through my room. I held my breath so that my sobs wouldn't escape me. When the door was shut and they had gone, I felt compelled to get out of bed and look at the room where they had been. Then I got under my covers, in the warm tent of my bed, and cried myself to sleep.

You'd think that I would hate my father after that, and turn against him, but I went along as I had been, desperately faking how I felt. Thinking about it, I suppose my drive to preserve our home was stronger than the revulsion of what had happened. I wanted to have my father in that house, part of my life, no matter what he had done. I did not condemn him. That has never been a part of my nature; it is my nature to forgive, to try to accentuate what is good, and not to pass judgment.

HOTCHNER: You never told your mother about this incident?

DORIS: This is the first time I have ever mentioned it to

anyone, telling you. But keeping it a secret didn't help because it wasn't too long after that that my father moved out. I was eleven at the time. My mother and father had lived together all those years and produced three children but they had nothing in common. Not a thing. The afternoon my father actually left the house, my brother helped him pack. My mother was deliberately not home. Paul was in and out of my father's room, carrying things to his suitcases. While they were packing they were having a long talk. I was down at the end of the hallway, watching all this, hearing the drone of their voices, but not invited by my father to be a part of it. I was crying hysterically, trying to keep it inside me the best I could. My brother was calm and matter-of-fact, as if my father were going off on a little business trip.

When my father was all packed, I went into the living room and hid behind the draperies, where I could watch the driveway without being observed. It was a lovely, soft drapery and I can still feel it wrapped around me as I pressed my crying face against the window and watched Paul help my father carry his bags into the car. There were no good-byes—my father didn't ask for me and all I wanted to do was hide there in the draperies and watch him. My father got in the car and I watched it move away down the long driveway that ran along the side of our house. Then the car turned into the street and disappeared and I felt that my life was disappearing with it.

My brother came into the living room and saw me hiding in the draperies. "What are you crying about?" he asked.

I couldn't believe that he wasn't crying.

HOTCHNER: How did you feel about your father after that? Did you hate him? Resent him? What?

DORIS: My father was such a rigid man, so remote, so ungiving toward me, and yet his leaving was an enormous loss to me. I loved him and he meant a lot to me. But I could no longer fantasize that the happy marriage I wanted for my parents was going to happen. That was my big dream as a girl— that my parents would have a happy marriage and that I would someday have a happy marriage too. It was the only real ambition I ever had—not to be a dancer or Hollywood movie star, but to be a housewife in a good marriage. Unfortunately, it was

Barbara Hutton with her newborn son, Lance, and her fourth husband, Count Reventlow.

Babs in her Tangier palace, married at the moment to Prince Doan, her seventh husband.

Dr. Max Jacobson with President John F. Kennedy during a Florida hike. On the ground resting are Prince Radziwill and Chuck Spalding. Jacobson gave injections to Kennedy, once inserting his needle directly into the President's throat in an attempt to cure him of laryngitis.

Van Cliburn almost lost a finger because of a Jacobson injection.

And as a result of his injections, Bette Davis had to have a section of her jaw removed.

Dr. Jacobson's needle ravaged Tennessee Williams.

Audrey Wood with four of her playwrights: Maurice Valency, William Inge, Carson McCullers, and Tennessee Williams.

Rod Steiger's ego threw fifteen actors out of work.

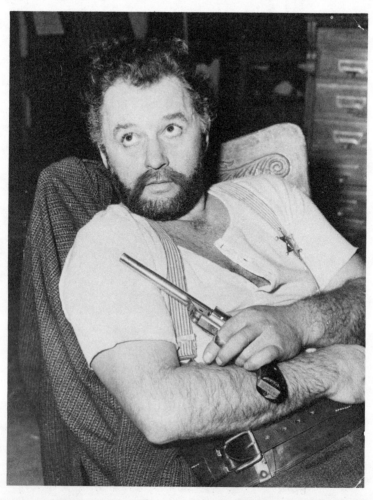

Jimmy Durante rehearsing a number with the Met's great Wagnerian soprano Helen Traubel.

Otto Preminger in Hong Kong with the only sights he wanted to see.

In Verona, with Ricardo Montalban, Susan Strasberg, Richard Beymer, Marty Ritt, and Eli Wallach. To my right is a teen-ager, a colonel's daughter from a nearby Air Force base who was an extra. Her name: Sharon Tate.

Sharon with Tony Curtis in *Don't Make Waves*.

Sharon married Roman Polanski, was pregnant with their child when brutally mutilated by the Manson crazies.

Candy Bergen was constantly upstaged by her "brother," Charlie McCarthy.

This is the face Doris Day showed to the world—happily beside Sinatra in *Young at Heart*.

But her sunny smiles—this time for Ronald Reagan in *The Winning Team*—belied the unhappiness of her private life.

Sophia Loren's father, shown here with her mother and sister, refused to legitimatize her . . .

. . . so in Carlo Ponti, twenty-four years her senior, she found a father substitute.

Burt Reynolds married Judy Carne, whom, he says, he shouldn't have married.

But Burt did not marry Sally Field, whom, he admits, he should have married.

Anthony Quinn's appetite for roles is voracious, ranging from *Viva Zapata* . . .

. . . to *Heller in Pink Tights* —so perhaps someday he will portray Hemingway.

Lorin Maazel, nine yea[rs]
old, conducting a
rehearsal of the
New York Philharmon[ic]

Bess Truman back home in
Independence, Mo.

Lee Marvin repeated his *Cat Ballou* performance at a state dinner at the
White House.

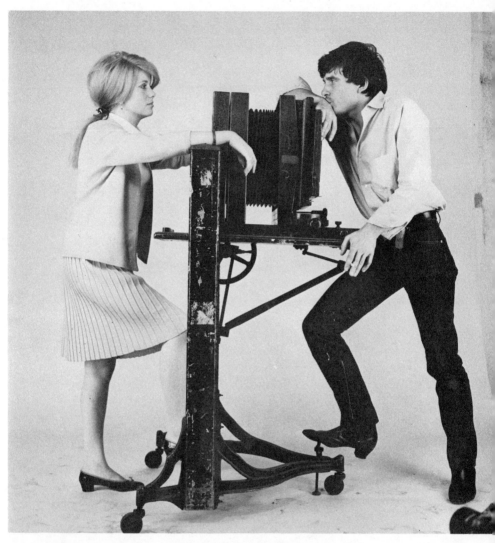

David Bailey was the only man Catherine Deneuve married but the only one of her three loves—Roger Vadim and Marcello Mastroianni were the other two—with whom she didn't have a child.

Dorothy Fields with Richard Rodgers and Irving Berlin.

Frank Loesser with the piano that exalted him and the cigarette that killed him.

Hemingway's zest for life was my legacy.

a dream that would elude me just as surely as it had eluded my mother.

After those revelations about her father,* Doris began to develop a different perspective on her life, and the nature of what she remembered and the depth and quality of her insights all changed. All of her relationships with men had been disastrous, and her fourth marriage, recently dissolved, was perhaps the most unfortunate of the lot; the real tragedy is that anyone so deserving of love, so giving of love, should have been so victimized.

It was my intention not ever to write about another movie star, being a believer in Heraclitus' advice not to pass twice in the same waters, but when for the second time in my life I found myself facing insolvency, this time in Paris, reluctantly I decided that renouncing Heraclitus was my only salvation.† I had gotten into this latest fix because, as the television networks say, of circumstances beyond my control. In the spring of 1977, I had received a trans-Atlantic call from Charley Ritz, whom I knew quite well from the many evenings we had spent together when Hemingway, who was an old friend of Charley's, had stayed at the Ritz. Charley Ritz was the only son of César Ritz, who had founded the hotel, and now, at eighty-three, having spent his life at the Ritz, Charley felt the time had come to have a book written about his father and the hotel and about all the great people who had stayed there. He had invited me to come and stay at the Ritz while I wrote his biography, and my publisher was enthusiastic about the book.

It took a while to finish whatever it was I was then writing, and to rent my house in Westport, with the result that by the time we were actually on our way, Charley Ritz suffered a stroke and died before I ever got to see him again.

---

*After revealing the details of her father's infidelity, Doris collapsed and canceled our sessions for two days, most of which time she stayed in bed.

†George Orwell's *Down and Out in Paris and London* is a classic demonstration of the purgatorial depths that insolvent free-lancing can reach. Orwell's specter of having to wash dishes in the steamy kitchen dungeons of the Ritz has served as motivation for my desire to maintain solvency.

CHOICE PEOPLE

So there I was in Paris, not able to return to my leased house, my work project buried with Charley. I eventually decided to write a novel that would largely take place in the Ritz during the Second World War, and I received a modest advance for it. But this was a time when the dollar was intimidated by the franc, and although I was able to augment my meager bank account with a few auxiliary endeavors, nevertheless the haughty official at the Morgan Guaranty Bank on the Place Vendôme was sternly reminding me that I was not maintaining the required minimum balance.

At this moment, with *The Man Who Lived at the Ritz* more in my head than on paper, again Morrow came to my rescue. This time the biographical offering was Sophia Loren, who lived only a few blocks from my apartment, on the Avenue George V. I hesitated, but only long enough to add up my son's tuition for the École Bi-Lang, the rent for our apartment on the Boulevard de Courcelles, the cost of produce on the Rue Lévi and of meals in our favorite restaurants.

The Sophia I met was a woman who had slowly and painstakingly built her persona. She had risen from the postwar ashes of the ghetto town of Pozzuoli, near Naples, and she had relentlessly dedicated herself, with the help of the fierce devotion of her ambitious mother, to becoming a movie star, and eventually a superstar. The first impression I had of Sophia, meeting her as I did in the salon of the Ponti-Loren triplex, a salon with damask-covered walls, a fresco of billowy clouds on the ceiling, floating above a luxurious blend of antique and modern furniture—my impression was of discipline. Her whole being seemed regimented to a concept she had of herself and of the life she lived. I do not mean for this to make her out to be artificial and contrived, for indeed she wasn't. She was uncomplicated, direct, and warm with me, to the extent that her discipline allowed her to be. But I felt that there were many secrets locked inside her that her discipline would not permit her to set free—and this proved to be the case.

She also severely confined me to those morning sessions in her living room. I never once saw her socially, never once had a meal with her or with Ponti, who kept a sharp eye on our undertaking. Many times I invited them to dinner, at my apartment and at restaurants, but they invariably refused, and Sophia also declined my invitations to have lunch. My interest was in observing Sophia in a social situation, but she never permitted it.* It was as if she were determined that I could only study her under the glass of her elaborate salon, with everything under tight control.

When she went to Cannes to attend the film festival, I pressured Ponti into letting me accompany them, but when I got to Cannes I found they had not provided me with a ticket to attend the gala, and afterward Sophia, Marcello Mastroianni, and others of their film group went off to a supper party in a restaurant without telling me where they had gone. I saw about as much of Sophia in Cannes as I did in Paris.

In the beginning of our talks, as Doris had, Sophia dismissed her father as inconsequential to her life. She had been born illegitimate, and she had seen her father only a few times during his life; he had refused to marry her mother, who staunchly pushed Sophia into a film career, remained optimistic when things were darkest, hustled the film offices to get parts for Sophia, was convinced that Dame Fortune would eventually look their way.

After several weeks of taping, during which time Sophia described her life almost by rote, using stock answers she had for years given to stock questions, I arrived one morning and dramatically tossed all our completed tapes in the wastebasket (I had duplicates). We have to do better than this, Sophia, I told her. A book must have depth, details, resolutions. I told her what Edna Ferber had said about women and their fathers, and I suggested that we talk about her father again, but more frankly. All right, she said, but I've really told you all there is.

HOTCHNER: Let's begin with that moment when your father lay dying in the hospital and you left the movie set to go to him.

---

*Doris, on the other hand, completely shared her life with me while I was writing the book. We ate together often in restaurants, and several times she attended dinners at our house. I even spent several days in Las Vegas with Doris and her friend Raquel Rael. One of the occasions that gave me valuable insight into Doris was a James Cagney film tribute that we attended together.

SOPHIA: My sister told me where he was and I rushed to his hospital room. I sat down on the bed beside him and held his cold hand.

HOTCHNER: Were your mother and sister there?

SOPHIA: Yes. I was surprised to see my mother there because she always hated him for having seduced and abandoned her. And there was my sister, also illegitimate, who had suffered terribly because of his refusal to give her his name until I paid him a million lire for it.

HOTCHNER: What is going through your mind as you sit in that hospital room, watching his slow death?

SOPHIA: Well, I think for so much of my life he has been a source of pain and rejection and humiliation, yet now, here at the conclusion of his life, whatever negative feelings I had about him have been erased by a wash of pity; and a glow of love has somehow managed to shine through.

HOTCHNER: Pity and love.

SOPHIA: Yes, pity and love. How seldom I saw him—how many times during my agonies of surviving he refused to help—yet, strange as it may sound, he meant a lot to me. As I look back now, I realize that I sought him everywhere. I married him. I made my best films with him. I curried his favor. I sat on his lap and snuggled him.

HOTCHNER: You say you married him—is your relationship with Ponti father-daughter?

SOPHIA: He's twenty-four years older, you know.

HOTCHNER: You speak of your best films—you're referring to De Sica?

SOPHIA: Yes, I truly believe that all the important men in my life were father figures.

HOTCHNER: Cary Grant too?

SOPHIA: Well, he is even older than Carlo, isn't he?

HOTCHNER: How many times did you actually see your father?

SOPHIA: Very few. Once when he came to Pozzuoli and brought me a little blue car. Once in a courtroom when he sued me for libel. And once when he had my mother and me arrested as prostitutes—it was his way of trying to get us out of Rome, where he lived, and force us to go back to Pozzuoli. Those are the only times I saw him, and yet he was important to my life.

HOTCHNER: Then perhaps your story should begin and end with your father.

SOPHIA: How strange!

HOTCHNER: It is something to think about.

SOPHIA: Yes, it is. There was one more time I saw him. Not long before he went to the hospital, at his request my sister arranged for me to visit him in his apartment in Rome. I had not seen him for many years, and I had never been to a place he lived in. I found him much older than his years. I believe he was suffering from cancer. He was very pleased to see me and took me all around the flat, showing me his possessions and mementos. We didn't have much to talk about, but it mattered a great deal to him that I see everything in his home. When it was time to leave, and we stood in the doorway saying good-bye, he took one of my hands in his and said: "Lella, I am very proud of you."

That was the only affectionate thing he ever said to me.

As a father myself, I sometimes think of the effect I've had on my two daughters. One of them has already written about me in a transparently disguised novel, and I don't come off favorably. I gave as much of my time and understanding and support as I could, as much love as I was capable of, and yet I was judged wanting. Whereas Sophia's father, who gave her nothing but grief, and Doris's father, who deserted her, both engendered understanding and love in their daughters.

This conundrum intrigues me, and so does Edna Ferber's enduring perspicacity.

19

Burt Reynolds Bares His Body and His Soul

The revelation of deep emotional linkage to their fathers has sometimes surfaced as strongly in men I have known as it has in women. Burt Reynolds is a case in point.

I had been knocking around Hollywood with Burt while he was making *The Man Who Loved Women* with Julie Andrews; getting to know him and his way of life, watching him at work, sharing meals with him, observing how he dealt with people on locations—exchanging a kind of affection with his fans—sometimes seeing him in his home.

Before I met him, I had been told that Burt's house was a monument to machismo, all red and black leather, heavy drapes, amber lights, deep-pile settees—but that was obviously before Burt's long involvement with Dinah Shore, during which time Dinah had inspired soft beige and white colors, elegant rugs, and modest lighting for Burt's splendid collection of cowboy and Indian sculptures by the great American artist Frederic Remington. But despite its transformation by Dinah, the house is unmistakably the lair of a bachelor, presided over by a Scottish houseman named Harry, a reformed soldier of fortune who has transferred his once fierce cosmic devotions to Burt's well-being.

The elegantly appointed dining room has obviously rarely, if ever, seen a dinner party, and although the sumptuous pool area with its burnished bar, tropical vegetation, and pristine tennis court is a party giver's dream, it has a reclusive feel about it that suggests Burt is not disposed to partying there.

In the basement, Burt has an attractive and superbly equipped workout room that is a muscle builder's delight. Gleaming Nautilus weighted pulleys, leather horses, tables with overhead weights, sit-up boards, leg muscle developers—name it, there it is, surrounded by a mirrored wall which enables the body builder to watch himself as he puffs and grunts to the rhythm of his weights.

One evening an instructor named Danny, in headband and knickers, his middle secured with a wide leather cinch band, was already in the gym when Burt and I arrived from the studio. As Burt stripped down to exercise trunks, he told Danny he'd wait for his pals to arrive, and ten minutes later they did—Jon Voight and John Travolta. Travolta had been on a heavy body-building regime for ten months under Sylvester Stallone's supervision while they were making *Staying Alive;* Burt had been at it for several months under Danny's tutelage; but this was Voight's initial workout and he was hesitant, wary, and envious.

The three of them were about a half hour into their exercises, Burt exuding bemused assurance, Travolta pleasure in his mirrored torso, Voight tight-lipped determination, when a short man festooned with layers of bulbous muscles entered the room and was given a reception befitting the King of Body Builders, which he is—Franco Columbo, Mr. Universe, an old friend of Burt's.

"Les me see what you do," he said with a lilting Italian accent.

The three men performed for him self-consciously, prep-school boys for the headmaster. He corrected their techniques, then lined them up in front of him and told them most of their exercises were a waste of time. You are big movie stars, he said, so in front of cameras you have many close-ups, no? Well, then, here is where you needa the muscles, here, the neck, the shoulders, all up here where is the close-ups. Whatsa the good down here the thighs and all that business? He proceeded to demonstrate exercises designed to give them close-up muscles.

Voight admired Travolta's cuts (the stomach indentations between developed muscles), his lats and his delts (other indentations). Travolta said nothing, maintaining a smug smile as he swung his body to and fro with the weights, watching his cuts, lats, and defs undulating in the mirror.

One afternoon, when Burt had no shooting scheduled, we met in his home, and with Burt stretched out on a living room couch with his dog at his side, the phones turned off, he spoke candidly and thoughtfully about his life. There is a disarming honesty and directness about him, but also there is in him a complicated mixture of being in awe of who he is and at the same time being disappointed in what he is not—but still hopes to be. This is what he told me that afternoon:

I ran away from home when I was in the eighth grade, but looking back on it, I can't figure out why I did, other than the thirst I had for adventure. I grew up in Riviera Beach, Florida, near Palm Beach. My father was the local sheriff; my mother ran our drug store. We lived in a tough neighborhood but we lived comfortably and although our family life was rather austere, there was no reason to run away. The family bank was a paper bag hidden in the kitchen, and I took a fistful of that money and was in my room counting it—it came to $110—when I heard my mother crying because they had discovered that the money was missing and they were very upset about it.

"It couldn't have been Bud (my nickname)," my mother was saying. "He wouldn't ever steal anything. Not Bud."

So what I did was to roll up that money and leave it on the front seat of the family auto on my way out to the highway to hitchhike. I caught a ride from a guy who asked me where I was going, and I said to see my uncle in South Carolina but I have no idea why I said that, since I had never been to South Carolina and I certainly didn't have an uncle there. So he let me out in Allendale, which is at the Georgia border, and I walked across the bridge, past a sign that said WELCOME TO SOUTH CAROLINA. But I no sooner got across that bridge than the sheriff pulled up and asked me where I was going. All I had was a cardboard box with some clothes in it. I told him I was going to see my Uncle Ralph.

"You know what we do with vagrants here?" the sheriff asked, and he pointed to a printed sign by the side of the road: NIGGER, DON'T LET THE SUN SET ON YOUR ASS IN THIS COUNTY. "You ain't a nigger, boy," the sheriff said, "but when you come in here vagrant we treat you like one." He threw me in jail for thirty days, and that cured me of wanting to run away.

I guess the important element missing from our home was any warmth, any love. Between my mother and father, yes—they really liked each other—but as for their relationship with me, I never heard the word *love* until I was thirty-five years old, and my father and I finally developed a rapport we should have had when I was living at home. As a boy, I felt affection, and I felt love, but there was no way to express it except with girls, and I guess I used to overdo it with them to compensate for never hearing or saying it with my family. Girls love to hear you say you love them, and there were a lot of them in high school and college whom I said I loved, but it wasn't an act with me. I really did love them when I said it, but it didn't last very long. But what I found out was that girls lose their virginity much earlier than fellows, probably because they're more sophisticated than men, but also because men are always pressuring them to have sex.

But there was one girl in high school who really stopped me in my tracks—Betty Lou. I often think about her to this day. She was the school beauty, a free-wheeling amoral nymph who came from the richest and most social family in town. I was a star on the football team, and in my junior year we were crowned king and queen of the Junior Prom. What I was planning on was to get a football scholarship when I graduated high school, and marry Betty Lou. It didn't bother me that when I called for her on a date, I had to go to the service entrance to get her; actually, considering who I was and where I came from, I felt I didn't belong at the front door of that big mansion she lived in.

At any rate, there we were at the Junior Prom, Betty Lou dancing tight up against me with that incredible body of hers, and while the orchestra was playing "Harbor Lights," I said, "Betty Lou, I really and truly love you," and she said, "You know something, honey? When you become a big football star at Florida State next year they're going to call you Papa Reynolds, because I just found out we're going to have a baby."

Right there in the middle of the American Legion Hall I stopped dancing, and with everybody looking at us, I gave her a big kiss. Then I grabbed my friend Steve, who stuttered, especially when excited, and I said, "Listen, I have to get to Georgia right away so I can marry Betty Lou." Georgia law allowed you to get married at sixteen. "But how do you know B-B-B-Betty L-L-Lou will m-m-m-marry you?" Steve asked. It was the right question to ask, because the following day when I turned up at Betty Lou's service entrance to elope with her to Georgia, her mother was waiting for me.

She said there wasn't going to be any Georgia, that she was going to Cuba with Betty Lou to have things "taken care of," and that I should forget about getting married. She said that when Betty Lou did get married it would be to a very rich man, but that in the meantime, the two of us could go on dating as before and have our fun, only I should be more careful about knocking up her daughter.

And we did continue to go on dates and have sex until, true to her mother's prediction, Betty Lou got married to a man from a "good family" who was as rich as they come. Betty Lou and her mother were completely amoral people, and Betty was so open and sweet and honest about her amorality that from then on I was always attracted to amoral people. Betty Lou was a rocket ship to the moon, unlike any other woman I have ever met, and I've met some. But it wasn't until I was in my early thirties that I met a woman who topped Betty Lou for amorality, and I'd say that that was one of the reasons I married her, my one and only marriage. Judy Carne was not just amoral, but she had the same kind of free-wheeling lack of inhibitions that had attracted me to Betty Lou, although in the case of Judy the amorality and free-wheeling zaniness eventually got out of control. I passed up a lot of great ladies whom I knew before

Judy, ladies with whom marriage might have worked, but looking back on it, I can see that in Judy I was taking on someone who was destined to self-destruct.

Until now, I have never said an unkind word about her, although she has done her share of bad-mouthing me. *The National Inquirer* paid her ten thousand dollars to sign an article about how I used to beat her, and then ten years later they gave her another ten thousand, and she did the article all over again. But the fact is that I always tried to help her in every way I could. After her terrible automobile accident, when she was almost paralyzed, I immediately came to her assistance and she promised to get off drugs, but she never could. She's been married several times, but every time she has a new crisis in her life, I get a phone call. Judy has a strange conglomeration of drives inside her—she loved men, women, life itself; she went to the Cordon Bleu cooking school and when she wanted to, she was a wonderful homemaker and cook. But then . . . well, there was that other side of her. There was a time when I went off to do a movie in Thailand, and when I returned I found two gay English hairdressers driving my car without a license, a big bull dyke lying on the rug in the living room stoned out of her mind, playing Monopoly with another bull dyke, and two unidentified guys smoking grass in the kitchen. Now, I am rather prone to hysteria when it comes to anyone using drugs in my house, so all I remember is that the two of them went sailing out the window—I don't recall if it was open or closed but I did assist them with great zeal—and then I went charging in on the two gay chaps, who are probably still running at full tilt somewhere between L.A. and Cape Cod. And that occasion marked the beginning of the end of our marriage.

Even though it wasn't much of a marriage, it left me badly traumatized and overwary about ever getting married again. Judy had not yet had her success on "Laugh-In," and there was no telling about her moods. We'd see a girl that I thought attractive, and Judy would say, "Let's go home and go to bed with her," and she meant it. She'd say, "I feel a little crazy. Let's get up on the piano and dance"—and she would. She was nutty, completely nutty, but there were also some things about which she was very wise. For instance, I used to use my fists a lot—somebody rubbed me wrong, I'd belt him—but one time a guy insulted her at a party and I punched him out, and when we got out to our car she said, "What you did is completely boring, Burt."

I said, "What do you mean? That jerk insulted you."

She said, "Why didn't you put him down with words instead of punches? Smacking somebody is a bore, but if you knock 'em down with words, something clever—what I'm trying to tell you, Burt, is that a black eye heals, but words wound you forever."

She was right, of course, and I learned my lesson: women are not impressed with beating on somebody, but they get turned on by a man who can put a boor in his place by what he says. Judy herself had a rapier tongue, a really fast, sure wit. She had grown up performing in English dives and dance halls; Lenny Bruce had been one of her running mates in London, and her rejoinders could be flamethrowers.

After Judy's criticism, I discovered how much I could achieve with words, and later on, when I appeared on talk shows, especially with Johnny Carson, I was able to project myself with repartee, proving Judy right about the superiority of words over macho deeds.

If only I had remembered that, I would never have committed the mistake of trying to project an image with that ill-advised nude center spread I did for *Cosmopolitan.* I had turned thirty-five, and in taking stock of myself, I realized that my career was just marking time. The films I was appearing in slid in and out of public view without leaving a trace of themselves. In restaurants, on the street, I was an unrecognized nonentity. I had just finished shooting a film that I had high hopes for—*Deliverance*—but it was a year away from release, so when, during an appearance on the "Today" show, while bantering with another guest—Helen Gurley Brown, who is the editor of *Cosmopolitan*—the subject of becoming the first male center-spread nude came up, I thought, What the hell, why not? Maybe this will make an impact and put my name in the air. Then when *Deliverance*

comes out, that ought to put me on the level where I
want to be.

When that issue of *Cosmopolitan* was published, I was
appearing on the stage in Chicago in *The Rainmaker*. I
expected a little flurry because of it, maybe a call from a
local television station, but on the day of publication it took
a corps of eleven policemen to get me from my hotel to the
theatre, which was a block away. When I made my entrance,
there were whistles and catcalls and female voices calling,
"Take it off!" Every night of the run, I had to stop the show
and ask the audience to show some respect for my co-star,
Lois Nettleton, and to give me a chance to perform the role
which they had bought tickets for. I hated to leave the
theatre at night because there would be mobs of three or
four thousand people outside the stage door waiting for me.
The assault on me by the media—television, radio, all that—
was overwhelming, but there was an unattractive, nasty tone
to it. I never felt so lonely in my life. There were nights,
trapped in my dressing room, not wanting to face that mob
outside, an anger would rise up in me and I would pick up
chairs, tables, anything I could get my hands on, and smash
them against the wall.

I had posed for the centerfold as a lark, but I was the
butt of every joke on television—on the Oscars that year
there were four Burt Reynolds gags. I guess my reaction was
to feel sorry for myself, that it wasn't fair that I had worked
so goddamn hard as a performer, had fallen down all those
stairs and been thrown out all those windows. I knew I was
getting better as an actor and I was convinced that someday
I'd be a really good actor, but I was thinking, When I die,
what they're going to write on my tombstone is: Here Lies
Burt Reynolds, The First Guy to Pose Nude in a Magazine.

When *Deliverance* came out, I did get considerable
attention for the role I played, but it was overshadowed by
all the cheap hoopla over the *Cosmo* thing. Of course, if I had
it to do over, I would never have posed, but who's to say
what combination of factors eventually get you where you
want to go? Not that I'm there. I'm not. Directors like
Francis Coppola, Sidney Lumet, Sydney Pollack, never give

me first crack at their scripts. But they will, I keep telling myself, they will.

On the following day we are having lunch in Burt's trailer: lean food and fruit drinks, which is Burt's diet ever since he discovered he had hypoglycemia, a condition involving a deficiency of sugar in the blood which has the effect of causing its victims to faint dead away—in Burt's case sometimes in the middle of a take.

I ask Burt why he seems to prefer "mature" women. He looks at me thoughtfully; Burt is invariably direct and outspoken: "Well," he says, "most women don't come into their own until thirty-five, and don't know who they really are until they're forty-five. Women over thirty-five are tremendously interesting to me; over forty-five, fascinating; and over fifty-five, irresistible. Of course, I'm talking about a very special kind of woman, a woman without desperation, one who has had just about every man she really wanted. For me, a young woman is a pretty little pattern; an older woman, a kaleidoscope. But that doesn't mean I can be pals with them. As friends, I'm more comfortable with a man. I guess that's because I'm more forgiving of faults in men than I am in women. Also, women are more manipulative—they know your weaknesses and exploit them; men don't have that insight. Women have X rays in their eyes."

"If you don't mind my saying so, Burt, you've been involved with several of these attractive 'mature' women since your divorce—Dinah Shore being one of them—but you pass them by. Is it because the best way not to fail again at marriage is by not trying?"

"No, the best way not to fail again is to be absolutely positive that when you do it this time, you're going to do it right."

"You're not going to get a written guarantee, you know."

"Sure, I know, but goddamn it, I want to get as close to a guarantee as I can possibly get, so I'm going to live with her and fight with her and be in love and be crazy . . ."

"Well, if that's true, you told me the only woman you've been truly in love with was Sally Field and you were with her long enough to know her damn well, so what . . ."

"I should have grabbed her when I could. Terrible mistake

that, terrible. But let me explain about Sally. I had seen her on 'The Flying Nun'—she was sort of a joke then, but I saw the actress in her and wanted to do a movie with her. But all I had to offer her was *Smoky and the Bandit.* She was at the point in her career when she yearned to do quality work, and this certainly wasn't it, but I charmed her into it. And while making that picture we fell in love—God! did we fall in love! The wise birds all thought that she was too short, too plain-looking, too flat-chested, too down-to-earth to be a star, but I found her funny and very sexy, and at first she thought I was crazy to think she was sexy but I made her *feel* sexy, and that's when she began to bloom. She was a giver, an incredible giver, but at the time, I took giving for granted because all the women I had ever known had completely given themselves to me and I thought that came with the territory.

"I was convinced that Sally was going to be a big star and I told her so. There was a special rapport between us that made that picture work. We never spent a moment apart. She would stay with me every night and then get up at six in the morning to go home and make breakfast for her two sons and get them off for school. Then she'd come back and stay with me until it was time to pick them up at school. Can you believe she did this for five years? Five years! I got along with her younger son, Eli, very well. We loved each other, but Peter was nine and he's a bright, perceptive kid who knew things like when to be sick to get attention. He could turn a look on me that said, Okay, movie star, when are we moving in and becoming a family so my mom can stop running back and forth all the time."

"Why didn't that happen?" I asked.

"Because after Sally gave that remarkable performance in *Sybil,* I knew it was just a matter of time for it to happen."

"For what to happen?"

"For her to become a big star and have to move on."

"I don't understand what you're saying."

"Okay, I'll spell it out for you. A script was sent to her for a film called *Norma Rae* which she gave to me to read. After I read it, I said to myself, 'The envelope please.' It has Academy Award written all over it. I knew right there and then that if she did the part, it would be all over for us. Sally had a desperate need to succeed. She had been in analysis since she was fourteen. She had a bizarre relationship with her stepfather and with her mother, whom she loves and adores but doesn't get along with, so that her intense love for her sons compensated for lack of love everywhere else. I could deal with being second to her sons, but I couldn't deal with being third because I knew stardom would get second billing. After winning an Oscar, her life would become four months shooting a flick in Spain with Warren Beatty, six months in Morocco with Jack Nicholson, whatever, and where would I fit in? A visitor to the set, or off in Texas or Idaho doing my thing with Dolly Parton or Goldie Hawn.

"Now, I've never told anyone this, because I'm really ashamed of it, but after I read *Norma Rae* I did everything I could to stop Sally from doing that picture. I told her certain scenes were too dirty, when in reality they were rather sweet and wonderful. I told her that her co-star, Ron Liebman, was so wrong for the part it would wreck the film. I criticized everything, trying to discourage her, lying about what I really thought, because I knew that the Academy Award was hers. She was nominated, of course, but I didn't accompany her to the awards ceremony. I sat home alone that night, like a wounded Citizen Kane, visualizing her dancing with Dustin Hoffman at the Academy Ball.

"We saw each other after that, but we were never the same. I had become obsessed with the notion that two stars could not coexist in the same galaxy, which is, of course, nonsense."

"Maybe it was your way of avoiding marriage."

"Probably was. We don't see each other at all now. But I miss her. I think about her. I know what I had."

"Were her children also a deterring factor?"

"Oh, hell, no! I'm dying to have kids. In fact, when I finish this picture, I'm going to Vietnam and with the help of Julie Andrews and Blake Edwards, who have two Vietnamese kids themselves, I'm going to adopt a couple of orphans. What I'd like to get are the ones who are half American, the ones nobody wants."

"You know what I'm thinking, Burt, is that you've really boxed yourself into a corner: you say you're only attracted to people who have talent, but you also say that when that talent asserts itself and they become successful, they no longer fit into your life pattern. Isn't that a self-defeating philosophy?"

"Yep, it sure is, and I either have to accept the fact that I'm that kind of selfish son of a bitch, or I'm going to have to grow up and realize that . . . Listen, I have talks with myself every day . . . really, I discuss it with myself. And this last year's been an amazing one for me, for I have come to realize that if one loves a person, really loves that person, then you love her not only in spite of her faults but also in spite of her talents. It's almost impossible for me to get involved with people who aren't in show business, to meet someone who is as interested in the arts as I am, who shares my passion for old movies, who loves books, wants to go down the Wild River in a canoe with me, and most importantly, to find someone who's not attracted to my image but to the person I am. I find that often when I reveal myself as I really am, with all the bullshit stripped away, they take off. 'I didn't know you're so quiet,' they say, or they think I'm not having a good time with them because I'm not on.

"At the moment, I have a wonderful relationship with Loni Anderson, an extraordinary woman, another 'mature' lady, with an eighteen-year-old daughter, who's been around the horn a few times. Loni and I have an easygoing, compatible relationship. When I first met her I didn't care for the flashy look she projected and told her so. She's changed her style of dressing and done all she can to please me, but, damn it! she has the potential of being an enormous star, not so much for her talent as her personality, in the tradition of Lana Turner. When the camera is on her, it falls in love with her, with that body of hers that could stop the Chicago Express, and when she becomes the star I know she'll be, I will probably do my shuffle-off number. I seem to have built this perfect psychic guillotine with which I perform my own beheading."

"What you're saying is that with your help Loni will become a star and then you'll back away from her as you did with Sally Field?"

"Yeah. I guess it's my death wish."

Harry entered the living room and apologetically announced that the person Burt had been trying to reach was on the phone.

While Burt was out of the room, I thought about Dinah

Shore's observation that Burt was the most vulnerable man she had ever known. It seemed to me that that vulnerability was enhanced by a forlorn loneliness—a stranger in his own town. He did not seem to have any really close friends, and yet there was a strong need in him for compassionate friendship, for a friend he could trust and confide in. All the people in his life seemed to be work-oriented, or married couples like the Montalbans and the Stewarts, whose lives he envied. Burt was the captain of his ship, all right, but he seemed to be riding at anchor, stranded in the chart room, puzzling over what course to map out, but in the meantime not going anywhere.

Ten years ago, Burt had said that what he feared most was that he might become an unhappy success, and when he returned to the living room I asked him point-blank if he thought those fears had been overcome.

The question threw him; he creased his brow in thought. "To be honest, I'd have to say I'm somewhere between unhappy and happy. Learning how to become a success is so much more difficult than adjusting to being a failure. Failure doesn't go away. It hangs on you and you organize all your energies to try to fight your way out of it. But success . . . I spend all my time trying to figure out, How do I enjoy this? Why am I not enjoying this? Why does this and that depress me? I find myself being self-conscious about success, analyzing it, but I know the best thing would be just to enjoy it, take it for what it is. But I can't. As I get older, I hope the pressure of success will decrease and I'll get better about it, but right now, to answer you, I'm not a happy success, no.

"I found a clue to myself in an experience I had recently when I went to an automobile racetrack to take a driving course. The kind of cars Paul Newman races. After some instruction, they put my group on the track to see what we could do. I know how to handle fast cars from my days as a stunt man, and going past the grandstand I was passing everyone, but when we finished our laps my overall time was not very good. Which puzzled me, because I thought I was really moving. The instructor came over and said, 'Burt, you were terrific on half the track, where it runs in front of the grandstand, but you were a turtle on the backstretch. You know why? Because there are spectators in the grandstand. Burt, we can't put spectators all over the course.'

"I guess that's pretty much how it is with success—you got to be able to go on your own in the backstretch. That's something I'm working on. Success is a bitch. You can forget about all those old-fashioned concepts like values and virtues, what counts and what doesn't, because success distorts everything.

"So does failure. When my marriage to Judy collapsed and we got divorced, I called my mother and told her that I had failed—the first person in our family to get divorced. Tell Dad that he's right about me—I'm never going to make it. My father is a big, gruff man who has been a police officer all his life and we had always had a kind of military school relationship, if you know what I mean. He was a tough disciplinarian and not much had ever gone back and forth between us.

"But now he got on the phone and said, 'Burt, come on home. I've got something to tell you.' Dad picked me up at the airport and I anticipated a long lecture, but he didn't say a word in the car driving to our house. Then when we got there, he poured a couple of glasses of brandy, and that was the first time in all my thirty-three years he had ever offered me a drink, or had ever had a heart-to-heart talk with me. I figured he was softening me up for his lecture, but to my surprise he began to tell me about all the mistakes he had made in his life, the failures he had had. In all my years at home, he'd always come on as this perfect man who was forever arresting people for their mistakes, so it must have been difficult for him to tell me about the times he had failed in his life. He told me that failure was necessary to understand the values of achieving anything, that everyone failed at one time or another, and that all that counted was the love and understanding of the people who cared about you, as he cared about me, his son.

"As a little boy, I had never dared shed a tear in front of this man, but now, for the first time in my life, I felt I could express my emotions, and the tears ran down my face as I listened to him. There were tears in his eyes too, and all of a sudden we were in each other's arms, holding tight, shedding our tears of love, and that moment gave me a strength that I am sure I can always draw on.

"We have a wonderful relationship now, my dad and I, and I sometimes think I ought to go home and have a couple of drinks with him and let him tell me about success. After all, the two are not so far apart, failure and success. And as a man, my dad is as successful as anyone I know."

20

Anthony Quinn and the
Long Pursuit

Every writing project, fiction or nonfiction, involves discarded pages and reams of file cards filled with unused information. The free-lancer accepts this waste as indigenous to his profession, but what he tries to avoid are those projects that never come to fruition, which means that after considerable research and writing the free-lancer has nothing to show for it, and the time (capital) he has invested is a dead loss.

My longest unfinished project involves Anthony Quinn, and after sixteen years there is no end in sight. Tony first appeared in my life in 1967, shortly after the publication of *Papa Hemingway,* convinced that portraying Hemingway would be the pinnacle of his career. We met in his suite at the Hampshire House, and with great force and assertiveness he told me of his lifelong identification with Hemingway, his devotion to everything he had written, his vision of how he would portray this giant among giants. For two hours Tony held forth, occasionally reading passages from *Papa Hemingway,* a bravura performance that was more caricature of Hemingway than accurate, but undeniably vital. From my point of view, the important thing was Tony's compassion for Hemingway, and I could tell that eventually, working on the role, he would be able to make the necessary adjustments. I wasn't looking for mimicry, but rather an approximation of Hemingway's life force, the essence of the man he was.

Tony and I parted with the understanding that since he was on his way to Hollywood, he would make arrangements with a studio for the production of the film. His enthusiasm and intense vitality seemed boundless, qualities that were certainly apparent in the memorable roles he had played—in *Viva Zapata!* with Marlon Brando, the role of the artist Paul Gauguin in *Lust for Life* (he won Oscars for both of these), the Arab chieftain in *Lawrence of Arabia,* the poignant prizefighter in *Requiem for a Heavyweight,* the pope in *The Shoes of the Fisherman,* a freewheeling adventurer in *The Guns of Navarone,* Zorba, Bombolini in *The Secret of Santa Vittoria,* and on the Broadway stage, King Henry II in *Becket* opposite Laurence Olivier. Tony had thrust himself into those parts as one would thrust an isotope into some inert mass to energize it.

A few weeks after our first meeting, Tony phoned from Santa Monica and urged me to come there immediately to meet with studio executives who, he said, were very enthusiastic about our project. I found Tony and his wife and three little children occupying an entire floor of the Miramar, a Santa Monica hotel that had certainly seen better days. Tony played the part of the benign patriarch to perfection. He also presided over our meetings with the studio people with the assertiveness of a matador addressing his peons before the corrida. These executives made notes, asked some financial questions, and said they would get back to us. All Hollywood meetings are concluded with that benediction: we'll get back to you.

Months passed. No word from Tony, so I presumed the studio executives were taking a long, circuitous route getting back to us. I had by now become accustomed to these Hollywood enthusiasms which flare brightly for a moment and then extinguish with a puff of smoke. I really think that's what causes the smog out there—all those incipient deals going up in smoke.

But then came another call from Tony. Could I fly out right away and spend a few days working with him on an outline? That's all that was needed to conclude our deal. A short outline. He knew just what they wanted. I didn't want to go but it was really very difficult to resist being swept up by the torrent of Tony's enthusiasm, so I reluctantly consented. It was then that I discovered that Tony was not calling from Hollywood, as I had presumed, but from Durango, Mexico, where he was making a period Western.

What a jaunt that was! After flying to Los Angeles, I had to transfer to a small plane that took me to the Mexican coastal town of Mazatlán, where a hired car took me on an arduous trip over winding mountain roads to Durango.

The location where Tony was filming was seventy miles outside the town, and we worked there every day for a week, writing an outline in between Tony's scenes, which involved battle heroics, so that most of the time Tony was covered with blood and grime; Tony also managed to find time to meet with the director of the film for the purpose of rewriting whatever scene that was scheduled to be shot on the following day. At each day's end we drove the seventy miles back to town, where Tony played with his little sons before they went to bed, invariably followed by a long, hearty meal, red wine flowing long into the night. Iolanda, his second wife, made sure the kitchen offerings were up to Tony's standards. Among the dinner guests was his twenty-year-old son from his first marriage, who had come for a visit. Tony's laugh was a window-shaking roar, his romp with his sons like a rugby skirmish; the whole house seemed to inflate when he walked in.

Tony would have kept me in Durango for weeks, working on that outline and talking about Hemingway—how he loved to discuss Hemingway!—but I had to leave to fly to Washington to attend a state dinner at the White House for Kurt Kiesinger, the then chancellor of West Germany. As we parted, Tony assured me that now that he had an outline our movie would be off the ground in no time.

I had come to realize that Tony was one of those rare people who bring to every new day of their existence a distillation of everything that preceded it—and since his birth in Chihuahua, Mexico, in 1915, Tony had certainly compressed a great deal of living into that span of time. Shortly after his birth, Tony's sixteen-year-old mother escaped from the chaos of Pancho Villa's revolution by traveling five hundred miles on foot to El Paso, carrying Baby Tony on her back all the way. There they were joined by Tony's nineteen-year-old father, an itinerant fruit-picker who was half-Irish—thus Tony's Irish name. The three of them rode freight cars to California, where they worked long hours for little money, picking oranges and sleeping under the trees at night. "My youth was all whirlwinds of sand and threatening rain," Tony recalled. Tony's father was struck by a car and killed in Los Angeles when Tony was nine, and after that it was mostly work for Tony, with school a sometime thing. "I was born to struggle," Tony said, "to fight odds. I used to faint from hunger, right on Hollywood Boulevard. One whole summer we lived on the beach on mustard greens and mussels. You didn't live in those days. You just tried to exist. Before I was eighteen, I had worked as a shoeshine boy, newsboy, carpenter, electrician, butcher in a slaughterhouse, taxi driver, cement mixer, truck driver, clothes cutter, boxer, and farm laborer. I was foreman of an apricot ranch when I was fourteen, with a hundred and fifty people under me. The best job I had was foreman in a mattress factory."

At fifteen, Tony was playing the saxophone at parties, and that led to playing the saxophone at Aimee Semple McPherson's Angelus Temple, where, in addition to playing sax, Tony started to preach. At sixteen, Tony, who weighed only 147 pounds, was a sparring partner for the gargantuan heavyweight Primo Carnera, who worked out with him for speed. Tony had a string of welterweight fights, for purses ranging from five to fifty dollars, but after sixteen wins he was knocked out and his manager ended his career because he felt seventeen-year-old Tony didn't have a killer instinct in the ring.

About this time Tony discovered that the reason people didn't understand him very well was because he had a congenital speech defect—his tongue was attached to the floor of his mouth by excess flesh. He had it corrected in an operation that he paid off in installments by working as a janitor in a drama school, and that's where he began to learn to speak properly and to develop an interest in acting. He got his first part in a play with Mae West that paid him ten dollars a week, and that led to a bit appearance as an Indian in Cecil B. de Mille's *The Plainsman*. A year later he married De Mille's adopted daughter, Katherine, but Tony, then twenty-two, refused to take any roles in his father-in-law's movies, and instead laboriously carved out his own career in Hollywood. Katherine and he had four children.

The turning point in his career, Tony said, was going to Italy to make *La Strada* with Fellini, for although he had won Oscars for his supporting roles in *Viva Zapata!* and *Lust for Life*, *La Strada* made him a star. And from then on he lived the life of a star, with six automobiles, a ninety-foot yacht, a mansion in Pacific Palisades, an East Side New York $300,000 townhouse, a twelve-acre estate in Ridgefield, Connecticut, an apartment in Paris; when he was making *The Guns of Navarone* in Rhodes, he purchased a five-hundred-acre isthmus there with two harbors.

He has given up most of these possessions, in favor of a sprawling villa outside Rome where he now lives with Iolanda, whom he met when she was working in the costume department for the film *Barabbas*, which Tony made in Italy in 1962. He has lovingly filled his villa with thousands of books, antiques, and paintings. Tony himself paints and sculpts very well, and recently he had a successful one-man show in Hawaii.

After I left Durango, I really believed that Tony would quickly arrange for our film to be produced, but I never heard from him again. Not a word.

Until, fourteen years later my phone rang and Tony said: "Hotch, I'm really ready to go with *Papa Hemingway*—meet me for lunch tomorrow at '21', will you? I've got great news." Just like that, as if Durango was yesterday.

Fourteen years had done nothing to dampen Tony's enthusiasm for playing Hemingway. "We're going to do it on the *stage*, Hotch, fuck those Hollywood bastards, it's gonna be the goddamnedest spectacle anyone ever saw, I already talked to Roger Stevens—we're all set to open at the Kennedy Center next fall, then we'll tour the entire country, Tony Quinn's farewell to acting, my final role, after that, only painting, what a tour! The production will cost three million, audiences will never have seen anything like it, a production that will knock their eyes out, every place but Broadway, fuck Broadway, only if they come crawling, Lennie Bernstein to do the music, or Sondheim, we'll get Jerry Robbins or Bob Fosse to choreograph and direct, and . . ."

"Wait a minute, hold on, Tony—what's that you're saying about music?"

"Well, that's what it is—a musical, a really big musical."

"You're going to sing and dance as Hemingway?"

"Yeah, why not?"

"Impossible. *Papa Hemingway* as a musical? Tony, you've gone too far."

"Wait a minute. If I'da come to you a few years ago and said: 'Hotch, listen, I've got a great idea for a musical—Eva Perón and the Argentine dictatorship—' "

"I would have said you were nuts," I admitted.

"There you go! Well, this is no more nuts than *Evita.*"

"But who's going to assemble all this, Tony? A musical is a very complicated piece of business."

"Don't worry. I'm working on it. I'll get Joe Stein, who wrote *Fiddler,* or Hugh Wheeler, who did *Sweeney Todd,* maybe Kander and Ebb for the music—you liked *Cabaret,* didn't you? Don't give it a thought, I've got a producer named Gladys Rackmill and she's lining up everything. Just let's shake on it. Okay?"

What the hell—I shook on it.

A year passed, during which time an occasional item about the musicalized *Papa Hemingway* appeared in the papers, but they were more hopeful than specific. Almost a year to the day after our "21" lunch, Tony called, his voice uncharacteristically subdued, and asked me to meet him at his apartment in the Adams Hotel. Tony has an entire floor of the Adams, a posh hostelry at Eighty-sixth and Fifth, half of the floor occupied by his painting and sculpting studios.

He was sad to report that the musical project had not gone as expected. A Hollywood screenwriter who had never done a musical had finally been engaged to write the script but it was a fiasco. Gladys had never found a composer and lyricist *but* Tony was undaunted. We can do it without music, you and I, he said, vibrancy coming back in his voice, his expressive face coming to life. I tried to throttle his excitement before it got up to full speed, but he zipped right past me. Fifteen years had not subdued his ardor, or stiffened my resistance. We met a couple of times a week all through the summer, and by fall I was halfway through a playscript. We even began to have talks with an organization about planning a tour, but suddenly Tony disappeared, and when he returned he told me that a revival of the musical version of *Zorba* had been proposed to him, along with a fifty-thousand-weekly guarantee, and that considering the great expense of casting his sculpture at the foundry on Long Island, he had decided to accept it. BUT! Listen, *don't despair!* In two years, after he had stuffed his pockets with *Zorba* gold, he would be ready to play Hemingway, because he was put on earth to play Hemingway, and it would be the greatest role of his career, et cetera, et cetera, et cetera.

The better I knew Tony the more I came to realize that the Outer Quinn—hearty, self-assured, papa bearish, bursting with plans and ideas, wary, tenaciously concerned with making money, idealistic, a dreamer and schemer, loving, brutal, passionate about women, hot-tempered, forgiving—this Outer Quinn is the temple watchdog for the self-doubting, frail, indecisive Inner Quinn, who is still that shy, speech-impaired boy from Chihuahua.

I like both of them. The Outer Quinn is a circus of commotion, while the Inner Quinn is a cousin of the St. Louis Depression boy who lives in me.

Tony and I may never do *Papa Hemingway*, but the wise free-lancer knows from experience never to say never. My patron saint, Lazarus, was one of the earliest free-lancers, and several times I have had projects that rose from ashes as dead as his.

The ashes of my first interview with the symphony conductor Lorin Maazel are a case in point. Just about the time I was going into the Air Force, I had heard a radio broadcast of a performance by Arturo Toscanini's renowned N.B.C. Symphony Orchestra, conducted by a ten-year-old musical prodigy named Lorin Maazel. For several years following that performance, Maazel was given wide publicity as he conducted most of the major orchestras in this country and Canada, a little boy in a velvet Lord Fauntleroy suit on a high podium, waving his junior-size baton.

But when, at fifteen, he could no longer be considered a child prodigy, the demand for his appearances stopped as abruptly as it had started. For several years he completely disappeared from public view, and it was at this point that I was given an assignment to interview him and write an article about the rise and crash of a prodigy meteorite.

I went to Pittsburgh for the interview. Maazel was attending classes at the University of Pittsburgh and playing the violin with a local quintet. He was bright and engaging and forthright about what puberty had done to his career. He said that he had a firm belief in his talent and he exuded a conviction that someday he would come into his own as an adult. I believed him, and I felt that it would be a disservice to write about him at that low point in his career. And, to be honest, I didn't feel that I could make a story about him interesting enough for publication. So I did not write about Lorin Maazel, failed prodigy, and chalked up the experience under the heading of Wasted Effort.

But a decade later I was pleasantly surprised to see an announcement in *The New York Times* that Maazel was going to conduct a performance by the French Orchestre National at Carnegie Hall, his first United States appearance since his prodigy days. I found out that in the intervening years he had been living in Rome and conducting in Europe. I also found out that he was now married and had a child. I felt that the time had come to dig up my old notes and carry them forward, the story now being one of resurrection rather than downfall. But what I was particularly interested in was whether Maazel would permit his child to be a performing prodigy if she had the same talent he had had.

HOTCHNER: Tell me about that time when you conducted Toscanini's orchestra.

MAAZEL: I was ten years old then, and Toscanini himself had invited me to conduct the orchestra, which had been handpicked by him, and was composed of the most accomplished musicians of that time. Although I had already conducted several symphony orchestras, including the New York Philharmonic, to have been invited by the great Toscanini to direct his renowned group was an awesome experience for the shy boy I was.

I entered the rehearsal hall where the distinguished musicians of the orchestra were already assembled, and mounted the podium. As I lifted my baton and looked up to face them, instead of readying their instruments, each musician pulled a lollipop out of his pocket and began licking it.

I recall, very vividly indeed, how deeply I felt this mockery, but outwardly I did not let them see how much their gesture had hurt my ten-year-old sensibilities. I gave the downbeat and persisted. They began to play but soon one of them intentionally played a wrong note. I conducted then, as I do now, from memory but I spotted the note as easily as if a score had been in front of me. I stopped the rehearsal and pointed out the error. After two or three more such efforts on their part, the musicians, who seemed stunned to discover that a ten-year-old boy could have committed such a complicated score to memory, stopped baiting me and performed with their customary effort.

HOTCHNER: Did you often have to face that kind of hostility?

MAAZEL: Yes, virtually every time I appeared before a new orchestra—and by the time I was fifteen I had conducted most of the principal symphonies in the United States and Canada—I had to face the same hostility from musicians who resented being led by a little kid in velvet pants and long curls. On one occasion the first violinist of an orchestra I was conducting asked to be excused from rehearsal early. "I have a little boy your age, Maestro," he said to me, emphasizing the "maestro" a little too hard, "who has the mumps." As he was leaving, I heard another violinist whisper to him: "Tomorrow bring a little mumps for our genius."

HOTCHNER: Why do you think they resented you so?

MAAZEL: And why shouldn't they have resented me, as did many adults who were not musicians? At the age of nine I had achieved what they had not accomplished with a lifetime of hard work. When I was four I had demonstrated the rare ability of having absolute pitch [being able to identify the pitch of any tone simply by hearing it]. At five I was playing violin concertos. At six I was already committing to memory, note by note, the scores of symphonies and operas. No adult could be offhand about a child like that. Either they openly resented my very existence or they gushed over me such floods that I was often in danger of drowning. I don't know which made me cringe the most.

HOTCHNER: Did you find children of your age hostile to you?

MAAZEL: Well, you can imagine what I had to face with other children. When I was not performing I attended a public school in Pittsburgh, where we had moved when I was eight. Now Pittsburgh is a pretty tough town and that school had its full quota of tough kids. So when this little genius with his long hair and fancy clothes went out for his first recess, the schoolyard bullies were licking their chops. But when the leader of the pack, who was a good head taller than I was, came sauntering at me, I stood my ground—it is my nature never to back off from anything, bullies or symphony orchestras. The bully taunted me, to the delight of the other kids who had gathered around; I let him get away with that, but when he gave my hair a yank, that did it and I let him have a roundhouse right smack on the button. I guess he was the most surprised bully who ever landed on his bottom. He picked himself up and we went at each other. I had a cut lip and a black eye by the time the teachers pulled us apart, but in a way I was prouder of those two blemishes than the medals and decorations I received for my musical accomplishments. Nobody in that schoolyard ever put me on again. I lost that fistfight but I won the respect of every kid in my class.

HOTCHNER: Do you think it was a mistake for you to have been put in a public school, considering the kind of life you led?

MAAZEL: To the contrary—I think my parents' decision to put me in that school rather than provide me with tutors or a fancy school was the saving factor of my prodigy-ridden boyhood; but I must confess that I had to consciously do *badly* in my studies in order to keep myself at the pace of the rest of the class. Even so, I slowly outdistanced the Pittsburgh school system and by the time I was fifteen I had completed high school.

HOTCHNER: I looked up "prodigy" in the dictionary, and this is the definition: "Endowed with extraordinary gifts or powers, a wonder; something abnormal or monstrous." Do you agree with that definition?

MAAZEL: Those two opposites sum up my boyhood. Although the adulation I received was naturally very gratifying, there was something monstrous and abnormal about not being able to live like other boys. Children want to conform, and as I grew older I began to despise the long hair and velvet pants that set me apart. I loved to play baseball and football, and I was good enough at these sports to have made the school team; how many afternoons I yearned to be out on the diamond instead of at the music stand under my parents' watchful eyes.

HOTCHNER: What's the sharpest memory you have of your boyhood?

MAAZEL: Of all remembered emotions, I'd say my recollection of loneliness is the sharpest. Set apart from other boys, and traveling so much, I had no chance to make friends. How I used to envy the boys who palled around together. I don't think any of them envied me.

HOTCHNER: What happened to you when you turned fifteen?

MAAZEL: I was not prepared for it—the glamorous world I had taken for granted vanished. I was dropped from the heights of adulation to the depths of obscurity, from entity to nonentity virtually overnight. A gangling teen-ager, his voice changing and down on his upper lip, is no longer the cute little freak that has novelty in the concert hall. Like many a prodigy before me, I had found that at the point when most young people begin their careers, mine was ended. This is the inevitable hell of being a child prodigy—it must end as childhood ends.

HOTCHNER: How can a teen-ager handle such a cataclysmic event?

MAAZEL: The answer is, he can't. You suffer terribly from this rejection; you don't know who you are. I had not lost my knowledge or skills—I was the same boy I had always been—but now, hurt and puzzled, I had been dropped, rejected, dumped into a state of obscurity I did not understand. With tremendous effort, over the ensuing years, I forced myself to concentrate on my college studies and forget the past; as a result, by the time I was graduated, I was ready to try to start a fresh career as an adult. I was lucky to make this recovery; for most child prodigies, the abrupt end of their childhood careers is a blow from which they never fully recover.

HOTCHNER: Do you have resentments? Do you feel you were exploited?

MAAZEL: Of course I was. I brought in considerable income and I brought praise and adulation to my parents, who worked hard at keeping me chained to my music and away from the more normal pursuits of boyhood. At this point I suppose I am expected to express bitterness and resentment toward them, but

I'm afraid I have to go against the current mode of prostrating oneself on the public psychiatric couch and blaming it all on Ma and Pa.

I can sympathize with what a prodigy means to an ordinary parent; what magic he injects into the life of a tailor or mechanic or post office clerk; what attention and money come to that parent for having produced this unique offspring. When I was eight years old I led a W.P.A. symphony orchestra in a performance of Tchaikovsky's "Marche Slav," and the conductor told my parents that I was a genius who must be given every opportunity to perform. The following year, Olin Downes, then the foremost critic in the country, watched me perform at the Interlaken Music Camp in Michigan and arranged for me to conduct Mendelssohn's "Italian" Symphony at the New York World's Fair. How can I blame my parents for responding to pressures like these?

HOTCHNER: Now that you yourself have become a father, would you allow your child to follow in your footsteps if she proves to be a prodigy?

MAAZEL: My answer is an emphatic NO. If my child has extraordinary talent, I will encourage her to her limits but *within herself.* By that I mean I will get her a fine teacher and take her to concerts and help her however I can but I will not subject her to the exploitation of performing in public. Why should any child be put through the ordeal of going through her tricks before a mass of ohhing and ahhing adults? Why should she be robbed of her playtime? Or subjected to the envy and hostility of adults who resent her talents?

Furthermore, any parent who pushes a gifted child beyond his natural interest-span runs the risk of turning that child's love of music or whatever his talent is into a hate of that talent. By the time the child approaches maturity, he will develop a revulsion for the very thing the parent hoped he was instilling in him. That almost happened to me—I came within a whisker of pursuing other interests for my career.

As the parent of a talented child, I would regard that talent as something that would enable her to enjoy life more fully; but as an aid to the *art* of living and not *making* a living. If her talent is such that it will lift her into the rarefied air of the artist, that's fine, but let it come to her after she has had the fun of girlhood.

The audiences of the world don't need children.

Maestro Toscanini came to the dress rehearsal of my performance with his N.B.C. Symphony—the only time he watched me conduct. Afterwards he came up to me and put his hand on my shoulder, a faint smile on his beautiful aesthetic face. "God bless you," he said. He repeated it, then again, and that's all he said before he left. I've often wondered how to interpret his words, whether they were offered as praise for my effort, or whether Mr. Toscanini, knowing the hellish road of the prodigy that lay ahead of me, was offering a benediction.*

In contrast to unfulfilled or long-delayed projects like Quinn and Maazel, there are those that are supposed to be difficult but which sometimes turn out to be easy as pie. For instance, Bess Truman. After the Trumans left the White House, Bess was not available to the press. Even while she was in the White House, Mrs. Truman granted few interviews, preferring to leave the limelight to Harry.

Back when I was first starting and scratching hard to make my way, Bess Truman was mentioned as a definite assignment if I could get to her—but I was warned that others had tried and it wasn't easy. I attempted to reach her through Mr. Truman's secretary, but I was told that an interview with Mrs. Truman was not possible.

About that time I went to St. Louis for my brother's wedding, and on an impulse, the day after the nuptials, I borrowed my mother's car and drove to Independence, Missouri, where the Trumans were living. A similar tactic had worked, if you recall, when I phoned Sinatra directly, but I knew there was no way to reach Mrs. Truman on the telephone. I had no idea what I would do when I got there, but even if nothing came of it, it gave me a chance to see Truman's birthplace; ever since his spectacular defeat of Dewey against enormous odds, Harry had been one of my heroes.

*Maazel went on to distinguish himself as conductor of the Cleveland Symphony, and only recently resigned that post to become artistic director of the Vienna State Opera.

I parked down the block from the Trumans' white frame house and walked toward the entrance. As I did, a car pulled up and Mrs. Truman, carrying a bag of groceries, got out, along with a man with a telltale Secret Service insigne on his lapel.

"Hello, Mrs. Truman," I said.

"Hello," she said pleasantly.

"I'm very pleased to see you. My name's Hotchner, I'm a writer, originally from St. Louis, and I'd very much like to talk to you. I phoned your husband's secretary but . . ."

"What was it about?"

"Just wanted to write about your life now—what happens to you and Mr. Truman when you change your address from Sixteen hundred Pennsylvania Avenue to a little town in Missouri."

"Well, no harm in that. Come on up on the porch." She gave the bag of groceries to the housekeeper who came to meet her, and we sat in comfortable chairs on the porch. It was hot, and she fanned herself with a painted bamboo fan. I asked her if she missed living in the White House. From what I had read about her, I had the impression that she was taciturn and not easy to talk to, but that certainly wasn't true. She spoke openly and pleasantly.

"Well, I certainly miss the White House today, I can tell you. I have just spent the afternoon trying to find a yardman, but I had no luck. I do some of the gardening myself—I work hard at my roses—but how nice it would be to have a few of those White House gardeners caring for our grounds.

"We have a power mower and I spent the early part of the summer trying to induce Mr. Truman to use it. Finally he did. Eleven o'clock of a Sunday morning, with all the Methodists and Baptists going by our house on the way to church, Mr. Truman got out on our front lawn in his shirt sleeves and began cutting the grass. When I looked out of the window and saw him I was horrified.

" 'Harry! Come in here this minute,' I called to him. 'You know what those churchgoers are saying.' There's no doubt in my mind he planned the whole thing deliberately to exonerate himself from ever touching that mower again. And he hasn't.

"This house doesn't look very big, but we have fourteen

rooms, and it would be extremely pleasant to have some of the wonderful staff we had in the White House to help run it. I certainly miss them. We only have our maid, who has been with us for twenty-eight years, and occasional cleaning help. Despite the fact that *Collier's* magazine recently said that I shop by phone and avoid the stores, the truth is that I drive to the grocers like most of the other housewives in Independence and I choose the meat and vegetables that look best. We have a couple of very good department stores where I do most of my other shopping.

"Now in this respect I don't know whether I miss the White House or not. It's true that this kind of chore wasn't a part of my life there—Mabel Walker, the housekeeper, would bring the menu to my desk at nine o'clock each morning and it would simply be a matter of approving it or changing it a bit—but I don't really mind having to shop, whereas there were certain White House chores that I did mind.

"What I minded most were the big receptions, where hundreds and hundreds of strange hands had to be shaken, and sometimes there were afternoon receptions and evening receptions on the same day. I do not miss them one bit.

"The mountain of daily mail that had to be answered with the help of my secretary and her staff—that's another task I certainly don't miss. The day-in, day-out schedule of appointments that kept me living by the clock—also not missed one bit. I was recently asked whether, when I now read in the papers about some function or activity taking place in the White House, or when I see a photo of Mrs. Eisenhower engaged in some activity which I once performed, whether I feel a twang of nostalgia. Well, I most certainly don't. I never enjoyed that side of White House life.

"But there are some things about the White House that I miss very much. The lovely cut flowers, fresh every morning, that filled the second-floor rooms. The new books that the Library of Congress sent over every week. (I am an avid reader and here in Independence I am limited by what our library has on its shelves.) And I miss our good friends, who would come regularly to visit, and whom we have known ever since we first came to Washington back in 1935. We know people here in

Independence, but we are not 'connected' with them, as you are with friends.

"When my husband and I recently returned to Washington for a brief visit, I was reminded how much I enjoy and how much I miss the physical beauty of the city. The wide, tree-lined avenues, the splendid buildings, the thrilling monuments—they lifted my heart the way they did the first time I saw them.

"Then too, the theatre, concert, and other cultural life of Washington is sorely missed by both Mr. Truman and myself. We have a very good Philharmonic in nearby Kansas City, and occasional theatre, but it cannot compare with the cultural climate of the capital. I do not miss Washington social life in its formal sense, but I do miss the informal social life I had with our many friends.

"I miss, too, certain aspects of my job as First Lady. It was a challenging, intensely interesting position, and I rather enjoyed tackling its many problems.

"Here in Independence, life is easier, slower, much more relaxed. People smile more. We have the luxury of undemanded time, but we also have the occasional dullness that goes with it. I am not much of a joiner, never have been, and clubs take little of my time. I go to church regularly, but I don't work in any of the groups. I play a little bridge, but not on fixed afternoons. The mail is still mountainous, but I have no secretarial help, so when I get snowed under I send an S.O.S. to Mr. Truman's office.

"We entertain occasionally, but usually in small groups. I have had as many as fourteen for sit-down dinner, and thirty for a buffet, but they were exceptions. My husband and I rarely go out in the evening since his operation, for he is quite tired when he gets home from the office. He has as many daily callers as he had in the White House, and he has his book to work on as well.

"Occasionally some of our Washington friends stop off to see us on their way west, and those are wonderful occasions. We talk about Washington and the things and people we miss there.

"For the truth is, I have two loves, and I would be happiest if I could live half-time in Washington, and half-time in Independence. My husband and I lived in the capital for a long time, and there are days when I miss it so much I feel blue."

Mrs. Truman's housekeeper came to the screen door and said that Mr. Truman was on the phone. We both stood up, and I thanked her for her kindness in inviting me on the porch to have a chat.

"Not at all," she said. "It's nice to talk to someone from the outside world, once in a while."

21

Lee Marvin Ties One On in the White House

I mentioned that I escaped from the Durango conferences with Tony Quinn in order to attend a state dinner in the White House in honor of Chancellor Kurt Kiesinger of West Germany. I have no idea what put me on the list of invitees. I had never met Kiesinger, or any other German notable, nor was I involved in any way with the Johnson administration. Someone said there were three representatives of the "arts" at the dinner: Raymond Burr, because Kiesinger liked "Perry Mason" on German television; Lee Marvin, because Kiesinger liked *Cat Ballou;* and I was there because *Papa Hemingway,* which had been translated into German, was one of his favorite books. I don't know—the explanation smacked of White House press agentry.

At any rate, I looked forward to being a guest at this high-level White House function. I had been in the White House only once before but not as a dinner guest at a state affair. I had written a play called *The White House,* which was performing in Philadelphia prior to its Broadway opening. It was kaleidoscopic in form, a kind of political vaudeville that depicted intimate moments in the lives of many of the presidents and their wives; the cast included Helen Hayes, Fritz Weaver, James Daly, and a young newcomer, Gene Wilder.

Lady Bird Johnson had come to Philadelphia to see the play, and liked it sufficiently to invite us to perform a section of it in the East Room for the entertainment of the wives of cabinet members, senators, Supreme Court justices, and the Joint Chiefs of Staff, whom she had invited for her annual luncheon.

It was thrilling for me to see Helen Hayes perform the scene wherein Dolly Madison, with the British about to burn down the White House in the War of 1812, saved Gilbert Stuart's portrait of Washington, an event that took place in the very East Room where Helen was performing that afternoon—and there on the wall was the actual Stuart portrait Dolly Madison had saved.

Getting back to that state dinner in 1968: I had a room at the Mayfair, which was only a short distance from the White House, and since it was a balmy May evening I decided to go there on foot. It's quite possible that no one had ever before walked to the White House for a state dinner. As I approached the southwest gate of the White House, there was a steady stream of chauffeur-driven limousines driving through. The officers at the entrance examined my invitation very carefully and, I thought, rather reluctantly let me enter. To avoid the limousines, I decided to take a shortcut across the lawn; as a result I was accosted by concealed Secret Service men at three checkpoints, each of whom, after scrupulously examining my credentials, advised me that I'd be better off in the future coming to these functions in a conveyance. By the time I got to the front door, my tux a bit wilted from the experience, I was inclined to agree.

The Marine Corps party band was playing in the foyer, and a smartly uniformed Marine guide led me into a spacious room where guests were being introduced to other guests by white-gloved Marine officers in their ceremonial best. Cocktails were being served in a unique manner—white-jacketed barmen circulated with trays on which there was an assortment of drinks, and no sooner had you drained off one drink than a tray bearer was at your elbow with a fresh supply. My Marine guide led me over to a group of three austere Midwesterners who exuded the monied upper social reaches of Shaker Heights and Grosse Pointe. As we were exchanging the usual bromides, an unrestrained growl came from my blind side: "Hotchner, what the fuck are we doing here with all these stiffs?" It was Lee Marvin; my three austere companions immediately drifted toward the nether reaches of the room. I had never before met Lee Marvin, but he talked to me as if I were his next-door neighbor.

"I just spent twenty minutes with two shitheads from the State Department, for Chrissakes," he growled. The growl seemed to be his normal speech.

Lee and I spent the rest of the cocktail hour together, Lee fending off with barbed insult any interloper. The only thing about the proceedings that seemed to please him was the endless readiness of the cocktail trays. To show his impartiality he drank from all of them. By the time we were summoned to dinner, he was very loose.

I was relieved to find that, in his condition, Lee was not at my table. I had been warned that the Johnson kitchen was nothing to write home about, but on this occasion, at least, the meal was quite good: lobster *en Bellevue* accompanied by Charles Krug champagne and a Pinot Chardonnay, tenderloin of veal *princesse* with *dauphine* potatoes accompanied by a Great Western *vin rouge*, a salad of greens with Tilsit cheese, and for dessert mint Cecilia with an Almadén *blanc de blancs*.

The guests right and left of me were pleasant, intelligent wives of administration officials, and by the time Kiesinger and Johnson had exchanged verbose, meaningless toasts and we had adjourned to the foyer for dancing to the Marine Band music, I had forgotten about Lee Marvin. But he hadn't forgotten about me.

"Listen, Hotch," he growled into my ear, "I'm gonna cut in on Lyndon—watch me." President Johnson was dancing the first dance with Mrs. Kiesinger.

"No, Lee," I said, "don't do it—I'm sure that would be frowned upon."

"Fuck 'em," he said, and started to make a move toward the President. I grabbed his arm.

"You see that blonde over there in the green sparkles? Let's see you get her on the floor—she's a damn sight prettier than Frau Kiesinger." I was using the kind of substitute distraction that had worked with my daughters when they were little.

"Betcha a buck," he said.

"You're on."

He crossed the floor in a less than straight path, almost bumping into Johnson, and he practically pulled the recalcitrant blonde onto the dance floor. After a couple of dances, the Johnsons withdrew to their upstairs quarters, and the Kiesingers departed for Blair House, where they were staying. Established protocol was for the band to play another half hour, until midnight, when everyone was expected to leave. And everyone did —except Lee Marvin.

He had already proposed giving me a lift in his car—"I got me an MGM limo longer than the fuckin' East Room"—and since I didn't relish another crossing of no-man's-land on foot, I had waited for him, but I hadn't anticipated his resistance to the curfew. An attractive young woman who was probably one of Johnson's press aides, or perhaps the Princess of Protocol, went over to Lee and very politely explained that the evening had run its course but that the band was required to keep playing until the last guest had left.

"Okay, fine," Lee said, well slurred by now, "but you gotta gimme the last dance."

She was a good sport about it, and while the Marine Band endlessly played "Good Night, Sweetheart," Lee, who, I suspected was not much of a dancer even when sober, bumbled around the dance floor with her as the White House staff and the Marine officers patiently stood by, watching them. Many of them turned annoyed looks on me, but I just kept a dumb semi-smile on my face that I hoped looked inscrutable, desperately regretting that I had not stayed in Durango.

Lee was right about the size of the black custom Cadillac that waited at the curb. The driver was a distinguished-looking black man named Preston. Lee introduced me: "Preston, my man, this is my old, old pal, Senator Hotchpotch, who owns a string of bawdy houses in Salt Lake City. Say hello to Preston, best fuckin' driver in the U. S. of A."

Preston chuckled. "Where to, Mr. Marvin?"

"Could he drop me off at my hotel?" I asked. "I'm just around the block from here."

"He could not!" Lee snapped. "You 'n' me gotta go have a nightcap. Take us for a glass of booze, Preston, *s'eeel vous plah*!"

"I'm sorry, Mr. Marvin, but it's after hours and all the bars are shut."

"At twelve fuckin' o'clock? Aw, you're kiddin'. In a town fulla thirsty senators? Let's have a look."

Preston drove by several bars, all of them closed. I was greatly relieved, because what I very much did not need at that moment was another drink. "Well, just drop me off, Lee, and . . ."

Lee moved up to the partition and growled directly into Preston's ear: "Now, Preston, don't give me that shit—you guys know where to get laid, drunk, or shot up, and I'm tellin' you right here and now, the distinc . . . distincwitched senator Mr. A. E. Hotchpotch, and the distincwitched actor Mr. Lee Marvelous are gonna have them a nightcap! Y' get me?"

"Well, maybe the private airport," Preston said. "I hear tell there's a club over there . . ."

"Attaboy."

There is a small airport on the outskirts of Washington that is restricted to private aircraft; Lee and I waited in the departure area while Preston went off in search of a bottle of after-hours whiskey. It was almost 2 A.M. by now, and the only people in the lounge were two men and a woman at the departure desk, where a single attendant was on duty. Lee grabbed my arm so hard I could feel my bones crunch.

"Looka that broad!" he exclaimed, sucking in his breath. "Just looka that!"

The woman at the counter to whom he was referring was indeed a gorgeous young redhead. The two men with her were big and paunchy. Lee made a zigzag beeline for them, and they were startled at seeing this familiar movie face coming at them. When Lee discovered that the men were about to board their private plane to go to East Hampton, Long Island, Lee gallantly offered to drive the young lady back to her place. They said they had already called a taxi but Lee insisted that he wouldn't hear of it. The girl, who on close inspection was even more beautiful than she had seemed from a distance, giggled and looked at Lee with eyes that showed real promise.

The flight dispatcher announced that the East Hampton plane was ready, the girl kissed the two men good-bye, one more meaningfully than the other, and Lee took her by the arm as we walked toward the car, Preston leading the way, a paper bag in his hand.

I offered to sit in the front seat but Lee insisted that I stay in the back with them. He poured the Wild Turkey into glasses he took from the Cadillac's bar, and proposed a toast to "this angel who's dropped down on us." Then wrapping his arm around the girl, he kissed her in a tentative way and said, "Mmmmmmmm."

"Get under way, Preston," Lee commanded.

As the engine started, the door on my side was yanked open and there stood one of the East Hampton voyagers. "We're canceled out! Bad weather in East Hampton," he announced. "Come on, Sugar."

He reached across and started to take her hand but Lee yanked it away and snarled: "Get lost! Let's go, Preston!"

Preston started to go but the man had a good strong grip on Sugar's arm and he began to run alongside the car, holding onto her. Lee had hold of her other arm and as the car began to pick up speed it was obvious they were going to yank the arms off poor Sugar, who was screaming bloody murder.

I began to yell for Preston to stop, STOP! at the same time trying to pry Lee's fingers from their deadlock on Sugar's wrist. The running East Hampton man succeeded in wedging himself inside the open door of the Cadillac just as Preston's humanitarian instincts overcame him and he stopped the car. With a final mighty tug, the East Hampton man yanked Sugar from Lee's grasp and tugged her out of the limousine. Preston immediately drove off as I closed the door.

Panting heavily from his exertion, Lee sat hunched in the corner, glowering at me. "You son of a bitch," he growled, "you no-good son of a bitch! I saw what you did. Get out! Stop the car, Preston! Get the fuck out!"

Preston stopped the car. I didn't know where I was but I was glad to get out of there. As I started to walk away, Lee opened the window and called to me: "Hotch, listen, I'm sorry, pal, come on back, we got lotsa Wild Turkey to fin'sh up, really, pal, I'm sorry as hell."

There was a cab coming with its "available" light on; it

stopped for me and I could hear Lee's voice still calling to me as we pulled away. I felt a little bad leaving him like that in his lonely Cadillac with his half bottle of Wild Turkey. It had certainly been an evening outside my anticipation. During that long ride back to my hotel, I remember, I hoped that I'd never get invited to another state dinner. Once in a lifetime, I decided, is more than enough.

22

Random House Shows Its Muscle and Gets a Hamstring

I have often wondered how my life would have gone if I had not strayed from the straight and narrow path of lawyering. I think that if, as a young lawyer, I had had the good fortune of getting on with a firm that specialized in trial practice, I might have become more interested in following my profession, but as it was, being the junior lawyer in a firm that primarily represented business corporations had a numbing effect on me.

It never occurred to me when I was in law school that lawyering is basically a service profession, and that you must be available at all times to minister to your clients' problems as they arise, whether they be traffic summonses or mortgage foreclosures. No, I only saw myself as a champion of the oppressed, protecting the little man against the connivances of omnivorous big business, heartless prosecuting attorneys, and sadistic cops. Imagine my disillusionment when I discovered that the law firm which had hired me represented, among many other corporations, the biggest chain of finance and loan companies in St. Louis, and several firms that sold furniture and major appliances on the installment plan; this meant that most of my time was spent going to Justice of the Peace courts (evil contrivances manned by illiterate judges and corrupt sheriffs*) to obtain writs

---

*Now mericfully abolished.

that garnisheed wages and replevined merchandise. These companies would wait until an object like a refrigerator was almost paid off, and then, with just a few dollars owing, as soon as the customer was even a day late in paying his installment, my job was to hurry over to one of the J.P. courts (usually located in rickety, run-down buildings in a seamy part of town) and pay a few bucks for a writ that would enable the sheriff to grab the refrigerator and return it to the company, which could then resell it at additional profit.

It was a disheartening experience for a young lawyer who fancied himself Clarence Darrow incarnate; I surreptitiously inquired about employment at other firms, but we were still in the backwaters of the Depression and the only jobs available were similar to mine, and offered the same beneficent sum of seventy-five dollars a month.

But I did have a couple of experiences during my year of practice that alleviated the humiliating tedium. Keeping Cysmanski off the hot seat for buggering his daughter was not the only one. Much more gratifying was my triumph on behalf of Sergeant Barney Burke of the St. Louis police department.

A partner in my firm, Lou Shifrin, was one of St. Louis's triumvirate of police commissioners, and as a result many policemen came to him with their legal problems. When I joined the firm, Shifrin, an arrogant and humorless man, told me that one of my duties would be to get rid of these policemen as diplomatically as possible. "Of course," he said, "if you want to take on any of their cases outside of your work for the firm, that's up to you. This firm does not deal at a policeman's level."

Most of the cops referred to me by Shifrin were involved in marital disputes, but after a few attempts at mediation by having both husband and wife in my office, I realized I wasn't cut out for it and I developed a nice technique for referring these policemen to other attorneys. (I used the same technique for cops involved in auto accidents, evictions, and kindred matters.)

But Barney Burke's problem was not related to any of these. A silver-haired, soft-spoken, downcast man, he told me about the tragic year he had just suffered through. At the beginning of the year, his wife of twenty-three years had died after a long illness, and he was left with the sole responsibility of caring for a daughter of nineteen who was a manic depressive and who had twice been institutionalized. His wife's illness, and the fees of a psychiatrist who was counseling his daughter, had left Barney heavily in debt, with his house mortgaged and most of his salary going directly to creditors.

Then there was the day he came home after a midnight shift and found that his daughter had hanged herself in the basement. There was an incoherent note beside the body. Despite her problems, Barney was deeply attached to his daughter and he took her death very hard. He had a thirty-thousand-dollar insurance policy on her life with the Metropolitan Life Insurance Company, which provided for double indemnity in case of death from other than natural causes, but when he had applied for this benefit, the insurance company had informed him that there was a clause in his policy that explicitly stated that double indemnity would not be paid if the death was caused by suicide.

I took a look at the policy and found that the clause did exist. "I've been to three lawyers and they've all said I had no case," Barney said. "But I paid all those premiums for twelve years and I really need the money to save my house and keep myself going. All those debts—two funerals and the hospital and all—I just wish there was some way you and Mr. Shifrin could help me."

He was such a down-to-earth, appealing man I didn't have the heart to take away his last hope. I told him to leave the policy with me and promised to give it some thought, but I warned him that I had received a draft notice and might have to go into the army in the near future. Of course, in my opinion his cause was virtually hopeless.

I spoke to Lou Shifrin about it, explaining about the clause. "Is there any question about its being suicide?" he asked, crankily.

"No, sir."

"Then, for Chrissakes, why give it a second thought?"

I didn't again think about Barney's problem until one Saturday afternoon a month or so later, when I was in our firm's library preparing a dry brief on some fine points relating to preferred stocks. It so happened that one of the law digests on the library table was open to the insurance section and Barney Burke came to mind. I turned to "Life Insurance—suicide" in the index and ran my eye down the case briefs until I found one reference that stopped me cold: "Suicides by persons of unsound mind." It was a case that had been decided by the Supreme Court of Missouri, and it held that if an insured of unsound mind commits suicide, there is a presumption that he does not know the nature of his act and therefore the standard insurance clause of double indemnity exemption by reason of suicide does not apply.

On Monday I called a senior partner of the prestigious law firm that represented Metropolitan Life, gave him the citation of the case I had found, and referred him to the psychiatric profile of the insured, which he had in his file. He called me back two days later and said that a check for an additional thirty thousand dollars was on its way over. He didn't apologize or explain. There was no question in my mind that Metropolitan Life knew about this Supreme Court decision, and I wondered how many beneficiaries of mentally disturbed suicides had been unjustly denied double indemnity because their lawyers were not aware of this obscure decision.

It was three days before Christmas when I took the check to Sergeant Burke, who was on duty in the jail hospital. He was sitting at a desk with his tunic unbuttoned, drinking coffee from a cardboard container. His round Irish face came alive when he saw me and he hurried to unlock the barred door.

"I brought you a Christmas present, Barney," I said, and I handed him the check.

He looked at it, then he looked at me, then he looked at the check again, and then he sat down with a thump and looked up at me with eyes that had seen a miracle. He tried to say something, but he couldn't. What he did was weep, I suppose from a release of the tension he had been living with for so long.

When he composed himself, his first concern was to pay me. The usual fee arrangement for an attorney in a case like this is one-third of the amount collected, but I said I'd be perfectly happy with five thousand dollars. Barney insisted that I take my full share. He said that twenty thousand dollars would get him completely out of debt, pay off his house, the hospital, the doctors, the psychiatrist, everything, and that since I was about to be drafted and army pay would be only twenty-one dollars a month I'd certainly need my full share.

"Just before you showed up today," Barney said, "I had been sittin' here thinkin' what a rotten Christmas it's gonna be with my wife and daughter gone, and me in hock, but you've made it a damn sight better, Counselor, and I thank you with all my heart." He tried to smile but it was the lopsided smile of a man who had been mugged by tragedy.

I told Lou Shifrin about the case, but he wasn't interested in the legal aspects of my triumph, only in the ten-thousand-dollar fee. "We will allow you to split it with us," he said.

"But I did this on my own, on a Saturday—I thought you said . . ."

"I gave you permission to work on it. The fee must be split with the firm, that's our policy."

I didn't argue with him. A five-thousand-dollar fee was a wonderful windfall. Two months later my draft number came up, and on the day I was inducted into the Air Corps, I gave the money to my mother and she used it for a down payment on a two-story brick house, a real honest-to-God home, thereby realizing a dream that she and my father had had all their lives.

Even though I never again practiced law, my legal training has been a boon to me, especially when what I have written has carried me into areas of legal controversy. One of these confrontations involved a lawsuit filed against me by Random House, in which I acted as my own attorney.

Now I am fully aware that lawyers are fond of a threadbare adage that goes, A lawyer who represents himself has a fool for a client. I chose to disregard this grim caveat, but before I put on goat's horns for having rushed into a courtroom where legal angels feared to tread, I want it known that I have a maxim of my own: he who would pay a lawyer a higher fee to represent him than the total amount at issue is indeed a fool of a client.

The background is this: In 1971, Random House, which had midwifed me into the publishing world, decided they did not want to publish a new manuscript of mine called *King of the Hill*. It was my fourth book for Random House. I had originally been recruited by Bennett Cerf, who became over the years my friend as well as my publisher. Of course, that was in the halcyon years when Bennett was his own boss and RCA peddled only radios and television sets, not books. My first Random House book was a modest adventure novel; my second book was *Papa Hemingway*, an enduring best seller in the United States and around the world; my third book was *Treasure*, an adventure novel that did reasonably well and had a hearty paperback sale; now my fourth book was to be an autobiographical account of a summer in my life during the Depression in St. Louis. Bennett died shortly after the *King of the Hill* contract was signed; it was a loss I felt very keenly. Even though I had the same editor as I had had on *Papa Hemingway* and *Treasure*, I was nevertheless apprehensive about the Random House changes that Bennett's death would provoke.

I turned in *King of the Hill* a month before the due date. First reaction: everything okay. Later reaction: the editor didn't feel that the book worked in the first-person voice of the twelve-year-old boy narrator and preferred that I write a new manuscript from the point of view of an adult. I refused, on the ground that this was not an editor's suggestion for reasonable revisions, but a demand for an entirely different book, to be written not in accord with my own artistic judgment but with theirs. We were at an impasse. Random House said that under the circumstances they felt they must reject the manuscript and return it to me.

To this point, all well and good. In my judgment, a publisher has no obligation to publish a manuscript he doesn't wish to publish, and nothing in our contract could be construed to oblige him to do so. But Random House went a step further: coincident with the return of the manuscript, they made a written demand that I return that portion of the advance I had received on signing the contract. They had given me $11,250 on signing, and by contract I was to receive another $11,250 on submission of the completed manuscript.

It was Random House's contention that their contract obligated me to return the initial $11,250, and exempted them from paying the second $11,250. The basis for their contention was a time-honored phrase that has appeared in virtually all publishers' contracts to the effect that the manuscript must be "in form and content satisfactory to the publisher." The contract did not specifically state what would happen in the event the publisher deemed the manuscript unsatisfactory. But immediately following the "form and content" clause, there was a provision that if the manuscript had not been delivered by the date prescribed in the contract, then the publisher could require the author to return that portion of the advance previously paid. That was the only specific provision for the return of the advance.

Through my agent, I informed Random House that I would not return the $11,250 for in my opinion that money was their risk in the venture. My risk was the two years I had spent on the book. I pointed out that if Random House's interpretation prevailed, it would mean that regardless of his contract, a writer would be writing on pure speculation; that after several years of living on the advance, paying taxes on it, and so forth, he would have to dredge up the initial lump sum on the whim of the publisher, a sum of money which very likely he no longer had nor could borrow.

Immediately, a lawyer for Random House, a member of the venerable firm of Weil Gotshal and Manges, called my lawyer and threatened suit. "Tell Hotchner," this venerable member of that venerable firm said, "that we are going to haul him into court and it will cost him much, much more in legal fees to defend himself than the $11,250 involved. So he better pay up." My lawyer advised me to settle.

I was outraged, for to my mind this was a kind of blackmail —writer being bludgeoned by rich and powerful publisher, bankrolled by even richer and more powerful communications giant.* It was then that I announced that, contrary to my better judgment, I intended to be my own lawyer. Everyone I knew, especially lawyer friends, shook heads and clucked tongues. I suppose in the back of my mind I never thought that Random House would actually go to trial because the manuscript they rejected was immediately published by Harper & Row to widespread favorable reviews. My total advance from Harper & Row was $10,000, so actually I received $1,250 less than if Random House had lived up to its contract.

Civil cases in New York move very slowly. For four years various motions and interrogatories were filed. I found that I rather enjoyed reaching way back to my pleading days to answer

---

*RCA subsequently sold Random House to S. I. Newhouse & Sons.

various documents. I even initiated a number of motions and interrogatories of my own. One entire day was consumed with my deposition, taken in the venerable Weil Gotshal and Manges conference room, in the presence of a court reporter and a trio of WG&M attorneys, one of them a senior member of the firm (the going rate for senior members at depositions must have been two hundred dollars an hour). At that time, I estimated the cost of all this, and it seemed to me that Random House's legal fees had already exceeded the $11,250 they were seeking as judgment. Of course, I had filed a counterclaim for the other half of the advance that Random House had never paid.

Finally, in January, 1977, the case was put on the trial docket before Judge Martin Evans of the New York State Supreme Court. In New York, where phraseology is often perverse, the Supreme Court is the lowest of the state courts. The case was to be tried without a jury. In the four years that had passed since this action had been filed some significant changes had occurred at Random House. Both Nan Talese, the editor who had rejected *King of the Hill,* and James Silberman, the chief editor who had demanded return of the advance, had left the company.

By way of preparation, I had discussed the law involved in my case with Irwin Karp, the general counsel for the Authors League, of which I am a member. Karp felt that this was a case of prime importance to all authors and generously offered to appear on behalf of the League as an amicus curiae—which meant that he wouldn't participate in the trial but that he would file a legal brief on my behalf.

I read the opinions in virtually all publication litigation related to my situation, and to my astonishment discovered (Karp confirmed this) that I had a case of first instance by the tail. By that I mean this: jurisprudence, as we practice it, is based on precedent. The better you can identify the facts of your case with one that has gone before, the better you can rely on the verdict in that previous litigation—provided, of course, it was in your favor. But if you find yourself in a situation that cannot be fully fitted into the contours of a previous case, if no set of facts substantially like yours has ever been decided before, then you have a case of first impression, a case which will make new law. I remembered enough from my law school days to recall that judges love such cases because their opinions bear unique weight and are often added to the holy script in law school textbooks.

Of course, there had been previous litigation that had involved squabbles between publishers and authors over advances. But in no reported case had there been a situation where a manuscript was turned in by an established, professional writer that conformed to what was expected in theme and substance, but which was rejected on the ground that the publisher wanted it entirely rewritten in a totally different way, demanding return of the advance if it were not. The issue in *Random House v. Hotchner* (Index No. 126-46/73) was clearly joined. It was virgin territory. As lawyers say, although I have no idea why, there was no previous case "on all fours with it."

The case came up for the first time before Judge Evans in January, 1977, but was put over until October. I left for Europe in February to work on the Ritz book. By September I was still at work in Paris, and I asked WG&M to postpone the trial until I returned in 1978. They refused on the ground that their client was ready for trial and it would be very expensive to have the trial later on. The logic of their position escaped me, since the cost of a trial is the cost of a trial whenever it occurs, but their refusal forced me to stop work and return from Paris.

In order to understand why Random House was acting so irrationally in persisting in this lawsuit, it is necessary to go back to what had happened after a previous lawsuit, filed by Mary Hemingway against Random House and me to enjoin publication of *Papa Hemingway.* Bennett Cerf was editor of Random House at that time, and I had an understanding with him that Random House's law firm (the selfsame Manges firm) would handle half the litigation, and my attorney, Mervin Rosenman, would handle the other half, each of us to pay our own attorney's fees.

But by the time the litigation and all the appeals had been exhausted,* Cerf had passed on and the presidency had been

---

*The decisions of the Supreme Court, the Appellate Division of the Supreme Court, and the Court of Appeals were all in my favor.

vested in a company man named Robert Bernstein, who took the position that I should pay all of my own attorney's fees plus half of the Manges fee. The lawyers had performed an equal amount of work, splitting the four causes of action among them, but Bernstein, whose voice went shrilly countertenor when excited, loudly proclaimed at our conference that he was sick and tired of writers taking advantage of Random House. I, in turn, had a few negative comments to make about publishers whose word was not their bond.

Ever since that exchange, Bernstein had been smoldering with animosity toward me, and when the *King of the Hill* advance came to his attention, he persisted in wanting his people to get me.

In the plane coming back from Paris, I was tormented with bleak ruminations about the foolhardiness of taking on the Weil Gotshal and Manges–Random House–RCA Goliath. I saw myself in the courtroom as David without a slingshot. During my one year in legal service, I had never tried a case or been involved in a courtroom proceeding; Cysmanski, if you recall, copped his plea before the jury was fully impaneled. The closest I ever came to a trial was in moot court in my second year of law school, and all I got out of that was a hung jury. I knew very well that the rules of evidence are strict, confining, frustrating, old-fashioned, and unpredictable. It is one thing to have a valuable fact or exhibit in your possession; it is quite another to get it admitted into evidence. WG&M was a firm that specialized in publication law; they represented Scribner's as well as Random House. They knew everything there was to know in the lawbooks that related to publishers and writers. The closer I got to New York, the bigger the specter of this trial filled the 707. I may well have been the first passenger at 36,000 feet to suffer from courtroom fright.

WG&M were very sure of themselves. At our preliminary hearing before Judge Evans in January, in an effort to avoid the trial, I had proposed what I thought was a fair compromise: I would pay to Random House fifty cents out of every dollar I received in royalties from Harper & Row, and I would also drop my counterclaim. The WG&M attorney, Robert Weiner, dismissed the offer with a deprecating flick of his left wrist. "We expect full recovery," he told the judge.

Back in January, I had also gone to see Horace Manges himself. Ironically, in 1966, Mr. Manges had personally appeared on my behalf, as well as Random House's, in our successful defense of the court action commenced by Mary Hemingway to try to suppress my memoir about Ernest. Since he was a former comrade-in-arms, I thought I might be on friendly grounds when I asked Manges if there were some way we could settle the *King of the Hill* affair. "Yes," he said, "you can pay us eleven thousand dollars."

"But that's not a compromise," I said.

His eyes behind his glasses were gray stones. "You've had the use of the money for all this time," he said. "We won't charge you interest."

Mr. Manges was an old man. He had spent his life in the publishing world. I had expected wisdom.

I had a hell of a time getting any witnesses. Just as doctors are reticent to testify against each other, so too are editors and publishers and agents (my own agent, Phyllis Jackson, whose testimony was quite vital to my case, had died several months before the trial started). I wanted to establish custom and usage in the industry in relation to rejected manuscripts, but if experienced people in the industry wouldn't testify, how could I do that? You cannot subpoena expert witnesses. I got turned down by most of the editors I knew, with the exception of Howard Cady, a senior editor at Morrow. I had hoped that Frances Lindley of Harper & Row, who had been my editor on the book, would testify, but she said she had important editorial conferences scheduled with a writer from Bulgaria and doubted she could make it.

That's all I had, other than myself, although how I was going to interrogate myself when I took the stand worried me. I asked several writers I knew if they would testify, but they all recoiled at my suggestion. One writer, himself battling Random House over another issue and knowing what I wanted, wouldn't even return my phone call.

With a defense like that, I didn't need Don Shula to tell me that I needed a hell of an offense. So I spent an entire week preparing for the cross-examination of the two witnesses Random House planned to call. By far the most important of these two was Nan Talese, who had been the editor on the book and who had signed the letter of rejection demanding return of the advance. My cross-examination of her would be complicated by the fact that she and her husband, Gay, were good and close friends of mine. On the witness stand, however, we would be combatants—friendly, nonvituperative combatants, I hoped. But in the unpredictable swirls and downdrafts of the court-room, things do not always turn out as expected.

The day before the trial, I discussed my overall strategy with Mervin Rosenman, who thought I was on the right track and was enthusiastically supportive.

But I got a contrary reaction from a woman attorney I talked to who was an expert in the field of literary law. "You are doing a foolhardy thing," she said. "You have an important case here and by going into the arena with Weil Gotshal and Manges, well, you're an amateur Christian against the lions. They will have a field day twisting you all around and destroying your position simply because you won't be able to fend for yourself. The old saying about lawyers who represent themselves is true. You should have an experienced lawyer."

"But the trial starts tomorrow," I said, my courage draining into my socks.

"You can get an automatic postponement if you tell the judge you've just taken on counsel."

"But the expense—only eleven thousand dollars is involved."

"I would do it for much less than that because, considering the importance of the issue here, I could get several organizations I know to contribute to your defense. It would wind up costing you very little."

"I better think about it."

"You don't have much time."

I dialed Mervin Rosenman with a sweaty forefinger.

"Don't be silly," he said. "You'll do just fine. Think positive, talk firmly, and don't forget to stand up when you address the court."

Only once before did I have a night like the night I had before the trial started. That was in Ciudad Real, in central Spain, the night before I was to dress up as a matador and go into the bullring. But on that occasion I had the great Antonio Ordoñez at my side. Now, on the morning of October 11, I dressed up as a lawyer (dark suit, subdued tie) and entered the courtroom all alone. The WG&M counsel table was filled with lawyers, papers, and bulging briefcases. I sat down at the opposite table and took out my legal pad, on which I had written questions I planned to ask.

The judge entered, we all stood up, and the trial began.

Judge Evans, black-robed, white-haired, thin-voiced, and low-keyed, asked the WG&M trial attorney, Robert Weiner, if he had an opening statement. A very brief one, Weiner said. This was a simple contract case; the defendant was obligated to produce a book to plaintiff's satisfaction; defendant did not produce said book; demand had been made for return of the advance; defendant had refused, although by contract he was obliged to return the money; plaintiff sought $11,250 in damages, plus costs. Weiner then started to call his first witness, but I found myself rising to my feet and requesting time to make my opening statement. "Yes," Judge Evans said, "Proceed."

"This is not at all the simple contract case that plaintiff would have you believe," I said. "Far from it. This is a case that goes to the very heart of the relation between publisher and writer. The vast majority of books that are published are published under an arrangement whereby a publisher advances money to a writer who then uses that money to live on while he researches and writes the manuscript that will eventually become a book. It is a unique partnership, the essential ingredient of which is the advance. It is the fuel that makes the system go. The publisher risks his money, the writer risks his time, and that mutuality of risk is what puts a book on the shelf. The plaintiff here is maintaining that he should have no risk at all—that if he doesn't like the manuscript he merely sends it back and gets his money back. Like one of those money-back guarantees that run in newspaper ads. Now, sir, if Random House's position prevails, then all risk would fall on the writer and his position would become purely speculative. If your Honor, in his decision, were to support Random House in this position, then the entire system of publishing would be in jeopardy. Most professional writers cannot undertake such total risk. The flow of books would be seriously impaired. The evidence will show that after two years' work I produced a competent, publishable manuscript for Random House, one that they nevertheless chose to reject. I do not dispute their right to reject it, but surely I cannot be asked to absorb the total cost of that rejection. This is the issue before your Honor. The facts involved here have never been precisely adjudicated before, and this case is being closely watched by the Authors League and other interested parties."

To my surprise, I felt right at home. The adrenaline pumped nicely. I had the inexplicable illusion that I had stood here many times before and the match was being played on my home court.

Nan Talese is an attractive, articulate, and knowledgeable woman. On direct examination, she testified that she had expected *King of the Hill* to be written from an adult's point of view and that she did not feel "enthusiastic" about it in the form in which I had written it.

"It was not in form and content satisfactory to you?" Weiner asked.

"No, it was not."

"And you returned the manuscript and asked the defendant to return the $11,250 that Random House had advanced him?"

"Yes."

Weiner asked me if I wanted to cross-examine. On a piece of paper directly in front of me, I had written in large letters: "FORM, CONTENT, RISK." That was to be the focus of my cross-examination—Random House's soft underbelly, where, I hoped, the shaft could pierce.

I quickly discovered that a person who conducts his own cross-examination has a considerable advantage over a lawyer who must act an alter ego role. The self-lawyer is in direct confrontation with the witness. Instead of his lawyer asking questions based on secondhand information, the person representing himself has been party to the deeds he is inquiring about. Thus, when I asked Nan: "Didn't I tell you thus and so?" and "Do you recall when you told me . . ." I was gaining an immediacy of response that gave me an advantage.

I also found that I took to cross-examination as naturally as a newborn to the teat. Few objections to my questions were sustained.

What is form? Form, Nan said, is a very broad term; it could mean anything from the physical manuscript to the type of book: poetry, criticism, fiction, nonfiction.

And substance? The theme, the subject.

"Did you object to either the form or the substance as you have just defined them?"

"Well, no . . ."

"It was the *style* you found fault with, wasn't it?"

"Yes."

"But where in the contract does it say anything about style? Can you show me the word?"

"No."

"In your opinion was the manuscript publishable as you received it?"

"Yes, but I didn't feel it was the book I had contracted for. I just didn't feel as enthusiastic about it as I felt I should have been. I felt some other editor in some other publishing house would publish the book with the enthusiasm it deserved."

"Was it on your authority that Random House demanded return of the advance?"

"I signed the letter, but Jim Silberman, the editor-in-chief, requested I write the agent asking for the return of the advance."

"Then it was Silberman's notion that writers take all the risk and the publisher has none?"

"Yes. Silberman and, I suppose, Robert Bernstein."

"What is your own feeling?"

"I believe the risk should be shared."*

I was sailing along, getting all the right answers, piling up points, eroding Random House's position. But just after lunch I got my first serious jolt as a trial tenderfoot.

It was vital to my cause to introduce into evidence the seventy or so reviews of *King of the Hill* which had appeared in newspapers and magazines across the country. I had clippings of the actual reviews (not photocopies) as they had been sent to

---

*There is no transcript of the trial, and what I am recording here is a reconstitution from copious notes and from memory.

me by the Literary Clipping Service, to which I had subscribed at the time. Holding this sheaf of reviews in my hand, I confidently asked the court reporter to mark them for exhibit as evidence. Weiner objected and the judge sustained him. I was stopped cold. "But, your Honor," I said, "these are the actual clippings from the newspapers themselves."

"How do I know that?" Judge Evans asked. "They could be admissible, but you haven't laid a proper foundation for them."

I was baffled and confused. "But surely, your Honor, if it's just a technicality . . ."

The judge was a bit testy. "Yes, it's a technical matter, but I can't be partial by helping either side. As it is, you cannot put the reviews into evidence."

"Then I'll ask for a ten-minute recess and find out how to do it," I said.

"Granted," he said.

I rushed to the pay phone in the hall and started phoning lawyers I knew until I found one who was in his office. "Swear yourself in and testify as to how you received the reviews and all that," this attorney said. "Then you will have laid the proper foundation."

To double-check, I phoned a second attorney and he suggested the same procedure.

I asked the clerk to swear me in, took the stand, and did as I had been advised.

"Objection," said Weiner.

"Sustained," said the judge.

I was stunned. "But . . . but," I groped in my darkness, "these reviews are vital evidence, your Honor."

"You haven't found the way to lay the proper foundation, and I can't help you. Let us proceed."

Seventy reviews, full of glowing praise, many written by distinguished reviewers—the point being that since critics for *The New York Times, The Washington Post, Los Angeles Times, The Boston Globe, Chicago Sun-Times,* et cetera, et cetera, had all found *King of the Hill* highly satisfactory, that would certainly damage Random House's position that the manuscript was unsatisfactory. But if I couldn't get the reviews into evidence, then legally they did not exist.

Desperation, not necessity, is what spurs me on in moments like this, and, finally, virtually at the last moment, I saw the light.

"Mrs. Talese," I said, "publishers rely on book reviews to publicize and advertise their books, don't they?"

"Yes."

"And how do you get these reviews you rely on? From a clipping service?"

"Yes."

"Then please look at this clipping and tell me if this is a clipping you would rely on."

"Yes. Random House subscribed to the Literary Clipping Service."

I asked the court reporter to mark the clipping as an exhibit. Weiner objected.

"Overruled," the judge said. There was the faintest of smiles on his face. "You found the way," he said.

Writing for the stage and television had taught me how to construct a telling climax for a scene. At the end of Nan's testimony, I asked her what she thought would happen if Random House or any other publisher offered a contract to an established writer that said, in plain words: "Here is X amount of dollars for an advance, but if we don't like your manuscript when you turn it in two or three or four years from now you must give back the money." Would he sign it?

"Probably not," Nan said.

"Would Philip Roth or Norman Mailer sign a contract like that?"

"No."

"Would your husband, Gay Talese?"

"No."

I started to walk away, then turned back for effect. "You know me very well, don't you? Would I ever sign a contract like that?"

"Certainly not," Nan replied.

Random House's second witness was another Random House editor, who admitted he knew nothing about the preparation of the manuscript and could only testify that Nan Talese had asked him to read it and he had agreed with her. I asked him about form and content. He said form was fiction or nonfiction

369

and content was the substance of the book. He explained in detail and his answers were different from those given by Nan Talese.

At the end of the first day's testimony, Judge Evans called Weiner and me to the bench. "When I sit without a jury," he said, "I like to indicate to the attorneys during the course of the trial how I'm leaning so that they can better prepare for the next day. I must tell you that right now I find myself favoring Mr. Hotchner's position." Weiner blanched.

"I think you will change your opinion tomorrow, your Honor," Weiner said, "because we plan to put Hotchner on the stand as our witness and we're going to prove that the manuscript he wrote was not the manuscript we agreed upon."

"All right," the judge said, "I'm open to persuasive evidence, but tonight I'd like you to look up the cases that deal with advances that are given to salesmen. What if the salesman doesn't earn in commissions as much as his total advance—must he return the unearned advance? I'd like you to look at these cases—it seems to me they're very relevant here."

I started to say that a salesman who didn't produce sales was different from a writer who did produce a publishable manuscript, but a gruff voice that sometimes monitors me told me to keep my mouth shut. It also said: Leave well enough alone.

One thing I was sure of: there was no way under the Centre Street sun that Weiner was going to prove his case with my testimony. In the past, I had been on the witness stand several times and held my own against some pretty good batterings. But that night I reviewed my deposition and all papers in the case carefully. My object went beyond holding my own with Weiner. I wanted my testimony to score the final, convincing points with Judge Evans.

When we reconvened the following morning, Weiner looked pale under his black beard. I asked him if he had a copy of the salesman brief that I could look at. He said, rather testily I thought, that he hadn't prepared one. Of course that told me which way those decisions had gone.

Weiner tried to be belligerent in cross-examining me, but I could tell his heart wasn't in it. He worked hard and fired rapid volleys of questions, but they fell like scattered shot in an open field. Finally, when I saw an opening, I steered my testimony around to that soft underbelly of form and content. In the midst of a lively exchange between us, Judge Evans took over the questioning. He asked Weiner to give his own definition of the words *form* and *content*. Weiner stood mutely before the judge, an aghast expression on his face. He finally said something to the effect that his witnesses had already defined those words. "No," Judge Evans said, "they each had differing definitions. Now I want you to tell me just what definitions you were relying upon when you brought this action." I felt sorry for Weiner. He was a decent man, and this humiliation did not belong to him, but to Robert Bernstein, who, as the head of Random House, had insisted on this litigation.

"They are just traditional words," Weiner finally managed to say after much bumbling around. "They don't have any meaning, just the word 'satisfactory' is what's important."

The judge was astounded. "You mean you have these two words in the contract that have no meaning?"

The more Weiner tried to explain, to extricate himself, the more he entangled himself in those fatal words. Finally, to put an end to his desperation, he said: "Your Honor, could we have a meeting in your chambers?"

We went into the judge's office. The judge took off his robe, and Weiner and I sat on either side of his desk. "When this case first came before me," the judge said, "I was ninety percent sure I was going to find for the plaintiff. I thought it was going to be a case of a writer not living up to his commitment. But, of course, that's not it at all. Did you look at those salesmen cases?"

"Yes, your Honor, but what I wanted to say is . . ."

"Well, you see, it's been held that a salesman's advances are nonrecoverable and I would think that a writer certainly deserves the benefit of those decisions. What's the difference?"

"Yes, your Honor, but what I want to say is . . ."

"Your own witness has admitted that the manuscript was publishable, and the fact that it *was* published by Harper and Row with all those favorable reviews—certainly Random House's rejection has to be on *reasonable* grounds."

Weiner finally got to make his statement. Hard cases make bad law, he said, and Random House wanted to avoid a written opinion based on the facts in this case. They were very much afraid, he said, that a negative opinion in this case, which dealt with a paltry $11,250, would have adverse repercussions on their contracts that involved advances of $400,000 and $500,000. Thus, they were asking permission to withdraw their lawsuit, pay all costs, and admit defeat if I would consent to withdraw my counterclaim.

Of course, it also occurred to me that by refusing to allow Random House to withdraw, which was my privilege now, I would certainly win a verdict with a written opinion in my favor. That would have been an even more satisfactory victory, but I knew that Random House would surely appeal a strong decision in my favor. I knew from experience that such appeals are very costly and time-consuming; a big corporation can keep a case on appeal for a long time. I could not possibly handle my own appellate brief, arguments before the appellate court, and all the other technical matters incident to the appeal. So I would have had to hire an appellate attorney, pay his considerable fees and the costs of printing briefs. But more important than the monetary cost was the cost to me of lost days and emotional disturbance. I wanted the Random House leeches out of my life. They had sucked enough of my time and my emotions.

The settlement was such a sudden and complete victory that it took some time for it to sink in. It meant that without putting on a single witness, I had triumphed. And in the best conceivable way—by forcing Random House to admit that they were wrong. That after a lifetime in the book world, Horace Manges was wrong not to have had some compassion for the writer's position. That Robert Bernstein, who liked to identify himself with liberal causes in nonmonetary matters that related to international literary affairs, was wrong to have stubbornly persisted in this lawsuit for five years without involving any of his own money, his time, or his emotions.

I phoned Irwin Karp at the Authors League to tell him the result and to thank him. He was overjoyed. "What you've done," he said, "is bound to make writers more courageous. They must stand up for their rights. I don't mean the few writers who get the big advances, but the ordinary, struggling writer who makes every kind of concession in his eagerness to get his book published. You've scored a spectacular victory for us, and I can tell you it's appreciated."

Next day, on the plane going back to Paris, I thought about the trial itself—the experience of having performed in a courtroom. I thought: You know, Hotchner, you would have made a pretty good trial lawyer. It was a hell of an experience. I wondered why more people didn't defend themselves. All you have to do is think positive, talk firmly, and stand up when you address the judge.

23

Catherine Deneuve Doesn't Know Who She Is

There is an ethereal side to free-lancing which can bestow unexpected rewards upon the writer; I'm referring to his daydreams, his ability to project himself into his fantasies. I don't mean to say that he can completely fulfill his fantasy world but if he is clever and persistent, the free-lancer can tinge almost any fantasy with a touch of reality.

Under the guise of writing about them, the free-lancer can go places, meet people, and participate in events that others can only dream about. A few years ago, for example, when I was living in Paris, it was my forlorn hope that somewhere, somehow I would run into Catherine Deneuve. I felt that she epitomized all that was glamorous, chic, debonair, and sexual in a woman of Paris. There was a depth of sadness in her eyes, an abandoned quality to her lips and hair, and a Renoir lustiness to her body that reached out to me in her Chanel ads and in her films, all of which I had seen.

The fact that she and I were inhabiting the same city (the same *quartier,* for all I knew!) without meeting filled me with frustration.

I asked my Paris friends about her, hoping one of them knew her and could tell me about her, but none did. She led a very private, eccentric life, it seemed, and not one of those I canvassed had ever even seen her. But she was in Paris, of that they were sure.

It was at that point that I rubbed the magic free-lancing lamp and conjured up a good genie in the form of a New York magazine editor to whom I had written extolling Deneuve as a cover profile. My suggestion was approved and I was told to get to her as soon as possible—the good old fantasy converter was about to do its work. I saw myself having lunch with her in an elegant restaurant, dawdling over our wine as she told me about her life and loves and dreams.

But Deneuve was elusive and it took me three weeks to locate her—and even then I didn't get to her, only to the press representative for a movie she had just started, *Love at First Sight*. The press agent arranged my initial rendezvous with Catherine at midnight on the Place de la Concorde. She was scheduled for night shooting, midnight until dawn, my interviews to take place inside her trailer dressing room in between takes.

But alas, on the very day of our midnight tryst the press representative phoned and told me not to come. The movie had been abruptly and unexpectedly suspended because the producer did not have sufficient capital.

"You mean he began a movie without having the money to make it?" I asked.

"Yes, that is sometimes the way here."

"But where is Miss Deneuve—can't I interview her anyway?"

"Nobody knows where she is."

"Perhaps you could call her apartment?"

"I have. There's no answer. She may have gone to her country place but, on purpose, she has no phone there."

For the next few weeks I called the press representative regularly but she had not heard from Catherine. Eventually I gave up.

But one afternoon the press lady called and said that if I was still interested, Miss Deneuve could see me. Yes, she was back in Paris, and yes, the film was supposed to recommence shooting in two weeks. I was given an address in St.-Germain-des-Prés on the Rue Bonaparte where it comes into the Place St. Sulpice. The free-lance fantasy converter had worked again.

The Deneuve apartment is on a high floor with a stunning view of the Church of St. Sulpice and the imposing fountain of the supine lions, both of which dominate the square. I wait in the living room: comfortable, expensive furniture, a mix of modern and art deco. Above the sofa, a large painting of a girl in the manner of Manet by an artist named Naviasky. Several large, exotic lily plants on tabletops.

Catherine enters the room quietly. She is wearing plum-colored willowy slacks and a classic blouse of Yves St. Laurent. There is a subdued, shy quality about her. She wears no makeup and her incredibly thick, blond hair falls haphazardly about her face.

I remark on the view. She looks out on it with pleasure. "It fascinates and distracts me," she says. "I've just moved here but it takes so long to get things done. I think it has to do with a woman's mind."

"What does?" I ask. "Getting things done?"

"Yes, a woman's mind is cluttered, much busier with inconsequentials than a man's, thus it's harder for her to operate on many levels as I have to. Mother, house manager, career, personal fun, social life, and enough of the solitude I find necessary." She has the accent of the Chanel commercials, but her command of English is effortless. She smokes a lot.

"Why did you call off our first meeting?" I ask her.

"Disappointment is my worst enemy. I cannot abide disappointment, and when my movie was canceled after a week's shooting, *zut*, just like that, *canceled*, that was a terrible bitterness. It cast me so low. I was numbed by it. I ran to the country and hid from myself. Thank God I have two women friends who understand the importance of being next to me but not talking. Men don't understand that there are things that I can only share with a woman. But disappointment shuts off my life flow. I don't know how to handle it. I can't say: Oh, well, it will be better tomorrow—even though I know it will be. That is intelligent—I am not intelligent about things like that. It is a physical thing. I feel it in my body. I can hurt people badly when I'm down, like a wounded animal. So I must be alone. Oh, not *completely* alone, that would be too frightening, but with one of my woman friends who will sit there in the silent room with me and share the anguish without asking anything or trying to make talk."

"But you have so much else to fill your life, haven't you? I mean, besides film-making."

"Oh, yes, the days are too short for what I want to do. Much too short. I am never bored. I am never not busy. The movie business robs me of time I need for myself. My days are too cluttered, as is my mind, but I never lose track of enjoyment. I manage always to enjoy life—except of course, when I am hit by the down times. Then I can do nothing else. I am collapsed. Life has no meaning. What the hell, there are ups and down for all of us—but perhaps my up is higher and my down is lower than the average person's, but dealing with it is the same."

"What's the furthest down that you've been?"

She looks away from me as a barely perceptible quiver goes through her. "When my sister died. She was a lovely actress, Françoise Dorléac—it was a horrible accident . . ." She looks out the window, down on the square below, where workmen are assembling a mosaic of stone pavements around the fountain. Finally: "I am still, in a way, down from that. Ten years ago. We are not prepared for death. I was raised a Catholic but they cheat you. They tell you morbid and heavy preachments about death but nothing that you can deal with when it happens. Other religions do it better: the Chinese, the Indians. All that dear departed crap, the heavy scene in church on the day of interment. My sister was a beautiful woman, my closest friend, my true love. Instead of sex education in the schools, they should give a course in death education. In living you find out about sex —but dying, how do you find out about that?"

"You are very vulnerable, aren't you?"

"Vulnerable? In what way?"

"Exposed to what can hurt you. You don't seem to defend yourself."

"My *bête noire* is guilt. I try to be so careful not to hurt other people's feelings. I try to feel how they feel but sometimes when I am enjoying my life and they are not enjoying theirs I feel guilty. Can you imagine that it makes me feel guilty because I am enjoying my life and they don't? I am basically so shy but I'm getting better. Socially. But I am just as insecure as I've ever been. I am a very insecure woman."

"But in your up times you are enjoying your life . . ."

377

"Yes, yes, so very shy but also very aggressive. I am a contradiction, I know, but I don't wait for things to happen. I am impetuous. I go for what I want. Is this at war with my shyness? Yes, I guess so. But what I really want, if I want it strongly, that dominates. If I must give my feelings I must. I cannot wait to test the waters. I throw myself in. That's how I became a mother. I wanted those two children from those two men. Marriage, and a father's presence, fatherhood, all that, was a secondary consideration. I was only seventeen when I was with Roger Vadim. I was so in love with him. He was the first man I had loved. I wanted a child from that love. I *needed* to have that child. Roger didn't want to marry me, not when I was pregnant. But it never even crossed my mind not to have that child. It was natural and beautiful and important to have that baby. Then after the baby was born, Roger wanted to marry but I rejected him. It was too late. Something important had gone out of it. I didn't think he wanted to marry me for the same reasons I wanted to marry him."

From the hallway we hear voices and Catherine excuses herself. "My mother and father are leaving. I must say good-bye to them." When she returns, I ask her about her father, Maurice Dorléac, who was an actor. "He's seventy-six but brimful of life. I really admire my father." But she parries my questions about him. "I don't want to go into things," she says. "There was an interview not so long ago where my father called me a hypocrite. We both became terribly upset about it. When I was growing up . . . well . . . we could not give to each other, my father and I. I was remote. I suppose I still am. I wish it had been different."

"Your mother was an actress?"

"Yes. Her name was Renée Simonot."

"So you have acting in your blood."

"Yes." She runs her hand through her hair and gives long thought to that. "The whole cathedral of my being was made for film-making. I love everything about it, the whole rhythm of making movies. Even the business talk. Contract talk. I love to hear grosses and below-the-line costs. I love the exaggerated quality of making a movie. It is physically exhausting, the same as if I had exerted great physical energy, but actually all I've done is perform a scene that took one minute, but to prepare emotionally, to get the body up to that moment before the camera starts, then to sustain it—it is the high jump, the pole vault, the high dive—standing there, measuring, thinking, psyching up, for as big an effort as you can give.

"But there is real danger in being an actress. It is not to act my life on the screen or I might find myself acting a part in life instead of being Catherine Deneuve. It is a terrible thing to lose reality to performing. Some people do live a life of pretense. Some actors I know. Lying is such an easy solution. Telling the truth often makes life so difficult. I have two writer friends whom I see a lot. We talk about the same facts, the same things, but they embellish them. They change them. They see them through magnified or interpreted eyes. I see them and deal with them just as they are. But then, what is truth? What are facts? Which of us is right?"

"But when you do perform in a film, do you give all of yourself to the part?"

"No, no, I don't. I don't want to give too much of myself for fear of going beyond my depth. I must have limits. Boundaries. But I also have a terrible fear of disappointing. I want to please. I *desperately* want to please, but if I gave everything to a film or to a person, I would retain nothing for myself—the mystery of who I am and what I want would be lost and something would have flown out of me. As long as I retain this margin of being, there is a sense of promise in me. A promise that there is more. That's intriguing. There's a certain excitement to that."

"Do you ask too much of the people you've become involved with?"

"No, I don't think so—I don't have to put people on a pedestal to admire them. I am realistic. I don't demand perfection. I only demand my own response and when my impulsive response is there, I don't hold it back. I give all there is to give."

"But you just told me you're afraid of that—that you have to hold something back for yourself. Isn't that a contradiction?"

"Yes, yes, I am a contradiction. I told you that. I don't think of consequences. If you try to measure the future you will never risk the present. Playing it safe. A ghastly game. Giving to others heals me, as the Indians healed themselves with herbs. They did not understand what the herbs did, how they operated, they only

knew their healing powers. So with me. I do not want to know
what there is about the process of giving that heals me. It is my
herb. I must not try to pick it apart. Just use it and know what
it does and be grateful."

Her children come into the room and she introduces them.
Christian, age fourteen, the son of Vadim, and Chiara, age four,
daughter of Marcello Mastroianni. They stay for only a moment.
"It is difficult for my son," Catherine says, "because I have to
be both mother and father to him, tough and gentle, and he
doesn't know at any particular moment which I'll be. We are too
passionate with each other. He is terribly shy but getting better."

"Does he see his father?"

"No, virtually not at all. Oh, a holiday or two, but he has had
no father in his life. Little Chiara, isn't she divine? How much
easier a girl is than a boy. Outgoing. Not a bit shy. I'm concerned, though, about Christian. Perhaps I'm too tense. If only
I could relax and roll with the buffets, just take things as they
come, not force anything, not be so organized, not try to do all
I try to do. But I can't. That's not me. I give a lot and I expect
a lot."

"This resurrected movie of yours—can you give a lot to
that?"

"Oh, yes. It's a part I adore. I look forward to it very much."

She walks me to the door. We shake hands. She smiles. "Will
you be there Friday when I pose for the cover picture for this
article you're going to write?"

"No, I don't plan to."

"Oh, I think you should come. The photographer will be
David Bailey, the only man I married and the only one with
whom I didn't have a child."

Reality has not shaken my fantasy one bit. I eagerly look
forward to Friday.

Clic-Clac is the improbable name of a photographic studio on
the Rue Daguerre. David Bailey sits on a table, drinking steaming coffee out of a mug while a young Chinese assistant adjusts
a white umbrella that is crookedly perched over a hot-lighted
chair in the center of the room. Bailey smokes incessantly. His

face is the face of a man who is using up his life as fast as he can and enjoying it. His expressive hands constantly attack his tousled hair.

We go to a bar on the corner to wait for Catherine, who is already a half hour late. Bailey's speech is pure Cockney, a joy to hear. "I comes from the East End o' London," he tells me, "a genuwine Cockney, not like Michael Caine, who's trying to pass. Everyone on the East End's a tailor. Me pa was a tailor, and I was an apprentice tailor. Only three options in life for a East End kid—be a tailor, a car thief, or play in a rock band. I didn't know I wasn't Jewish till I was fourteen. Anyways, from when I was four years old, I started messin' around with cameras—a little purloined stuff that happened to fall in me hands. At fourteen I announced I was gonna be a photographer, and me mates on the street said: 'Oh-oh, maybe Bailey's going a little queer.' Then, I started to get interested in birds—the ones what fly—and when I was fourteen and a half I announced I was also gonna be a ornithologist, and they all said: 'That does it, Bailey *is* queer.' I now have sixty parrots in me house in London. I'm a parrot fancier, that's what I am."

What Bailey actually is, is the world's foremost photographer of beautiful women. His contribution to the Sixties, as a personality, was considerable; he was the prototype for the lead character in Antonioni's exquisite film *Blow-Up.* "When I was a kid," Bailey is saying as he dumps a glass of cognac into his coffee, "they was twins on the East End who ran things tight. If someone had to be killed, they was killed. The twins 're now serving thirty years but not for any of the things they did. I know about the killings and I'd say not one of them wasn't justified. They only killed evil men."

"How did you meet Deneuve?" I ask.

"I was assigned to do her bare-ass for a *Playboy* center spread. She didn't want to. Had to be coaxed. None of 'em wants to. None that I know."

"Have you remarried?"

"Want to see my wife?" He hands me a large, tabloid-shaped magazine called *Ritz,* which has a black-and-white head shot of Deneuve on the cover. "First wife on the cover, second wife inside." He turns to an inside page where there is a full-length photo of a Japanese beauty in a bikini poised on a diving board. I comment on her beauty. "Want to see more of her? Turn the page." Another shot of his Japanese wife, this time nude.

"Why did you and Deneuve get married? I mean, instead of just living together?"

"Why not get married? What's the difference between getting married and not getting married? Divorce. So what the hell's that? Another kind of good-bye, that's all. You know what they all miss about Cat'rin? Her great sense of humor. She's a very funny lady. She's laughs. First-rate comedienne, but they always ask heavy questions, and you know the French, they *love* to talk heavy so that's all you ever read about Cat'rin: Miss Deneuve, what would you say is the meaning of life and all that shit."

"She says she's too organized, too driven to work. Is making money important to her?"

"Nah, hell, Cat'rin doesn't care any more about money than I do. If she gets a hundred thou she's likely to go across the street and buy a trinket with it. Same's me. She's generous where it counts. Might turn off all the lights to save on the electric bill. I mean, she's bourgeois in the best sense of the word. Probably what attracted her to me. Probably never in her life saw a specimen like me."

Deneuve arrives two hours late but Bailey doesn't seem to mind. They hug and greet each other with honest fondness. "Where you been?" Bailey asks. "In the sack?" Deneuve is trailed by a young, handsome Italian named Chico, who is carrying a freshly pressed blouse on a hanger. He is her hairdresser-makeup man on her movies. Bailey fluffs her hair. "You been primpin', ain-chu?"

"Three hours under the blast furnace," Deneuve says. Bailey takes off his jacket to go to work and Deneuve admires his sports shirt. She is obviously at the top of one of her up periods, much more animated than she was at our previous meeting. Her movie is set to start shooting again ten days hence and her spirit is rejuvenated. Her hours at the hairdresser's and Chico's subtle makeup have conspired to make her beauty quite overpowering.

She seats herself under the hot, white lights but Bailey

doesn't like the reflection from the white umbrella over her head; he asks his Chinese assistant to put up a silver one. Bailey studies her under the silver light and she smiles at him, an old and knowing smile. "There's gold in that light," Bailey says. "You see gold in that light?" he asks me. I don't see any gold. Bailey goes over and pokes his head under the umbrella; the thin inside struts are gold. Bailey fusses with the umbrella.

"I did a commercial, Cat, only this time I was *in* it. Sat up till three A.M. learning my eight lines but they wouldn't stick. Nervous as hell, didn't sleep all night. When I got to the studio in the morning I discovered they'd changed all the lines."

"Now you know how it is, David," Deneuve says, and laughs at him. I look at her in the viewfinder of Bailey's camera and her beauty intensifies.

Bailey is working all around her, adjusting every little detail. They have enormous affection for one another. "You want some mood music, love?" he asks. "Let's have some mood music," he says to his assistant. "What'll it be, Cat? How about red roses?"

"Oh, yes," she says, responding to some past sacrament. "Red roses for a blu-u-ue lady."

"No got," the assistant says. "All right for Dylan doing *Kodachrome*? We got that."

"Now, that's fitting, ain't it?" Bailey says, and the music starts to play. Bailey is just about ready but there's a phone call from London. "You want to do Lux, love?" he calls out to Deneuve, his hand over the mouthpiece.

Deneuve's eyes flash. There is an edge to her voice. "No, I already said no."

Bailey listens on the phone. "For no amount of money?"

"For *no* amount of money."

Bailey listens some more. "Really no amount of money, love? They're talkin' *money.*"

"For all the money there is. I already told them. Calling you won't help. I made a mistake with Mercury. It's a product and it is wrong to do a product, an automobile, a bar of soap. Chanel is all right, that is a mystery. A scent. That's all right, but Mercury was a mistake and one mistake is enough."

Bailey is suddenly ready to work. The lights flick off, leaving Deneuve isolated in the white spot under the silver umbrella.

She leans forward toward the camera, thrusting her beauty at it. Bailey slides himself into and around the tripod of his camera, his body literally fusing with camera and tripod. Deneuve and he are only a few feet apart. The hot circle of light binds them in its brilliant cocoon as the camera begins to trip at a rhythmic pace, *ka-tung, ka-tung, ka-tung,* Bailey making urgent sounds, *ka-tung, ka-tung,* as Deneuve responds to him, the camera's rhythm a sensuous metronome, *ka-tung, ka-tung,* an insistent force demanding their response, leading them on, *ka-tung, ka-tung* until suddenly the roll of film is finished and the camera goes silent with the passion of that moment safe inside it.

Catherine and I are having lunch at Lasserre, a three-star restaurant noted for its food as well as its physical beauty, a feature of which is the frescoed ceiling, which periodically opens, revealing baskets of hanging geraniums framing the open sky. I invited Catherine here to try to cheer her up a little, for her movie has again been canceled, this time permanently, and she is very down.

We start with a Kir champagne and *saumon frais marine à l'aneth.* The exquisite bouquet of salmon cheers her a bit. "My daughter, Chiara, wanted to come to lunch with us," she says. "I take her everywhere—she thinks she's my age, and that my friends are her friends. She is so dear, like a flower just opened."

"You should have brought her."

"Next time—but not to Lasserre, which is for serious eating. The thing about me as a mother—I like to be *with* a child but not *play* with a child. I'm no good at that. I like to have her as part of my world but I can't be part of hers."

M. Pierre, the director of Lasserre, recommends a combination of mousse of eel and mousse of crab, and Catherine is delighted with the suggestion. But even as she smiles at M. Pierre, it is only a mask that is penetrated by her sadness.

"You enjoy food, don't you?" I ask.

"Oh, yes. And I care very much about how food looks. Here they present it so beautifully—it is art. I also like the country look of food, heaped on a platter, surrounded by mounds of vegetables. When I'm at my country place I like to cook for my children and my boyfriend—oh, that terrible word, 'boyfriend'

—it sounds so bad in English—in French we have it better—
'*fiancé.*' We don't use it in the formal sense, but in English it's
a very serious word."

The *sommelier* comes to discuss the wine and although Catherine says she should not have any because she has a serious
meeting at four o'clock, I easily seduce her with a bottle of
Lasserre champagne that comes from their own vineyards. The
champagne, I figure, might do her some good.

"Would you like to live in the country?" I ask.

"Full-time? Maybe. I love to garden, especially to raise a sea
of yellow petunias; the prettiest sight for me is white butterflies
darting through the yellow petunias. I have a friend who is going
to give me some cuttings from his Polar Bear rhododendrons,
which bloom all summer. That's exciting. But . . . well, here it
is summer and I'm not in the country because I can't enjoy any
of these lovely things when I'm depressed like this. But why am
I so destroyed by a thing like this movie? A part of me gets up
every day and goes to do the film. Yes, puts on makeup and acts
for the camera and the rest of me watches in disappointment."

"Vadim says that you have a slight tendency to be masochis-
tic but with a sense of humor, not Russian."

There is a touch of anger to her voice. "Vadim! He does not
weather well. The book he wrote, all he could do was gossip
about his ex-wives—Brigitte Bardot, Jane Fonda, me, and the
Danish actress, Annette Stroyberg. Oh . . . I was too young with
Vadim and really too young with Bailey."

"You and Bailey still love one another, don't you?"

"We were such opposites. Bailey's idea of country was a
one-hour drive to lunch somewhere. He couldn't relax. Always
traveling. Always working. So we had no country place where I
could work the soil with my hands—that's what I like best, to feel
the warm soil crumbling in my hands."

The waiters serve us warm *escalopes* of fresh foie gras in a
delicate champagne sauce, surrounded with peeled, pitted white
grapes.

"Then why not go work in your garden and forget the un-
pleasantness of this abandoned movie?"

"Because when there is not a big thing in my life—a film, a
new love affair, whatever—a big, consuming thing—then I can't

enjoy the little things. But when there is a big thing going for me, I can enjoy everything."

"But soon there will be a new movie, there's always another movie—you know that."

"About tomorrow, I have no excitement—only curiosity. Who said that, Cocteau? The trouble is I'm a Libra, passive and love-prone. I don't dream. Can you imagine that? Not to dream?"

We eat in silence for a while. I don't want to ask her anything else. She is too vulnerable, and too sad.

"I will tell you something," she says, finally, her voice lifeless. "I have no idea who I am, and what I want, where I'm going or how I'll get there."

The halves of the ceiling start to part and she watches pensively as the sun comes streaming into the dining room. A small white butterfly flits among the geraniums. "I'm in my early thirties now," she says, her eyes on the butterfly. "But my fear is that one day I'll just be a forty-year-old cynical woman going from affair to affair."

The halves of the ceiling start slowly to close. "When I'm making a movie, I am all right. I feel wonderful. I know I am a good actress and I feel the flow of life moving through me and into the camera. But when there is no movie, in the between times, I do not have a sense of being. I do not know who I am. I do not know where I want life to take me. I could go anywhere, do anything, but I don't know where I want to go. Isn't that sad?"

As the closing ceiling moves past the geraniums, the white butterfly retreats from the flowers, hovers for an instant, and then gracefully rises into the disappearing sky.

24

Richard Rodgers' Love Affair with Nefertiti

The creation of a musical has always intrigued me. There is something about the enhancement of written characters with songs and dances that excites my imagination. I wrote musical sketches in high school, and in college I created the book and most of the lyrics for a satire on prizefighting called *Down in Front.* As previously noted, a listing of this show on my Air Force qualification card led to my being assigned to write the book for the Air Force musical *Three Dots with a Dash,* but when I became involved in professional writing, I was never able to create the risk time necessary to write a musical.

In a sense, all free-lancing requires risk time, but magazine articles and books are usually written under contracts that alleviate some of that risk, whereas the financial onus of playwriting rests squarely on the playwright. For however long it takes him to write his play he is completely on his own. And the writer of a musical increases that risk because even after his work has been satisfactorily completed, it doesn't have any meaning without the interweaving of music and lyrics which are more important to the musical than the libretto.

The success of *Papa Hemingway* provided me with my first risk period, thanks to its long tenure on the best-seller list and its publication in twenty-five countries around the world. I could now afford to devote six months to a musical project, if I could find one.

I don't recall who arranged it, but somehow I was introduced to Dorothy Fields, who had written the words for some of the finest popular songs ever composed: "On the Sunny Side of the Street," "I Can't Give You Anything but Love, Baby," "The Way You Look Tonight," "Lovely to Look At," "I'm in the Mood for Love"; and with her brother, Joe, she had coauthored *Annie Get Your Gun, Something for the Boys, Mexican Hayride, Sweet Charity,* and other Broadway musicals. I don't think more joyful lyrics were ever written than

> Grab your coat and get your hat,
> Leave your worry on the doorstep,
> Just direct your feet
> To the sunny side of the street.

It was a song I often heard and sang during the Depression, a marvelous spiritual antidote for what the song calls "those blues on parade." And another of Dorothy's lyrics that lifted Depression *malaise* was:

> I can't give you anything but love, baby,
> That's the only thing I've plenty of, baby.
> Dream awhile,
> Scheme awhile,
> We're sure to find
> Happiness,
> And I guess,
> All the things we've always pined for . . .

The purpose of that first meeting with Dorothy in 1968 was to discuss an idea she had for a new show, but considering who she was and how underqualified I was, I felt like an imposter as her maid admitted me to Dorothy's beautiful apartment overlooking Central Park. She was a cheerful, amusing woman with a warm, easy smile, a quick mind, and an air of expectation. We sat at the window, the green of the park spread far below us, as she told me about the research she had done on the Peace Corps, which was the subject of the musical she wanted to do.

She had visited a Peace Corps unit in South America and she

had specific suggestions as to how a show could be built around a group of young Americans who are stationed in a remote area to help the underprivileged natives. There was a time when she would have tackled the book herself with her brother, she said, but he was dead now and she had lost her enthusiasm for writing librettos, only wanting to pursue her passion for creating lyrics. She had already spoken to her friend the composer Burton Lane, and if the subject interested me, the next step would be to meet with him.

"Ever since *Finian's Rainbow*," she said, "Burt has been saying that he wants to do another show, but he turns down everything. So finicky. But if I didn't offer it to him so he could turn it down, he would be offended. Burt, I love Burt, but for a man who writes such cheerful music, he's glum. He broods. For Burt, disaster lurks behind every half-note."

The more I thought about a group of young Peace Corps kids as the basis for a show, the more I liked it, so that by the time Dorothy and I met with Burton Lane I had developed some specific ideas. Burt is a tall man with a somber mien but I found that his skepticism and wariness were accompanied by a pleasant, low-keyed manner, an easily provoked smile, and a willingness to be convinced.

By our third meeting I had developed an outline for a first act, with detailed descriptions of the principal characters; prodded by Dorothy's infectious enthusiasm, Burton was beginning to discuss possible song placements. It was altogether the most enthralling writing experience I had had, enhanced by the unique sensation that came from working with others rather than in my customary solitude.

At the end of a month of meetings, it was agreed that we had progressed to the point where I could begin to write the actual scenes. At the same time, Dorothy and Burt were going to start work on certain songs that were firmly rooted in those scenes.

While this work was in progress, Dorothy and I met every day, but I learned not to go past four o'clock, for that's when, punctually, Dorothy poured herself a glass of sherry. Faster than Jekyll hopped from Hyde, Dorothy went from sobriety to inebriation. I never knew anyone with such low tolerance for alcohol.

When Dorothy was on the road with a new show, everyone

knew that all the work on the songs had to be accomplished in the morning. However, when *Sweet Charity* went out West to play in a casino at Las Vegas, the casino producer, not knowing about Dorothy's sobriety curfew, invited her for opening night dinner before the show. The producer ordered drinks (Dorothy requested her favorite, a grasshopper, which combines crème de menthe and crème de cacao). As the drinks were being served, the producer was called to the telephone, and when he returned a few minutes later, Dorothy was gone. He was standing there in front of the table, mystified, when the waiter came up to him and pointed *under* the table—and there was Dorothy, in a heap.

With the waiter's help, the producer sat Dorothy in a chair and the two of them carried her in this manner to the elevator, managed to get to her room, and put her to bed.

Two hours later, the producer was called to the phone and he was surprised to hear Dorothy's voice on the other end.

"Dorothy! How are you feeling?"

"Not so hot," Dorothy answered. "If you don't mind, I don't think I'll go to dinner with you."

When I had completed the first three scenes, I sent copies to my collaborators; Dorothy immediately registered her approval. Burt had some quibbles, but not important ones, and I happily plunged on.

And that's about the time when we were put out of business. It was Dorothy's fault, but a fault of such innocence there should be a softer word for it. What had happened was that Dorothy had gone to lunch with her good "friends" Robert Fryer and Lawrence Carr, who had produced two musicals of Dorothy's, *Redhead* and *Sweet Charity*. At the time of their lunch with Dorothy, Fryer and Carr had a musical on the road in Philadelphia called *Hot Spot*, in which Judy Holliday played a government worker, and the show was in serious trouble; they told Dorothy about their show and Dorothy told them about ours.

One week after that luncheon, the Fryer and Carr musical had been drastically rewritten, and lo and behold! Judy Holliday had become a Peace Corps worker. Despite the changes, the show flopped and brought down our embryonic musical with it.

Dorothy was disconsolate; she felt that she had betrayed us.

She hadn't, of course. She had simply made the fatal mistake of trusting alleged friends, who on Broadway are in very, very short supply.

Although we never did do a musical, Dorothy and I shared enjoyments over the ensuing years. There was a birthday party one summer, in a Water Mill restaurant, attended by a host of her musician friends. The composer Cy Coleman performed amusing high jinks on the keyboard, and someone sang a medley of songs by Frank Loesser, who was present. He was a short, swarthy man who smoked incessantly and coughed a lot. I had long been in awe of his remarkable talent, and I spent most of the evening talking with him. He told me witty stories about the tribulations of getting *Guys and Dolls* on the stage, stories about *How to Succeed in Business Without Really Trying* and about the squabbles he had had with Ray Bolger while they were giving birth to *Where's Charley?* Loesser was frequently interrupted by paroxysms of coughing, a rasping, strangling cigarette cough that flushed his face and doubled him forward. Then, recovered, he would light a fresh cigarette and draw it deeply into his protesting lungs. "The docs want me to give it up," he said. "I'll outlive all of them." He didn't. The cigarettes killed him, as I knew they would.

I painfully remember how, when I was a boy, my father's nicotine addiction slowly accelerated to the point where he woke several times a night to smoke cigarettes, sitting on the toilet seat in the bathroom, his roiling, choking cough stabbing the quiet night. And then came that day when the principal called me to his office to go in a police car to the hospital. My father lay near death, having suffered a massive coronary; the doctor said he would be gone within the hour.

My mother, brother, and I sat in the grim corridor outside intensive care, staring at the clock on the gray wall, conditioning ourselves for my father's death. Each time the doors swung open and a white coat emerged, my breath caught in my chest and I squeezed my mother's cold hand.

But my father survived the hour, and the night, and all the following day. That night, when I went back to our two rooms at the Harlan Court, I went through all the pockets in my father's clothes and collected the cigarettes I found there in unfinished packs. There were Camels and Fatimas and Chesterfields; the bottoms of my father's suit pockets were lined with tobacco shreds. I went through the dresser drawers and found more cigarettes, and in a kitchen cupboard there were two full packs remaining in a carton.

With mounting fury, I stripped every cigarette from that apartment and then I took them out on the little balcony outside the front room and, sobbing, crushed them with all my might, cursing them, pounding them to shreds on the iron railing of the balcony, and then I flung them into the night, flung them as far as I could. Goddamn you! Goddamn you! Goddamn you! I shouted as I hurled death from that balcony.

My father recovered. The doctor, of course, said it was a miracle. My father lived a long time after that, but in a chronic state of fear. He could no longer work at his trade as a traveling salesman, and the best he could do, besides a little light housework, was to try to sell watch straps for a few hours a day to local jewelry shops. We became totally dependent on my mother's earnings, and on what I could scrounge from a variety of odd—and I mean *odd*—jobs. As a boy, starting life, I found it incomprehensible that a man in the vigorous years of his existence would deliberately destroy himself by sucking in the smoke of burning leaves.

And that's what I thought about the day Frank Loesser died. Thinking about him, and his extinguished talent, rekindled the fury that I felt that night when I flung my father's cigarettes from the balcony.

After the Peace Corps fiasco, I was resigned to the fact that my one musical opportunity had passed me by, but a few years later another chance presented itself, this time with Richard Rodgers. It was Dorothy who brought us together in his office at Fifty-seventh and Madison. He had been having serious and protracted medical problems; there was a deep indentation along his chin and neck where part of his jaw had been removed, and one of his legs dragged a bit when he walked, but he was brisk and straightforward. I was as nervous meeting him as I had been meeting Hemingway, but he immediately put me at ease with his candor about himself.

"I have not had an easy time since Oscar died," he said. He was referring to his longtime collaborator, Oscar Hammerstein II, who had written the lyrics for *South Pacific, Sound of Music,* and *The King and I.* "I did *No Strings* with Sam Taylor writing the book. I rather enjoyed doing my own lyrics but the book was weak. And then I tried to do a show with Alan Jay Lerner, but it became . . . well—very peculiar. I am someone who is organized and once I start on a show I can be counted on to do my work. But Alan . . . well, he never produced anything. We talked a lot and he made promises . . . but he was spending a lot of time with Max Jacobson, Dr. Feelgood, getting those shots. Alan spent half his life at Dr. Jacobson's office, he did his writing there, can you imagine? He was always chock-full of energy but weeks passed, months passed, and I had nothing to work on except promises.* So now I've given up on him. I want to get a show going, and I've got an idea that I hope you'll like. I saw your play *The White House,* and the way you did those sketches, especially the ones with Helen Hayes, and the use you made of political songs, I liked that very much. So maybe we can get together on this idea of mine."

Rodgers' notion was to do a musical about the beautiful Egyptian queen Nefertiti and the king Akhenaton. It was an unusual subject for a musical, for the focus of their lives was their revolutionary espousal of the concept of a single god who was an ethereal, noncorporeal god who dwelt in the spiritual heavens. There was romance in the premarital courtship of Nefertiti and Akhenaton, but the thrust of the show would be in the violent confrontation between them and the entrenched priests.

It was certainly a departure from anything Rodgers had ever

---

*During the period Lerner was working with Rodgers, according to a report in *The New York Times,* there was a trial in the Court of Domestic Relations during which Lerner's wife, Michelene, had testified that her husband had become addicted to injections from Dr. Jacobson "that helped him to write faster." She told a packed courtroom that her husband had told her that "maybe they [the injections] will destroy me but they make me see life in a good light." The *Times* reported that Mrs. Lerner said her husband visited Dr. Jacobson's office at all hours of the day and sometimes stayed all night. She also told the court that her husband had persuaded her to take the shots also, but that she had quit after two months because "the shots made me feel bizarre, very high."

done before, but to be honest, I can't think of any subject I wouldn't have tackled for the opportunity of working on a musical with Rodgers. We met again the following week, during which time I had uncovered some interesting material. At that meeting we agreed to go forward, and we signed a paper that wedded us to the project. At last, a musical, and with Richard Rodgers, no less—a musical that would be steeped in the exotica of ancient Egypt. I went to the Metropolitan Museum of Art and studied the celebrated painted bust of the beauteous Nefertiti. I walked through the Egyptian rooms, sopping up the atmosphere. There was a tomb likeness of Akhenaton and appurtenances from his realm. I read all the material on the subject I could find. And then I started to prepare an outline.

Richard and I met in various places—his office, his home in Connecticut, a temporary office he had at the New York State Theater, his New York apartment. It was thrilling to watch him shape the outline to accommodate the songs he was planning. Unfortunately, this took longer than I had anticipated because meetings often had to be canceled because of Richard's health.

But once the songs were in place, I was able to start on the scenes, which we had already discussed in detail. Richard approved of these and began to work on the music. I was so excited I could think of nothing else. The musical totally consumed me. The characters were fleshing out and the events were dramatic and suspenseful. I finished the first act and Richard said we certainly had a good show in the making. I basked in anticipated glory, floating on musical air, up high, in one of those big brightly colored balloons.

An announcement of our musical appeared in *The New York Times* and I can truthfully say that nothing about myself that I had ever seen in print gave me a comparable thrill:

HOTCHNER WRITING FOR RODGERS
    A. E. Hotchner, author of the book "Papa Hemingway" and the incoming play "The Hemingway Hero," is writing the book for Richard Rodgers' new musical, which will deal with the life of Queen Nefertiti of Egypt (circa 1375 B.C.). Diahann Carroll is being mentioned for the leading role.
    The first act has been submitted to Mr. Rodgers, who will be the producer and composer. He was not certain yesterday

whether he would provide the lyrics, too, as he did for his music in "No Strings." Miss Carroll was starred in that show.

But as I started on the second act, the balloon I had been riding began to lose altitude. I came in one day with a scene that we had discussed. Richard read it and said: "How does it happen that you didn't discuss this with me?" Of course, I certainly had, and I told him so, but he said I was mistaken, that all this was new to him, and he suggested that we develop it in a different way. I didn't pursue the matter. We worked out a different outline and I rewrote the scene along the revised lines.

Our next meeting was two weeks later. I had sent Richard the new scene in advance, to give him more time to evaluate it, but what transpired at this meeting was painfully disheartening. Richard seemed vague and uncharacteristically confused about what was happening in the script. His energy level was very low and I had difficulty hearing him when he spoke. After a few minutes we agreed to meet another time.

It was obvious that Richard was undergoing some kind of physical trauma. I discussed it with an internist friend of mine, and he said that in light of Richard's age and the operations he had had, followed by the slight stroke, it was possible that he was having circulatory problems that restricted the flow of blood to his brain. This would account for the memory lack, vagueness, and confusion that I had described. The doctor said that there were drugs to counteract this condition but he presumed that Rodgers' physicians had already prescribed them.

Richard and I met several more times, his condition fluctuating: on one occasion he would be sharp and aware, on another vague and remote. He never mentioned the music and I suspected he had stopped working on it. It broke my heart but I realized that it was pointless to continue.

I went to see him one afternoon at his country home, which was near mine in Westport. He moved slowly and took deep breaths. We sat beside the pool that fronted the lush nature preserve of the Audubon Society. It was a majestic vista that I looked at through his eyes and it made me feel sad.

I said that unfortunately I had to postpone our undertaking because I had to go to work on a new book that I had previously contracted for. He said that was perfectly all right because there was a revival of *South Pacific* at the New York State Theater that required his attention. His wife, Dorothy, brought us ice tea and we chatted awhile. I was reluctant to leave, for I knew I would never see him again. I admired him very much, for his talent, of course, but especially for his courage. Against tough odds he was certainly fighting as good a fight as you could ask of a man.

I gave him a little memento of our abandoned venture: a miniature replica of Nefertiti that I had purchased at the Metropolitan Museum's gift counter. He rubbed his fingers over it affectionately and smiled upon her.

25

The Ghost of J. Edgar Hoover
Haunts the Corpse of
Ernest Hemingway

There was an item in *The New York Times* one morning that ran a cold tremor through me; as I read it, I felt a devastating embarrassment, for I had been cuckolded by the ghost of J. Edgar Hoover and it was difficult to imagine any fate more demeaning than that. What I had been guilty of was intermingling the tyranny of an evil mind (Hoover's) with the aberrations of a mind in revolt against itself (Hemingway's); guilty of ascribing paranoia to the oppressed rather than the oppressor; and I had ignored the simple truth that a persecution complex is not always imaginary, but that it can derive from being persecuted.

Twenty-two years after the fact, *The New York Times* article established indisputably that I had confused some of Hemingway's bizarre complaints with dementia, that I had failed to realize that something can be made bizarre by distortion, and that I should not have looked upon Hemingway's behavior as a conclusion but only as a clue to be closely examined under a magnifying glass.

The New York Times piece revealed that an FBI file on Hemingway had been opened under the Freedom of Information Act, and the 124 pages of FBI reports in that file indicated that from 1942 until his death, Hemingway was under surveillance by the

397

FBI—which meant that all those times that Ernest protested to me about the persecution of the "Feds," when I ascribed his angry denouncements of the FBI to the hardening of his obsessions into delusions, I was jumping to a conclusion and denying Ernest the benefit of doubt.

The very first time I met Ernest in Havana, at the bar of the Floridita, he mentioned the presence of the FBI. "One time we were in here," he recounted, "bar crowded, everyone having a good time, when in came three eager young gents to have a drink at the bar, and they have FBI written all over them. So I send word to the trio of musicians who play and sing here, and at the stroke of midnight they break into 'Happy Birthday' in English, everyone joining in, and when we get to 'Happy birthday, dear FBI,' those three J. Edgars nearly caved in. They cleared out fast."

And the following day, when Ernest and I went out fishing on his boat, the *Pilar,* he told me about his anti-submarine activities during the war. "From 1942 to 1944 we turned her into a Q-boat and patrolled the waters off the north shore of Cuba. Anti-sub. Worked under naval intelligence. We posed as a commercial fishing boat but changed *Pilar*'s disguise several times so it didn't look like any one boat was fishing too much. Had thirty-five hundred dollars' worth of radio equipment in the head; the actual head was however you could manage over the side. We had machine guns, bazookas, and high explosives, all disguised as something else, and the plan was to maneuver ourselves into a position where we were hailed and ordered alongside by a surfacing U-boat. A U-boat not on alert could have been taken by our plan of attack. Crew was Spanish, Cuban, and American, very good at their jobs, all brave, and I think our capture attack would have worked."

"But you never got a chance to try it out?"

"No, but we were able to send in good information on U-boat locations and were credited by naval intelligence with locating several Nazi subs that were later bombed out by Navy depth charges and presumed sunk. Got decorated for that."

In the FBI files was a copy of a letter from J. Edgar Hoover addressed to the FBI bureau chief in Havana: "Any information which you may have relating to the unreliability of Ernest Hemingway as an informant may be discreetly brought to the attention of Ambassador Braden. In this respect it will be recalled that recently Hemingway gave information concerning the refueling of submarines in Caribbean waters which has proved unreliable."

There is another letter in the files, signed by Hoover, which reads: "Hemingway's judgment is not of the best, and if his sobriety is the same as it was some years ago, that is certainly questionable."

Over the years the FBI continued to file reports on Ernest's activities, but it was the reports on the last year of Hemingway's life that particularly upset me. During the time I had been in Madrid with Ernest in the early fall of 1960, he had started to behave in a rather irrational manner, but I attributed this to his generally depressed frame of mind. But when I went to visit him in Ketchum, Idaho, later that fall, he had become obsessed with the suspicion that he was being followed. When my train pulled into the Shoshone station, I expected to find Ernest and a doctor friend of ours in the bar across from the station where we always had a drink before starting the long drive to Ketchum, but not this time. A friend of ours, Duke MacMullen, met me and led me to his car. Ernest was sitting in the front and said we should leave as soon as possible.

I asked where our doctor friend was.

"He wanted to come but I wouldn't let him."

"Why?"

"The Feds."

"What?"

"Feds. They tailed us all the way. Ask Duke."

"Well . . . there was a car in back of us out of Hailey . . ."

"That's why I wanted to get you out of the station area. Was afraid they'd make their move and pick us up."

"But, Ernest, that car turned off at Picabo," Duke said.

"Probably took the back road. That would take them longer, so I wanted to be out of Shoshone when they got there."

"But, Papa," I said, trying to collect myself, "why are federal agents pursuing you?"

"It's the worst hell. The goddamnedest hell. They've bugged everything. That's why we're using Duke's car. Mine's bugged.

Everything's bugged. Can't use the phone. Mail intercepted. What put me onto it was that phone call with you. You remember we got disconnected? That tipped their hand."

"But long-distance calls are often cut off. How can that mean . . . ?"

"I have a pal with the phone company in Hailey. He traced the disconnect for me. It was here, at this end, not the New York end."

"But what does that have to do with it?"

"For God's sake, Hotch, use your head—you placed the call, didn't you? A legit disconnect would be at your end. But the disconnect was *here,* in Hailey, where our phone calls are relayed. That means the Feds were monitoring the call *here* and that caused it to cut out."

As we turned off the main highway into Ketchum, Ernest said in a very quiet voice: "Duke, pull over. Cut your lights."

Ernest rolled down his window and peered across the street at the bank. It was lighted and you could plainly see two men working in back of a counter. Ernest had his head partially out of the window, fixedly watching them. Then he carefully rolled up his window and told Duke to move on.

"What is it?" I asked.

"Auditors. They've got them working over my account. When they want to get you, they really get you."

"But how do you know about those men? That it's your account?"

"Why would two auditors be working in the middle of the night? Of course it's my account."

"But what have you done? What will they find?"

"Hotch, when they want to get you, they get you."

In *Papa Hemingway* I treat this episode as the first significant onset of the persecution paranoia that eventually resulted in Ernest's hospitalization at the Mayo Clinic, where he underwent a series of shock treatments. It never crossed my mind that the FBI could indeed have been tailing Ernest in another car, and the two men in the bank were dispatched there by J. Edgar Hoover to get the goods on Ernest. Just as it never occurred to me that the incident at the Christiana Restaurant a few nights later was anything but a figment of Ernest's persecution complex. It was the only time during my stay in Ketchum that we went out for dinner.

Ernest seemed at ease as he pleasurably recounted some amusing stories about his days in the old Ketchum when there was gambling and it was as wide open as a gold-rush town, when he suddenly stopped in the middle of a sentence and said we had to pay up and go. Mary Hemingway, who had been enjoying her one evening out, her meal half-eaten, asked what was wrong. Ernest gave his head a little nod toward the bar. "Those two FBI men at the bar," he mumbled. "That's what's wrong." Mary asked how he could possibly know they were FBI men and Ernest told her to keep her voice down. "Don't you think I know an FBI man when I see one? We've got to get out of here, Hotch."

I went to find the waiter and on the way passed a table where Chuck Atkinson, who owned the restaurant, and his wife were having dinner. I asked Chuck whether he knew the two men at the bar. "Sure," he said, "they're salesmen. Been coming through here once a month for the last five years. Don't tell me Ernest is worried about *them.*" He shook his head sadly.

When I told Ernest they were salesmen, he scoffed: "Of course they're salesmen. The FBI is noted for its clumsy disguises. What do you think they'd pose as—concert violinists? Come on, Mary. You can have coffee back at the house."

Reports in the FBI file indicated that Hemingway certainly was under surveillance during this period, and it was possible that Ernest was correct in identifying those men at the bar as FBI agents. It was also apparent from reading the FBI reports that Ernest had been followed all during the chaotic period when his attempts at suicide had resulted in his confinement in the psychiatric section of the Mayo Clinic. The most revolting of all these FBI revelations was the fact that even while Ernest was in the hospital, Hoover continued his unrelenting persecution of him.

When I flew to Rochester, Minnesota, to visit Ernest at the clinic, a few months before his death, his immediate and most anguished complaints were that his room was bugged, as was the phone in the hall, and that "one of the interns is a Fed in disguise." I'll never lose the image of his face, etched deeply with anguish and fear, as he told me about these oppressions.

Of course, I ascribed them to his unbalanced mental state, as did the Mayo doctors to whom I spoke, although someone in authority at Mayo must have approved the stationing of an FBI agent in the hospital, disguised as a member of the staff.

In the files was a report sent to Hoover by the special agent in Minnesota, informing him that Hemingway had entered the clinic under an assumed name and giving him details about the psychiatric treatment Ernest was receiving; the report corroborates Ernest's suspicion that there was indeed an FBI agent operating from inside the hospital.

What was particularly heinous about that disclosure was that by its irrational surveillance, which intensified Ernest's fears and obsessions, the FBI obstructed Ernest's chances of overcoming his delusions and thereby contributed to the forces that eventually drove him to commit suicide. Which, one must conclude, was what J. Edgar Hoover intended.

I myself have had only one encounter with the FBI. This occurred during the 1960 season, when I produced and wrote a series of special Hemingway dramas which Buick sponsored on CBS. I had been given an office in the CBS building on New York's West Side, and I was busily at work there one day, preparing *The Gambler, the Nun, and the Radio* for the start of rehearsals, when my secretary came in and said that a Mr. Smith and a Mr. Jones of the FBI were there to see me.

Suspecting a gag of some sort, I went to the outer office, where two neat, well-scrubbed gentlemen, hats on their laps, awaited me. They showed their identification cards, which I looked at very carefully. They said they needed about an hour of my time; for what? I asked.

"When you were in the Air Force, did you not live in Greenwich Village on Wooster Street in the house of one Bernadine Inzoraan?"

"Yes."

"It's about that."

"About Bernadine?"

"Well, about that house, everything about it."

We made a date three weeks hence, when *The Gambler, the Nun, and the Radio* would be completed. In the interim, I puzzled over what could possibly be of interest to the FBI about that house on Wooster Street.

I had been introduced to Bernadine by Tina de Roos, the Dutch ballet dancer who was my girl friend. In those war years small apartments were impossible to find, but Tina discovered that there was an unoccupied room on the top floor of a house owned by her friend Bernadine Inzoraan. I would have moved in with Tina in her place but the Air Force required proof of a self-maintained residence to qualify for the per diem additional pay which was essential for anyone stationed in New York City.

Bernadine was an attractive woman of thirty or so, with a shock of the most lustrous amber hair imaginable. Her narrow house on Wooster Street, four stories high, was adjacent to a stable, which housed a dozen of the nags that pulled carriages in Central Park. There was a barren room on the fourth floor off a hallway that also gave onto a small bathroom. I said it would be fine but that I had no furniture. Bernadine said that was not a problem—they would throw a furniture party for me. In the hallway outside the room there were stacks of tiles which Bernadine had hand-painted and baked in her kiln (she was a well-known ceramic artist), and she said that if I could manage with all the tiles stored there, the apartment was mine for fifty dollars a month.

I enjoyed living there. The furniture party provided me with more than enough domestic comforts (in fact, I had a surplus that I donated to the Salvation Army). The flat itself was only three blocks away from Tina's place, and it was easy to get to Thirty-third and Park, where the *Air Force* offices were located. Bernadine's husband, Alain, was in the Merchant Marine on the run to Murmansk, and appeared infrequently. Her mother, an imposing, imperial woman referred to as "The White Princess," was a Russian émigré who dressed only in white and was disposed toward reciting dramatic accounts of her czarist days.

Once every month, like clockwork, Bernadine gave a cocktail soiree, to which I was invariably invited. Russian delicacies were served under the supervision of The White Princess, a string trio played Mozart, and the guests were an attractive homogeneous mix of Village artists and well-heeled foreigners with exotic accents. I was the only one there in uniform, but Bernadine made a point of introducing me to people, thereby making me feel at ease in the group.

Those times when Alain Inzoraan came back from sea, he often took stacks of Bernadine's tiles with him on his return trip to Russia. Using superlatives drenched with her thick accent, The White Princess extolled the popularity of her daughter's tiles in the Soviet Union, describing her as an artist whose tiles spoke "to the core of Russian souls."

When I moved to Paris to become chief of *Air Force*'s European bureau, I gave up the Wooster Street apartment and never again visited the house, nor did I ever again see Bernadine, The White Princess, Tina, or any of the people I used to see at the soirees.

I told all this to the FBI agents when we met, and they dutifully wrote down what I told them in their notebooks. They said they were interested in some of the guests who attended those soirees, and they handed me a stack of photographs, asking me to indicate the ones whom I recognized. I said I couldn't do that unless I knew precisely what they were looking for.

"The house on Wooster Street has been torn down," one of the agents said, "but we have developed reliable information that it was the focal point of espionage activities of Russian agents during the war. Bernadine Inzoraan was the coordinator, and the so-called White Princess, who, in fact, was not Mrs. Inzoraan's mother, was in charge of the operation. The house on Wooster Street was used as a monthly drop by the various Soviet spies in the New York–Washington area. They would come to those monthly cocktail parties for the dual purpose of leaving material to be couriered to Moscow and to get new instructions. The mix of people that Mrs. Inzoraan provided was perfect cover for their operation, and having you there in your Air Force captain's uniform was very useful."

"Now about those tiles that were stored outside your door," the other agent continued, "they contained some of the most sensitive information that the Russian agents were able to obtain during those years. The espionage reports that were left with The White Princess at the parties were put on microfilm and then baked into those tiles by Bernadine Inzoraan. Then Mr. Inzoraan would take them with him on his trips to Murmansk, where they were delivered to the KGB."

By this time my mind was reeling from these revelations; I always felt that there was something strange about those soirees, that they were repeated in precise thirty-day cycles, and, considering the limitations of obtaining wartime comestibles, that they were so lavish. But all that was not so strange that it aroused my suspicions. I suppose any suspicions that might have formed were allayed by the eccentricity of The White Princess, who was a personification of the Mad Woman of Chaillot.

I looked through the stack of photographs, some of which were blurred and indistinct, taken, I presumed, with undercover cameras. Some of the faces were familiar, regulars who came to the cocktail parties every month. There was a photo of a man and woman, smiling, that the agents were particularly interested in. Yes, I was sure that they were there quite often. No, I didn't know their names, but they were certainly part of the group. One of the agents turned the photograph over and showed me the names on the back: Sobell, Bernard, and Sobell, Marilyn.

The agents did not reveal any of the other identities. They marked those photos that I recognized and thanked me for my cooperation. I asked what had happened to the Inzoraans and The White Princess; they said the FBI had been searching for them but could not find a trace of them, and it was presumed that they had long ago defected to Russia.

After the FBI men departed, I sat at my desk for a while thinking about those parties, trying to remember any incidents that in retrospect seemed strange. Then I remembered something. Tina and I had been invited to a birthday party. Phil Thompson's birthday. Phil had gone to Washington University with me, and married now, with a couple of babies, he lived in a garden apartment in the Village. His obesity and high blood pressure had disqualified him for military service and he was prospering as an account executive at the advertising firm of Young & Rubicam.

We were late for the birthday party ("a surprise so *please* be on time") and I had neglected to get a present. As I left my room, some of Bernadine's newest, most colorful tiles struck my eye. I decided Bernadine wouldn't begrudge me a couple of them to give to good old Phil for his birthday. I stopped downstairs to ask her permission, but she was out. It had been my intention to tell her about the tiles, and to pay for them, but I didn't see Bernadine for several weeks after that and I forgot about those tiles.

Phil Thompson died shortly after the war, and I had no idea what had become of his family. But I began to fantasize about what priceless microfilms might have been in those two tiles that I gave him. Perhaps by pinching those tiles I had prevented Russia from obtaining a Pentagon blueprint for a new fighter plane, or from being able to break our code.

The way I eventually worked it out in my own mind, I was a hero for having prevented those two tiles from getting to the Russians; but in my heart I knew that I had been a naïve dupe for a couple of clever spies who ran their operation right under the nose of Captain A. E. Hotchner of the United States Air Force.

26

Marlene Dietrich Is Singing "La Vie en Rose"

It has not been easy panning for gold in the riverbed of my experiences, sorting through all the silt of the poseurs, flashes in the pan, cowards, imposters, and hypocrites, the euphuists, imitators, and narcissists. But I have been lucky to find so many nuggets on the screen of memory.

There is an attic room in the Normandy-style house where I live, built by Simon Guggenheim in 1925, in which I keep mementos of the people who have left their mark on me. It has been a long time since I have rooted among these dusty keepsakes:

A bronzed bust of Hemingway that I commissioned for the "Buick Playhouse" television specials, a good strong likeness executed by the sculptor Robert Berks.

A watercolor by Ludwig Bemelmans, "March on Fifth Avenue," the wind blowing umbrellas inside out, hats flying, doormen whistling for cabs, one of the paintings drummed out of *Cosmopolitan* by Herb Mayes.

A black plaster-of-Paris mask of Paul Newman's face as he appeared in *The Battler*, eyebrows heavy with scar tissue, broken nose, cauliflower ear, a grotesque mask of pugilistic mutilation.

A book about Nefertiti, her colorful portrait on the dust jacket, a present from Dick Rodgers inscribed: "Good luck to both of us."

Two long-barreled Berber tribesmen rifles, stocks inlaid with ivory and jewels, purchased in Tangier while I was stalking Barbara Hutton.

Antonio Ordoñez' *traje de luces,* suit of lights, ivory with black-and-gold decoration, which I wore into the bullring that fateful day in Ciudad Real. I put it on now, the jacket much heavier and tighter than I remembered, place the black matador's hat on my head, unfold the black-and-silver cape which I take from my manager, Ernesto Hemingway, and for the moment I relive walking in the *paseo* across the bullring's expanse in unison with Dominguin and Ordoñez. And on the wall is the poster that announced the event—Plaza de Toros—Ciudad Real—Mano a Mano, Antonio Ordoñez y Luis Miguel Dominguin, Sobresaliente, El Pecas; how Ernest enjoyed that afternoon! El Pecas, solemn in his matador costume, speaking *sotto voce* to his manager out of the corner of his mouth. Ernesto warning El Pecas to be wary of the enraged bull jumping the fence into the *callejón* where they were standing.

An album of Marlene Dietrich's memorable opening night at the Café de Paris in London (on the album cover, "To Hotch, with love, Marlene"), which she gave me when I saw her in her dressing room after the show. I now put the record on an old turntable which my son, Timothy, has discarded here in favor of a more sophisticated record player; the excitement of that London evening fills the attic. Noel Coward's rhymed introduction, mellifluously delivered, then Marlene's sensuous voice singing: "Go see what the boys in the back room will have. . . ."

A wicker chest, a leftover stage prop from the Rod Steiger fiasco, *A Short Happy Life,* and inside it is my old officer's shirt with tarnished leaves on the epaulets; also in the chest, a 16-gauge shotgun in its leather case, the shotgun a present from Hemingway, who had it made for me by his old friend Pedro, Madrid's renowned gunsmith. We chose the wood for the stock, burled walnut with geometric swirls, my initials inlaid under the stock in gold, intricate scrollwork on the silver breech and trigger guard, Pedro carefully measuring my arms from shoulder to elbow, from elbow to fingertips, noting my weight and height, Ernest giving him precise specifications for the gun, its balance, its recoil, its accuracy, with the knowledge and intensity that was so characteristic of him. I take the gun from its case and assemble it; the burnished walnut stock has the patina of old silk, and as I hunker the gun into my cheek and swing it fluidly with a flight of imaginary birds, I am overcome with sad remembrance of those glorious days when Ernest and I hunted pheasants among the dry stalks of Hailey's autumnal cornfields.

Dietrich is now singing "La Vie en Rose."

A leather-bound copy of *Annie Get Your Gun,* a present from Dorothy Fields, the leather dry and beginning to scuff.

A stack of cardboard pigeons, white on red, red eyes the size of ball bearings, targets Ernest and I shot at in shooting booths at small town fairs while we motored through the South of France. If the shooter, using a dilapidated .22, completely eradicated the red of the pigeon's eye with three or four shots, depending on the generosity of the proprietor, he would win the booth's grand prize, a bottle of champagne. Ernest and I plunked the eyes from a lot of these cardboard pigeons during that trip. Looking at them now, with their neatly obliterated eyes, I could see Ernest presenting the champagne, which was of very questionable vintage, to members of the audience that always gathered around us at the shooting booths.

Marlene is now doing her version of "Lili Marlene."

A photograph of Newman and me on the dock at Harbour Island in the Bahamas, several large bonefish in our hands, smugness on our faces.

A peculiar musical instrument called a Marxophone, a simpleminded zither with a series of stationary numbered striking hammers and a little book to tell you which numbers to strike to play a melody; it had belonged to Charley Lederer (given to him, he said, by Gregory Peck, who in turn had gotten it from his grandfather), whose skill at playing it I admired. Charley insisted that I take it as a present (Charley was the most generous man I've ever known) but I refused. When I left for New York the following day, however, there it was in its case on my seat in the plane (a typical Charley Lederer ploy).

Two more keepsakes from Ernest. His good-luck horse chestnut, which he gave me the last time I saw him at the Mayo Clinic; I rub the smooth chestnut against the side of my nose, a trick Ernest had shown me, and the chestnut takes on a shine as lustrous as the day it dropped off a tree in the Tuileries. The other little memento, a tiny intricately carved ivory box, round with a hinged top; open it and there's a small heart inside, the color of agate but of a strange substance.

Marlene is singing "Das Lied ist Aus" and the agate-colored heart, in the palm of my left hand, has a force in it that I can feel all the way up my arm. Perhaps to my heart? Ernest said there was a certain secret about that box, but he never told me what it was. It came into my possession as a result of my last visit to see him at the Mayo Clinic. He told me there was something of his that I must have. It was in the top drawer of his dresser in his New York apartment, he said, a little ivory box with a secret and sacred history but he didn't mention the heart inside it. He made me promise to phone him as soon as I got the box because it was important, *important* that I have it.

The following day when I returned to New York, I went to his apartment, an apartment I had found for him at Sixty-second and Fifth, occupied only when he and Mary were in New York; I almost didn't find the box, which was tucked inside a pair of wool socks. Reaching Ernest on the telephone at the hospital was very difficult. He did not have phone privileges and I had to get special permission to talk to him from Dr. Rome, who was in charge of his treatment.

"I have the box, Papa, it's beautiful . . ."

"You found the heart?"

"Yes. It's made of a strange substance, isn't it?"

"It must always be kept in that box."

"All right."

"Keep it in a dark place."

"Tell me about the box, Papa—where does it come from?"

"The box is just decoration. It's the heart."

"But what about the heart? Why is it so special?"

He didn't answer.

"Papa?"

"I can't talk on this phone, understand? This phone is not secure. There's a fucking FBI fink on the line, itching to bust my ass for J. Edgar Hoover."

"But how can I find out about the heart, Papa?"

"You'll figure it out. A smart St. Louis boy can figure it out.

One thing we know for sure—since it ain't black it can't be the heart of J. Edgar Hoodoo."

"Papa, can you write me about it?"

"No, the FBI reads everything."

"When I see you . . ."

"You won't be seeing me, Pecas."

"Oh, sure . . ."

"Remember to keep it in a dark place."

"What?"

"The heart."

"Oh, sure, but, Papa . . ."

The voice of the hospital operator cut in. "Mr. Hemingway, your allotted time has expired."

"You hear that, Hotch? My allotted time has expired."

"But, listen, Papa, you have to tell me . . ."

"I'm sorry, Mr. Hemingway, I have to terminate . . ."

"So long, Pecas, my allotted . . ."

The line went dead.

Dietrich has stopped singing.

At the very back of the attic is the leather-bound television set Gary Cooper gave me. I take out my handkerchief and dust it off and plug it into a wall socket. I pull up its antenna and raise the little hood that covers its tiny screen. While it is warming up, I know, I simply *know* what is going to materialize on its screen. I haven't turned it on since Coops gave it to me, but I know what is coming—I can feel it in my bones: Gary Cooper walking slowly down the deserted, dusty street, Coops against the odds, and winning, as he always did—except once.

But as the garbled static clears and a snowy picture develops, it is not Coops but Lee Marvin sneering at Newman in *Pocket Money,* just as he sneered at me when he banished me from his limousine in the middle of that Washington night. Lee Marvin. It is true life mocking me for my weakness for fantasy, curdling my sentimentality, but as I sit there on the dusty floor of the dim attic hunched over Coops's little television set, I realize that the force of these people whose lives have touched mine is solidly inside me, their voices, laughter, and wisdom, a treasure peculiarly mine: Dorothy Parker's bitter-sweet cynicism, Durante's irrepressible affection, Ingrid's beautiful courage, Doris' warmth, Newman's honest friendship, Tony Quinn's dedication, Coop's uncomplicated loyalty.

I pick up Hemingway's little ivory box; the heart lies nestled within, a pearl in its shell, a delicate legacy, enigmatic, but I feel confident that someday, somehow, I am going to solve the mystery and meaning of Ernest's heart.

Picture Credits

Ursula Hotchner, *Picture Editor*

Page 139, TOP, Walter Sanders, *Life;* BOTTOM, Bob Landry, *Life;* 141, TOP, Wide World Photos; BOTTOM, Bettmann Archive; 142, TOP, Larry Burrows, *Life;* 143, BOTTOM, Pictorial Parade; 144, TOP LEFT, Wide World Photos; TOP RIGHT, A. E. Hotchner; BOTTOM, Dmitri Kessel, *Life;* 145, TOP and BOTTOM, Bettmann Archive; 146, TOP, Pictorial Parade; BOTTOM, Bettmann Archive; 147, TOP, Consulaat Generaal der Nederlander; 148, TOP, Bob Landry, *Life;* BOTTOM, Bettmann Archive; 149, TOP, Loomis Dean, *Life;* BOTTOM, Wide World Photos; 150, Allen Grant, *Life;* 151, TOP, Allan Grant, *Life;* BOTTOM, Stephen Colhoun; 152, BOTTOM, Pictorial Parade; 293, TOP, Wide World Photos; BOTTOM, Bettmann Archive; 294, TOP, Mark Shaw; BOTTOM, Bettmann Archive; 295, TOP, Bettmann Archive; BOTTOM, W. Eugene Smith, *Life;* 296, TOP, O'Neill Theatre; BOTTOM, Pictorial Parade; 297, TOP, W. Eugene Smith, *Life;* BOTTOM, A. E. Hotchner; 298, BOTTOM, Pictorial Parade; 299, TOP and BOTTOM, Pictorial Parade; 303, TOP, Museum of Modern Art; 304, TOP, Wide World Photos; BOTTOM, Francis Miller, *Life;* 305, Pictorial Parade; 306, Pictorial Parade; 307, TOP, Lisa Larsen, *Life;* BOTTOM, Martha Swope, *Life;* 308, A. E. Hotchner.